A SEA OF
WORDS

A SEA OF WORDS

*A Lexicon and Companion to the
Complete Seafaring Tales of
Patrick O'Brian*

THIRD EDITION

Dean King
with John B. Hattendorf
and J. Worth Estes

*An Owl Book
Henry Holt and Company
New York*

Henry Holt and Company, LLC
Publishers since 1866
115 West 18th Street
New York, New York 10011

Henry Holt® is a registered
trademark of Henry Holt and Company, LLC.

Distributed in Canada by H. B. Fenn and Company Ltd.

Frontispiece: Detail of *Sea Battle with Rock of Gibraltar Behind*
(courtesy of the Mariners' Museum, Newport News, Virginia)

Library of Congress Cataloging-in-Publication Data

King, Dean.
A sea of words : a lexicon and companion to the complete seafaring tales of Patrick
O'Brian / Dean King ; with John B. Hattendorf and J. Worth Estes.—3rd ed.
p.   cm.
"An owl book."
Includes bibliographical references.
ISBN 0-8050-6615-2
1. O'Brian, Patrick, 1914– —Dictionaries.   2. O'Brian, Patrick, 1914–
Aubrey/Maturin novels.   3. O'Brian, Patrick, 1914– —Language—Glossaries, etc.
4. O'Brian, Patrick, 1914– —Characters—Dictionaries.   5. Maturin, Stephen
(Fictitious character)—Dictionaries.   6. Aubrey, Jack (Fictitious character)—
Dictionaries.   7. Historical fiction, English—Dictionaries.   8. Naval art
and science—Dictionaries.   9. Sea stories, English—Dictionaries.
I. Hattendorf, John B.   II. Estes, J. Worth, 1934–   III. Title.

PR6029.B55 Z74   2000
823'914—dc21
00-040946

First Edition 1995
Second Edition 1997
Third Edition 2000

Maps by Jackie Aher

Printed in the United States of America

9 10 8

A Note on the Third Edition

All men owe honor to the poets—honor
and awe, for they are dearest to the Muse
who puts upon their lips the ways of life.
—Homer, *The Odyssey*, book 8

I would like to dedicate this final edition of *A Sea of Words* to Patrick O'Brian (1914–2000), creator of the Aubrey-Maturin novel series. I have added many new entries for *The Hundred Days* (HarperCollins, U.K.; W. W. Norton, U.S.A., 1998) and *Blue at the Mizzen* (1999). It is for the better understanding and enjoyment of O'Brian's magnificent epic of the Royal Navy during the age of Napoleon that I wrote this book and *Harbors and High Seas*.

Macte Virtute, Patrick O'Brian.

Contents

CONTENTS

List of Illustrations

Preface to the Second Edition

The Curiosity That
Patrick O'Brian Inspires in Us

While walking from the village of Buriton to Ashgrove Cottage,
Stephen Maturin observes that the Hampshire landscape is "ordinary
country raised to the highest power." Indeed, the rolling, wooded
South Downs of southern England are subtly splendid. But for the
O'Brian reader, this countryside is raised yet another notch in its
appeal—by the author in the fiction he has set there.

Readers have many reasons to rejoice in the Aubrey-Maturin novels, for Patrick O'Brian has the gift not only of raising the ordinary to
a higher power but of making the extraordinary human. In his central
characters we admire their honor, dignity, skills, and knowledge, and
we empathize with their foibles and flaws. In his plots we escape into
a world where etiquette and order seem to rule, relishing for instance
the formalities of a Navy officers' banquet—and the inevitable trans-
gression of those formalities—and where even war has its civilities.
And of course O'Brian, his sense of humor never curtailed, frequently
sends us into fits of laughter.

Of all things we admire, though, the most rewarding is perhaps
the curiosity that O'Brian inspires in us. For me, these novels have
sparked many learning adventures, among them visits to Mystic
Seaport, where I saw a capstan turned to a shanty and watched a

mainsail unbent, to the Musée de la Marine in Paris, which displays spectacular 15-foot-tall ship models, and to the National Maritime Museum in Greenwich, where the Battle of Trafalgar recurs in a narrated panorama through the sternwindow of a French first rate. On my way down to Portsmouth for a stroll on the decks of Nelson's *Victory* (whose round tumblehome greatly increased my appreciation for Maturin's shipboarding talents), I even stopped in the village of Buriton.

It is in *The Reverse of the Medal* that Maturin alights here from the Portsmouth night coach one fine morning for a walk across the fields and through the woods to Ashgrove. I quickly discovered why, in addition to its proximity, he might have paid an extra three shillings to be dropped off in this quaint farming village. The famous historian Edward Gibbon (1737–1794), who lived in a manor house by the pond and across from the Norman rectory, once wrote, "No more typical scene of 18th century England could be found." It's still true today.

After eating a "full-cooked" English breakfast at the Master Robert Inn—a walker's meal if ever there was one—I visited the village's peaceful flint-wall Norman church. The morning sun glistened on the dew-soaked tombstones as I prepared to strike off over the fields. Soon the sign for the South Downs Way, a national footpath, pointed up a tree-covered cart track, and I took it. As I dodged the deep, muddy ruts of the track, a covey of pheasants burst from a ragged hedge onto a cow pasture.

At the top of the cart track, I reached a lane guarded by two gnarly, silver-barked beech trees whose sagging branches were weighted by the half centuries they had seen. This was a lane that meandered over hills, through forests, and past farms. It was a lane for pleasant walking, and as my goal was to discover what I could about Ashgrove Cottage, a fictional place, I took my time. Like Maturin I was alone, and I did as I pleased. That included savoring ripe blackberries beside the road.

Soon I heard the clopping of horses. Around the bend, on big brown mounts, came four women in field boots and riding caps. Out front a perky, unblinking brunette greeted me with an irrepressible "Hello," long on the first syllable. Behind her, side by side, were a sturdy, upright blond and a stout, silver-haired matron, the very countenance of the landed gentry, and bringing up the rear, a plumpish youngster. Surely, I thought, this was the Williams family out for a day's ride. As I stifled a sudden desire to ask if they knew of a certain Jack and Sophie Aubrey, it occurred to me how delightful it is to go in search of fact and find fiction.

Eventually I reached Butser Hill, the highest point on the South Downs Way, and, looking south over the rippling Downs, I fancied I could make out Spithead and the Isle of Wight, just as Aubrey could from his observatory. My journey was well rewarded, and I couldn't help but think of Maturin's words as he traversed the same countryside: " 'Why do I feel such an intense pleasure, such an intense satisfaction?' . . . [H]e searched for a convincing reply, but finding none he observed 'The fact is I do' " (*The Reverse of the Medal*, p. 178). I'm sure that Maturin's profound curiosity and the opportunity to carelessly, purely indulge it were at least part of that intense satisfaction.

Indeed, curiosity seems to be a staple characteristic of O'Brian readers. From the comments and inquiries that poured in after the initial publication of *A Sea of Words*, it became apparent that the book had merely wetted that curiosity. Hence, *Harbors and High Seas: An Atlas and Geographical Guide to the Aubrey-Maturin Novels*, which explores the routes and the places where O'Brian leads his characters, and *Every Man Will Do His Duty*, an anthology of firsthand accounts from the men who fought the battles. Among them are Thomas Cochrane's account of the cruise of the *Speedy*, upon which much of the action of *Master and Commander* is based, as well as accounts of the Glorious First of June, the battles of Cape St. Vincent and Trafalgar, and the frigate action between the *United States* and the *Macedonian*.

The second edition of *A Sea of Words* simply attempts to answer many more of the questions generated in reading these thought-provoking novels: What are the marthambles, and is there a historical basis for the chelengk that Aubrey receives from the Grand Turk? Who is Maturin's famous patient the Duke of Clarence, and who the remarkable, precocious British prime minister William Pitt the Younger? On which days were honorary salutes required of all British warships, and what precipitated the Gordon Riots?

In this edition you will find many more entries regarding natural history, music, geography, and actions of the Napoleonic wars and the War of 1812. There are entries from *The Commodore* and *The Yellow*

Admiral, neither of which was published when the first edition of *A Sea of Words* came out. This edition also refocuses on what I consider to be the seminal book of the series, *Post Captain*.

In this second edition you will also find many more translations of foreign words and phrases. In cases where passages have several foreign phrases together or near one another, the whole string has been translated together with elipses linking them, so that by looking up the first foreign word of the passage, you will find all of the necessary translations. The new "Time Line of the Napoleonic Wars, the War of 1812, and the Fight for Independence in Chile" (see the appendix, page 483) should help readers place the events of the novels in the context of the history of the era.

I humbly confess to a number of corrections as well and thank all of the well-informed amateurs and experts who kindly wrote to suggest additions and modifications and to pose questions. With the help of the learned professors John B. Hattendorf and J. Worth Estes, these suggestions and queries have been addressed whenever possible.

Of course, there is much more relevant, fascinating information that simply would not fit into this one book, nor half a dozen like it. But it is my hope that *A Sea of Words* will continue to inspire readers to read and reread O'Brian, to explore the many great fiction and nonfiction books written about the period, and to set off on their own adventures of discovery, traversing the landscapes and seeing in person the important places and artifacts of this great age of history, one that Patrick O'Brian's Aubrey-Maturin novels so brilliantly bring to life for us.

—Dean King

Foreword

Dean King

"No man could easily surpass me in ignorance of naval terms," claims Stephen Maturin early on in *Master and Commander*, Patrick O'Brian's first Aubrey-Maturin novel. Indeed, Maturin's continuing ignorance of the ways of the sea and nautical terminology is one of the chief sources of humor in the series—and a very clever one, for it allows us, in our own ignorance of 18th-century naval cant, to associate ourselves with the novels' paragon of intelligence.

" 'So that is a mainstay,' said Stephen, looking at it vaguely. 'I have often heard them mentioned. A stout-looking rope, indeed.' " Likewise confronted, we can imagine ourselves uttering these lines with Maturin's boggled look and feigned disinterest. Later, in *Post Captain*, Maturin wistfully concludes, " 'Your mariner is an honest fellow, none better; but he is sadly given to jargon.' "

When reading the Aubrey-Maturin novels, the question "How much vocabulary do I really need to know?" inevitably arises, and it recurs again and again. If you're anything like me—a certified lubber—you raced through the first three novels glued to the plots, inventing definitions, or what you convinced yourself were at least reasonable approximations, and reassuring yourself at each instance of Maturin's touching lubberliness.

The fact is you don't *have* to know more about the historical and nautical background to enjoy these books. But there comes a time when most of us suddenly realize we *want* to know more. Cross-catharpings? Lord Keith? Mauritius? Part of the great beauty of these tales is that they spark a thirst for knowledge; suddenly an era that initially seemed very remote—that of the French Revolutionary and Napoleonic wars—becomes very immediate. I found myself wanting to know more almost every time I turned the page. What I needed were maps and nautical manuals, instructive illustrations, and historical essays. There definitely was no one good source.

What I found when I began researching this companion book, however, was a great wealth of resources right here in the United States. Both the Mariners Museum in Newport News, Virginia, and the New York Yacht Club in New York City, for instance, were able to provide me with editions of *Falconer's Universal Dictionary of the Marine* and *The Naval Chronicles*, the very volumes that O'Brian so studiously pores over in writing his books.

Even more important to the success of this venture was that two eminent American scholars of the period—John Hattendorf, Ernest J. King Professor of Maritime History at the Naval War College, in Newport, Rhode Island, and Worth Estes, Professor of Pharmacology at Boston University—agreed to contribute essays and review the text. Hattendorf's "The Royal Navy During the War of the French Revolution and the Napoleonic War" and Estes's "Stephen Maturin and Naval Medicine in the Age of Sail" are invaluable to anyone who wishes to better understand the Aubrey-Maturin era.

Of course, understanding the full meaning of every term O'Brian uses would take the better part of a career. And this is not necessary to enjoy the books. But even a humble attempt to learn more enhances the reading experience. It brings us closer to the author's passion both for the age of Admiral Lord Nelson and for the very act of exploring that time. When you open this book, I hope that your imagination calls up the smell of the musty volumes of *The Naval Chronicles*, the feel of their rough-trimmed pages and of the thin layers of rice paper that for two centuries have attempted, often successfully, to keep the ink of the wonderful engravings in place.

The excitement of peeling back time and existing in the past, a thrill that O'Brian has so obviously reveled in for decades, can be experienced by better grasping the primary tools with which that past was preserved: words, many now out of use, with connotations fast fading. And when a sailor admonishes Maturin and Martin to "mind the paintwork. . . . They would not like to have the barky mistaken for a Newcastle collier," it's gratifying, if not essential, to know that a "barky" was sailor slang for a vessel well liked by her crew and that a "collier" was a bluff-bowed and broad-sterned ship originally intended to carry coal.

A few things must be said about this companion book. First, no claim can be made of comprehensiveness. Our survey of O'Brian's books found more than 8,000 words that could use defining for modern readers, including the names of some 400 ships, 500 people, and 1,200 places. Obviously we had to focus our efforts, and we chose nautical, medical, and natural history terms, though we didn't limit ourselves to those.

Second, we have tried to use as little jargon as possible in describing the terms. But we haven't sidestepped it entirely. You will quickly pick up the basic terminology that recurs in the definitions of the more specialized words. In that way, the learning of sailing terminology grows exponentially. You build with each new term, and before you know it, it all crystallizes. You have ascended through the morass of rigging to the maintop, and as you look down, the ship becomes a coherent organic entity. At that point the vocabulary becomes manageable. The act of, say, "hauling in the cable and fishing the best bower at the starboard cathead" is easily recognizable as pulling in the anchor and hanging it on the bow, indeed, a specific anchor on a specific part of the bow.

Third, O'Brian uses a variety of spellings and hyphenations for many words, so it pays to be a little flexible when searching for a term in *A Sea of Words*. Also, a word that appears in many forms in the books probably does not appear in all of those forms here. For instance, we define "spanker" and "boom" but leave it to the reader to resolve "spanker-boom" (the boom of the spanker). Also, when O'Brian himself provides an explanation for a term in the text, we usually do not redefine it, simply to save precious space for the many other terms.

Finally, there is more than one way to use this book. Looking up words as you go is rewarding, but browsing through the lexicon to familiarize yourself with the lingo in between book readings is perhaps even better. Part of the beauty of O'Brian's books is the deft way in which he weaves the languages of the sea and science into the narrative. Stopping to consult a reference book too frequently disturbs the intimacy between reader and tale, and between reader and author.

By all means, *do* read the two introductory essays before you read the next O'Brian novel. You may be surprised at how many more of O'Brian's details you pick up when you return to the fiction.

As for the sea salt, there's this little cottage on the Outer Banks of North Carolina, just over a dune from the crashing surf. On the porch is a graying two-seater hammock swing where my wife, Jessica, and I have been known to hoist volumes of O'Brian. Pelicans soar overhead in age-old vees and the weather raises Cain whenever it wants to. And yes, the sun and the sea salt wrinkle the pages of our paperbacks. I hope you put this book to good use in a similar reading spot.

Acknowledgments

The authors would particularly like to thank Greg Easley for his many hours of research and Jessica King for her careful editing. Also, Elizabeth Aquino, Raney Aronson, Whittney Bradshaw, David Miller, Jayne Riew, Nancy Steed, Durk Steed, Paula Skreslet and Andy Trees, for their input.

Thanks also to the institutions that made this book possible, including the New York Yacht Club, the University of Virginia, the Mariners' Museum, and the Boston Medical Library; and especially to David Seaman at the University of Virginia Electronic Text Center; to Joe Jackson, the Librarian of the New York Yacht Club; and to Tom Crew and the staff of the Mariners' Museum.

Special thanks to David Sobel, Jonathan Swain Landreth, and Jody Rein.

For the second edition, a very warm thanks to all of the readers who so graciously wrote in with suggestions for additions and revisions. We appreciate your high standards and hope we were able to live up to them.

ACKNOWLEDGMENTS

A special thanks to Jessica King for editing all of the language entries and for her French, Spanish, and Italian translations, and to Worth Estes for his Latin translations.

Our highest regards to John Harland, author of *Seamanship in the Age of Sail*, whom we consulted concerning the technical details of ship maneuvering and who kindly contributed his time in fine-tuning a number of those entries. We heartily recommend his book to any readers who wish to delve deeper into the technical details surrounding the wooden ships of this era. My gratitude also to Logan Ward for his many editorial contributions.

Finally, in compiling the first edition of *A Sea of Words*, it did not occur to me to do the obvious—that is, to offer my deepest thanks and heartiest congratulations to Patrick O'Brian and his publishers, HarperCollins, U.K., and W. W. Norton for their splendid work. Their long-sustained dedication and high standards of achievement serve as a beacon in the dark to all of Mr. O'Brian's readers. Without the Aubrey-Maturin books, of course, this book would not exist.

The Royal Navy During the War of the French Revolution and the Napoleonic War

John B. Hattendorf

When a sailor was swimming on the surface of the open ocean, his horizon was a mere 1.1 miles away. But climbing to the maintop—about 100 feet above the water on a 74-gun ship—extended the distance he could see to nearly 12 miles. The height of any object on the horizon, whether ship or shore, also increased that distance. Perched in the rigging of a large ship, a lookout might see the sails of another large ship at 20 miles, even if the ship was hull-down (with only its sails visible above the horizon).

Height was the key. Yet a person's range of view could be affected by many circumstances, such as fog or even loud distractions on deck. At long distances, the atmosphere could create strange refractions, causing mirages.

For a naval man, there is a direct analogy between climbing the mast to extend the horizon at sea and climbing up the hierarchy of command to view the wider operations of the Navy. The top of the Royal Navy hierarchy was not in a ship at sea, but ashore, in London. It was only from there that one's vision was global, encompassing the Navy's numerous theaters of operation and distant exploits. And it was from there that the Navy's basic directions emanated—everything from grand strategy to pay, from ship construction to uniforms, from navigation charts to food allowances. Officers of the Crown, including naval officers like Jack Aubrey, were ultimately governed by Parliament, the King's Cabinet, and the King himself.

King, Cabinet, and Parliament

For all those who served in the Navy, King George III stood at the pinnacle of command. Not only was the King a symbol of sovereignty, but he also played a tangible role in day-to-day affairs. Maintaining the prerogative of the Crown to appoint its own ministers, George III was an important influence on national policies and was certainly able to prevent the government from taking measures in which he did not acquiesce. Although after his first bout with insanity in 1788, George III began to leave an increasing amount of business to his ministers, he retained considerable influence over national policy and ministerial appointments throughout the years of the French Revolution and the Napoleonic wars.

In the King's name and through his authority, the prime minister and the other ministers in the Cabinet collectively exercised the executive power of government through the means provided by Parliament. In this, the Cabinet was controlled on one side by the King and on the other by Parliament. When a cabinet was appointed and received the King's support, it could normally expect the support of a majority in both the House of Commons and the House of Lords as well as a victory in the next general election, providing that it did not prove incompetent, impose undue taxation, or fail to maintain public confidence. When any of these were joined by public outcry over a defeat in battle or disappointment in foreign policies, Cabinet ministers were clearly in political danger.

Because of its representative nature and its exclusive ability to initiate financial measures, the House of Commons was the stronger of the two Houses of Parliament, but the House of Lords, usually siding with the King, retained enormous power. Its assent was essential to the passage of any law. In the 18th century, when most Cabinet ministers, including the head of the Navy, were Lords, it was normal for the Cabinet's views to be more in harmony with those of the House of Lords. Together, the two could kill inconvenient measures arising in the Commons.

The Cabinet dealt with questions of broad naval policy and strategy, including finance, ship construction, and logistical support, obtaining funding from Parliament and sometimes even giving broad operational directives to the Admiralty and to senior naval commanders.

The Lords Commissioners of the Admiralty

Traditionally, the Crown vested the powers and functions of the Admiralty in the office of Lord High Admiral. An ancient office of state, it had not been held by an individual since 1709. Instead, these powers were delegated to a board of seven men who were the "Commissioners for Executing the Office of Lord High Admiral," or "Admiralty Board." Of these seven, three were usually naval officers, called professional Lords, and four civilians, or civil Lords. In theory, each commissioner was equal in authority and responsibility, but in practice the person whose name appeared first on the document commissioning the board was the senior member, or First Lord. During this period, the First Lord was more often a civilian member of the House of Lords than a naval officer.

First Lords of the Admiralty, 1788–1827

John Pitt, 2nd Earl of Chatham . . . . Jul. 16, 1788–Dec. 19, 1794
George John Spencer, 2nd Earl Spencer . . . . Dec. 19, 1794–Feb. 19, 1801
Admiral John Jervis, 1st Earl of St. Vincent . . . . . . Feb. 19, 1801–May 15, 1804
Henry Dundas, 1st Viscount Melville. . . . . May 15, 1804–May 2, 1805
Admiral Charles Middleton, Lord Barham . . . . May 2, 1805–Feb. 10, 1806
Hon. Charles Grey, Viscount Howick . . . . Feb. 10, 1806–Sep. 29, 1806
Thomas Grenville. . . . . Sep. 29, 1806–Apr. 6, 1807
Henry Phipps, 3rd Lord Mulgrave . . . . Apr. 6, 1807–May 4, 1810
Charles Philip Yorke . . . . May 4, 1810–Mar. 25, 1812
Robert Saunders Dundas, 2nd Viscount Melville. . Mar. 25, 1812–May 2, 1827

Source: J. C. Sainty, Admiralty Officials, 1660–1870 (1975).

In 1805, Lord Barham was the first to assign specific duties to each of the professional Naval Lords, leaving the civil Lords to handle routine business and sign documents. Under the Lords Commissioners of the Admiralty, the senior official was the First Secretary of the Admiralty. Usually an elected member of the House of Commons, he was the senior civil servant. More often than not, it was the First Secretary who communicated the decisions of the Commissioners to naval officers in the fleet, although from 1783, a Second Secretary assisted in carrying out the administrative burdens of the office.

The Admiralty Office

The heart of the Admiralty was the Admiralty Office on the west side of Whitehall. It was a neighbor of the War Office, which administered the Army at a building called the Horse Guards, both overlooking St. James's Park to the rear. In this location, the Admiralty was close to the nerve centers of national power: 10 Downing Street (the Prime Minister's residence), the Treasury, the Houses of Parliament, St. James's Palace, and the residence of George III.

Designed by Thomas Ripley, the Master Carpenter to the Crown, the Admiralty Office was built between 1725 and 1728 to replace one that had stood on the same site. Masked from the unruly mob on the street by a stone screen added in 1760, the brick building's tall portico and small courtyard were often filled with arriving or departing naval officers and chastened messengers bringing news from the fleet.

It was a place where naval officers' careers were made or lost. As O'Brian describes a visit by Jack Aubrey to seek a commission from Lord Melville in *Post Captain*, that tension is palpable: "The plunge into the Admiralty courtyard; the waiting room, with half a dozen acquaintances—disconnected gossip, his mind and theirs being elsewhere; the staircase to the First Lord's room and there, half-way up, a fat officer leaning against the rail, silent weeping, his slab, pale cheeks all wet with tears. A silent marine watched him from the landing, two porters from the hall, aghast."

The Admiralty Office's oak-paneled boardroom was the site of the Admiralty Commissioners' daily meetings. Saved from the earlier building, a working wind-direction indicator mounted on the wall over the fireplace served as a constant reminder of the fleets at sea, while charts covering the walls kept the Commissioners abreast of the various theaters of action. Together, the Commissioners deliberated at a long table, preparing the fleet for war, selecting its commanders, and making officer assignments. While the Board itself did not make strategic decisions, the First Lord was involved in this process as a member of the Cabinet, and the Admiralty Secretary often forwarded the Cabinet's instructions on strategy and fleet operations to the fleet commanders.

The Admiralty managed a wide range of other administrative and judicial duties as well. For this, the First Secretary of the Admiralty supervised a bustling office with many clerks, visitors, and activities, making it a prime target for spies; indeed, security leaks were a problem.

On the other hand, the Admiralty itself had need of foreign intelligence, which Admiralty officials obtained in several ways. Some of it came from the ordinary sources of government intelligence: Post Office officials in London and Hanover who opened foreign letters and diplomatic agents and colonial officials abroad who forwarded information to the secretaries of state, who in turn forwarded it to the Admiralty. The Admiralty's own sources included the reports of officers abroad, who supplemented their observations with information from merchant seamen and others in the ports they visited. Additionally, the First Lords often privately employed spies to make secret reports. When Lord Spencer became First Lord in 1794, one of his first observations about the Admiralty was the need to assign a clerk the specific responsibility of coordinating the different sources of foreign intelligence.

In 1786, the growing Admiralty bureaucracy expanded into a new yellow brick building joined to the Admiralty on the south. Here on the ground floor were three large state rooms for the First Lord's official entertaining. Above that, two floors housed mainly the private apartments of the First Lord but also the Admiralty Library.

The Admiralty was not the only office that managed naval affairs. There were a variety of other boards and offices in London that dealt with specific aspects of the Navy. The most important of these was the Navy Board.

The Navy Board

The Principal Officers and Commissioners of the Navy, who formed the Navy Board, worked in the Navy Office building at Somerset House in the Strand. They were concerned with three main areas: (1) the material condition of the fleet, including building, fitting out, and repairing ships, managing dockyards, purchasing naval stores, and

leasing transport vessels; (2) naval expenditure, including the payment of all salaries and auditing accounts; and (3) the health and sub-
sistence of seamen. The last function was delegated to subsidiary
boards, also located at Somerset House:

- The Sick and Wounded Board, or the Commissioners for taking
  care of Sick and Wounded Seamen and for the Exchanging of
  Prisoners of War.
- The Commissioners of the Victualling, who were responsible for
  acquiring, storing, and delivering food supplies to the fleet.
- The Transport Board, which hired merchant vessels to carry
  troops and supplies, took over from the Sick and Wounded
  Board the responsibility for prisoners of war in 1796. The two
  boards merged in 1806. Originally composed of three senior
  naval officers, the Transport Board also included a civil administrator and a physician after 1806.

The Ordnance Board

An entirely independent board at the Ordnance Office with locations
both at the Tower of London and at the Warren, next to Woolwich
Dockyard down the Thames from London, the Ordnance Board was
responsible for supplying both the Army and the Navy with guns
and ammunition. Headed by the Master-General of the Ordnance,
this board contracted with private foundries to make cannon; supervised gunpowder plants at Faversham and Waltham Abbey; managed the arsenal at Woolwich, where guns were received, tested, and
issued; and appointed and supplied gunners to ships. The Ordnance
Board worked closely with the Admiralty, its principal channel of
communication on sea affairs, in determining with the Navy Board
and its subsidiaries the specifications of armaments for naval vessels
and in coordinating the timely delivery and convoy of supplies as
well as the construction and victualing of Ordnance vessels.

The Size of the Navy

Together, these offices and boards managed the support and direction
of a large number of officers, seamen, and ships. Today, as then, it is difficult to ascertain exactly how many men were in the Navy. Parliament
authorized a certain number in its annual vote, a certain number were
assigned to vessels, and then there were actual musters, where the men

on board each ship were counted. These muster counts varied from month to month and often were not completely kept or fully compiled for the Navy as a whole. The following figures, however, give an approximation (no figures are available for 1814 and 1815).

Ships and Men in the Royal Navy, 1793–1813

Year	Number of ships	Number of men authorized	Number of men assigned	Number of men mustered
1793	390	45,000	69,868	69,416
1794	420	85,000	87,331	73,835
1795	483		100,000	96,001
1796	534	110,000	114,365	106,708
1797	587	120,000	118,788	114,603
1798	660	120,000	122,687	114,617
1799	694	120,000	128,930	
1800	729	120,000	126,192	118,247
1801	735	120,000	125,061	117,202
1802	746	130,000	129,340	118,005
1803	608	50,000	49,430	
1804	623	100,000	84,431	
1805	726	120,000	109,205	
1806	789	120,000	111,237	119,627
1807	865	130,000	119,855	
1808	921	130,000	140,822	
1809	979	130,000	141,989	
1810	976	145,000	142,098	
1811	960	145,000	130,866	
1812	898	145,000	131,087	138,204
1813	899	145,000	130,127	

Source: Numbers of ships as of January 1 each year from Roger Morriss, The Royal Dockyards During the Revolutionary and Napoleonic Wars (Leicester: Leicester University Press, 1983), table 1, p. 12. Remaining data from Christopher Lloyd, The British Seaman (London: Longmans, Green, 1968), pp. 288–89.

Ships and Tactics

The Navy of this period was made up of a wide variety of ships with specific roles to play. Some were designed for combat, others for support activities. The most important combat vessels were those designed to fight an organized enemy fleet in a line of battle; they were called line-of-battle ships or ships of the line.

Battle Tactics. Navies had developed the line of battle in the 17th century. Simply described, it involved sailing ships in a line, bow to stern, as the most efficient way of concentrating their gunfire, at the same time protecting the ships' weakest points. The bow and stern were the least protected parts of the ship, carrying only a few guns, and volleys received there could damage the ships' weakest structural points if aimed low at the rudder, stern, or bow, or, if aimed high, could travel the whole length of the deck, killing men and wreaking havoc with the sails and rigging.

It was these factors that made the tactic known as "crossing the T" so effective. In this maneuver, one battle line passed, at a 90° angle, ahead of the opposing battle line, each ship firing its broadsides at the enemy ships' bows and masts and along their decks. This maneuver was not an easy one to undertake because the approaching ships were themselves vulnerable to heavy gunfire. It helped to have the weather gauge, that is to say, to be to windward of the opposing fleet, because that allowed the swiftest approach and the advantage of choosing when to initiate the engagement. But one could not always dictate one's position when encountering an enemy, or, for that matter, predict wind shifts. In general, however, while the British preferred the weather gauge, the French more often preferred the lee, because they tended to concentrate on reaching a destination to get troops or to convoy merchant ships rather than on seeking battle.

There were some other significant national differences in naval gunnery. Most prominent among them, perhaps, was the fact that in general the French fired at the masts, rigging, and sails of British ships, aiming to disable the enemy's motive power, while the British usually fired on the French warships' hulls. It was far more difficult to hit the hull of an enemy ship, but piercing the hull often created the heaviest damage, possibly sinking the ship.

Most battles took place at relatively close range. They often didn't begin until the ships were as close as 1,000 yards, and sometimes this distance was reduced to 500 yards when the guns were double-shotted (firing two rounds at once). Closer ranges were termed "musket shot range" (within 300 yards) and "pistol shot range" (within 50 yards).

Sometimes, ships of the line were engaged in blockade operations, designed either to keep the enemy's ships in port or, alternatively, to draw them out to fight. There were two types of blockades: close and open. An open blockade, usually by smaller ships of the line off an enemy port, such as Toulon in the Mediterranean or Brest in north-western France, gave the impression that the port was not carefully watched or that there was a chance of battle success for the enemy. At the first sign the enemy fleet gave of moving out of port, a fast ship was sent to bring up the blockader's battle fleet to engage them.

A close blockade with ships of the line, such as the one Nelson conducted off Cadiz in July 1797, was difficult, dangerous, and tedious work for the blockaders. Such a blockade was meant to keep an enemy fleet at anchor in port. Jack Aubrey was typical of many officers who expressed their displeasure in such work. Not only did it lack the élan of battle, but it was difficult to control a large line of battle in shallow and confined waters close to shore.

Rated Ships of the Line. Broadly speaking, the ships of the line were also the rated ships, falling into five or six classes. All of them were normally commanded by a sea officer trained in navigation, seamanship, and gunnery and holding the official rank and title of Captain, that is to say, a Post-Captain. There were gradations of seniority among these men, depending upon their length of service and experience, but all were Post-Captains.

The biggest ships in the Navy, the first-rate ships of the line, were all armed with 100 or more heavy cannons on three decks, with lighter guns on the forecastle and quarterdeck. In 1807, they carried a total complement of about 837 naval officers and men, plus 170 Royal Marines (a special corps of soldiers who served on naval vessels and were called the Royal Marines from 1802). The largest British ship of this period, carrying 120 guns, was H.M.S. *Caledonia,* launched in 1808. Nelson's flagship, the 100-gun H.M.S. *Victory,* was among the biggest ships when it was launched in 1765. In addition to being fighting ships, these large ships had additional naval roles, often carrying an Admiral and his staff either at sea or in port and serving as symbols of naval power and diplomatic prestige.

The next class of ships of the line, the second rates, carried 90 to 98 guns, usually 98, with heavy guns on three decks, lighter armament on the quarterdeck, forecastle, and poop, and a total complement of about 738 naval officers and men, and about 150 Marines. Most naval officers did not like these three-deck ships, since they did not perform as well as either the first or third rates under sail. When Admiral Lord Keith was commanding the Mediterranean Fleet (1799–1802), he preferred as his flagship the two-deck third-rate ships *Audacious* and *Minotaur* to the *Foudroyant,* a three-deck second rate.

Third rates, also ships of the line, usually carried 64, 68, 74, or 80 guns, with the heavy guns on two decks and lighter guns on the quarterdeck and forecastle. Among these, the 74 predominated, carrying a complement of 590 to 640 naval officers and men, plus 125 Marines. Fourth-rate ships carried 50 to 60 guns on two decks and were technically rated as ships of the line, but during this period they were rarely used in the line of battle. In fact, they were rapidly disappearing from the fleet, having been used in peacetime largely as flagships for small overseas squadrons or as large vessels for patrol work. A fourth rate carried a complement of about 343 naval officers and men, plus 59 Marines.

The Composition of the Royal Navy, 1793–1815
(as of January 1)

Year	1st rates (100+ guns)	2nd rates (90–98 guns)	3rd rates (64–80 guns)	4th rates (50–60 guns)	5th rates (32–48 guns)	6th rates (20–32 guns)	Unrated (sloops and others)
1793	5	19	114	22	90	41	99
1794	6	19	117	22	94	42	120
1795	6	20	120	20	112	41	164
1796	6	19	117	30	118	44	200
1797	7	19	120	25	130	47	239
1798	8	20	130	25	135	49	293
1799	8	21	137	23	132	51	322
1800	9	19	136	26	132	47	360
1801	8	19	139	26	134	47	362
1802	8	19	138	26	141	44	370
1803	7	15	126	20	124	33	283
1804	7	15	129	20	128	33	291
1805	8	14	131	23	142	34	374
1806	8	15	139	22	153	36	416
1807	8	15	145	20	166	41	470
1808	8	14	165	19	175	46	494
1809	8	15	170	18	179	40	549
1810	8	15	177	17	185	40	534
1811	9	17	177	15	181	38	523
1812	9	15	181	14	173	30	476
1813	9	16	188	13	165	31	477
1814	9	12	183	19	180	40	493

Source: *Adapted from Roger Morriss,* The Royal Dockyards During the Revolutionary and Napoleonic Wars *(Leicester: Leicester University Press, 1983), table 1, p. 12.*

Frigates. Like destroyers in modern navies, frigates were the most glamorous ships. They were the fleet's fast fighters, involved in all sorts of duties and high drama. Not part of the line of battle, they fought the majority of single-ship actions, convoyed merchantmen with valuable cargoes, raided rich enemy fleets, served as the eyes of the battle fleet, and carried earth-shattering news from all quarters of the globe. There were many different types and designs, but nearly all were fifth rates with 32 to 48 guns on a single deck. Some of these, known as razee frigates, were built as larger ships but had upper decks removed to create single-deck frigates. A fifth rate carried a complement of 215 to 294 naval officers and men, plus 42 to 48 Marines.

In this period, the United States Navy earned a reputation for the quality of its frigates, the most famous, the 44-gun U.S.S. *Constitution*, being launched in 1797. The military successes of the *Constitution* and her compatriots, the *Chesapeake, Constellation, Congress, President*, and *United States*, rocked the morale of the British Navy during the War of 1812.

There were some sixth-rate frigates of 20-some guns in the Royal Navy, the most common type carrying 28 guns. Jack Aubrey's *Surprise* was one of these. A sixth rate carried a complement of about 135 to 195 officers and men, plus 30 Marines.

Unrated Ships and Vessels. A wide variety of other types of warships did not fall under the system of rated ships, the principal ones being sloops, bomb vessels, fireships, brigs, cutters, and gunboats.

Sloops. Unlike the current sailing sloop, which carries only a single mast, in the Royal Navy at this time a sloop of war had two or three masts, all carrying both square and fore-and-aft sails. When it had two masts, it was said to be "brig-rigged," and with three, "ship-rigged." Sloops varied widely in appearance, but they carried 10 to 18 guns and were generally commanded by sea officers with the rank of Commander. There were more than 200 of these ships in the Navy during the latter part of this period. Sometimes they carried out the patrol duties of frigates, but, being relatively small, they were also commonly used close to shore for raiding and cutting-out expeditions to capture particular ships. Sloops ranged in their complement of men from 42 to 121 officers and men, with 15 to 20 Marines.

Bomb Vessels and Fireships. Only a small number of these very specialized ships existed in the Navy. Designed to carry heavy ordnance for bombarding cities and fortifications, bomb vessels were named for volcanoes or some other entity that evoked fire and brimstone. When not being used for this purpose, they were employed as sloops. Fireships, also used as sloops when not in their special role, were intended to be set on fire and sent in among an enemy fleet to ignite its ships. No vessels were actually used for this purpose during these wars, but several were kept in readiness. One fireship was used to fire rockets in 1809. Bomb vessels carried a complement of about 67 officers and men, and fireships carried 45 to 56 officers and men.

Brigs. A brig was a smaller version of the brig-rigged sloop of war, and its distinctive feature was square sails on two masts. Brigs usually carried 14 short-range carronade guns and were commanded by Lieutenants.

Cutters. Designed for speed, these vessels carried about ten guns and a lot of sail. Most of them bore both square and fore-and-aft sails on a single mast. Some, however, used a distinctively American schooner rig taken from a type used at Bermuda, having a very large triangular sail, and, with only four to six guns, were categorized as schooners. Cutters carried a complement of 45 to 60 officers and men.

Gunboats. The term "gunboat" comprised a wide variety of vessels that were used primarily for local defense. They were relatively small and carried at least one or two guns mounted in the bow or stern. The smallest being not much bigger than a ship's boat and the largest approaching the description of a cutter or schooner, gunboats carried a complement of 45 to 50 officers and men.

Yachts. This type of vessel was not a pleasure vessel, but a relatively fast, sleek sailing craft designed to carry high officials on state visits. They carried a complement of 50 to 67 officers and men.

The Royal Dockyards and Ropeyards

The capacity to construct and repair ships was vital to the Navy. By the 1750s, Britain's dockyards had become the largest industrial organization in the world and remained so until the vast changes brought by the Industrial Revolution in the 19th century. A key part of these establishments, which were under the authority of the Navy Board, were the ropeyards that manufactured the miles of cordage required to rig and operate the ships of the Navy.

At home, the largest concentration of these dockyards was in southern England, at Deptford, Woolwich, Chatham, Portsmouth, and Plymouth, but there were also a number strategically located around the world, the largest being at Malta in the Mediterranean, Halifax in the North Atlantic, Jamaica and Antigua in the Caribbean, and at the East India Company outposts at Bombay in the Indian Ocean. In 1814, they employed a total of 17,374 civilian yard officers and laborers. During the two wars, they built 119 ships (supplementing those built by commercial dockyards) and repaired and outfitted many more.

Sea Officers: Commissioned and Warrant

Sea officers came from every class of society, but without a doubt promotion was dependent upon one's being liked by senior officers and having connections.

In O'Brian's Aubrey-Maturin novels this is readily apparent, and usually to Jack Aubrey's disadvantage. In *Post Captain*, at Aubrey's disastrous interview with Lord St. Vincent, the First Lord of the Admiralty, St. Vincent rebukes Aubrey for his doggedness in pursuing post rank and for the attempts of his father and others to curry favor on his behalf: "General Aubrey has written forty letters to me and other members of the Board and he has been told that it is not in contemplation to promote you. . . . Your friends pepper us with letters to say that you *must* be made post. That was the very word the Duke of Kent thought fit to use, put up to it by Lady Keith." Throughout the novels, Aubrey's connections and actions are double-edged swords. Others far less accomplished than he at warfare but neater in their personal affairs and with better connections are promoted faster and receive the plum assignments.

All sea officers held written documents that gave them their rank and authority. The most important officers received commissions from the Admiralty, and the less important officers, such as Surgeons and Masters, received warrants from the Navy Board or other authorities. Normally, these commissions were given for each assignment or appointment, not just upon first receiving the rank.

Admirals. Admirals, also known as flag officers because they flew a colored flag denoting their rank, were in the highest category of sea officers. They had long been divided into three sets of three groups each. There were three squadrons, each of which flew a different colored ensign. In order of seniority, they were the Red, White, and Blue squadrons. Each squadron had an Admiral, Vice-Admiral, and Rear-

Admiral. An Admiral commanded the main body of the squadron and flew the Union flag at the mainmast head; a Vice-Admiral commanded the van and flew his flag on the foremast; and a Rear-Admiral commanded the rear and flew his flag at the head of the mizzenmast.

In the first part of these wars, however, the position of the most senior post, the Admiral of the Red, was not filled, as it was reserved by tradition for the Lord High Admiral or Admiral of the Fleet. From 1805, both the positions of Admiral of the Fleet and the newly created post of Admiral of the Red, coming next below, were filled. At his death in 1805, Horatio Nelson, as a Vice-Admiral of the White, was about halfway up the Admirals' hierarchy.

Between the Admirals and the established lower officers was another category, the Commodores.

Commodores. This rank was neither permanent nor a necessary step for promotion between Captain and Rear-Admiral. A Commodore was a Captain holding temporary command over a squadron, who had authority similar to that of a Rear-Admiral. Instead of a flag, a commodore flew a swallow-tailed broad pendant, also called a broad pennant. After 1805 there were two distinct types of Commodores: (1) a senior Captain who was appointed Commander-in-chief of a station or a detached squadron and therefore outranked any flag officer who came within his jurisdiction, and (2) a senior Captain appointed by his Commander-in-chief to command a division under him. All Commodores reverted to the rank of Captain upon hauling down their broad pennants and relinquishing their duties.

Captains. A sea officer with the rank of Captain, also called Post-Captain, reached this "post rank" by being appointed to command a "post-ship," one of the first- to sixth-rate square-rigged ships. The term "post" was used to differentiate from officers who commanded unrated vessels and were called captains, even though they may have been only Lieutenants or Commanders in naval rank or even masters of merchant vessels. A Post-Captain's seniority started on the day he first took command of a rated ship, and if he lived long enough to reach the top seniority, he was, by tradition, entitled to flag rank, that is to say to be made an Admiral. This bottleneck created some obvious difficulties for the Admiralty, which in 1747 circumvented the tradition of automatic promotion by simultaneously promoting Captains they preferred not to have at sea to Rear-Admirals and retiring them without ever having them serve at sea as a flag officer or add the distinctive Red, White, or Blue Squadron color to their rank. Officers in this situation, such as Admiral Haddock in O'Brian's *Post Captain*, came to be known as "yellow" Admirals.

Commanders. The rank below Captain was Commander. The institution of this rank in 1794 caused some confusion, since up to that point, any commanding officer was properly the commander of his vessel, regardless of his rank, and was called captain.

From 1794 onward, those promoted to Captain came only from among those who held the rank of Commander. Officers holding the rank of Commander commanded sloops of war, vessels smaller than rated ships but larger than the cutters and gunboats commanded by Lieutenants.

Lieutenants. The most junior of the traditional sea officers' ranks in the Navy, a Lieutenant was originally the Captain's deputy, literally a "place-holder." While a small nonrated ship might have only one Lieutenant, a first rate carried up to six. So it was common for a Lieutenant's commission to specify his relative position, for example as First, Second, or Fourth Lieutenant on a particular ship. The Admiralty issued a new commission every time a Lieutenant's relative position changed. For promotion above the rank of Lieutenant, a sea officer often needed either to have the patronage of an Admiral or political influence in London or to distinguish himself in some extraordinary manner as an officer. That is why a positive mention in a Captain's letter following a victorious action was so important.

Midshipmen. Ranking just below Lieutenants, Midshipmen were not commissioned sea officers. From 1794, all newly rated Midshipmen were considered to be prospective commissioned sea officers, but this was not the case before that year. During the period of O'Brian's novels, there were still a number of Midshipmen in the service who were of the pre-1794 type and had no aspirations of being Lieutenants. After 1794, the regulations required that one must serve two years as a Midshipman as well as pass an examination to become a Lieutenant. From 1802 to 1814, Midshipmen who served as second in command to a Lieutenant commanding a small vessel such as a gunboat or cutter were called sub-lieutenants.

Cadets. There was a very small group of prospective commissioned sea officers who held this title while attending the Royal

Naval Academy (after 1806, the Royal Naval College) in Portsmouth for up to three years of training before going to sea as Midshipmen.

Masters. Holding warrants, Masters were generally of a lower social class than those who aspired to become commissioned sea officers, but in pay and status they were closely equivalent to Lieutenants. They were specialists in navigation and pilotage, and in order to serve in successively larger ships, had to pass progressively more difficult examinations set by Trinity House, a corporation chartered in 1514 to superintend pilotage, maintain buoys, and license seamen. Masters were qualified to stand deck watches and to command naval vessels engaged in operations other than combat. By 1808, they were considered "warrant officers of commissioned rank" and joined sea officers in messing in the wardroom. They were assisted by Master's Mates.

Surgeons. The Navy Board qualified Surgeons through an examination at the Barber-Surgeons' Company, and they were responsible to the Sick and Wounded Board under the Navy Board. They were the only medical officers on board individual ships, but the Navy Board did appoint Physicians to serve with large squadrons and at naval hospitals. From 1808, Surgeons, like Masters, were considered equivalent to commissioned officers. They were assisted by Surgeon's Mates, who after 1805 were called Assistant Surgeons.

Pursers. Receiving warrants from the Admiralty, Pursers were responsible to the Victualling Board but were not required to be examined. In the double capacity of an official and a regulated private contractor, the Purser managed the supply and issue of victuals, clothes, and ship's stores. Pursers were frequently assisted by Purser's Stewards and Purser's Yeomen. In 1808, they, like Masters, obtained equivalency with wardroom officers.

Chaplains. Also holding warrants from the Admiralty, Chaplains were examined by the Bishop of London before being accepted by the Navy. From 1808, they obtained wardroom status and from 1812 were qualified to receive pensions. The Articles of War required that religious services be performed every Sunday according to the rites of the Church of England, but religion was not widely and openly accepted among the ranks as an important factor in the Navy. Some naval officers took up the Anglican evangelical movement in this period and tried to bring religion to seamen, but many sailors thought these officers brought bad luck to their ships and derisively called them "blue light" ships.

Chaplains often also served as teachers, though some ships did carry Schoolmasters qualified by Trinity House and holding warrants of a lower status from the Admiralty. They were assigned to teach all young people on board ship. Originally on the same pay level as Midshipmen, Schoolmasters had their pay raised in 1812.

Boatswains, Gunners, and Carpenters. These warrant officers were usually less educated than Masters, Surgeons, and Pursers and were not wardroom officers. Boatswains were specialists in sails, rigging, ground tackle, and the skills associated with cordage, held Admiralty warrants, and were responsible to the Navy Board. Gunners were warranted by the Ordnance Board and were responsible to it for the ships' guns and ammunition, while Carpenters were primarily concerned with the maintenance of the hull, masts, and yards and were responsible to the Navy Board. Unlike the others, Carpenters often began their careers as apprentice civilian workers in the dockyards before qualifying for warrants from the Navy Board to serve at sea. The Carpenter, Boatswain, Purser, Gunner, and Cook were considered "standing officers" of a ship, and in principle, warranted to it for the ship's lifetime, whether she was in commission or not.

Cooks. In the 17th century, Cooks held warrants, but at the beginning of the 18th century, they descended to an inferior status. Usually untrained seamen, they were often recruited from the ranks of the injured and disabled.

Daily Life on a Warship

The daily routine of life at sea was monotonous. By tradition, the day officially began at noon, when the date and day of the week were changed on the log-board. Just before noon on a clear day, the Master, Master's Mates, and Midshipmen measured with their quadrants the angle of the sun as it reached its highest point off the horizon, thus determining latitude and correcting the time kept by any chronometers on board. Noon was reported to the Captain, and eight strokes were struck on the ship's bell, followed by the Boatswain's "pipe to dinner," executed on his high-pitched silver whistle.

The day itself was divided into watches of four hours apiece, measured by a sandglass and marked by a ringing of the bell: eight bells at twelve o'clock, one bell at twelve-thirty, two at one o'clock, three at one-thirty and so on, until eight bells was reached at four o'clock, and the cycle started again.

Sailors stood their duty hours in watches, four hours on and four off, throughout the day and night. Shortly before four A.M., the Quartermasters, who had among their duties keeping time and steering the ship, awoke the Midshipmen, Mates, and the Lieutenant of the watch coming on duty, and shortly thereafter, the Boatswain stood at the hatchways and piped "All hands," and shouted: "Larboard (or starboard) watch, ahoy. Rouse out there, you sleepers. Hey. Out or down here." Stumbling out of their hammocks, the members of the watch quickly dressed and came on deck for muster before going to their assigned stations. They relieved the wheel and the lookouts, hove the log to determine speed, and recorded all the information on the log-board.

Shortly after four A.M., the Carpenter and Boatswain came on deck to begin their repair work, while the Cook lit fires in the galley and began the preparations for breakfast, often the oatmeal gruel called "burgoo" or "skillagolee," an unloved concoction frequently of poor oatmeal and bad ship's water. (Sometime after 1805, Cooks were able to serve it with butter or molasses to make it more palatable.) Another breakfast offering was dark, thick "Scotch Coffee," burned ship's biscuit boiled in water.

At about five A.M. the watch began to wash down the decks and polish the planks with a heavy holystone. Nooks and crannies were polished in the same way with small bits of the same type of stone, called prayer books. Following the holystoners came other sailors with brooms, swabs, and buckets to dry the decks, while others polished the brass fittings so that they gleamed in the first rays of dawn. Other seamen flemished down the lines into neat and orderly coils.

At seven A.M., this work was about finished, and the decks were drying as the First Lieutenant came on deck to supervise the remaining work of the day. At about seven-thirty A.M., the Boatswain's Mate piped "All hands, up hammocks," and the rest of the crew came on deck. After the last of the hammocks were stowed, the Captain came on deck and eight bells were struck for eight o'clock. With his approval, the Boatswain piped breakfast for the crew. After half an hour, they returned to their duty, and the new watch came on deck, bringing with them bags and chests from the lower deck to allow cleaning there.

During the forenoon watch, between eight A.M. and noon, many of the crew worked in "messes," groupings based on their mess tables, preparing the main meal of the day, to be served at noon. Others might have helped the Master and the Captain of the Hold restow the provisions in the warship's small hold, below the orlop deck, to make the ship sail more efficiently. Or they might have performed some other maintenance chores such as retarring the rigging or repairing a damaged cannon. Those not on watch could sleep, socialize, or mend their clothes.

By eleven, six bells, the Captain, having examined the Midshipmen's logs and the Gunner's, Purser's, Boatswain's, and Carpenter's accounts and having conferenced with the First Lieutenant and others, might call all hands to witness punishment, in which case the Boatswain rigged a grating for flogging a seaman.

After the observance of noon, dinner was served to the crew, who used sea chests as benches while eating. Later, the fife might play a tune on his flute while the crew received their liquor rations from tubs on the main deck and took them down to the mess tables below. The issuing of grog, a mixture of rum and water, began in the 1740s as a means to control liquor consumption in the Navy. The men usually received two rations a day totaling a pint, but it was not the only drink. Beer, rationed out at the rate of a gallon a day, was far more popular than grog but usually available only in home waters or up to a month out at sea. In the Mediterranean, the seamen often received a pint of wine as their alcohol ration.

While the crew ate at tables below deck on weekly rations of ship's biscuit, salt beef, pork with pea soup, and cheese, the officers had better fare. In the wardroom, they ate together sitting on chairs at a well-set table, each often attended by a servant. Instead of sharing the rations the Admiralty provided the crew, the officers appointed one of their own as the mess caterer, and he purchased their food ashore, using their mess subscriptions. Sometimes these mess subscriptions, billed to each officer, ran as high as £60 per year (more than half a Lieutenant's annual pay) and allowed officers to enjoy such luxuries as tea, sugar, and wine.

At one-thirty P.M., the watch on deck was called to duty, leaving those off watch to do what they wished, or, alternatively, all hands were called to be exercised for ship's drills: fire, boarding, sail handling, gunnery, etc.

At four in the afternoon, the watch changed again. This four-hour period was divided into two two-hour watches, called dogwatches.

During this time, a short evening meal was served, along with the second portion of grog. Just before sunset, the drummer beat to quarters and all hands reported to their battle stations for inspection by the officers. At this time, the Master of Arms often arrested anyone who was being rowdy or who had managed to drink too much of a friend's rum. Offenders were put on the black list and often placed in irons through the next day. After the ship was reported as being in good order, the men were released from their battle stations and recovered their hammocks from stowage in the netting.

At eight o'clock, the watch was changed, those just finished turning in for a few hours of sleep before the middle watch (midnight to four A.M.). Lights were extinguished so that the ship could not be seen from a distance, and the Master at Arms began his series of nightly rounds through the ship. All was quiet, except for the regular sentry reports of "all's well" from various stations.

And so the pattern continued day after day, month after month, year after year, broken only by battle, the occasional call at port, or an emergency that required all hands to work together in maneuvering the ship.

An Overview of the War of the French Revolution

The War of the French Revolution involved the formation of two coalitions against France and nearly a decade of fighting before a temporary peace was concluded in 1802. After a year of uneasy truce, however, war broke out again, this time continuing for more than a decade. To differentiate the two wars, the first is called the War of the French Revolution; the second, the Napoleonic War. Each of these, in turn, had its own subdivisions.

At first Britain hesitated to get involved. As the revolution swept across France and the Bastille fell to the mob in 1789, the British government explicitly refrained from any involvement in the internal affairs of France. London abandoned this detachment only at the end of 1792 and took little direct action until after Louis XVI's execution in 1793. Finally, the French republican government, having started wars with Austria and Prussia the previous year, declared war on Britain and on the Dutch Republic on February 1, 1793, and British leaders confirmed the necessary course of action.

The War of the First Coalition, 1793–1798

Joining as partner in the First Coalition with Austria, Prussia, Holland, and Spain, Britain chose a diffuse strategy. Following precedents from the period of 1689 to 1714, Britain tried to starve France into submission. At a time when France was facing a major crop failure, the Admiralty sent orders to stop all French merchant ships and any neutrals carrying grain to France. It was this order that sent Admiral Lord Howe in search of French Admiral Villaret-Joyeuse, then convoying American grain from the Chesapeake Bay. Engaging him on the "Glorious First of June" in 1794, Howe's line of battle sliced through the French line and engaged it from leeward, capturing six ships and sinking one. But Howe paid little attention to the merchant ships, which reached France with the much-needed grain.

In the West Indies, Vice-Admiral Sir John Jervis with Lieutenant-General Sir Charles Grey set about capturing French colonies. Moving rapidly, they took the island of Martinique in February 1794 and then Guadeloupe. But the French quickly retook the latter. In 1796, Rear-Admiral Sir Hugh Christian continued British successes by capturing the islands of St. Lucia, St. Vincent, and Grenada. And in February 1797, Rear-Admiral Henry Harvey and Lieutenant-General Ralph Abercromby took Trinidad from the Spanish.

In the Mediterranean, Admiral Lord Hood's squadron took advantage of Toulon's discontent with the new revolutionary regime, seizing the city and, with it, France's most important naval dockyard for the Mediterranean fleet. But British forces were unable to maintain their position and soon withdrew all the way to Lisbon, Portugal too far away to function as a base for effective naval operations in the western Mediterranean. When a revolt on the island of Corsica, led by Paoli, suggested that the island might serve as a base for blockading Toulon, Hood orchestrated an amphibious assault in 1794 to achieve that end. It was there, while directing fire on land at Calvi, that Captain Horatio Nelson was wounded and lost the sight of his right eye. Although British forces took the island, they were forced out again just two years later.

At that point in 1796, the Royal Navy retired from the Mediterranean to await another opportunity. Some members of the coalition interpreted Britain's withdrawal as a failure to support the alliance. Under this pretext, Austria withdrew from the coalition in 1797, joining Holland, Prussia, and the Dutch Republic, which had already made peace in 1795. From 1797 to 1799, Britain remained France's only opponent.

Operating from Portugal's Tagus River in 1797, Admiral Sir John Jervis learned that the Spanish fleet was sailing northward to join the French at Brest, possibly intending to invade Britain. With a fleet of 15 ships of the line, Jervis found the Spanish fleet of 27 ships, commanded by Don José de Cordova, 24 miles southwest of Cape St. Vincent, Portugal, on February 14. Jervis led his line, close-hauled, past detached units of the Spanish line, intending to reverse course and attack from the windward gauge. While this maneuver was taking place, Nelson, fearing that the enemy might escape, wore his ship and headed straight for their main body. This unexpected move confused the Spanish and contributed to their defeat. Coming at a very low point in Britain's war effort, news of the victory boosted morale tremendously. Nevertheless, the Navy faced an even greater challenge when sailors of the Home Fleet anchored at Spithead off Portsmouth, affected by some of the ideas of the French Revolution, mutinied in the spring of 1797, demanding better pay and conditions. The mutiny spread to the fleet anchored at the Nore. Both incidents were quelled without a major disruption, but they created serious doubts over whether British seamen would willingly fight the Dutch or French fleets.

Following the French conquest of the Dutch Republic in 1795, Britain began seizing Dutch shipping to prevent France from using Dutch resources against her. This policy bore fruit in Commodore Peter Rainier's seizure of the Dutch East India Company's settlements at Amboyna and the Banda Islands in the East Indies in 1796 and in Vice-Admiral Sir George Elphinstone's attack on Cape Town in the Dutch colony at the Cape of Good Hope in September 1797. On October 11, 1797, a Dutch squadron of 16 ships of the line and eight frigates under Vice-Admiral Jan de Winter left the island of Texel on the northern Dutch coast and sought an engagement with British Admiral Adam Duncan. Duncan defeated Winter off Camperdown on the Dutch North Sea coast.

By 1798, Austria seemed ready to rejoin the war against France and repeatedly asked Britain to return her naval forces to the Mediterranean. In the intervening years, however, France had strengthened herself in the Mediterranean, and the demand on

British naval forces in other important theaters had increased. Still, in the hope of protecting Naples from France and influencing Austria to join a new coalition, the Cabinet in London ordered the Admiralty to send a squadron to the Mediterranean. Lord St. Vincent wisely chose Rear-Admiral Horatio Nelson's. The daring move deprived the British Home fleet of its strategic reserve, leaving nothing to meet the French fleet if it broke through the British blockade of the northwestern French port of Brest. At the same time, it left the West Indies vulnerable to the Spanish, and the North Sea to the Dutch.

The stakes were high, but the British had gambled on the right man. With a stroke of good luck, a long, frustrating, and misdirected search blossomed into a smashing victory. With 14 ships of the line, Nelson found the French fleet with 13 ships of the line under Vice-Admiral François Brueys at anchor in the protected Aboukir Bay near Alexandria, Egypt. The Battle of the Nile resulted on August 1, 1798. Sailing in shallow water on the shore side of the anchored ships, Nelson succeeded in taking all but two of the French ships and destroying the flagship *L'Orient*, which blew up, killing Admiral Brueys.

The War of the Second Coalition, 1799–1801

The Battle of the Nile was not enough in itself to mobilize the creation of the coalition needed to defeat the extremely powerful French forces, but the dramatic victory, coming at a critical time for diplomacy, did play a role. Throughout 1799, allied British, Austrian, and Russian diplomats forged a policy for the coalition's offensive. Their strategy called for encircling France with concentric attacks from the Channel, the Alps, the North, and the Mediterranean. But the chief naval component, Admiral Lord Keith's fleet, which was to attack from the Mediterranean, was soon diverted after Bonaparte's great victory at Marengo in June 1800 caused the Cabinet in London to reconsider. Britain's strategic focus shifted from offensive, coalition warfare to one allowing options in case the coalition failed. Land operations in Holland and amphibious attacks in Brittany became relatively more important, and the Mediterranean became primarily an area for defensive action. In September 1800, the successful capture of the island of Malta, lying as it does at a major choke point in the passage between the eastern and western Mediterranean, solidified Britain's defensive positions.

In March 1801, Lord Keith landed General Abercromby's expeditionary force in Egypt to contest French presence there. Abercromby's seizure of Alexandria gave Britain a strong bargaining chip for future peace negotiations. Despite this, it seemed that nothing could diminish France's ability to dominate the Continent. Russia abandoned the coalition and formed a League of Armed Neutrality with the Baltic powers. The assassination of Czar Paul in March 1801 and the British attack on Copenhagen in April of that year served to destroy the league, but Bonaparte's continued military success forced both Austria and Naples to agree to come to peace terms.

The Peace of Amiens, 1802–1803

Following William Pitt's political defeat, the new ministry under Prime Minister Henry Addington signed the preliminary peace agreement on October 1, 1801. Under the terms of the treaty signed at Amiens in March 1802, Spain regained Minorca, the Knights of St. John recovered Malta under Russian supervision, and Bonaparte evacuated Naples, the Papal States, and Egypt. France gained the most advantages, retaining most of her Continental conquests and giving up none of her overseas gains, while Britain retained only Trinidad and Ceylon, yielding her conquests at the Cape of Good Hope, Egypt, Malta, and in the West Indies at Tobago, Martinique, Demerrara, Berbice, and Curaçao.

For Britain, the Amiens treaty was a necessity, but it soon became obvious that Napoleon was not satisfied. He clearly intended to dominate the Mediterranean, capture Russian trade, and exclude Britain from the Levant trade while also threatening her in India. When Britain returned Minorca to Spain, Napoleon quickly moved to annex Leghorn (Livorno) and the island of Elba, appearing only to wait until Britain surrendered her strategic position in Malta before taking even more.

An Overview of the Napoleonic War

After a short period of peace, war against Napoleon erupted again. This time, it would take a dozen years and three more coalitions before peace was achieved in 1815. The immediate cause of the outbreak of hostilities was Britain's decision in 1803 not to evacuate Malta in accordance with the Treaty of Amiens.

But the new war was not just a renewal of the old dispute. Britain had fought before to contain the French Revolution. From 1803 to 1815, her objectives were different. This time, she fought to defeat Napoleon's bid to unite Continental Europe under his control and to build up French maritime strength in the process. As Napoleon marched his army into Germany, Britain watched. But she also sent a strong squadron under Nelson to the Mediterranean to observe the French fleet at Toulon, an expedition under Sir Samuel Hood to the West Indies to capture St. Lucia, and a squadron under Commodore John Loring to aid black troops rebelling against France on Santo Domingo.

The War of the Third Coalition, 1805

In 1804, the French began to prepare for an invasion of Britain. Simultaneously, Spain joined France, potentially providing naval superiority in the Channel and the Mediterranean. In the face of this, Britain worked to form a Third Coalition. Nelson watched the French fleet based at Toulon, not knowing where they would strike: Sardinia, Sicily, Naples, Egypt, or elsewhere. When the French fleet sailed from Toulon, Nelson followed them all the way to the West Indies and back. At the same time, squadrons commanded by Sir Robert Calder in the Bay of Biscay and by Lord Cornwallis in the Channel also helped prevent Franco-Spanish naval forces from joining together to form one superior fleet powerful enough to provide the support Napoleon would need to successfully invade Britain. Checked here, Napoleon canceled his invasion plans and marched his army from the northwest coast of France east against Austria. At Ulm, he quickly defeated the Austrians before Austria could become an effective member of the Third Coalition.

Thwarted in its original purpose of supporting the invasion of Britain, the Franco-Spanish fleet left Cadiz and sailed east to enter the Mediterranean. There, with the French armies in Italy, the fleet intended to help recover Sicily and reinstate French control of the Italian peninsula. The 33 French and Spanish ships of the line under Vice-Admiral Pierre Villeneuve and Admiral Don Federico Gravina, however, were intercepted by Nelson off Cape Trafalgar before they could enter the Mediterranean. On October 21, 1805, with 27 ships of the line and four frigates, a cutter, and a schooner, Nelson destroyed 16 ships and captured four others. Tragically for the British, Nelson was struck by a bullet from the French ship *Redoubtable* about an hour after the fighting began. He died three hours later in the course of his greatest victory. His last signal, made at 11:43 in the morning, was "Engage the enemy more closely."

The stunning victory prevented Napoleon from dominating the Mediterranean. Nevertheless, he continued his military success, crushing the Austrians at Austerlitz in December 1805, forcing her out of the war, and ending the Third Coalition.

The Fourth Coalition, 1806–1807, and the Naval War After Trafalgar

From 1804 to 1806, British war strategy was built on coalition with other European states, but Britain's Ministry of 1806 and 1807 took a different approach. Although Britain briefly participated in a fourth coalition, between October 1806 and the Peace of Tilsit in July 1807, the new government wanted to take independent action, using overseas and distant naval and amphibious actions to turn the war.

After the Battle of Trafalgar, the weakest point in Britain's Mediterranean naval strategy was Sicily, which she had been defendsing since 1804. Britain could neither defend so large an island adequately nor afford to give it up. Constantly threatened by French military forces in southern Italy and by the French fleet at Toulon, Sicily remained a deadweight on the Royal Navy. Because of this, the Royal Navy's blockade of Toulon, keeping the French squadron in port, remained a key goal. Meanwhile, to keep France from attempting to dominate Turkey, Vice-Admiral Sir John Duckworth backed British diplomatic negotiations with the Sultan at Constantinople in 1807 by bringing his squadron into the Dardanelles and attempting unsuccessfully to compel the Turks to make peace with Britain's ally, Russia.

In that same year a new Ministry came to power in London and changed the focus of British strategy. It returned to the earlier emphasis on European affairs and began to build a new coalition. With this in mind, leaders in London saw that the Baltic was an area of concern. Fearing that Napoleon might take control of Denmark and the Baltic approaches to the North Sea, the Cabinet ordered Admiral James Gambier to attack Copenhagen in September 1807 and to seize the Danish navy's ships and supplies to prevent their use by the French.

Following this, Lord Saumarez sailed in early 1808 for the Baltic to support Sweden against Napoleon.

Napoleon's agreement in 1807 with Czar Alexander I in the Treaty of Tilsit altered the strategic situation for Britain. Shortly afterward, she changed her focus again, this time to southern Europe, sending an army to Portugal, as France attempted to occupy it. As in Denmark earlier, Britain was concerned about the possibility of Napoleon seizing Portugal's navy and using it against Britain. To prevent this, Rear-Admiral Sir William Sidney Smith and his squadron arrived in Portugal and escorted the Portuguese royal family and its navy to safety in Brazil.

The Fifth Coalition, 1809

For a few months in mid-1809, Britain was allied with Austria, but this arrangement ended with the French victory at Wagram. The main thrust of British strategy in 1809 focused on the Low Countries and a large amphibious assault on Walcheren island in the Scheldt River estuary. Through this operation, the British hoped to remove the French threat from Antwerp, reduce the resources that the French could obtain to support their maritime power, and parallel Austria's military campaign against France in the Danube valley. A huge undertaking, the Walcheren landing involved some 44,000 men and 235 armed vessels. But because of bad weather, wide-spread illness, poor planning, and ineffective leadership, the expedition was a disaster for Britain.

The Peninsular War, 1807–1814

Following the outbreak of war in Portugal in 1807, the first British troops arrived in July 1808 with support from the Royal Navy. However, military operations were halted in a short time, following the convention at Cintra. In the autumn of 1809 a new ministry came to power in London; as usual, there were strategic changes, particularly a new emphasis on the war in Portugal and Spain. In 1810, Napoleon made his last serious attempt to shift the balance in the Mediterranean, with a determined attempt to seize Sicily. This challenge and the necessity to continue supporting forces in the Iberian peninsula made the Royal Navy's task even more complex. A revolt in Spain offered an opportunity to expand operations out from Portugal, and this theater became the British focal point.

In other areas in this phase of the war, the Royal Navy provided differing contributions to the war effort. Small warships and privateers became key elements as they attacked French merchant ships and protected British trade. At the same time, Napoleon's Continental blockade threatened to damage the British economy and industrial production, which was the basis for her war effort and allowed her to provide financial subsidies to allies as well as to maintain her own military and naval power.

Between 1808 and 1810, British expeditions captured French Guiana, Martinique, Guadeloupe, and Santo Domingo, while other expeditions sailed from India to take the Indian Ocean islands of Mauritius and Réunion, in a successful move to stop French privateers based in those islands. This was followed, in 1811, by the East India Company's expedition to the island of Java. By that year, all the places in which Napoleon might reasonably have pressed Britain outside of Europe had been preemptively seized by Britain. Consequently, Britain was safely able to reduce her forces overseas.

The War of 1812, 1812–1815

However, Britain's emphasis on stringently controlling trade and maintaining her rights as a belligerent in the war against France had an effect on other nations. Between 1812 and 1815, while still fighting Napoleon, Britain faced a war with the United States over neutral trading rights and the impressment of seamen from American vessels. These issues had caused tension earlier, as on June 22, 1807, when H.M.S. *Leopard* (50-guns)—the ship that Jack Aubrey would later command in *Desolation Island*—had opened fire on the 33-gun frigate U.S.S. *Chesapeake*, which was carrying American Commodore James Barron to command U.S. naval ships in the Mediterranean. Totally unprepared, the American warship surrendered. But the incident caused a great public outcry against Britain in the United States.

The United States declared war on Britain in June of 1812. While active fighting against Napoleon continued, Britain tried to keep the conflict on a low burner. Nevertheless, the Royal Navy maintained a blockade on the eastern coast of the United States and had to increase convoy protection to prevent attacks by Americans. In the summer of

1812, U.S. Navy frigates enthusiastically engaged British warships. In a series of spectacular single-ship actions, the 44-gun American frigate U.S.S. *Constitution* captured the 36-gun H.M.S. *Guerrière* on August 19 some 700 miles east of Boston and took the 44-gun H.M.S. *Java* off the coast of Brazil on November 29. On October 25, 1812, the 44-gun U.S.S. *United States* also captured the 38-gun *Macedonian* in the mid-Atlantic. These victories raised American spirits in a war that was going badly ashore.

As Britain's operations against France in the West Indies ended, British troops and warships were sent from that region to fight in North America. In addition to convoying these troops, the Navy supported British military operations along the U.S.-Canadian border, in the Chesapeake Bay area at Baltimore and Washington, and in Louisiana. Meanwhile, on the Great Lakes, the small vessels that the Americans had quickly built achieved notable success at the Battle of Lake Erie in August 1813. The two countries negotiated peace at Ghent in 1814, neither side winning the objectives for which it had gone to war.

The War of the Sixth Coalition, 1812–1814

As Napoleon's authority in Europe began to crumble following his disastrous campaign in Russia in 1812 and 1813, the Ministry in London seized the opportunity to form a new coalition. Naval activity increased in northern European waters to support military activity there, but the emphasis on defense in the Mediterranean and support of the offensive in the Peninsula remained until Napoleon's abdication in the spring of 1814.

The War of the Seventh Coalition, 1815

The peace lasted for nearly a year, but Napoleon broke it with his escape from Elba and return to power for what is now known as the Hundred Days. In the face of this new crisis, the Ministry and the allies chose to concentrate British military forces under the Duke of Wellington in the Low Countries, traditionally an area of strategic concern. Just before Napoleon's defeat at Waterloo and his final abdication, the British squadron in the Mediterranean laid plans to support a rebellion in Provence against France. Although that proved unnecessary, British naval power had already proved what it could do. It had contributed significantly to the broader strategic effort that carried the allies to victory over Napoleon on land. In the years that followed, Britain dramatically reduced her naval forces in a long period of peace but still remained unchallenged as the possessor of the most powerful navy in the world.

Stephen Maturin and Naval Medicine in the Age of Sail

J. Worth Estes

In Patrick O'Brian's novel *H.M.S. Surprise,* Dr. Stephen Maturin laments, "Medicine can do very little; surgery less. I can purge you, bleed you, worm you at a pinch, set your leg or take it off, and that is very nearly all." Although he gives 18th-century surgery less credit than it probably deserves, he is not far off the mark when it comes to the practice of what we now call internal medicine. Maturin and his contemporaries relied largely on bitter remedies, some introduced as many as 2,500 years earlier. In fact, almost all medicines prescribed during the last years of the Enlightenment were ineffective by modern criteria. Nevertheless, Jack Aubrey and his crews placed unqualified faith in Dr. Maturin, even if he was skeptical of the worth of his own prescriptions. One must wonder why they did so.

Doctors and the Royal Navy

When Maturin joined the Royal Navy, its ranks included about 720 Surgeons. By 1814, as the Napoleonic wars neared their end, 14 Physicians, 850 Surgeons, and 500 Assistant Surgeons were caring for 130,000 men on shore and at sea. Doctors who aspired to Royal Navy service had to be examined before they were deemed acceptable, but the oral exams were perfunctory and few doctors managed to fail them. Depending on where they had obtained their training, and on their social status, Navy doctors were ranked as Physicians, Surgeons, Apothecaries, or Assistants (or Mates). Because Surgeons and Apothecaries were considered to be craftsmen, or artisans, they ranked below Physicians, who, unlike Maturin, did not deign to use their hands.

The most prestigious medical education in Britain and France, leading to standing as a Physician, was obtained at universities. Although Edinburgh was often recognized as the premier medical school in the English-speaking world, only Oxford and Cambridge could offer their medical graduates the qualification necessary for licensure in London (however, other doctors did practice there). Many Royal Navy Surgeons were trained at the Scottish universities of Edinburgh, Glasgow, and Aberdeen; the rest were probably trained as apprentices, and some of those obtained additional training by taking university courses, by attending private lectures and demonstrations by leading practitioners such as John Hunter in London, or by "walking the wards" of major London hospitals, to learn from the observations and opinions of senior medical staff as they visited their patients each day.

It is not entirely clear how or where Dr. Maturin obtained his professional credentials. He seems to have acquired his premedical education at Trinity College in Dublin. Maturin tells Dr. Butcher, of the *Norfolk*, that he studied medicine in France, and elsewhere he says that he has walked the wards at the Hôtel Dieu in Paris, a hospital that had been famous since the Middle Ages. Indeed, Maturin says he "has dissected with Dupuytren"; if so, it must have been while they were both students, because Guillaume Dupuytren (1777–1835) would have been a bit younger than Maturin, and he did not join the staff of the Hôtel Dieu until 1808. Although he had become one of France's leading surgeons by the end of Napoleon's reign, Dupuytren did not achieve his reputation as an innovative surgeon until several years after Maturin first met Aubrey.

Dr. Maturin may have earned an M.D. degree in Paris, but he is credited with it in only one dispatch from the Admiralty to Aubrey. The Admiralty may have assumed that Maturin had a formal academic degree because he held the rank of Physician, but it was not required in order to practice medicine in 18th-century Britain (except in London, where the requirement was often overlooked anyway). Indeed, some universities, most notoriously Aberdeen, granted the M.D. to those who would pay a fee for it rather than attend classes. Maturin had other credentials, however. In *Post Captain* the Physician of the Fleet praises two of his works: One was on the surgical removal of bladder stones, and the other was *Tar-Water Reconsidered*, Maturin's reflections on, or perhaps his own experiences with, the panacea made by mixing the tar extracted from Scotch pine with water. Tar-water was devised in 1739–40 by the philosopher George Berkeley, Bishop of Cloyne, who promoted it as a panacea.

Shortly after Maturin joined the Navy, his partner at a dinner party asked him, "How come you to be in the navy if you are a real doctor [i.e., a Physician]?" Maturin's reply, dosed with puns, was nonetheless honest: "Indigence, ma'am, indigence. For all that clysters [i.e., enemas] is not gold on shore. And then, of course, a fervid desire to bleed for my country." Indeed, Maturin was politically motivated and in dire need of a job. It was within Aubrey's power to rectify the latter.

Until the Navy's medical services were reorganized in 1806, Surgeons were warranted by individual ship captains, not commissioned by the Admiralty. Nevertheless, they were billeted along with the other officers in the wardroom. Their base salary was £5 per month, plus £5 for every 100 cases of venereal disease they treated, along with an equipment allowance of £43 as well as an allowance for a personal servant. Thus, including expenses, the Surgeon of a third-rate warship might have an income of more than £200 per year when his share of prize money was factored in. The venereal disease component of the naval Surgeon's salary was financed by fining men with gonorrhea ("gleet") or syphilis ("pox," or "great pox"). Because naval Physicians, most of whom, unlike Surgeons, held academic degrees in medicine, were regarded as gentlemen, they were not required to be examined before acceptance into the Navy and were better paid. Moreover, they had some authority over Surgeons.

Serving at Sea

In addition to caring for the sick and wounded, Surgeons were responsible for maintaining cleanliness on the ship. They saw to it that pressed men, often dirty and poorly clothed, were properly cleaned. They fumigated the sick-bay and whole decks when neces-

Plate showing the placement of a tourniquet to apply maximum pressure to the large arteries of the arm and leg. "The tourniquet here is of the simplest kind, and can be readily applied by any byestander," stated William Turnbull in *The Naval Surgeon*, Figure 1 *(courtesy of the Boston Medicine Library, Boston Massachusetts).*

sary, usually by burning brimstone (sulfur), and they oversaw the ventilating machines that supplied fresh air to the lower decks and kept them dry. Although Surgeons knew that inadequate food was a major contributor to shipboard illness, strict monetary limits often hampered their ability to improve rations. Most were also concerned about shipboard drunkenness, but seamen insisted on retaining the grog perquisite, amounting to a half pint of rum mixed with one quart of water twice daily. However, it was not only the seamen's preference that kept rum as standard issue: They needed liquids, and beer and water did not keep well at sea.

Naval Surgeons saw most of their patients in the sick-berth, or sick-bay. It was usually located in a space partitioned off by fixed walls or canvas between decks. Most housed several men as well as the Surgeon's desk, drugs, and surgical instruments; the largest had their own cooking and latrine facilities. The sick-berth of the third-

A set of amputating knives and bone saws and a Petit tourniquet, tightened by a brass screw to prevent blood loss during an amputation. Reproduced from William Turnbull, *The Naval Surgeon*, Figure 3 *(courtesy of the Boston Medical Library, Boston, Massachusetts).*

rate H.M.S. *Centaur,* for instance, had 22 hanging beds as well as a drug dispensary. But that of the contemporary frigate U.S.S. *Constitution* seems to have had only four beds and no separate dispensary.

The medical day aboard warships was determined by both custom and regulation. The Surgeon's Mate visited the sick-bay before breakfast to attend to the patients' needs. At eight o'clock—which was the end of the morning watch and after the gun deck had been cleaned—the loblolly boy rang a bell on each deck to summon to sick call those who were slightly indisposed, or were under treatment for venereal disease, or had superficial ulcers; men who were injured or who fell seriously ill during the day could report to the Surgeon at any time. He took morning sick call at the mainmast, where he and his Mate examined those who presented themselves. Then they made their daily rounds of men already in the sick-bay, while the boy fed, washed, and shaved the bedridden patients. The Purser or his steward sometimes dispensed drugs to those who had continuing prescriptions for them, or to men who simply thought they needed a little something to make them feel better.

The Mate spent the rest of his day preparing and administering medicines in the sick-bay, dressing wounds and skin ulcers, and bleeding men who needed it. He was also responsible for maintaining the ship's surgical instruments, for keeping accurate records of medicines and expenditures, for inspecting the cook's pots and pans, and for supervising the loblolly boy. In addition to supervising the care of the sick and injured, the Surgeon's routine duties included overall responsibility for his Mates and boys, personally visiting every patient at least twice a day, and, depending on who was in charge at the Admiralty or at the Sick and Wounded Board, keeping accurate records on each patient admitted to his care.

During sea battles, the Navy Surgeon's workplace was the cockpit, a space permanently partitioned off near a hatchway down which loblolly boys and other crew members could conveniently carry the wounded for triage and treatment. Not all ships had such a space, so planks were sometimes laid across unused guns to serve as operating tables. The deck of the cockpit was strewn with sand prior to battle so that the Surgeon and his Mates would not slip in the blood that invariably accumulated there despite the sand-filled buckets positioned to catch it during amputations.

Serving on Board Hospital Ships or at Hospitals

The hospital ship was usually a reconditioned ship of the line no longer suitable for fighting. Each had a Physician and a Surgeon, three Assistant Surgeons, ancillary personnel such as nurses, cooks, and washers, and occasionally an Apothecary. The best-appointed hospital ships had wards for segregating patients with the various fevers, diarrheal diseases, venereal diseases, and itches, as well as for the dying.

A few doctors served at Navy hospitals ashore. By the end of the Napoleonic wars, hospitals had been established in every major overseas base. Service was more profitable there than at sea; hospital surgeons were paid £500 a year and given a free residence. Dr. Maturin saw several patients at Haslar, the first major naval hospital in Britain, near Portsmouth on the south coast. Designed for 1,800 patients when built in the 1760s, its population grew to over 2,100 in the 1780s and was still growing in 1800. Its patients were attended by two Physicians, one Apothecary and his two Assistants, and two Surgeons with seven Surgeon's Mates and three Assistants. Probably the largest hospital in the world at that time,

Haslar had 84 medical and surgical wards, plus special wards for contagious diseases. The other major hospital for the Home Fleet was at Plymouth. When construction began in 1758, it was planned for 600 men, but it had 1,250 beds in 1795 and more by its completion in 1806.

The Navy's overseas hospitals had the worst reputations, especially those in the West Indies, to which the Admiralty routinely sent poorly qualified doctors. Two of the best overseas hospitals were those at Malta and Minorca, where Maturin, like his historic counterparts, sent seriously ill patients when possible and necessary. But most naval hospitals, like many civilian hospitals at the time, were notoriously dirty, uncaring to patients, and staffed by drunk and debauched nurses who stole whatever they could. Until 1805, when they were prohibited from maintaining private practices, even the doctors were frequently inattentive to their charges.

Finally, a small handful of Navy doctors served as official naturalists on both warships and those sent on missions of exploration. Maturin's continued attempts to observe new species of plants and animals, and to collect specimens and reports to send home, is in that tradition.

The Disease Burden of the Royal Navy

Reforms in medical staffing and victualling procedures by the Navy between 1780 and 1800, many of them the work of Dr. Sir Gilbert Blane (1749–1834), a Royal Navy Commissioner for the Sick and Wounded Board beginning in 1795, helped lower its sick rate from about one in three in 1780 to about one in eight by 1804 and one in eleven in 1813. Certainly a portion of this accomplishment can be attributed to Blane's introduction of limes as a scurvy preventive soon after he took office in 1795.

The pathophysiologic theories on which Dr. Maturin and other physicians trained in the 18th century were unlike our own ideas of specific diseases with specific causes and specific treatments. Several levels of factors were said to cause disease. To begin with, "predisposing causes" related to the seasons, the weather, and the patient's constitution (body build, gender, age, inherited traits, and way of life). For instance, in the case of seamen, according to Dr. Charles Turner Thackrah, one of the earliest physicians to be concerned with occupational health:

[Sailors] are generally very healthy and robust, hardy and enterprising. Living well, and enjoying good air and exercise, their diseases are few, and commonly of an inflammatory kind, as . . .
Pneumonia &c . . . the most prevalent complaints, as the cause of
death, are the sequelae of [such] diseases . . . next to these I may
mention disorders of the bowels, as Colic, Diarrhea, and Dysentery. (*The Effects of Arts, Trades, and Professions on Health and
Longevity,* 2d ed. [1832; reprint, Canton, Mass.: Science History
Publications, 1985], p. 71)

The second level of causes of a patient's symptoms, their
"antecedent causes," included two kinds of airborne factors: "miasmas," invisible disease-producing particles that emanated from decay-
ing animal and vegetable matter—from rotting carcasses, privies, and
swamps for example—which were contrasted with "contagions," or
"effluvia," equally invisible particles generated by and emitted from
patients afflicted with any of a number of fevers. The sepsis that often
killed men wounded in battle, even after successful amputation, was
among the Surgeon's most serious encounters with contagions.

Disturbances in amount or quality of what were called the "six
non-naturals"—air, kinds of food and drink, amount of diet, sleep,
exercise, and mental state—formed the third level of causes of symptoms. Abnormalities or mere changes in any of these factors could produce illness, by, for instance, obstructing natural routes of elimination
or by increasing or suppressing normal physiological activities.

One or more of these three factors—predisposing causes, antecedent causes, disturbances in the six non-naturals—was assumed to
bring about a patient's "immediate causes" of illness, the disturbances in body function that produced the symptoms on which a
physician based his diagnosis. Diseases were not then diagnosed or
classified according to their etiologies, as they are today; instead the
patient's symptoms *were* the doctor's diagnosis.

Illness was described principally in terms of imbalances. The earliest, but still widely held, theory that governed 18th-century physicians' interpretations of their patients' symptoms had emerged from
a concept of disease causation first elaborated in ancient Greece in the
fifth century B.C., when physicians explained their patients' symptoms in terms of the "four humors": blood, phlegm, black bile, and
yellow bile. Each humor was associated with two qualities that could

be assessed by observation: blood with heat and moisture, phlegm with moisture and cold, black bile with cold and dryness, and yellow bile with dryness and heat. That is, symptoms were thought to be the result of humoral imbalances, manifested as excessive or deficient body heat or moisture. The humoral theory, still accepted in Maturin's time, held that in order to restore health and stability to the sick body, its imbalances had to be counteracted with drugs or foods with opposite properties.

But there was another set of factors to consider too. A new theory emerged in the 1690s, postulating that illness can also represent imbalances in the irritability of the solid fibrous components of blood vessels and nerves, as expressed by their tone (innate strength and elasticity). Both vessels and nerves were considered to be hollow tubes propelling their contents through the body with forces proportional to the tone of their fibers. The body was healthy when blood or the "nerve fluids" could circulate freely, and when sweat, urine, and feces could be expelled freely, and so forth. On the other hand, paralysis was attributed to weak nerves, while the increased body heat associated with fevers, the most common serious illnesses of the 18th century, was attributed to increased arterial irritability or tone. In short, a fast pulse became the hallmark of fever. Medical historians have labeled this the "solidist theory."

Finally, the study of the chemistry of respiration that began in the 1770s led to the interpretation of rapid breathing as one more manifestation of fever. That is, the discovery of oxygen and carbon dioxide led to the conclusion that the body "burns" food by combining it with oxygen (which actually means "acid-forming") to make carbon dioxide. Adding these chemical concepts to their previous theories, doctors now looked at a new set of balances—between acids and bases—allowing them to explain the apparent reciprocal actions of basic and acidic drugs. These three concepts—humoral, solidist, and chemical—were not mutually exclusive, and most therapies were interpreted within the frameworks of all three simultaneously.

In the case of fever, the physician's first therapeutic goal was to reduce the irritability or hyperactivity of the heart and arteries, as evidenced by the fast pulse. Initial treatment consisted of the so-called depletive, evacuant, or antiphlogistic regimen. For instance, Maturin often prescribed emetic, antispasmodic, cathartic, and narcotic drugs to rid the body of whatever noxious factors had disrupted its balances and to calm hyperactive fibers. Such therapy also relied on avoiding anything that would "feed" the internal fires of the inflammation, such as red meat and exercise, on "cooling" drugs, and on measures designed to reduce tension and tone in the arteries, especially bleeding.

The second major therapeutic mode consisted of stimulating, or "tonic," measures, remedies thought to strengthen the heart and arteries, in order to speed removal of whatever pathogenic factors had weakened the body, especially during convalescence from a fever, once its "crisis" had passed. Such methods included a wide variety of tonic drugs including red wine, one of Maturin's favorites, as well as cold water and electricity: all were assumed to speed recuperation by increasing the patient's depleted strength.

Dr. Maturin's chief task was to restore to normal the balances among his patients' humors, the tensions within their nerves and blood vessels, and the acids and bases their bodies generated from food. Diet was as important as drugs for these purposes. Foods were evaluated not only in humoral terms as hot, cool, wet, or dry, but also for their stimulating or sedative properties and for their acid, alkali, and salt content. Because fever exemplified heightened tones, it was treated with a "low diet" (meatless) that was easily digested and lacked "stimulating" properties. Patients with "colds," on the other hand, were fed foods, such as red meat, that would increase their body heat; both notions are still implicit in the ancient admonition to "feed a cold and starve a fever."

Humors and tones were often adjusted to prevent illness. For instance, although bleeding was generally reserved by most doctors for the worst cases of fever or injury, Maturin liked to bleed all men as they crossed the Tropics of Cancer or Capricorn toward the equator, "as a precaution against calentures [fevers] and the effects of eating far too much meat and drinking far too much grog under the almost perpendicular sun." He also preferred the hands to eat a meatless diet while sailing between those latitudes.

Although sailors were predominantly young, healthy men, they were still susceptible to most acute contagious diseases. In addition, chronic illness contributed to the loss of considerable manpower at sea. The medical journal of U.S. Navy Surgeon Peter St. Medard, kept on board the 36-gun frigate *New-York* during a cruise to the Mediterranean from 1802 to 1803 (during the Barbary Wars), provides us with factual insights into the medical thinking of Maturin's day. In it, St.

Medard recorded—as all U.S. Navy surgeons had been directed to do by the Secretary of the Navy—the name, rank, diagnosis, treatment, and result for each patient he saw among the 350-man crew over a 16-month period.

As on Aubrey's ships, the most frequent diagnoses on St. Medard's cruise on *New-York,* were the catarrhs (i.e., bad colds), influenza, consumption (tuberculosis), and pneumonia; these respiratory ailments accounted for nearly 50 percent of all diagnoses made in the British and American navies. Other leading diagnoses included malaria (then called intermittent fever because the typical attacks of shaking chills and fever recurred every 24 or 48 hours), diarrhea, dysentery (painful and bloody diarrhea), and bilious fever (characterized by jaundice and correctly attributed to some primary disorder of the liver). Syphilis and gonorrhea, which were predictable risks of shore leave almost anywhere, completed the list of the most common illnesses in all navies of the time, although rheumatism and related debilitating conditions such as lumbago and sciatica could remove significant numbers of men from a ship's work force for many weeks on end.

As Jack Aubrey was well aware, the most frightening illnesses (except for scurvy) were exotic tropical infections, especially malaria, yellow fever, cholera, and perhaps plague. Most commanders and their Surgeons considered some of these to be occupational hazards of specific stations visited by the Royal Navy. For instance, yellow fever was associated with the West Indies, dysentery and liver disease (probably hepatitis) with the East Indies, malaria with both stations, and respiratory illnesses with the cold home waters surrounding the British Isles. The worst of the continued fevers (so called to differentiate them from intermittent fever) was typhus, also known as ship fever or gaol fever. All of these, as well as the common respiratory illnesses, were potentially fatal, as was scurvy, although it took much longer to kill.

Scurvy was a special hazard at sea, chiefly on ships not sufficiently provisioned with fresh fruits and vegetables. Considered a result partly of damp decks and clothes, it was also thought to be contagious because the number of afflicted crew increased steadily (until a source of vitamin C was provided). After 1795, when the Royal Navy's ships were regularly supplied with citrus fruits, scurvy was unusual, but it still occurred, particularly on long voyages when resupply was impossible.

Maturin and Aubrey were confronted with several outbreaks of scurvy. One occurred on the *Leopard*, and Maturin easily recognized its typical symptoms: The four afflicted men were glum, listless, and apathetic, their gums were spongy, their breath was offensive, their old wounds reopened, and blood seeped from capillaries in their skin. Knowing that the men were getting their "sovereign lime-juice" mixed into their daily grog, Maturin was baffled by the outbreak— until he discovered that the victims had been trading their grog rations for tobacco.

Another problem Navy doctors had to contend with was mental illness, which was thought to afflict one in a thousand seamen—a rate seven times greater than among the general population. Doctors often attributed insanity to head injuries, which, in turn, they blamed on intoxication. Because the symptoms of intoxication could resemble generalized hyperactivity, alcohol was assumed to be a stimulant, not the general depressant we now know it to be.

The Medicine Chest

Medicine chests for Navy ships contained up to 100 of the more than 200 remedies prescribed by doctors on land and sea; the specific contents of each ship's chest differed somewhat according to the Surgeon's personal preferences. All of the drugs that Dr. Maturin gave his patients are known to have been used throughout the Royal Navy as well as in the American Navy, although some of Maturin's remedies, such as powder of Algaroth, Lucatellus's balsam, polypody of oak, and polychrest, were considered archaic by 1800.

The most frequently used remedies were tonics that, according to solidist thinking, strengthened a body weakened by disease, especially during convalescence from a fever. For this purpose, the favored drug was cinchona, also called Peruvian bark. It had entered medical practice in the early 17th century as a cure for the intermittent fevers—that is, malaria (indeed, today we know it contains quinine, which is still used to treat malaria). Because it was so successful for that purpose, doctors came to prescribe the bark for virtually all other fevers, although we now know that it would have been completely ineffective against them.

The next most frequently prescribed drugs were cathartics, which were assumed to flush out unbalanced humors with the feces and relax the abnormal tensions that had constricted their patients' intestinal fibers, causing constipation. Typical of this class of drugs were calomel (mercurous chloride), jalap, medicinal rhubarb, castor oil, and cream of tartar (sodium potassium tartrate), a strong cathartic that was the most active ingredient of Maturin's black draught.

Doctors also gave emetics, drugs that induce vomiting, to remove foul humors from the stomach, as well as to strengthen what they took to be weak stomach muscle fibers. Tartar emetic (antimony potassium tartrate) was administered for the same purposes, as was ipecac, which we still use to remove poisons from the stomach.

Diaphoretics, which Maturin called "anhidrotics," made patients "sweat out" their unbalanced humors. At the same time these drugs— especially those made with antimony, like James's Powder, a patent medicine that Maturin sometimes prescribed—were assumed to strengthen the blood vessels that supplied the sweat glands in the skin.

Opium and opium preparations such as laudanum (an alcoholic solution of opium also known as Thebaic tincture), were correctly regarded as sedative, antidiarrheal, and analgesic. Tolerance and addiction to opium were well known. Dr. Maturin used laudanum frequently as an escape from his worries. He appears to have been addicted to it, and it is unclear how he managed to wean himself from it. He believed that the coca leaves he discovered in Peru helped him overcome his reliance on opium, a common misconception even in the late 19th century.

Because syphilis was almost an occupational hazard of sailors, Navy Surgeons stocked various mercury salts with which to treat it. Most victims required prolonged therapy with oral mercury preparations, such as calomel or Maturin's "blue pill," and with unguents made with mercuric chloride. All mercurials were cathartic and diaphoretic, providing clear routes for the elimination of the contagious factor responsible for the affliction. However, it is unlikely that such treatments could have eradicated the syphilis organism.

Most doctors reserved two forms of treatment for their most seriously ill patients, especially those with the worst fevers or injuries. The first was the drug class called blisters, or epispastics, usually alcohol solutions of powdered cantharides beetles (sometimes called Spanish flies). When placed on the skin, this preparation does raise a large, painful blister. In humoral theory it was thought to draw foul humors into the blister fluid; solidist reasoning concluded that the artificially induced inflammatory blister would also neutralize the naturally occurring inflammation that had caused the patient's symptoms by the process Maturin called "counter-irritation."

The other relatively drastic treatment doctors favored was bleeding on the humoral grounds that it removed chemically or otherwise unbalanced blood that was producing symptoms and on the solidist grounds that it reduced tension of the hyperactive fibers of the fevered cardiovascular system. That is, releasing some of the patient's blood was assumed to reduce the friction (between the blood and the walls of the arteries) that was producing the patient's increased body heat. Doctors usually removed 12 ounces at a time but up to twice that amount from their sickest patients.

Maturin's remedies were not designed to counteract well-defined disease processes, as modern drugs do. Instead he and his contemporaries used drugs to adjust or fine-tune a patient's internal equilibria, his physiological balances, regardless of what might have disrupted them in the first place. The occurrence of catharsis, vomiting, sweating, or blisters after the administration of a corresponding drug simply confirmed that the remedy had indeed altered the humors, tones, and acid-base balance of the body in the intended way. However, few of these treatments could have provided truly effective cures.

Trauma and Surgery

During the ten years of naval warfare with France that culminated at Trafalgar in 1805, the Royal Navy had 1,483 men killed and 4,266 wounded in battle. That is only about 6 percent of the Navy's total losses during that time; those from disease and individual accidents accounted for 82 percent, and major accidents (for example, sinking) 12 percent. Thus, although the Navy called most of its doctors Surgeons, because their principal task was to repair battle injuries, their surgical skills were needed far less frequently than were their general medical skills.

Although Maturin was trained as a physician, not a surgeon, he had at least read the most influential works on naval surgery that had been published by the time he met Aubrey, including the works of Gilbert Blane, James Lind, William Northcote, and Thomas Trotter. Among the common occupational risks of life at sea that might require manipulative surgical treatment were burns, inguinal hernias, falls from aloft, limbs crushed under falling barrels or by suddenly tightening ropes and chains, and injuries incurred during fights. Burns, which occurred not only in battle but also when guns misfired during exercises, were usually cleaned and dressed with olive oil. Hernias were reduced by manipulating the loop of intestine that had been forced into the scrotum so that it returned to the abdominal cavity, where it could be retained with a truss. Surgeons removed wens and superficial tumors and incised and drained large boils and abscesses. They occasionally cut through the lower abdomen and into the bladder to remove stones, as Maturin did on the *Polychrest*, and some removed cataracts from the eye, although most sailors were not old enough to need this operation. Navy Surgeons were also often required to examine men condemned to be flogged to ascertain whether they were fit for the punishment, and to treat their back wounds afterward.

Because dentistry had not yet separated from regular medical practice, doctors were also often called on to pull teeth, one of Maturin's least favorite chores. For this purpose they used a clawlike device called a turnkey, or pelican, which gave them maximum leverage.

Doctors of Maturin's time understood the basic principles of inflammation, even if some of their methods for dealing with it now seem bizarre. For instance, believing that blood could turn to pus during the inflammatory process, they bled seriously ill or wounded patients in order to reduce the accumulation of pus. The bacteria that actually cause its formation had not been discovered. But generally, Surgeons had sound principles concerning wound treatment: They controlled hemorrhage by tying off bleeding arteries, removed foreign bodies from wounds, and cleaned the wound sites. They thought some chemicals, such as nitrates, had "antiseptic" (literally, "anti-inflammatory") properties, but they had no sure way of preventing infection. They attempted to close wound edges by clearing them of dead tissue and suturing them together. Afterward they inspected and changed dressings as often as possible to minimize inflammation and pus.

Ironically, more battle wounds occurred when ships fought at a distance than in close engagements. Cannonballs that had traveled a long distance caromed off masts and railings, creating dangerous large splinters. If surgeons could get to the arteries severed by these flying splinters, they could usually tie them off to stop the bleeding. For instance, during the fight with the Algerine pirate ship *Dorthe*

Engelbrechtsdatter, Maturin ties off the "spouting femoral artery" in the leg of one of the Sophies.

Surgeons removed bullets with specially constructed "bullet forceps" or other tools, sometimes probing blindly through a muscle mass or into a wound in the chest or abdomen. They almost never opened those body cavities because they were well aware that the risk of fatal inflammation (infection) at those sites was nearly 100 percent. Men who were seriously burned by misfired guns, by explosions, or by very fast missiles that brushed their skin were treated with olive oil and ointments to soothe the affected areas and to prevent exposure to air.

During sea battles, the decks and cockpits could grow nightmarish. In his journal, Robert Young, Surgeon of the 64-gun H.M.S. *Ardent* at the battle of Camperdown, which began at about one P.M. on October 11, 1797, vividly describes the gory scene:

I was employed in operating and dressing till near 4.0 in the morning. . . . So great was my fatigue that I began several amputations under a dread of sinking before I should have secured the blood vessels. [Young had no Surgeon's Mates to assist him.]

Ninety wounded were brought down during the action. The whole cockpit deck, cabins, . . . together with my [operating] platform and my preparations for dressing were covered with them. So that for a time they were laid on each other at the foot of the ladder where they were brought down, and I was obliged to go on deck to the Commanding Officer to . . . apply for men to go down the main hatchway and move the foremost of the wounded further forward . . . and thus make room in the cockpit. Numbers, about sixteen, mortally wounded, died after they were brought down. . . . Joseph Bonheur had his right thigh taken off by a cannon shot close to the pelvis, so it was impossible to apply a tourniquet; his right arm was also shot to pieces. The stump of the thigh, which was very fleshy, presented a dreadful and large surface of mangled flesh. In this state he lived near two hours, perfectly sensible and incessantly calling out in a strong voice to me to assist him. The bleeding from the femoral artery [the main artery of the leg], although so high up, must have been very inconsiderable, and I observed that it did not bleed as he lay. All the service I could render this unfortunate man was to put dressings over the [wound] and give him drink. . . .

Melancholy cries for assistance were addressed to me from every side by wounded and dying, and piteous moans and bewailing from pain and despair. In the midst of these agonising scenes, I was able to preserve myself firm and collected, and . . . to direct my attention where the greatest and most essential services could be performed. Some with wounds, bad indeed and painful, but slight in comparison with the dreadful condition of others, were most vociferous for my assistance. These I was obliged to reprimand with severity, as their voices disturbed the last moments of the dying. . . .

An explosion of a salt box with several cartridges abreast of the cockpit hatchway filled the hatchway with flame and in a moment 14 or 15 wretches tumbled down upon each other, their faces black as a cinder, their clothes blown to shatters and their hats afire. A Corporal of Marines lived two hours after the action with all the [buttocks] muscles shot away, so as to excavate the pelvis. Captain Burgess' wound was of this nature, but he fortunately died almost instantly.

After the action ceased, 15 or 16 dead bodies were removed before it was possible to get a platform cleared and come at the materials for operating and dressing, those I had prepared being covered over with bodies and blood, and the store room blocked up.

I have the satisfaction to say that of those who survived to undergo amputation or be dressed, all were found the next morning in the gunroom, where they were placed, in as comfortable a state as possible, and on the third day were conveyed on shore in good spirits. . . . (Christopher Lloyd and Jack L. S. Coulter, *Medicine and the Navy, 1200–1900*, vol. 3, *1714–1815* [Edinburgh: E. and S. Livingstone Ltd., 1961], pp. 58–60)

The *Ardent* suffered the most losses of the British fleet in that action, 41 killed and 107 wounded, including among the dead her captain.

Another firsthand account, by seaman Samuel Leech of H.M.S. *Macedonian* when she was defeated in a one-sided battle by the American frigate *United States* in October 1812, focuses on the Surgeon:

The first object I met was a man bearing a limb, which had just been detached from some suffering wretch. . . . The surgeon and his mate were smeared with blood from head to foot: they looked more like butchers than doctors. Having so many patients [36 were killed and 68 wounded], they had once shifted their quarters from the cockpit to the steerage; they now removed to the wardroom, and the long table, round which the officers had sat over so many a feast, was soon covered with the bleeding forms of maimed and mutilated seamen. . . .

Our carpenter, named Reed, had his leg cut off. I helped to carry him to the after wardroom, but he soon breathed out his life there, and then I assisted in throwing his mangled remains overboard. . . . It was with exceeding difficulty I moved through the steerage, it was so covered with mangled men and so slippery with blood.

We found two of our mess wounded. We held [one man] while the surgeon cut off his leg above the knee. The task was most painful to behold, the surgeon using his knife and saw on human flesh and bones as freely as the butcher at the shambles. (*Ibid.*, p. 61)

Hemorrhage was the greatest immediate hazard of battle wounds, especially those made by swords, bayonets, or large splinters. Bleeding from limbs was stopped by canvas tourniquets tightened by turning a screw to compress a brass plate positioned over the bleeding artery. Bleeding from the head and torso could be controlled only by compression bandages. Only after bleeding had been minimized could the surgeon proceed to correct the damage.

Eighteenth-century surgeons could perform a wide range of operations. The most frequent capital operations (those with the greatest risk of death) were amputations. Simple fractures and dislocations of arms and legs were reduced and splinted, but compound fractures associated with open wounds were likely to be followed by gangrene, which required operation. By 1800 some surgeons were able to cut through the muscles of the thigh with a knife and saw through the femur beneath them so rapidly that patients felt the excruciating pain for no more than two minutes.

Some operations were not standard, of course—on the contrary, they had to be improvised according to the nature of the patient's wound. For instance, a few surgeons made successful extemporaneous attempts to remove the entire arm along with the shoulder blade and collar bone; other joints were also removed, but rarely.

Trepanning, or trephining, was another rare capital operation. It involved cutting a disk about an inch or so in diameter from the skull to remove bone that had been fragmented by blunt trauma or shot, and to relieve pressure on the swelling brain beneath. Dr. Maturin won his reputation during his first voyage with Aubrey by this operation, which he later said he had performed "many times" without failure. Indeed, not long after he trepanned Joe Plaice for a depressed skull fracture, the Surgeon himself was knocked out when his head struck a gun on a Pacific island controlled by potentially hostile American whalers. Mr. Martin, the chaplain, could feel no underlying fracture and diagnosed a blood clot as the cause of Maturin's continuing coma. The Americans' surgeon, Dr. Butcher, was about to trepan Maturin in order to remove the clot when the patient was mercifully and humorously jolted into consciousness when a bit of snuff accidentally fell into his nostrils.

Because general anesthesia was not introduced until 1846, surgeons had to strap their patients into place or have them held down during major operations. They may have used rum or opium to minimize the patient's response to pain and to relax his muscles, but evidence of the routine use of such general depressants is difficult to find. Of course, many patients became suitably unresponsive after going into shock when the pain became sufficiently intense.

Olive oil was usually applied to burns, to keep the skin soft while it healed. The more complex ointments commonly applied to surgical sites were made with mixtures of oils and fats; lead salts were included in some of them because they were thought to help keep the wound dry. If that succeeded, and if the wound could be kept clean, surgical patients had a good chance of actually benefiting from their doctors' skills, even though the doctors were unaware of the relationship between bacteria and pus.

What Good Could Dr. Maturin's Medicine Do?

With the exception of a small handful of drugs, such as opium and cinchona, it is clear that Maturin and his contemporaries were unable to provide truly effective remedies for the majority of their nonsurgical patients. Nevertheless, most of them recovered. Fairly early in his naval career, Dr. Gilbert Blane could conclude that:

> there is a tendency in acute diseases to wear themselves out, both in individuals that labour under them, and when the infection is introduced into a community [such as the crew of a ship]. Unless there were such a *vis medicatrix* [healing power of nature], there would be no end to the fatality of these distempers . . . and those who happen not to be infected at first, become in some measure

callous to its impression, by being habitually exposed to it. . . .
Thus the most prevailing period of sickness is when men are new
to their situation and to each other. (*Observations on the Diseases
Incident to Seamen* [London: Cooper, 1785], pp. 66–67)

Blane, a strong proponent of keeping and examining naval medical
statistics, was right. In the absence of devastating epidemics of illnesses like smallpox or yellow fever, about 90 to 96 percent of adult
patients in the 18th century, civilian or naval, recovered after being
treated by their doctors, regardless of what the physicians did.

Dr. St. Medard's clinical notes on U.S.S. *New-York* bear this out. His
patients with bad colds recovered the most rapidly, followed by those
with uncomplicated diarrhea. Dysentery cases recovered more
slowly, as did those with "bilious disorders" (probably hepatitis).
Patients with typhus and other severe infections recovered the most
slowly and the least frequently. But the great majority did recover,
even though the only truly effective drug St. Medard had was the
quinine in the cinchona he gave patients with malaria, who recovered
about as promptly as those with bad colds.

The only major illness on *New-York* that her Surgeon could not
treat successfully was scurvy, because he had no lemons, limes, or
oranges on board. The other common illnesses eventually disappeared, thanks chiefly to the body's built-in immune and tissue
repair mechanisms. Scurvy was the only condition whose course
could not possibly have been affected by the body's usual repair
mechanisms. It has only one cure or preventive, vitamin C.

The concept of the healing power of nature was not unknown to
either Peter St. Medard or Stephen Maturin. Indeed, they and their
colleagues saw their task as helping nature accomplish its job.
Because their contributions to the restoration of healthy balances in
humors, tones, and acidity were effective in 19 out of 20 patients, neither doctors nor their patients had any reason not to believe that they
had contributed to their patients' recovery.

It probably would have been hard to convince Jack Aubrey, who
had great confidence in Stephen Maturin's professional skills, that it
was chiefly the surgical skills of naval doctors that contributed to the
survival of wounded men at sea, and that the drugs they prescribed
according to unproven (and unprovable) theories were effective only
because the body is often able to heal itself. But perhaps that unblem-
ished confidence worked to Aubrey and his crews' benefit.

MAPS, TYPES OF SAILING SHIPS, SHIP DIAGRAMS, AND A WARSHIP'S BOATS

Atlantic Ocean

North
Sea
Gulf of
Riga
Copenhagen
Baltic Sea

English
Channel
Camperdown
Bay of
Biscay

Cape
St. Vincent
AZORES
Cape Trafalgar
MADEIRA
CANARY IS.

Black Sea

Mediterranean
Sea
The Nile
(Aboukir Bay)
Acre
Cairo
Alexandria

B A R B A R Y

TROPIC OF CANCER

AFRICA

CAPE
VERDE
IS.

Freetown

Whydah

Gulf of
Guinea

Southeast Trades

EQUATOR

ASCENSION

ST. HELENA

Nile R.

Red Sea

Arabian
Sea

GREENWICH MERIDIAN

(0 DEGREES LONGITUDE)

TROPIC OF CAPRICORN

SOUTH
AFRICA

Capetown
Cape of
Good Hope
(Cape of Storms)

Indian Ocean

Westerlies

TRISTAN DA
CUNHA

Miller Cylindrical Projection
Scale on the Equator 1: 90,000,000

Graphic
Linear
Scale

0   1000
0°   0°
15°   15°
30°   30°
45°   45°
60°   60°
75°   75°
0 100 200 300 400 500 600 700 800 900 1000
Statute Miles

Atlantic Ocean

GREAT
BRITAIN

North
Sea

Stockholm

JUTLAND

Copenhagen

IRELAND

Newcastle-
on-Tyne

FUNEN

Baltic Sea

Gulf of
Riga

Dublin
Cork

The
Nore

Camperdown

ZEALAND

London

Amsterdam

Plymouth

Dover

Land's End

Portsmouth

Spithead

Le Havre

English
Channel

Quiberon

Paris

AUSTRIAN
EMPIRE

Brest

FRANCE

Venice

Trieste

Bay of
Biscay

Marseilles

Corunna

Bordeaux

Toulon

ELBA

Adriatic Sea

ITALY

Ferrol

CATALONIA

CORSICA

Rome

Epirus
Mts.

Cape
St. Vincent

Madrid

SPAIN

Port Mahon

MINORCA

Naples

Lisbon

PORTUGAL

Málaga

Palma

SICILY

IONIAN
IS.

Faro

Cádiz

MALLORCA

Cape
Trafalgar

Algeciras

Algiers

SARDINIA

Mediterranean
Sea

MADEIRA

Strait of
Gibraltar

Valletta
MALTA

Salé

B

A

R

B

A

R

Y

CANARY IS.

AFRICA

GREENWICH MERIDIAN
(O DEGREES LONGITUDE)

TROPIC OF CANCER

N

INSET

jackie aher © 1995

✗ naval battle sites

INDIA

Calcutta

TROPIC OF CANCER

Red Sea

Arabian Sea

Bombay
Poona
Goa

Malabar Coast

Bay of Bengal

LACCADIVE IS.

Madras

CEYLON

AFRICA

MALDIVES

EQUATOR

SEYCHELLES
MAHÉ

Indian Ocean

Southeast Trades

MADAGASCAR

MAURITIUS
RÉUNION

RODRIGUEZ

TROPIC OF CAPRICORN

Cape
St. Marie

N

Jackie aher © 1995

Types of Sailing Ships

The following sketches are from *Naval Costumes*, published in 1840 by the master ship designer Sir William Symonds, R.N. (1782–1856). Symonds became surveyor of the Navy in 1832. His structural alterations, much discussed at the time, revolutionized naval architecture.

36-gun frigate

18-gun corvette

16-gun brig

Spanish xebec

English lugger

ketch

packet barque

American schooner

American sloop

Dutch galliot

dogger

Greek polacca

French chasse-marée

Mediterranean felucca

Lisbon bean-cod

The Decks and Square Sails of a 74-Gun Ship

Sails

(1) mainsail or main course, (2) main topsail, (3) main topgallant, (4) main topgallant royal, (5) foresail or fore course, (6) fore topsail, (7) fore topgallant, (8) fore topgallant royal, (9) mizzensail or mizzen course, (10) mizzen topsail, (11) mizzen topgallant, (12) mizzen topgallant royal, (13) spritsail or spritcourse (lying under the bowsprit), (14) sprit topsail (lying under the jib-boom), (15) lower main studdingsail (when studdingsails are carried, they are extended beyond both sides of the arms on either the foremast or mainmast, or on both), (16) main topmast studdingsail, (17) main topgallant studdingsail, (18) fore lower studdingsail, (19) fore topmast studdingsail, (20) fore topgallant studdingsail.

Decks and Cabins

(A) poop deck, (B) quarterdeck, (C) waist, (D) forecastle, (E) upper deck, (F) gun deck, (G) orlop, (I) Captain's cabin, (J) Admiral's apartment, (K) wardroom, (L) gunroom. Ship diagram adapted from Rees's *Naval Architecture*.

The Fore-and-Aft Sails and Selected Rigging of a 74-Gun Ship

Sails

(1) main staysail, (2) main topmast staysail, (3) middle staysail, (4) main topgallant staysail, (5) fore staysail, (6) fore topmast staysail, (7) jib, (8) mizzen staysail, (9) mizzen topmast staysail, (10) mizzen topgallant staysail, (11) driver or spanker.

Rigging

(12) fore staysail sheets (the standing fall of the fore staysail sheets, which are bent through the clew of the sail, is made fast around a timberhead, or eyebolt, on the forecastle, while the leading part comes in through a block made fast to the eyebolt), (13) fore staysail halyards (the standing part of the halyards, which reeve through a single block bent to the head of the sail, belays to the head of the foremast, while the leading part reeves through a block lashed to the rigging under the top and leads down at the back of the mast), (14) fore staysail downhaul, (15) fore topmast staysail sheets, (16) fore topmast staysail halyards, (17) fore topmast staysail stay, (18) jib halyards, (19) jib stay. Ship diagram adapted from Rees's *Naval Architecture*.

Masts, Sails, and Rigging

This illustration from Serres's *Liber Nauticus* shows the elements of a square rig. On the far left are the disassembled parts of a mast: (1) the lower mast, (2) topmast, (3) topgallant, (C) cap, and (B) top. The center illustration shows part of the hull and the assembled mast seen from the larboard, or left, side: (A) the step of the mast, (B) the maintop, (C) the cap, (D) the crosstrees, (E) the cap, (F) topgallant masthead, (G) the truck, (H) the main wale, (I) the gun ports, (K) the main channel, (L) the shrouds (verticle lines), (M) the ratlines (horizontal lines), (N) the foothook, or futtock, shrouds, and (O) the backstays. The illustration on the right shows the rigged mast viewed from the stern with the running rigging and the principal sails: (P) pendant, (Q) clew lines, (R) lifts, (S) topgallant sail, (T) topsail, (U) course of mainsail, (V) reefpoints, (W) horses, (X) leech lines, (Y) braces, and (Z) stirrups.

This illustration from Serres' *Liber Nauticus* shows a capstan, used for hauling up the cables and other heavy pieces of equipment.

Water line

A Warship's Boats

Sir William Symonds drew the various boats of H.M.S. *Pique,* a fifth rate captured from the French.

barge, 30 feet

launch, 30 feet

barge, 32 feet, lateen-rigged

first and second cutter, 25 feet

jolly boat, 18 feet

gig, 30 feet

dinghy

aback A sail is aback when it acts to drive a ship in the direction of the STERN.

abaft Toward the after part, or STERN, of the ship. Used relatively, as in abaft the BEAM: on the stern side of an imaginary line across the middle (or WAIST) of a vessel.

Abd-ar-Rahman I (*731–788*) The first Umayyad emir of Córdoba (756–88). The only survivor of the Abbasid massacre of his family in Damascus, he fled from Syria and eventually entered Spain, where he defeated the emir of Córdoba at Alameda and seized power. He reorganized the state and attempted to unite the various Muslim groups. His great mosque at Córdoba—finished by his son and successor, Hisham I (757–796)—is a monument of Moorish architecture, known for its complex interior of low rounded arches with alternating black and white stones.

Abercrombie, General Sir Ralph (*1734–1801*) Scottish-born general. Studied law in Edinburgh and Leipzig, but joined the Dragoons in 1756 and fought in the Seven Years' War. Member of Parliament for Clackmannanshire, Scotland, 1774–1780. After serving in Holland in 1793 and commanding an expedition in the West Indies, he commanded British forces in Ireland and Scotland. In 1801 he was appointed to command the expedition to the Mediterranean. He died on board H.M.S. *Foudroyant* of wounds suffered during the successful landing of Anglo-Turkish troops at Aboukir Bay in Egypt.

ablation   The removal of any part of the body by surgery.

able seaman   A general term for a sailor who has a great deal of experience in performing the basic tasks of sailing a ship. In the Royal Navy in the 18th century, the most senior, best paid, and most prestigious of the three basic RATES of sailors: able seaman, ORDINARY SEAMAN, and LANDSMAN.

Aboukir   An island and bayou on the Mediterranean coast of Egypt located to the east of Alexandria and to the west of the Rosetta Mouth of the Nile. The Battle of the NILE was fought in Aboukir Bay on August 1, 1798.

Abraham-man   Among sailors, one who feigns sickness. Possibly an allusion to the parable of the beggar Lazarus, in Luke 16.

Abraham's bosom   From Luke 16:22, the abode of the blessed dead, where the beggar Lazarus was carried by the angels.

abroad   Spread, as in "all sail abroad."

Absit, o absit omen   May it not, oh may it not be an omen (Latin).

abune   Provincial form of "above."

Acacia   A genus of leguminous shrubs or trees with white or yellow flower clusters found in the warmer regions of the Old World. *Acacia senegal* yields gum arabic, also known as gum acacia, a water-soluble gum used in preparing pills and emulsions and making candy and as a general thickener and stabilizer.

accommodation-ladder   A flight of steps at the GANGWAY to enable officers and visitors to enter and exit the ship.

accoucheur   One who assists women in childbirth.

Achilles, **H.M.S.**   Launched in 1798, a 74-gun ship that captured the 90-gun Spanish FLAGSHIP *Argonauta* and recaptured the former British third-rate *Berwick* from the French at TRAFALGAR in 1805 while under the command of Captain Richard King. She remained in service until 1865.

achromatic   Colorless. An achromatic lens or telescope is one that refracts light without separating it into its constituent colors.

a-cockbill *or* **cockbill**   Having the tapered ends cocked or turned upward. Said of the anchor when it hangs from the CATHEAD, ready for dropping and of the YARDS of a vessel, when they are placed at an angle to the deck. The latter denotes mourning.

Acre *or* **Saint-Jean-d'Acre**   An ancient port with a fortress northwest of Mount Carmel between Tyre and Haifa in present-day Israel. It was taken by the Crusaders in 1191 and besieged by Napoleon in 1799.

Actaeon   In Greek mythology, Actaeon was a hunter who was turned into a stag and killed by his own hounds after he accidentally saw Artemis, the virgin huntress, bathing. Thus, a cuckold, from the play upon his becoming horned.

Actian games   Ancient Roman gymnastic competition and musical festival.

acting-order   An order to act in a certain capacity. More specifically, a temporary appointment to a vacant position made by one entitled to do so but not necessarily confirmed by the superior authority, as in a field promotion.

acushla   A term of endearment, like "dear heart" or "my darling." Originally from Irish *cuisle*, "pulse of the heart."

adagio   A direction for the musical time in which a piece is to be sung or played: slowly, leisurely, and gracefully.

Adanson, Michel (*1727–1806*)   A French naturalist and the author of *Les Familles naturelle des plantes* (1763). Adanson's system of naming and classification was later superceded by that of LINNAEUS.

Adansonia   A genus of large trees containing only two species: the BAOBAB, monkey-bread, or Ethiopian sour gourd of western and central Africa and the cream-of-tartar tree, or sour gourd, of northern Australia.

ad captandum vulgus   To win over to the masses (Latin).

Addington, Henry, Lord Sidmouth (*1757–1844*)   The Tory Prime Minister (1801–1805) who negotiated the Treaty of Amiens with Napoleon. Taking effect in March of 1802, it contained provisions for the return of all British colonial conquests to France, except for Trinidad and Ceylon; in return, France promised to leave Egypt. The treaty collapsed and war recommenced in April of 1803.

Admiral   A naval officer of FLAG RANK. The fleet commander or the commander of one of its principal divisions. Until 1864, the rank structure for Admirals was based on traditional red, white, and blue squadrons, each of which contained van, middle, and rear divisions, commanded by Admirals, Vice-Admirals, and Rear-Admirals, respectively. Beneath Admiral of the Fleet, the highest rank, the rungs on the ladder of promotion were as follows:

Admiral of the Red
Admiral of the White
Admiral of the Blue

Vice-Admiral of the Red
Vice-Admiral of the White
Vice-Admiral of the Blue

Rear-Admiral of the Red
Rear-Admiral of the White
Rear-Admiral of the Blue

Admiralty   The administrative department superintending the Navy, directed by the Lord Admiral or Board of Admiralty. During the Napoleonic wars the Admiralty became a center of operational command, with a constant inflow of dispatches and information and a constant outflow of orders. On the roof of the Admiralty, the TELE-GRAPH could send a signal reaching SPITHEAD in three minutes on a clear night or day. Various telegraph lines connected to other Naval centers, and a fleet of schooners and cutters laid ready to carry messages to the fleets and squadrons deployed in home and foreign waters. Also, the building housing the administration, located in Whitehall, London. In England, the Lords Commissioners of the Admiralty, together with the First Secretary of the Admiralty, formerly carried out this function. The Admiralty was incorporated as part of the Ministry of Defence in 1964. *See also* page 3.

The Admiralty, Whitehall

Adriatic Sea Five-hundred-mile arm of the Mediterranean Sea between the east coast of Italy and Croatia, Bosnia, and the Dalmatian coast. At its northern point lie Venice and Trieste.

advice-note A commercial form, partly printed and partly written, used to advise consignees of the arrival of their goods and to request removal of same from the station.

adze A carpenter's or cooper's tool, like an ax with the blade set at right angles to the handle and curving in toward it, often used by shipwrights for the shaping of wooden beams.

aetat Of or at the age of; aged (a particular number of years).

aetiology *or* etiology The cause(s) of an illness or abnormal condition. Also the branch of medical science that investigates the causes of diseases. In a larger sense, the science or philosophy of causation.

affusion The act of pouring a liquid on or into; a method of administering baptism. Also a remedy for fevers whereby water, usually between 50°F and 70°F, is poured onto the patient.

after-cabin The cabin in the after part of the ship used by a Captain, COMMODORE, or ADMIRAL, having superior accommodation and usually its own companionway.

afterguard   The men stationed on the QUARTERDECK and POOP to work the after sails, generally composed of ORDINARY SEAMEN and LANDSMEN.

a fortiori   Even more strongly (Latin).

aga   In Muslim countries, especially under the Ottoman empire, a commander or chief officer. Originally a military title, it was also used for civil officers and as a title of distinction.

***Agamemnon,* H.M.S.**   A 64-gun ship launched in 1781 and commanded by Nelson from 1793 to 1796. After surviving both the battles of Copenhagen and TRAFALGAR, she ran aground and was abandoned in 1809.

Agave   A genus of plants that includes the American aloe and whose flower-stem can reach a height of up to 40 feet.

âge ingrat   The awkward age, as in the teenage years (French).

agent provocateur   An agent employed to induce or incite a suspected person or group to commit an incriminating (often political) act, especially by seducing, decoying, entrapping, or impressing them.

Agnus   Lamb, that is, the lamb of God, Jesus (Latin).

Agnus Dei   In Latin, "lamb of God." A part of the Roman Catholic Mass so named because it starts with the words "Agnus Dei." Also the music set to it. Now also used in the Anglican service.

aguardiente   A coarse brandy made in Spain and Portugal.

ague   An acute or violent fever, usually malaria, marked by periodic paroxysms with cold, hot, and sweating stages. At first more associated with the feverish stage, the term later became synonymous with a fit of shivering, a chill.

a-high-lone   A way of emphasizing the word "alone."

Ah tutti contenti saremo cosí   Ah, and so we shall all be happy at last (Italian; from the final chorus of Mozart's *The Marriage of Figaro*).

aide-de-camp   An officer who assists a general in his military duties, conveying his orders and procuring information.

The great albatross, *Diomedea exulans*, the largest of all sea fowl

aide-mémoire   A memorandum or précis (French).

aigrette   A tuft of feathers such as that borne by the egret and some other birds. A spray of gems, or similar ornament, worn on the head.

***Ajax*, H.M.S.**   Launched in 1798, a 74-gun, third-rate ship that fought in General Abercromby's Egyptian expedition of 1801 and at TRAFALGAR in 1805. Burned and exploded with 250 hands on board during the DARDANELLES expedition in 1807.

akavit *or* **aquavit**   A colorless or yellowish alcoholic spirit distilled from potatoes or other starch-containing plants. Akavit is the schnapps of Scandinavia.

alba mistura   Literally, white mixture, an ointment made of olive oil, white wax, and white lead (lead monoxide).

albatross   A family of large web-footed seabirds related to the PETRELS and SHEARWATERS and inhabiting the Pacific and southern oceans. The 14 species of albatross include the mollymawks, gooney birds, and the great albatross, *Diomedea exulans*, to which the name is usually applied. The largest of seafowls, with a wing-span up to 15 feet, great albatrosses have dark-gray or gray-brown and white plumage, large hooked bills with horny plates, and prominent tubular nostrils. They are capable of very long flights, sometimes following ships at sea for weeks, scavenging the ship's refuse and eating squid, drinking seawater, and sleeping on the ocean's surface. It was once believed by sailors that albatrosses contained the souls of dead sailors, and so killing one was thought to bring bad luck. "The Rime of the Ancient Mariner" by Samuel Taylor COLERIDGE, written in 1798, told the tale of a seaman who tragically killed an albatross: "Ah! well a-day! what evil looks/Had I from old and young!/Instead of the cross, the Albatross/About my neck was hung." Also, a burden or encumbrance, causing deep anxiety.

Albères   The easternmost section of the Pyrenees Mountains, between France and Spain.

Alca impennis   *See* great AUK.

a-lee *or* **alee**   On or toward the LEE or sheltered side of the ship; away from the wind. Helm's a-lee: the response of the helmsman when ordered to bring the bow into the wind in order to TACK.

aleph   The name of the first letter of the Hebrew alphabet.

Aleppo button   A disease, also known as oriental sore, endemic in parts of Asia and Africa and caused by infection with *Leishmania tropica,* a parasite transported by sand flies. Various regional synonyms are used for the disease, for example, Baghdad boil, Delhi boil, Biskra button, and many others.

alexipharmic   Originally an antidote against poisons, but by the 18th century it had come to mean a medicine made with variable ingredients used primarily in fevers, that is, as a FEBRIFUGE.

Algaroth   Powder of antimony oxychloride, used as a caustic to scarify superficial wounds.

Algiers   Ancient Mediterranean port on the BARBARY Coast that served as a base for Algerine or Barbary pirates, who attacked European and American merchant ships and sold Christian captives into slavery. The city was bombarded by the British fleet under Admiral Lord Exmouth in 1816.

Ali Pasha (1741–1822)   A Turkish brigand known as the Lion of Janina (or Iannina, presently Ioànnina, Greece), he used ruthless means to become the PASHA of Janina in 1788 and held power over much of Albania and Macedonia and beyond. He intrigued with England and France during the Napoleonic wars. Byron and others described his barbaric yet cultured court.

aliquid amari   Something bitter or disagreeable (Latin).

allegro   One of the five grades of musical pace and character: brisk, lively, the quickest after presto.

allowance   In military use, money paid for various purposes or services and distinct from pay.

Almack's Club   A club in London's Pall Mall, founded by pub owner William Almack in 1762 to provide meals, newspapers, and gambling. It split into two other clubs, BOODLE'S and BROOKS'S, in 1764.

almoner   An official distributor of the alms of another. The name of a functionary in a religious house or in the household of a bishop, prince, or other person of rank. Sometimes applied to the chaplain of a hospital or other institution.

Almoravian draught   The name of this medicine is derived from that of the Berber dynasty, which ruled much of North Africa and Spain from 1056 to 1145. Its ingredients are not known.

alopecia   A medical term for baldness.

Altair   The eagle star, found in the northern constellation Aquila. One of the three stars that form the Summer Triangle (the three brightest stars in the summer sky).

Altiplano   The high tableland that lies between the western and eastern cordilleras of the Andes in Bolivia, Peru, and Argentina.

altitude   The height of a body in the heavens expressed by its angular distance above the horizon, a measure once taken at sea using a QUADRANT or SEXTANT and used to help determine a ship's longitude and latitude.

altumal   The mercantile style or dialect. Altumal cant is the language of petty traders and tars. It derives from the Latin word *altum,* "the deep," i.e., the sea.

amaranth   A purple color, that of the foliage of *Amaranthus,* a genus of ornamental plants with purplish or greenish flowers.

Amati   A violin, viola, or violoncello from the workshops of the Amati family in Cremona, Italy, which operated from about 1550 to 1700. Nicolò Amati (1596–1684) trained the masters Antonio Stradivari and Andrea Guarneri.

amber   Found chiefly along the southern shores of the Baltic, a yellowish translucent fossil resin that often entombs the bodies of insects. When rubbed it becomes noticeably electric, and when burned produces a pleasant smell. Often used for jewelry.

ambergris   A waxlike substance of marbled ashy color produced in the intestines of the sperm whale and found floating in tropical seas. It is odoriferous and used in perfumery.

Amboyna   A seaport in Indonesia's Molucca Islands that was taken from the Portuguese by the Dutch in 1605. In 1623, English traders who had settled there were killed by the Dutch in the Massacre of Amboyna. The port was captured by the British in 1796 and again in 1810.

***Amethyst,* H.M.S.**   A fifth rate built in 1799 and wrecked in 1811.

amidships   In the middle or toward the middle of a vessel.

Amiens, Peace of   The treaty between Britain and France that marked the end of the War of the French Revolution. Most of the conquests that each side had made since 1793 were to have been returned. The peace lasted only a short time, with the Napoleonic War breaking out in 1803.

amor vincit omnia   Love conquers all (Latin).

***Amphion,* H.M.S.**   A fifth rate built in 1798. The previous *Amphion*, also a fifth rate, blew up on September 22, 1796, in Hamoaze, Plymouth, most of her crew perishing.

Amphitrite   In Greek mythology, goddess of the sea, wife of Poseidon, and mother of Triton.

ampulla   A small bottle or flask.

Anabaptist   A Protestant sect that arose in Germany in the 16th century. Its members advocated the baptism of adult believers only and the separation of church and state.

anan An expression used when a listener has failed to catch the speaker's words or meaning and would like him to repeat what he said; the same as "I beg your pardon."

anastomosis Intercommunication between vessels, channels, or distinct branches of any kind by a connecting cross branch. First applied to communications between arteries and veins in animals.

anchor-ring The large ring on the shank of an anchor for attaching the anchor CABLE.

Andalusia A southern province of Spain, the last stronghold of Moorish Spain.

andante A musical movement that is moderately slow and distinct.

Andromeda A constellation of the northern hemisphere, representing the mythical Andromeda, daughter of Cepheus and Cassiopeia and wife of Perseus, who rescued her from a sea monster.

anemometer An instrument for measuring the force of a wind; a wind gauge.

an-end In the direction of the length; directly ahead.

anfractuosity Sinuosity, circuitousness, as in a winding channel or passage.

Angelus A devotional exercise said by Roman Catholics at morning, noon, and sunset that commemorates the mystery of the Incarnation and consists of short verses and responses and the Angelic Salutation repeated three times.

anguli scapulae The lower, sharper angle of the shoulder blade.

anhidrotic A medicine or action that inhibits perspiration.

anhinga Any bird of the genus *Anhinga*, fish-eaters related to the cormorant but with long, slender necks and pointed bills, especially the American snake-bird.

animalculae Tiny, usually microscopic, organisms.

anisette A liqueur flavored with aniseed.

anker A measure of wine and spirits, used primarily in Northern Europe, varying in amount from country to country, but in England equal to ten old imperial gallons (equivalent to ten U.S. gallons).

annelid A member of the phylum Annelida, usually elongated, segmented invertebrates such as earthworms, various marine worms, and leeches.

Anson, Admiral George (*1697–1762*) While attacking Spanish shipping in 1743 during the War of the Austrian Succession, Admiral Anson took a treasure-laden MANILA galleon called *Nuestra Señora de Cobadonga* with 1,313,843 PIECES OF EIGHT. His PRIZE share enriched him for life. In 1744 at SPITHEAD, Anson finished his three-year and nine-month circumnavigation of the globe, the first part of which is chronicled by his chaplain, Richard Walter, in *A Voyage Round the World* (1748). (The voyage also provides the historical setting for Patrick O'Brian's first seafaring novel, *The Golden Ocean.*) Anson served as First Lord of the Admiralty from 1751 to 1756 and from 1757 to 1762.

antaphrodisiac An agent, usually a medicine, that counteracts carnal desire.

Antares The red supergiant star, the brightest in the constellation Scorpius and in the southern sky. Antares is said to be the heart of the scorpion.

Antilles Arc of tropical islands in the Caribbean Sea from the southern point of Florida to the coast of South America, also known as the WEST INDIES.

antimonials Drugs made with various salts of antimony. Because they caused vomiting, catharsis, and sweating, they were thought to disperse fever and strengthen the body.

antimony A metallic element used to make many medicines, especially tartar emetic, prescribed for the treatment of fevers. It causes vomiting, sweating, and catharsis, depending on the dose and the chemical form specified.

antinomy A contradiction in a law or between two equally binding laws, statutes, or principles.

antiphlogistic An anti-inflammatory treatment used in the early stages of most fevers; *see* "Stephen Maturin and Naval Medicine in the Age of Sail," page 31.

antiphon A short verse or sentence sung by one choir in response to another.

Antipodes   A term used in Britain to refer to Australia and New Zealand, so called because they lie at the opposite end of the earth (or antipodes) from England. Also, specifically, the Antipodes Islands, a group of uninhabited rocky islands in the South Pacific Ocean, 350 miles off the southeastern coast of New Zealand.

antiscorbutic   Of use against scurvy.

anti-trades   Winds that blow steadily in the opposite direction to the TRADE WINDS. In the northern hemisphere the anti-trades blow from the southwest; in the southern hemisphere, from the northwest.

Apicius, Marcus Gabius (first century)   A Roman gourmet who squandered away his fortune on feasts and then, faced with a need to economize, killed himself instead.

apogee   The point in the orbit of the moon at which it is farthest from the earth; by extension, the highest point.

Apollo   The sun god of the Greeks and Romans, and the god of music and poetry.

aponeurosis   A fibrous white membrane that sometimes sheathes a muscle and sometimes connects a muscle to a tendon.

apoplexy   Usually called a "stroke." Caused by sudden obstruction of a blood vessel or hemorrhage within the brain, the syndrome can produce fainting, unconsciousness, and loss of speech and muscle function. The damage may be permanent or temporary.

Apothecaries' Hall   On Blackfriars Lane, the hall of the Apothecaries' Society, a city livery company (guild).

appetence   A natural affinity, as between chemicals. Thus, appetite or desire.

apse   A semicircular or polygonal recess, arched or dome-roofed, especially at the end of the choir, aisles, or nave of a church.

aqua regia   A mixture, produced by heating four parts of hydrochloric acid and one part of nitric acid, that can dissolve gold or platinum.

Aragon   A region and former kingdom of northeastern Spain.

Arcades ambo   Two people of the same tastes, professions, or character, often used derogatorily. The Latin means literally "both Arcadians," i.e., two pastoral poets or musicians.

Arcadian   Referring to Arcadia, a mountainous district in the Greek Peloponnesus idealized as a place of rural contentment. Thus, ideally rural or rustic. Also, a person living a simple, quiet life.

Arcturus   The brightest star in the northern constellation Boötes; formerly, also, the whole constellation, and sometimes Ursa Major, the Great Bear, near which it is located.

arcus senilis   A narrow opaque band encircling the cornea in the eye, common in old age.

Ardea goliath   A very large heron, known as the goliath heron, reaching 59 inches in height and having a reddish head and neck. The goliath heron lives in Africa and feeds during the day.

Argand lamp   Invented by Aime Argand in the 1780s, a lamp with a cylindrical wick, allowing a current of air to pass to both inner and outer surfaces of the flame and thus providing better combustion and brighter light.

argosy   A merchant vessel of the largest size and burden, especially those of Ragusa (now Dubrovnik) and Venice.

Arma virumque cano   I sing of arms (that is, warfare) and man (Aeneas, the Trojan prince who escaped and founded Rome); Latin, the opening words of Virgil's *Aeneid.*

Armenian bole   Pale red earth originally said to come from Armenia, used in astringent medicines and in tooth powders.

Arminian   Of, belonging to, or following the doctrine of Jacobus Arminius, a Dutch Protestant theologian who opposed the views of Calvin, especially on predestination. After Arminius's death in 1609, his doctrines were condemned by the synod of Dort in 1618–1619, but they quickly spread and were accepted by many of the reformed churches.

armourer   A maker of armor or manufacturer of arms. An official who has charge of the arms of a ship.

arrack   In Eastern countries, a liquor usually distilled from fermented coconut-palm sap or from rice and sugar fermented with coconut juice.

arrowroot   A tropical American plant with tuberous roots native to certain West Indian islands. Especially *Maranta arundinacea,* an herb with fleshy and nutritious tubers.

arsy-versy   Backside foremost, upside down, contrariwise.

arthropod   Invertebrate animals with segmented bodies and limbs, such as insects, arachnids, and crustaceans.

ARTICLES OF WAR
The Articles of War were regulations of the Royal Navy that first appeared officially in 1652 and were revised in 1661, 1749, and 1866. They comprised a varied collection of admonitions and rules that dealt mainly with the misconduct of officers and were later expanded to seamen. The Articles of War were supposed to be posted in every ship of the Royal Navy and read once a month to the ship's company.

According to *Falconer's Marine Dictionary* (1815): "After reciting several acts of parliament relating to the government and discipline of the navy, and declaring them to be repealed, it [the Articles of War] states: That, for the regulating and better government of his Majesty's navies, ships of war, and forces by sea, whereon, under the good providence of God, the wealth, safety, and strength of this kingdom chiefly depend; be it enacted by the king's most excellent Majesty . . . [t]hat from and after the 25th day of December, 1749, the articles herein following, as well in time of peace as in time of war, shall be duly observed and put in execution, in manner herein after mentioned."

The Articles of War paraphrased:

Article One states that all commanders, captains, and officers shall cause the public worship of Almighty God, according to the liturgy of the church of England established by law, to be solemnly, orderly, and reverently performed in their respective ships; and shall take care that prayers and preaching be performed diligently and that the Lord's Day be observed according to law.

Article Two condemns profane oaths, cursings, execrations, drunkenness, uncleanness, and other scandalous actions "in derogation of God's honour, and corruption of good manners."

Article Three states that any person who "shall give, hold, or entertain intelligence to or with any enemy or rebel" without proper authority and is convicted by a COURT-MARTIAL will be punished by death.

Article Four states that any letter or message from the enemy or a rebel must be conveyed to a superior officer within 12 hours of the opportunity to do so.

Article Five condemns all spies and anyone who aids a spy or conspires to help an enemy or rebel.

Article Six states that no person in the fleet shall give an enemy or rebel money, victuals, powder, shot, arms, ammunition, or any other supplies whatsoever, upon pain of death or such other punishment as the court-martial shall think fit to impose.

Article Seven states that all original papers of any ship taken as a PRIZE must be preserved and delivered to the Court of Admiralty or other authorized commissioner to determine that the prize is a lawful capture.

Article Eight states that nothing should be removed from a prize, except to better secure it, until it is lawfully condemned.

Article Nine states that when any ship or vessel is taken as a prize, none of the officers, mariners, or others aboard her will be stripped of their clothes or in any way pillaged, beaten, or abused.

Article Ten condemns any FLAG OFFICER, captain, or COMMANDER who upon the likelihood of engagement fails to make the necessary preparations and encourage his inferior officers and men to fight courageously, and states that any person who treacherously or cowardly yields or cries for QUARTER will suffer death.

Article Eleven forbids any person to disobey orders of a superior officer in time of action.

Article Twelve condemns any person who through cowardice, negligence, or disaffection withdraws or stays back in time of action, or who does not do his utmost to take or destroy every ship that it is his duty to engage.

Article Thirteen forbids anyone because of cowardice, negligence, or disaffection not to pursue an enemy, pirate, or rebel or come to the aid of a friend.

Article Fourteen forbids any person in the fleet from delaying or discouraging an action or service "upon pretence of arrears of wages, or upon any pretence whatsoever."

Articles Fifteen and **Sixteen** set death as the punishment for deserters to the enemy and forbid any captain to harbor a deserter from another ship of the Royal Navy.

Article **Seventeen** commands all officers, seamen, and ships convoying merchant ships to do so faithfully and condemns any sort of extortion.

Article **Eighteen** forbids His Majesty's ships and their officers and men from receiving and transporting goods or merchandise for personal commercial purposes.

Articles **Nineteen** and **Twenty** forbid mutinous assembly, sedition, failure to report anyone who utters mutinous words, and contemptuous behavior to a superior officer.

Article **Twenty-one** orders that any "complaint of the unwholesomeness of the victuals, or upon other just ground," be quietly made known to a superior officer and that the officer should then do whatever is in his power to rectify the situation.

Article **Twenty-two** forbids quarreling with, striking, drawing a sword on, or offering to draw swords with a superior officer.

Article **Twenty-three** forbids quarreling and fighting between the men.

Article **Twenty-four** forbids the waste and embezzlement of a ship's stores and provisions.

Article **Twenty-five** sets as death the punishment for arson of anything not belonging to an enemy, pirate, or rebel.

Article **Twenty-six** orders the punishment of anyone who willfully or through negligence grounds or strands a ship.

Article **Twenty-seven** forbids sleeping on WATCH and negligence in performing duty.

Article **Twenty-eight** orders death as punishment for anyone convicted of murder.

Article **Twenty-nine** orders death as punishment of the "unnatural and detestable sin of buggery or sodomy with man or beast."

Article **Thirty** condemns any form of robbery.

Article **Thirty-one** forbids any officer or other person in the fleet to make or sign a false MUSTER or MUSTER-BOOK, to command someone else to make a false muster, or to aid or abet another person in making or signing such.

Article **Thirty-two** orders all provost-martials belonging to the fleet to apprehend criminals and detain prisoners as ordered to the best of their ability; all others in the fleet "shall do their endeavour to detect, apprehend, and bring to punishment all offenders, and shall assist the officers appointed for that purpose."

Article Thirty-three states that any flag officer, captain, comman-der, or LIEUTENANT belonging to the fleet, convicted of behaving in a scandalous, infamous, cruel, oppressive, or fraudulent manner, unbe-coming the character of an officer, shall be dismissed from His Majesty's service.

Articles Thirty-four and **Thirty-five** state that anyone "being in actual service and full pay, and part of the crew in or belonging to any of his Majesty's ships or vessels of war" is liable to trial by court-martial for offenses and to the corresponding punishment as if com-mitted on board ship at sea.

Article Thirty-six states, "All other crimes not capital, committed by any person or persons in the fleet, which are not mentioned in this act, or for which no punishment is hereby directed to be inflicted, shall be punished according to the laws and customs in such cases used at sea."

Additional paragraphs address such issues as the pay and wages of British seamen captured by the enemy, the conduct and procedures of courts-martial, and command following shipwreck.

Artemisia   In *The Surgeon's Mate* (p. 247), Maturin makes reference to two Artemisias. One is the Queen of Caria (d. *c.* 350 B.C.) who mar-ried her brother Mausolus and succeeded him to the throne upon his death; the mausoleum she built in his memory at Halicarnassus was one of the Seven Wonders of the (ancient) World. The second is the fifth-century Queen of Halicarnassus and Cos, who joined the Per-sian fleet of King Xerxes and fought bravely against the Greeks at the Battle of Salamis.

artificer   A mechanic in the Royal Navy.

asafoetida *or* **asafetida**   A bitter, strong-smelling hardened resin of the *Ferula asafoetida,* a plant of the carrot family from North Africa and Central Asia, having many uses in medicine, including as an anti-spasmodic and general prophylactic against disease.

Ascension Island   In the Atlantic about 280 miles northwest of St. Helena, a triangular-shaped volcanic island of about 35 square miles. Turtle and birds' eggs were its chief export.

Ascitans   A heretical sect of the second century that danced around an inflated wineskin, inspired perhaps by Matthew 9:17.

ascites   Abnormal accumulation of fluid within the abdominal cavity; DROPSY of the abdomen, caused most often by heart or liver failure.

Ascot   In England, a village near Windsor in Berkshire and the site of fashionable horseraces held each June; also applied to hats, dresses, and other items suitable for wearing in the Royal Enclosure at Ascot or associated with the event.

Ashgrove Cottage   The Aubrey home in Hampshire. Ashgrove faces north, on poor soil, and is frequently deep in mud. Still, on a good day the grounds are picturesque, and from his observatory Aubrey can peer down at the shipping around Portsmouth and the Isle of Wight. Ashgrove has convenient access to the main Portsmouth-to-London road at the nearby towns of Petersfield, BURITON, and Cosham.

asp   A small venomous hooded serpent, found in Egypt and Libya. Also a species of viper found in parts of Europe.

Asperges me, Domine, hyssopo ... et super nivem dealbabor   Sprinkle me, Lord, with hyssop (an aromatic plant used in biblical Hebrew purification rites) . . . and I shall be whiter than snow (Latin, Psalms 51:7).

asphyxia   Suffocation.

Assassins   A band of Ismaili Muslim fanatics living in Syria at the time of the Crusades whose goal was the creation of a new Fatimid caliphate. From a string of mountain fortresses, they were sent to terrorize orthodox Muslims and Christian Crusaders alike by SHEIKH-AL-JABAL, the Old Man of the Mountain, and subsequent leaders. The Assassins' campaign included the murder of politically important people, thus in English the term came to mean a politically motivated murderer.

Ast illi solvuntur frigore membra/vitaque cum gemitu fugit indignata sub umbras   But as for him, his limbs lay limp and cold, and indignant life fled into the shadows with a groan (Latin, the ending of Virgil's *Aeneid*).

Astley's Royal Amphitheatre   A popular house of entertainment, featuring at times clowns (among them Grimaldi), acrobats, conjurors, and equestrians. A favorite of Londoners, it burned in 1803 and was rebuilt.

ataraxy   Peace of mind; stoical indifference.

Athenry   One of the oldest towns of County Connaught, Ireland, 13 miles east of Galway.

athesphatos oinos   Marvelous quantities of wine (Greek).

athwart   Across from side to side, transversely; usually, but not necessarily, in an oblique direction. From side to side of a ship.

a-trip   Said of YARDS when they are raised up to the MASTS and ready for crossing, of TOPSAILS when hoisted and ready for trimming, and of an anchor when it is just clear of the ground in WEIGHing.

a-try   *See* LIE A-TRY.

attar   A very fragrant essential oil obtained from the petals of flowers, especially roses; fragrance.

auctor   Originator, author, leader (Latin).

audit ale   A special ale brewed at some of the colleges at Oxford and Cambridge and served on audit day, when students had to pay their bills.

auger   A carpenter's tool for boring holes in wood, with a long pointed shank having a cutting edge and a tapered screw point.

auk   A diving bird of the family Alcidae, which includes the guillemot, puffin, razor-bill, little auk, and the extinct great auk. Inhabiting mainly the colder parts of the northern oceans, auks are predomi-

The razorbill, a type of auk (*from* Encyclopaedia Britannica, *1771*)

nantly black, white, or gray with short wings and legs and webbed feet. The great auk, a flightless bird about 30 inches long, nested in great concentrations on North Atlantic islands. Unafraid of humans, it was easily clubbed to death and was often corralled on board for slaughter by sailors, fishermen, and sealers. Auk feathers were used for bedding, the carcasses for oil, and the eggs for food. Each nesting pair produced only one egg per season, and the colonies dwindled rapidly before 1800. The last two known specimens were captured on an island near Iceland in 1844.

aurora   The rising light of dawn. Also, a luminous atmospheric phenomenon, consisting of arches of light and occurring near or radiating from the earth's northern or southern magnetic poles, caused by the emission of light from atoms excited by electrons accelerated along the earth's magnetic field lines. Popularly called the Northern or Southern Lights or merry-dancers or streamers. The Southern Lights are also called aurora australis, and the Northern Lights, aurora borealis.

auscultate   To listen, especially when physicians, on rare occasions, examined the chest by applying an ear directly to it; this was called "immediate auscultation." After the stethoscope was invented (see LAENNEC), the use of that instrument as an intermediary tool caused its use to be referred to as "mediate ausculation." Although listening is essential to the earlier technique of PERCUSSION, the word "ausculation" is not ordinarily used in conjunction with it.

austral   Belonging to the south, southern; also, influenced by the south wind, warm and moist. Of or pertaining to Australia or Australasia.

Autre pays, autre merde   Different country, different "shit," Aubrey's bungled version of the French saying *autres temps, autres moeurs* (manners change with the times).

avifauna   Collective term for the various kinds of birds found in any district or country.

aviso   A dispatch boat. Also, a notification, dispatch, or formal advice.

avoirdupois   The standard system of weights used in Great Britain for all goods except precious metals, precious stones, and medicines. The avoirdupois pound contains 7,000 grains. The avoirdupois weight of the U.S. agrees with that of Great Britain in the pound, ounce, and dram, but the U.S. hundredweight contains 100 pounds and the British hundredweight 112 pounds; the ton, 20 hundredweights, differs accordingly in the U.S. and Britain.

awning   A canvas rooflike covering providing shelter from the weather on deck. Also the part of the POOP deck that is forward of the BULKHEAD of the cabin.

azimuth compass   A compass for taking bearings of both heavenly and terrestrial bodies.

Azores   Volcanic islands in the North Atlantic about 800 miles off the coast of Portugal and settled by the Portuguese beginning in the 15th century.

B

Bab el Mandeb The 20-mile-wide strait between the Red Sea and the Gulf of Aden.

babirussa Found in the East Indies, a species of wild hog (also known as hog-deer, Indian hog, and horned hog), whose upper canine teeth, in the male, pierce the lip and grow up and back like horns.

back To turn a sail or a YARD so that the wind blows directly on the front of the sail, retarding the ship's forward movement.

back and fill To go backward and forward.

backing Motion in a backward direction. Said of the wind, shifting in a counterclockwise direction in relation to a vessel's course. When the wind shifts in a clockwise direction, it is called veering.

backstay A long rope, part of the standing RIGGING, that supports a MAST and counters forward pull. Attached to the upper MASTHEADS, backstays slant a little toward the STERN, extending to both sides or to the CHANNELS of the ship, where they are fastened to backstay-plates.

bagnio A brothel.

bahadur   An Anglo-Indian term meaning a great man or distinguished person; often used as a title before an officer's name. From the Hindi word meaning "hero" or the Persian word for "brave."

bailey   The external wall enclosing the outer court and forming the first line of defense of a castle. In a wider sense, any of the circuits of walls or defenses that surround the keep. Also, either of the two- or three-walled courts within the innermost wall surrounding the walled courts.

bailiff   An officer of justice who is subordinate to a sheriff and who executes writs and arrests. A warrant officer, especially one who arrests debtors.

bairn   Scottish word for a son or daughter.

bait   Of travelers, to stop at an inn to feed the horses, but also to rest and refresh themselves; to make a brief stay or sojourn; to feed, take nourishment.

baize   A coarse woolen cloth used for linings, coverings, curtains, and clothing.

Bakewell tart   A baked sweet consisting of a pastry shell lined with a layer of jam and filled with a rich almond-flavored sponge cake. Named for the town in Derbyshire where it originated.

ballast   Gravel, sand, stones, iron, lead, or any heavy material placed in the hold of a ship to improve her stability. "In ballast" means laden with ballast only.

ball-scoop   A surgical instrument for removing small shot from superficial wounds.

balsa   A very buoyant raft or fishing float made from the wood of the balsa tree and used chiefly on the Pacific coast of South America.

balsam   An aromatic oily or resinous medicinal preparation, usually for external application, for healing wounds or soothing pain.

Baltimore Clipper   Name given in the United States to a fast SCHOONER or BRIG-RIGGED vessel, with raked MASTS and a sharp BOW, of about 90 to 200 tons and 35 to 120 feet on deck.

band   A slip of canvas stitched across a sail to strengthen the parts most liable to pressure.

Banda Isles   A group of 12 small volcanic islands in the Molucca Archipelago.

bandicoot   A large Indian rat as big as a cat and very destructive.

banker   A ship employed in cod fishing on the Bank of Newfoundland.

Banks, Sir Joseph (*1743–1820*)   Botanist who accompanied Captain James COOK on his voyage (1768–1771) to the Pacific in H.M.S. *Endeavour*. The *Endeavour* landed in New South Wales at Sting-Ray Harbour in 1770, and Cook claimed the east coast of Australia for Britain. Cook later renamed the harbor BOTANY BAY in honor of Banks's many discoveries there. Banks was president of the ROYAL SOCIETY from 1778 to 1820.

Banksia   A genus of Australian evergreen trees and shrubs. Also, common name of a species of climbing rose, originating in China, that bears small white or yellow flowers in clusters. It was named after Lady Banks, the wife of Sir Joseph BANKS. The labrador, gray, or jack pine, *Pinus banksiana*, named after Sir Joseph Banks, is also called banksia.

banns   Public announcement in church of an intended marriage so that those who know of any impediment can voice their objection.

Bantu   Of or pertaining to an extensive group of peoples inhabiting the equatorial and southern regions of Africa and the languages spoken by them.

banyan *or* banian   In the English Navy, a day on which salt meat was replaced by fish or cheese, a practice begun during the reign of Elizabeth I (1558–1603) to reduce costs. The term derives from the Banians, Hindu traders who abstained from eating meat because they held animals to be sacred. Also, the banyan is an East Indian tree of the mulberry family with branches that send out shoots down to the soil, where they root and grow into secondary trunks.

Banyuls   A sweetish red or tawny dessert wine made in the communes of Banyuls-sur-Mer in southern France.

baobab   A broad-trunked tropical tree (*ADANSONIA digitata*), also called monkey-bread and Ethiopian sour gourd, found in Africa and long naturalized in Sri Lanka, formerly Ceylon, and some parts of India. Very slow-growing, the baobab reaches up to 60 feet in height and 30 feet in diameter, and some grow to be several thousand years old. Its trunk and lower branches are soft and spongy and can store a great deal of water, inuring them to long dry seasons. The flowers are pollinated by bats. Many animals use the baobab for food and shelter. Its acid fruit looks like a gourd and is edible, and its bark is used to make paper, rope, and cloth.

Barbary The Islamic countries along the north coast of Africa, from the western border of Egypt to the Atlantic Ocean. The Barbary States included Algeria, Tunisia, Tripoli, and sometimes Morocco. *See also* ALGIERS *and* TANGIERS.

Barbados leg A form of ELEPHANTIASIS that occurs in hot climates, caused by *Wuchereria bancrofti,* minute parasitic worms that are transmitted by mosquitoes.

barca-longa A large Spanish fishing boat, common in the Mediterranean, rigged with single LUGSAILS on each of two or three MASTS, and reaching up to 70 feet in length.

Barclay de Tolly, Mikhail, Prince (*1761–1818*) A Russian field marshal of Scottish descent, he became minister of war in 1810 and commanded the Russian forces against NAPOLEON in 1812. His policy of continuous retreat deep into Russia and his defeat at Smolensk resulted in his being replaced by Field Marshal Mikhail Kutuzov, Prince of Smolensk. After Kutuzov's death in 1813, he was again placed in command of the Russian forces, distinguishing himself at Leipzig and in the capture of Paris.

bare poles With no sail set, with furled sails, as in "with or under (bare) poles." Said of a ship in a storm that has taken in all of her sails because of the violent winds.

barge In naval usage, a FLAG OFFICER's boat or one fitted for ceremonial purposes. Also, a long, narrow boat, generally with no fewer than ten oars, carried on a MAN-OF-WAR. *See* illustrations, pages 70 and 71.

barge-pole A long pole used to propel a barge.

bark *also* **Jesuits'** *or* **Peruvian bark** The bark of various species of the cinchona tree, which contains quinine. Ground into a powder, it was highly effective in the treatment of malaria and became a mainstay in the treatment of almost all other fevers, although not truly curative for them. For nautical meaning, *see* BARQUE.

barky   A sailor's term for a vessel well liked by her crew.

barley water   A drink made by boiling down pearl barley. It is used to soothe or protect irritated mucous membranes.

Barmecide   One who offers imaginary food or illusory benefits. Barmecide was the family name of the princes ruling at Baghdad in the 8th century. In *The Arabian Nights* a story is told of a prince who put a succession of empty dishes before a beggar, pretending they contained a delicious meal—a fiction the beggar humorously accepted.

barometer   An instrument for measuring atmospheric pressure. The marine barometer had a column of mercury in a glass tube that was suspended in gimbals to prevent the ship's motion from affecting it. In general, when the mercury rose in the glass column—a "rising glass"—it signified high pressure or improving weather; a "falling glass" meant falling pressure and bad weather. *See also* GLASS.

baronet   The holder of a title of honor that is the lowest that is hereditary, below a baron and above a knight, carrying the title "Sir," and, to differentiate from knights, the abbreviation "Bart." after the surname, as in Sir John Spencer, Bart. A baronet is a commoner, the intention being "to give rank, precedence, and title without privilege."

baronetcy   A baronet's position or rank; a baronet's patent.

barouche   A four-wheeled carriage having a seat in front for the driver and facing seats for two couples.

barque *or* bark   A three-MASTed vessel with the FOREMAST and MAIN-MAST SQUARE-RIGGED and the MIZZENMAST FORE-AND-AFT rigged. Also sometimes used for the BARCA-LONGA of the Mediterranean and other small sailing vessels.

barrel   A revolving cylinder or drum around which a chain or rope is wound in various machines and appliances.

bar-shot *or* bar   A shot consisting of two half cannonballs joined by an iron bar, used at sea to damage MASTs and RIGGING.

Bartholomew Fair   This festival, named after one of the 12 apostles, was held on the 24th of August, from 1133 to 1855, at West Smithfield

(Bartholomew Fair) in London. Known for quality presentations and theater but also its rowdiness, it was closed by the city in 1855.

Bartolo (*1314–1357*)   Bartolo of Saxoferrato was an Italian jurist, legal commentator, and professor at Perugia. He wrote a famous commentary on Justinian's Corpus Juris Civilis.

bas bleu   French for bluestocking, a woman with intellectual or literary interests. The term comes from the Blue Stocking Society, an 18th-century English club whose members—mostly female—met to discuss literature, art, and other intellectual matters. One of the club's popular speakers was Benjamin Stillingfleet, whose habit of wearing unconventional blue stockings gave the club its name.

bashaw   A grandee, a haughty, imperious man. From the title of rulers of BARBARY Coast countries.

bashi-bazouk *also* **bashi-bazo**   A mercenary soldier belonging to the skirmishing, or irregular, troops of the Turkish army, notorious for lawlessness, plundering, and savage brutality.

basilisk   A fantastic reptile, also called a cockatrice, alleged to be hatched by a serpent from a cock's egg. Ancient authors stated that the basilisk's hissing drove away all other serpents and that its breath, and even its look, was fatal.

Basque Roads   Roadstead off the French coast near Rochefort on the Bay of Biscay where the Battle of Basque Roads (or Battle of Aix Roads) took place in 1809. Although an English victory, Captain COCHRANE contended that had Admiral GAMBIER been more enterprising, the victory could have been much more devastating.

Bastille   A prison-fortress built in Paris in the 14th century. The storming of the Bastille on July 14, 1789, touched off the French Revolution.

bastardy order   Order made by a magistrate for the support of an illegitimate child by the putative father.

Batavia   City and seaport on the northwest coast of Java, now Djakarta. Capitol of the Dutch possessions in the East. Built on marshy grounds and long considered unhealthy.

Batavia salve   A topical ointment made of unknown but probably exotic ingredients, associated with the Dutch East Indies.

bate   To lower in amount, weight, or estimation; to reduce.

bateleur   A small eagle of Africa and Arabia, whose name (*bateleur* is French for "tumbler") comes from the birds' aerial acrobatics, including somersaults, loud wing clapping, and screaming dives. About two feet long, the bateleur has a black crested head, a red face, and long, pointed wings. It hunts for small mammals, reptiles, especially snakes, and carrion.

Bath   A well-known city in the west of England, famous for its hot springs. Bath was a center of social life in 18th-century England.

battel   Board and lodging expenses, and tuition when applicable.

batten   A narrow strip of wood nailed to various parts of the MASTS and SPARS to preserve them from chafing. A similar strip used to fasten down the edges of the tarpaulin fixed over the HATCHWAYS to keep out the water in bad weather. Also, a wooden bar from which hammocks are sometimes slung.

battle-lantern   A ship's lantern made of thick horn to prevent fire and explosion, so called because one was placed at each gun to light up the deck during a night engagement; a fighting-lantern.

baulk   A roughly squared beam of timber. Sometimes used specifically to designate Baltic timber, which is roughly dressed before shipment.

Bay of Biscay   The Atlantic Ocean immediately west of France and north of Spain, where British blockaders of Napoleon's ports spent much time. Well known for its ferocious storms and heavy seas.

Beachy Head   At 575 feet above sea level, Beachy Head, in East Sussex, is the highest headland on England's southern coast and a well-known landmark. The French defeated an Anglo-Dutch fleet off Beachy Head in 1690.

beadle   A messenger of justice, a warrant officer. An under-BAILIFF.

beak *or* **beakhead**   A small platform at the fore part of the upper deck; the part of a ship forward of the FORECASTLE, fastened to the STEM and supported by the main KNEE. In warships the sailors' lavatories, or "heads," were located here.

beam   One of the horizontal transverse timbers of a ship that support the deck and hold the vessel together. Also, the breadth of a ship.

A ship running before the wind (*from Sir William Symonds's* Naval Costumes)

When preceded by LARBOARD or STARBOARD, it designates the side of a vessel or that direction. A beam wind is a wind hitting the side of a vessel at a right angle to its centerline.

beam-ends The ends of a ship's BEAMS. "To be laid on the beam-ends" means to have them touching the water, so that the vessel lies on its side in imminent danger of capsizing.

beamy Of a ship, broad in the BEAM. Wide.

bean-cod A small Portuguese fishing vessel with a sharply curved BOW. *See* illustration, page 63.

bear For sailors, a word associated with direction and the maneuvering of a vessel. To bear down on something means to head toward it; to bear up is to put the vessel before the wind, which is accomplished by turning the helm to the vessel's windward—or "up"—side (as the wind in the sail forces the leeward side lower, toward the water); to bear off is to avoid something; to bear away is to change course when

CLOSE-HAULED and put the vessel before the wind. Also, a large padded stone used for scrubbing the decks.

beat   To sail toward the wind on successive TACKs.

beat to quarters   *See* QUARTERS.

beck   To make a sign of recognition, respect, or obeisance; to nod, make a slight bow; to curtsy.

becket   A simple contrivance, often a loop of rope with a knot on one end and eye at the other, but also a large hook or wooden bracket, used to hold loose ropes, TACKLE, oars, SPARS, etc., or for holding or securing the TACKs and SHEETs of sails and for similar purposes. The rope handle of a wooden bucket.

Beckford, William (*1759–1844*)   The eccentric English author of the classic Gothic novel *Vathek* (published in English in 1786), also known for having built Fonthill Abbey, a grand palace of the English Gothic revival.

Bedlam   Corruption of the name of St. Mary of Bethlehem Hospital, a London lunatic asylum where the Navy discharged up to 50 men a year for treatment in the early 19th century.

Beechey, Sir William (*1753–1839*)   English portrait painter to Queen Charlotte beginning in 1793. Among his well-known works are *Brother and Sister* and *Cavalry Review in Hyde Park*. His son, Frederick William (1796–1856), became a noted naval officer and geographer.

beetle   A mallet with a heavy head, usually of wood, used for caulking seams between planks, driving wedges or pegs, ramming down paving stones, or for beating, flattening, or smoothing.

before the mast   A descriptive phrase applied to common sailors, who were berthed in the FORECASTLE, fore of the FOREMAST.

before the wind   Said of a ship sailing with the wind directly astern.

béguin   Affection, a crush (French).

behindhand   In arrears, insolvent, in debt.

Behn, Aphra (*1640–1689*)   A dramatist, poet, and novelist known as the "Incomparable Astrea," she is believed to have been the first English female professional writer, particularly known for coarse comedies, such as *Forc'd Marriage* (1671), *The Rover* (1677), and *The Roundheads* (1682). Her personal experiences included growing up in the West Indies, serving as a spy in Antwerp, and imprisonment for debt.

belay   To make fast, or secure, a running rope, especially one of the small ones used for working the sails, around a cleat, BELAYING PIN, or KEVEL. Also, to disregard, as in "belay the last word."

belaying pin   The wooden or iron pins around which ropes of the running RIGGING are coiled, also sometimes used as weapons. Normally kept in holes on a rail, called a FIFERAIL or pinrail, around the mast.

Belcher neckerchief   A blue neckerchief with large white spots and a dark blue center spot or eye, named after the celebrated pugilist Jim Belcher; sometimes applied to any multicolored handkerchief worn around the neck.

belike   Like, likely.

bell   *See* SHIP'S BELLS.

belladonna   Literally, beautiful lady, the Italian name for deadly nightshade, *Atropa belladonna*, long used as a poison. The medical uses of its major active ingredient, atropine, included inducing sleep, analgesia, and dilating the pupil before cataract extraction. It is no longer used for those purposes, but it is prescribed today for others.

Bellerophon, **H.M.S.**   A 74-gun ship launched in 1786 and nicknamed "Billy Ruffian" by sailors. Commanded by Captain John Cooke at TRAFALGAR, *Bellerophon* fought in the LEE line and suffered 132 dead and wounded, including her captain, who was killed. On July 15, 1815, NAPOLEON gave himself up to Captain Frederick Lewis Maitland of *Bellerophon* and sailed in her to Torquay and then to PLYMOUTH before transferring to another ship for the voyage to ST. HELENA. Leaving the ship on August 7, Napoleon took off his hat to the officers and men of the *Bellerophon*. In Patrick O'Brian's fiction, while Jack Aubrey was serving on the *Bellerophon* in 1797, he and the ship's MASTER mapped the port at St. Martin's, France, which proved fortuitous later during a daring CUTTING OUT mission, as described in *The Letter of Marque. See also* CHIMAERA.

Bellona, **H.M.S.** A third rate built in 1760 and broken up in 1814.

bend To make fast. To bend a sail means to make it fast to its proper YARD or STAY.

Benedictine Of or belonging to St. Benedict or the religious order founded by him around the year 529. One of this order of monks, also known from the color of their dress as "black monks."

benefice A church office that receives the revenue of an endowment. Land granted in feudal tenure, a fief.

Bengal A province of Hindustan that includes the delta of the Ganges.

Bengal light A blue light used for signaling and illumination.

ben't Said of a story that is appropriate, happily invented, even if untrue.

Benthamite A subscriber to the philosophical system of Jeremy Bentham (1748–1832), an eminent English jurist and writer on law and ethics, who taught that the only good is pleasure and that the highest morality is the pursuit of the greatest happiness for the greatest number of people.

Bentinck, Captain John (*1737–1775*) Inventor of the Bentinck sail, Bentinck BOOM, and Bentinck SHROUD. The first was a triangular COURSE, used as a storm canvas, that was supplanted by the FORE-AND-AFT storm STAYSAIL in the Royal Navy, although it remained in use in the U.S. Navy somewhat longer. The Bentinck boom spread the foot of the FORECOURSE of COLLIER BRIGS, and simplified the operation of going about, since there were no TACKs and SHEETs to worry about. Bentinck shrouds ran from one side of the top to the CHANNELS on the other side, providing extra support to the TOPMAST RIGGING.

Berber Name given by the Arabs to the aboriginal people west and south of Egypt. Any member of the North African stock to which belong the aboriginal races of BARBARY and the Tuwariks of the Sahara.

berth Sufficient space to allow a ship to swing around at the length of her moorings; the place where a ship lies when at anchor or at a wharf. Also, the room or apartment where the officers or ship's company mess and reside. A sleeping place in a ship.

berth-deck   The deck that contains the sailors' hammocks.

bespoke   Ordered, commissioned, arranged for. Spoken of, talked of. Also, engaged to be married.

best bower   The port, or "working," anchor of the two usually identical anchors, carried at the BOWS of a vessel, the other anchor being the SMALL-BOWER.

betel   The leaf of the shrubby evergreen plant (*Piper betel* or *Chavica betel*), which is wrapped around slivers of areca nut and lime and chewed as a stimulant by the natives of India and neighboring countries.

beth   The second letter of the Hebrew alphabet.

beylik *or* **beylic**   The dominion or jurisdiction of a bey, an Islamic official.

bezant   A gold coin first struck at Byzantium or Constantinople and current in England until the 14th century.

bezoar   A layered calculus, or hard mass, found in the stomach or intestines of some animals, usually Persian goats, and used as a counter-poison. An expensive panacea at one time, it had been abandoned by most European physicians by about 1700.

bhang   The native name of the Indian variety of common hemp, *Cannabis sativa,* or marijuana, which possesses narcotic and intoxicating properties. In India the leaves and seed capsules are chewed or smoked, eaten in a sweetmeat mixture, and sometimes drunk in an infusion. The name is sometimes extended to an intoxicating substance prepared from the resin of the plant, called hashish by the Arabs.

bib   A bracket under the TRESTLETREE of a MAST, resembling a child's bib with the mast as the "neck."

Bible   A squared piece of stone used to grind the deck with sand in order to clean it. A small HOLYSTONE.

bight   The loop of a rope, as distinguished from its ends; the part between the ends.

bilander   A two-MASTed merchant vessel distinguished by a trape-zoidal MAINSAIL. Bilanders were used in Holland for coast and canal traffic.

bilbo   A long iron bar with sliding shackles to confine the ankles of prisoners and a lock for fixing one end of the bar to the floor.

bilge   The bottom of a ship's hull, the part on either side of the KEEL that is more horizontal than perpendicular; the lowest internal part of the hull. Also, the foul water that collects in the bilge through leakage or otherwise and becomes noxious.

bill-boards   Projections of oak plank secured to the BOW of the ship behind the CATHEADs for the FLUKE of the anchor to rest on. When the anchor has been stowed on the bill-board, it is said to be FISHed, and the TACKLE by which this is done is called the fish-tackle.

billet   An appointment, post, or berth.

billet doux   Love letter (French).

billet-head   A round piece of wood fitted to the BOW or STERN of a whale boat around which the line is secured when the whale is har-pooned; a scroll head.

binge   To rinse, as in to "binge a cask."

binnacle   A box, found on the deck of a ship near the HELM, that houses the compass.

Bio-Bio River   In central Chile, a 238-mile river flowing from the Andes into the Pacific at Concepción.

Biscayan   A native of any part of the shoreline of the BAY OF BISCAY; a Biscayan ship. Also, an inhabitant of the Basque province of Biscaya, or Vizcaya, in Northern Spain.

bisque de homard   Lobster bisque (French).

bistoury *or* bistory   A scalpel that is made in any of three forms: straight, curved, or probe-pointed.

bit   A sum of money; money.

bitter-end   The inboard end of a ship's anchor CABLE. The last and direst extremity.

bittern   Any of several long-legged wading birds having mottled brown plumage and noted for their deep, resonant cry. Specifically, the European species nicknamed "mire-drum" or "bull of the bog" for the boom it utters during breeding season.

bitts   A strong pair of oak posts close to the mast for securing items of running RIGGING, such as the foretopsail-SHEET bitts. When at anchor, the CABLE was hitched around the massive RIDING-BITTS, usually two sets of them, one behind the other.

blackamoor   A dark-skinned person, especially a Negro.

blackcap   Any of several birds with black heads or crowns.

Black Dick   *See* HOWE, Admiral Lord Richard.

black draught   A strong cathartic made of cream of tartar (sodium potassium tartrate), coriander, and, in some formulations, other ingredients.

blackguard   A rude or unscrupulous person.

blacking   A paste or polish applied to a surface to make it black.

blackjack   A tankard, often of tar-coated leather, for drinking beer or ale.

black list   A list of delinquents to whom extra duty is assigned as a punishment.

black pudding   Blood sausage.

black-strake   A band of planks painted with TAR and lamp black, immediately above the wales, which were extra layers of planks bolted in certain places to the ship's side for protection against chafing and impact.

blackstrap   An inferior kind of port wine. Also a drink consisting of a mixture of rum and molasses.

Blane, Sir Gilbert (1749–1834)   Physician who helped eradicate SCURVY from the Royal Navy by encouraging the consumption of lemon juice and who is credited with greatly improving the Navy's health and sanitary conditions. Blane collected naval medical statistics and wrote *Observations on the Diseases of Seamen* (1785).

blanquette de veau   Veal stew in a cream sauce (French).

blateroon   A babbler.

blauwbok   A large antelope found in South Africa and known for its distinctive ash-gray hair over a black hide.

blewit   A kind of edible mushroom.

Bligh, William (*1754–1817*)   Admiral Bligh is most famous for surviving three mutinies. The first occurred in 1789 three weeks out of Tahiti aboard H.M.S. *Bounty*, a former merchant ship loaded with breadfruit trees. Bligh, who was foul-mouthed and unliked by his crew, was set adrift along with 18 others in a 23-foot open boat, which he proceeded to navigate on a 41-day journey, landing safely at Timor. Later, he commanded one of the ships during the mutiny at the NORE in 1797. He became Vice-Admiral of the Blue in 1814, despite being arrested by his soldiers in 1808 when he was Governor of New South Wales, Australia.

bloater   A smoked half-dried herring.

block   A pulley or combination of pulleys mounted in a wooden or metal case and used to increase the mechanical power of the ropes running through it, especially in the RIGGING of ships and in heavy lifting.

bloody flux   Dysentery, characterized by bloody, painful diarrhea caused by any of several microbial organisms.

Blücher, Gebhard Leberecht von (*1742–1819*)   Prussian field marshal who fought against NAPOLEON in the disastrous campaign of 1806, surrendering with honor near Lübeck. In the dark days that followed, he helped re-create the Prussian opposition to Napoleon. He was a leader in the War of Liberation (1813–14). Although ill and subject to delusions, he won brilliant victories at Wahlstatt and Möckern and played a part in the defeat of the French at Leipzig. Crossing the Rhine, he led his army to Paris. In the WATERLOO campaign of 1815, he was defeated at LIGNY but arrived at a crucial moment in the Battle of Waterloo and helped make it a victory for the allied forces.

bluebottle   A fly (*Musca vomitoria*) with a large bluish body; the meat-fly or blow-fly.

blue devil   A baleful demon; despondency, depression of spirits; the apparitions seen in DELIRIUM TREMENS.

blue draught   A solution of copper sulfate used as an astringent and tonic, especially for consumption (tuberculosis), although it almost always causes vomiting.

bluejacket   A sailor (from the color of his jacket). The term is used especially to distinguish seamen from MARINES.

Blue-Nose   A nickname for a native of NOVA SCOTIA. A Canadian, especially Nova Scotian, ship.

blue ointment   An ointment for syphilitic chancre and rash made with metallic MERCURY, hog's lard, and mutton suet.

blue peter   A blue flag with a white rectangle in the middle, signifying the letter *p* in the international code, hoisted to signal that the ship is ready to sail, especially to recall the crew.

blue pill   A strong remedy for syphilis made with CORROSIVE SUBLIMATE; *see* MERCURY.

bluff   Of a ship, having little inclination in the BOWS.

blunderbuss   A short gun with a large bore, firing many balls or slugs and effective within a limited range without exact aim.

Boadicea (*d.* A.D. 60)   The British queen of the Iceni Celts in East Anglia, Boadicea led a revolt against the Romans, but her army was eventually defeated, and she poisoned herself. She is the subject of poems by Tennyson and Cowper and of the 17th-century tragedy *Bonduca* by John Fletcher and Francis Beaumont.

Boanerges   The name given by Christ to the two sons of Zebedee. Hence, a loud vociferous preacher or orator.

board   In sailing, to sail as CLOSE TO THE WIND as possible; the course of a ship when TACKing. "To make boards" means to tack; "to make short boards" means to tack frequently. Also, to enter a vessel, generally used in the sense of attacking it or officially entering it to examine papers.

boarding axe   A weapon with a steel axehead and a spike used for cutting an enemy ship's RIGGING and STAYS, thus hindering its ability to maneuver.

boarding-netting   Nets fastened to the side of the ship to repel boarders.

Board of Green Cloth   The financial office of the Royal Household, named for the green-covered table at which its business was originally transacted. Consisting of the Lord Steward and his subordinates, it controlled various matters of expenditure and had legal and judicial authority within the sovereign's royal court, having "power to correct all offenders, and to maintain the peace of the VERGE or jurisdiction of the court-royal, which extends every way two hundred yards from the gate of the palace" (*Wharton Law Lexicon*). Also, the term is associated with naval COURTS-MARTIAL, which also sometimes used a green cloth on the table.

boards   In bookbinding, rectangular pieces of strong pasteboard used for the covers of books. If a book has these covered only with paper it is said to be in boards; if covered with cloth, it is said to be in cloth boards; and if the boards are covered with leather, parchment, or the like, the book is said to be bound.

boat-cloak   A large cloak worn by officers on duty at sea.

boatswain *or* **bosun** *or* **bos'n**   A multipurpose PETTY OFFICER, usually one of the best seamen, whose responsibilities included inspecting the ship's sails and RIGGING every morning and reporting their state to the officer of the WATCH. If new ropes or other repairs were needed, he also informed the FIRST LIEUTENANT. The Boatswain was in charge of all deck activities, such as weighing or dropping anchor or handling the sails and he issued orders using a silver boatswain's pipe. "His vigilance should ever be on the alert, and his eyes should be everywhere," noted *The Naval Apprentice's Kedge Anchor* (1841). "He should be active of limb, quick of sight, and ready in the exercise of his mental faculties."

bob *or* **bob-wig**   A wig with the bottom locks in short curls or "bobs," as opposed to a "full-bottomed wig." Also, bob *only*, a curtsy.

bobstay   A heavy rope that draws the BOWSPRIT down toward the STEM and counteracts the force of the STAYS of the FOREMAST, which pull up.

Bob's your uncle   A slang phrase meaning everything is perfect.

Boccherini, Luigi (1743–1805)   Italian violoncellist and composer born in Lucca. He composed at the courts of the Infante Don Luis in Madrid and Frederick II "the Great" in Prussia. Best known for his chamber music.

boggart *or* **boggard**   A specter, goblin, or bogeyman, especially a goblin or sprite that haunts a gloomy spot or scene of violence.

Bohea   Black tea from the Wu-i hills of China, from where it was first exported to England; applied also to tea of similar quality grown elsewhere. The name was given in the beginning of the 18th century to the finest black teas.

boletus   The common name for the club fungi, a red or brown umbrella-shaped mushroom, some of which are poisonous and others edible. The boletus is common throughout the United States and Europe.

bollard   A wooden or iron post on a ship, a whale-boat, or a QUAY, for securing ropes to.

bolster   Any of a variety of objects used to prevent chaffing in the RIGGING, SHEETS, and anchor line, and on a ship's sides. For example, a small cushion or bag of tarred canvas used to prevent the STAYS from being chaffed by the movement of the MASTS, and a piece of wood covered with canvas for the EYES of the rigging to rest on the TRESSLETREES.

boltered   Clotted or clogged with blood, especially having the hair matted with blood.

bolt-rope   A rope sewn around the edge of a sail to prevent the canvas from tearing.

bolus   A round medicinal lozenge, often a cathartic of unspecified ingredients. The term was often used disparagingly for a useless or inconvenient remedy of large size.

bomb   A small war vessel carrying mortars for throwing bombs and also known as a bomb-galliot, bomb-ketch, bomb-ship, bomb-vessel, or bombard. *See also* KETCH.

bonito   A striped tuna, common in tropical seas, that grows to about three feet and lives chiefly on flying fish.

bonne bouche   A tidbit, from the French expression *garder quelque chose pour la bonne bouche,* to save something until last.

bonne mot   Aubrey's pidgin French for *bon mot,* a witty remark or saying.

bonnet   An additional piece of canvas laced to the foot of a sail to catch more wind. Although this arrangement was used in the 17th century, it was obsolete by the early 19th century.

bonny-clabber   Milk that has soured naturally.

bonus nullius   No good (that is, of no use), Latin.

booby   A fish-eating, island-dwelling bird of tropical and subtropical coasts and the northern Pacific. Up to 40 inches in length, boobies are closely related to gannets and have short legs, white plumage with dark tails, and brownish black, long, pointed wings. They sleep on the water and visit land primarily for breeding. Their brightly colored conical bills with sharp, slightly curved tips are ideal for their mode of fishing, which involves speedy dives from up to 100 feet above the surface of the water. Also, the native name in Australia for the wattlebird, a honey eater with pendulous ear wattles. Booby also means a lubber, a clown, a nincompoop.

Boodle's   Men's club founded in 1762 by Edward Boodle. Originally on Pall Mall on the site of ALMACK'S Club, it moved to its current location at 28 St. James's Street in 1783. Among its members were William Pitt the Younger and the Duke of Wellington.

boom   A long SPAR run out from different places in the ship to extend the foot of a particular sail, such as the JIB-boom, flying jibboom, and STUDDINGSAIL boom. Also refers to the part of a ship's deck where spare spars are stowed; the ship's boats are stowed "on the booms." Of a sail, set to a boom instead of to a YARD; of a SHEET, fastened to a boom. To boom out means to extend the foot of a sail with a boom. To boom off is to push a vessel off with a pole.

boom-iron   An iron ring fitted on the YARDARM, through which the STUDDINGSAIL boom slides when rigged out or in; a similar ring by which the flying JIB-boom is secured to the jib-boom, or this to the BOWSPRIT.

boomkin   *See* BUMKIN.

boor   A peasant, countryman. From the Dutch word *boer*, "farmer."

boot-top   To clean the upper part of a ship's bottom by daubing it over with a coat or mixture of tallow, sulfur, resin, etc. Boot-topping is chiefly performed where there is no dock or when there is not enough time to clean the whole bottom.

borborygm *or* **borborygmus**   Rumbling in the bowels.

Boreas, **H.M.S.**   A 28-gun sixth-rate ship commanded by NELSON in 1784 on a voyage to the WEST INDIES. Launched in 1774, she became a supply ship in 1797 and was sold in 1802.

boreen   A lane, a narrow road. Also, an opening in a crowd (chiefly Irish).

Borgia, Lucrèce (*1480–1519*)   The Duchess of Ferrara and the sister of Cesare Borgia (1476–1507), the duke who spread terror in Italy and was praised by Machiavelli in *Principe*. The daughter of Cardinal Rodrigo Borgia, later Pope Alexander VI, Lucrèce married three times for political purposes.

boring iron   A tool used for piercing, perforating, or making a bore-hole.

Borneo   An island in the MALAY Archipelago. Borneo is the third largest island in the world and was frequented by English, Dutch, and Portuguese traders in the 16th and 17th centuries.

Bossuet, Jacques-Bénigne (*1627–1704*)   France's greatest pulpit orator. His funerary orations were classics of French Baroque prose. Wrote tracts in support of absolutism.

bosun   *See* BOATSWAIN.

bosun bird   The arctic SKUA (*Cataractes parasiticus*). Also, a tropical bird, *Phaeton aethereus,* with a whistlelike call and two long feathers in the tail, called by sailors the MARLINE-SPIKE because it resembled one.

bosun's chair   A chair formed from a board, much like the seat of a swing, that can be hauled aloft and that a sailor sits on when working aloft.

Botany Bay   Inlet in NEW SOUTH WALES south of what is today Sydney, Australia, and so named for the flora discovered there in 1770 by Captain COOK's passenger, the renowned botanist Joseph BANKS.

bottle-jack   A bottle-shaped device for roasting meat.

bottom   A contract similar to a mortgage, in which a shipowner borrows money to enable him to complete a voyage and pledges the ship as security for repayment.

boules   A French game of bowls, which is played with heavy metal balls tossed in the air.

bounty   A gratuity given to recruits on joining the Army or Navy; a reward to soldiers; PRIZE MONEY for capturing an enemy ship.

Bourbon   A member of the royal family that long held the thrones of France (1589–1793 and 1814–1830), Spain (1700–1808, 1814–1868, and 1874–1931), and Naples (1735–1805 and 1815–1860).

bow *or* bows   The forward end of any craft, beginning on both sides where the planks arch inward and ending where they close, at the STEM or PROW.

bow-and-quarter line   The position of ships in a column when each successive vessel has its BOW a little to one side and behind the BEAM of the one in front.

bow-chaser *also* chase *or* chase-piece   A long gun with a relatively small bore, placed in the BOW-port to fire directly ahead. Used especially while chasing an enemy vessel to damage its sails and RIGGING.

bower *or* bower anchor   The name of the two largest anchors, the BEST-BOWER (STARBOARD) and SMALL-BOWER (LARBOARD), carried at the BOWS of a ship. Bower also refers to the CABLE attached to these anchors.

bow-grace   A kind of frame or fender of old junk placed around the BOWS and sides of a ship to prevent injury from floating ice or timbers.

bowler   In cricket, the player who bowls or propels the ball at the wicket, something like the pitcher in baseball.

bow-line *or* bowline   A useful type of knot that produces a loop and will not slip. Also, a rope fastened with a bowline to about the middle of the perpendicular edge on the WEATHER side of a square sail and secured forward to keep the edge of the sail steady when the ship is sailing CLOSE-HAULED. A SQUARE-RIGGED ship sails "on a bowline" when her COURSE is as close as possible to the wind.

bowman   The oarsman who sits nearest the BOW of a boat.

bowse   To haul down on a TACKLE, for instance after a TACK.

bowsprit   A large spar running out from the STEM of a vessel, to which the FOREMAST STAYS are fastened and from which JIBS are set.

Bow Street Runners   The first organized police force in London, established in 1748 by the writer Henry Fielding, who was then chief magistrate at Bow Street. They were empowered to serve outside of the City in 1757. Incorporated into the Metropolitan Police in 1829.

box-haul   A method of going about that involved throwing the sails aback, sailing backward, and turning the ship on her heel. It was used only in an emergency.

box the compass   To name the points, half points, and quarter points of the compass in proper sequence in a clockwise direction beginning at north (N, NbE, NNE, NEbN, NE, NEbE, ENE, EbN, E, etc.).

Boyne, **H.M.S.**   A 98-gun second rate that accidentally burned at Spithead in 1795. The crew was saved.

brace   A rope or line attached to the end of a YARD, used to swing, or TRIM, the sail. To move or turn a sail using braces. To brace up means to bring the yards nearer to FORE-AND-AFT by HAULing on the LEE braces. To brace in was to bring the yard more square. Also, a timber used to strengthen the framework of a vessel.

brace-pendant   Lengths of rope or chain into which the YARDARM brace-BLOCKS are spliced.

Brahmanism   The principles and practice of the Brahmans, the highest, or priestly, caste among the Hindus.

brail up   To HAUL up the foot or lower corners of a sail by means of the brails, small ropes fastened to the edges of sails to truss them up before FURLing.

breach   The breaking of waves on a shore or over a vessel.

bread-barge   An oval tub in which bread is placed for mess.

bread pill   Bread crumbs rolled into small pills, used for treating many gastrointestinal disorders, but essentially a placebo.

breadroom   A place partitioned off below the lower deck for keeping the bread.

break bulk   To begin to unload cargo.

bream   To clear a ship's bottom of shells, seaweed, ooze, etc., by singeing it, thus softening the pitch so that the debris can be scraped off.

breast-hooks   Thick pieces of timber, curved like KNEES and used to reinforce the BOWS of a ship.

breech   To secure a cannon by means of a BREECHING. Also, the back part of a gun.

breeching   A stout rope attached by a THIMBLE to the CASCABEL of a gun and securing the gun to the ship's side. *See* illustration, page 214.

Bréguet   A watch made by Abraham Louis Bréguet (1747–1823), a renowned French watchmaker of Swiss origin.

Brest   The chief naval base and dockyard for the French Navy operating in the Atlantic, located in northwest France and frequently blockaded by the British Channel Fleet.

brickbat   A fragment of brick, a useful missile when stones are scarce. An uncomplimentary remark, criticism.

bridle   A stout CABLE by which a vessel is secured to MOORINGs. A short piece of rope by which a BOWLINE is attached to the LEECH, or side edge, of the sail.

bridle-port   A port or port-hole in a ship's BOW through which BRIDLES may be run or chase-guns fired.

brig   A two-masted vessel, SQUARE-RIGGED on both MASTs, setting on a boom a large main STAYSAIL (known as a brigsail), but lacking a COURSE on the mainyard. The SHEET of the FORE-AND-AFT brigsail is secured to a BOOM. A SNOW was similar but did set a course on the MAIN; it had no mainstaysail, but it did have a loose-footed (no boom) fore-and-aft sail set on a "snowmast." A hermaphrodite brig has a brig's foremast and a SCHOONER's mainmast. *See* illustration, page 57.

brightwork   Polished metalwork, usually brass.

brimstone   Formerly the common name for sulfur.

Bristol   In southwest England on the Severn River, one of the country's most prosperous ports after London and home to fleets of traders that imported vast amounts of fruit, wine, oil, and many other products from around the world.

bristol card   A kind of pasteboard with a smooth surface suitable for art.

Bristol-fashion   Shipshape.

broach to   To veer or inadvertently to cause the ship to veer to WIND-WARD, bringing her BROADSIDE to meet the wind and sea, a potentially hazardous situation, usually the result of a ship being driven too hard. A ship arriving in this unhappy situation by YAWing to LEEWARD rather than windward was said to have been "brought by the lee."

broad pendant   A swallow-tailed pendant flown by a COMMODORE. The pendant—red, white, or blue depending upon the SQUADRON of the commodore—was originally 14 times as long as it was wide but was shortened gradually to two times its width.

broadsheet   A large sheet of paper printed on one side only.

broadside   The side of a ship above the water, or with the side of the vessel turned fully toward. The whole array or the simultaneous firing of the artillery on one side of a ship. Hence, a volley of verbal abuse.

Broke, Sir Philip Bowes Vere (*1776–1841*)   The British Rear-Admiral best known for his battle on June 1, 1813, with the U.S. FRIGATE *CHESAPEAKE* off Boston. Broke, who first served under NELSON and JERVIS, became known for his intense gunnery training, which served the *SHANNON* well in its duel with the *Chesapeake*. Two brutal broadsides wracked the *Chesapeake*, causing heavy casualties and helping to win the fight. Broke was a hero in Britain, having avenged recent British defeats in similar actions. He was made a BARONET but because of a battle wound, never again served at sea.

bromeliad   Any plant belonging to the family Bromeliaceae, which are chiefly tropical American and herbaceous plants such as the pineapple and Spanish moss.

bronchus   Each of the two main branches of the trachea, or windpipe.

Brooks's   A men's club created when ALMACK'S Club split into two new clubs, BOODLE'S and Brooks's, in 1764. Known as a place of excessive gambling, Brooks's moved from Pall Mall to 60 St. James's Street in 1778 and later became a meeting place of the WHIGS. Patrick O'Brian is a member.

brow   An inclined plane of planks, or GANGWAY, between a ship and shore used for entering and leaving.

Brummagem   A local vulgar form of the name of Birmingham, England, used to refer to a FARTHING, GROAT, or HALFPENNY. An allusion to counterfeit groats produced there, and by extension, counterfeit, sham, a cheap or showy imitation.

bubo   An inflamed swelling or abscess in glandular parts of the body, especially the groin or armpits. A common sign of the bubonic plague.

buck-basket   A basket in which cloth, yarn, or clothes are bucked (washed by being boiled in lye).

Buckler's Hard   A shipbuilding site near PORTSMOUTH on the Beaulieu River in Hampshire, in the south of England, used during the 18th and 19th centuries.

buff *or* **buff-leather**   Leather made of buffalo hide, but also applied to a stout leather made of ox hide, dressed with oil and having a characteristic fuzzy surface and a dull whitish-yellow color. Buff was formerly much used for military attire.

bugalet   A small, two-masted SQUARE-RIGGED vessel used along the coast of Brittany. The after mast, which was the larger one, carried a large square sail and a TOPSAIL, and the FOREMAST, a small square sail. It could also carry one or two JIBS.

bugger   A sodomite. In vulgar language, a term of abuse or insult; often, however, simply "chap" or "fellow." Also refers to something that is a great nuisance.

Bugio   Probably Bougie, the French name for a seaport of northeast Algiers.

buke   Obsolete form of "book."

bulbul   Any of the medium-sized, dull-colored PASSERINE birds of the family Pycnonotidae, native to Africa and South Asia. Famed songsters having short necks and wings, bulbuls are popular as cage birds in the Middle East. Often found in Persian poetry, the word *bul-bul* is frequently mistranslated as "nightingale."

bulkhead   One of the upright partitions serving to form the cabins in a ship or to divide the hold into distinct watertight compartments for safety in case of collision or other damage.

bullock   Originally a young bull or bull calf, but later, a castrated bull, an ox. Applied loosely to a bull or bovine beast.

bulwark   The raised woodwork running along the sides of a vessel above the level of the deck.

bum   A BAILIFF.

bumboat   A scavenger's boat, employed to remove filth from ships lying in the Thames. A boat employed to carry provisions, vegetables, and small merchandise for sale to ships, either in port or lying at a distance from the shore. Also used to carry prostitutes to ships in port.

bumkin   A short BOOM projecting from each side of the BOW of a ship, to extend the lower edge of the FORESAIL to WINDWARD. Also, similar booms for extending the MAINSAIL and the MIZZEN.

bumper   A cup or glass of wine or other drink filled to the brim, especially when drunk as a toast.

bung   A large cork stopper for the mouth of a cask; also a sobriquet for the sailor who was responsible for supplies stored in the hold.

bunt   The middle part of a sail formed into a bag so that the sail may gather more wind. When the sail is being FURLed, the bunt is the middle gathering that is tossed up on the center of the YARD.

bunting   Fabric made of coarse wool often used for flags. Also, naval slang for a signaler.

buntline   One of the lines used for HAULing up the foot of a sail in FURLing.

burgoo   To seamen, a thick oatmeal gruel or porridge. Easily cooked and cheap to provide, it was frequently served excessively at sea, and so unloved by seamen.

Buriton   A village in Hampshire near the London-Portsmouth route. In 1811 Buriton consisted of 48 houses and 72 families, 56 of which were employed in farming, primarily cereals as well as turnips and rape.

burr   A rough or dialectal pronunciation, a peculiarity of utterance.

bursten   Alternate form of "burst."

burton   A small TACKLE consisting of two or three BLOCKS or pulleys used to set up or tighten rigging or to shift heavy objects.

buss   A small, strong vessel of about 60 tons prevalent in the North Sea fishing industry in the 17th and 18th centuries.

Bustamente, Rear-Admiral don José   Commanding a squadron of four frigates, the *Medea* (40) and three 34s, *Fama, Clara,* and *Mercedes,* Bustamante was responsible for carrying nearly six million pieces of eight and a valuable cargo of tin, copper, seal oil, skins, and vicuña wool (a payload estimated to be worth anywhere from one million to two million pounds by various historians) to CADIZ from MONTEVIDEO in the year 1804. Although Spain was technically at peace with Britain, it had a special agreement with France and war with Britain was imminent. On October 5, Sir Graham Moore on board *Indefatigable* (44) and three other British FRIGATES—the *Lively* (38), Captain Hammond; the *Amphion* (32), Captain Sutton; and *Medusa* (32), Captain Gore—waylaid the squadron about 30 miles southwest of Cape Santa Maria, Portugal. A Lieutenant Arscott attempted to persuade Bustamente to surrender but failed, as the impatient Moore fired a gun signaling Arscott to return. O'Brian's account of the ensuing action in *Post Captain* is largely historically correct.

In his memoirs, Vice-Admiral William Lovell (who was not present at the action) writes: "I always did think . . . that it was a cruel thing to send only four frigates to detain four others, when by increasing the force by two or three line-of-battle ships, this might have been effected without loss of blood, or honour to the Spaniards. . . . It would have been humane to have sent such a force as would have put resistance out of the question; for what man, who was not a traitor, could yield without fighting (and with such a valuable cargo on board), to a force, in all appearance, not greater than his own. It was an untoward event" (*Personal Narrative of Events from 1799 to 1815,* p. 37). Prior to the event, Maturin recommends to the Admiralty that just such a superior force be sent.

bustard   A member of a family of birds remarkable for its great size and running power. The great bustard is the largest European bird and was formerly common in England, though now nearly extinct.

butt   A cask for wine or ale, varying from 108 to 140 gallons. Also, a measure of capacity equaling two hogsheads—in ale usually 108 gallons, in wine 126 gallons—but these standards were not always precisely adhered to. A cask for fish, fruit, etc.

butt *or* **butt-end**   The end of a plank in a vessel's side that joins or butts on to the end of the next, or the juncture of two such planks. Also, a small BLOCK consisting of two wings containing rollers for a chain to pass over.

butterbox   A derisive British nickname for a Dutch seaman.

Byng, Admiral John (1704–1757)   Having failed to prevent the French from taking MINORCA in 1756, Admiral Byng was COURT-MARTIALed and shot on the QUARTERDECK of H.M.S. *Monarch* on March 14, 1757, for lack of resolution. The execution was strongly decried after the fact as an act of face-saving by the government and is mocked in Voltaire's *Candide*.

by the wind   As near as possible to the direction from which the wind is blowing.

C

cabbage white   A white butterfly whose larvae feed on cabbage.

cabinet pudding   A pudding made of bread or cake, dried fruit, eggs, and milk, usually served hot with a sauce.

cable   The strong thick rope to which a ship's anchor is fastened. Also, a HAWSER or rope smaller than a BOWER used to move or hold the ship temporarily during a calm in a river or in a sheltered haven. Also, a unit of measurement that differs from country to country. In the Royal Navy it is equal to 100 fathoms or one tenth of a sea mile (approximately 200 yards, or 185 meters).

cable-laid   Originally said of a rope of nine strands, made by laying up three plain ropes together left-handed. Today, three-stranded ropes twisted together in the opposite direction to the twists of the individual ropes. *See also* HAWSER-LAID.

cablet   A small CABLE or CABLE-LAID rope less than ten inches in circumference.

cable-tier   The place in a hold, or between decks, where the CABLES are coiled away.

Cacafuego   Literally, "shit fire" (Spanish). The 32-gun XEBEC-FRIGATE that Aubrey boldly attacks in the SOPHIE. The event is based on Thomas COCHRANE's attack on the *El Gamo* in the *Speedy.*

cachexy   Malnutrition or wasting caused by disease.

cacothymia   A vicious state of mind; a form of insanity resembling what might now be labeled psychopathic behavior.

cadenza   In music, a flourish of indefinite form given to a solo voice or instrument at the close of a movement or between two divisions of a movement.

Cadiz   The seaport on Spain's southern Atlantic coast that head-quartered the Spanish treasure fleet. The site of a famous raid by Sir Francis Drake in 1587, it was blockaded by England in 1797 and 1798, and in 1800 it was bombarded by NELSON.

caecum *or* **blind-gut**   In humans, most mammals and birds, and many reptiles, the first part of the large intestine, which forms a pouch into which the ileum opens from one side.

Cagliari   Seaport on the south coast, and capital, of Sardinia.

caiman   Any of a group of large tropical American reptiles of the crocodile family that are closely related and similar in appearance to alligators.

Cainites   A gnostic sect of the second century, probably from the eastern area of the Roman Empire. The Christian theologian Origen declared that the Cainites had "entirely abandoned Jesus." They believed that Yahweh (the God of the Jews) was evil because the world he created was perversely designed to prevent the reunion of the divine element in man with the unknown perfect God. The Cainites revered such rejected figures as Cain, Esau, and the Sodomites, whom they considered to be bearers of an esoteric, saving knowledge (gnosis). The Cainites are sometimes called libertine gnostics for believing that true perfection, and hence salvation, comes only by breaking all the laws of the Old Testament. Because it was difficult to violate all of them during a single lifetime, they did not look for salvation on earth but rather escape from it.

caique A light boat or SKIFF propelled by one or more rowers, common on the Bosporus. Also, a LEVANTINE sailing vessel.

Calais A city and port on the northwest coast of France. Just 20 miles across the English Channel from Dover, it is the closest Continental port to England and the site of many battles over the centuries.

calamary Squid.

calcareous Of the nature of, composed of, or containing calcium, calcium carbonate, or limestone. Also, growing on limestone or in soil impregnated with lime. Chalky.

calcification Conversion into lime. Also, the hardening of a structure, tissue, etc., by the deposit of salts of lime, as in the formation of teeth and in many forms of petrifaction.

calculus, vesical Bladder stone.

Calder, Sir Robert (*1745–1818*) Admiral Calder joined the Royal Navy at the age of 14 and was knighted after carrying home the dispatches following the Battle of CAPE ST. VINCENT in 1797. In 1805, Calder, commanding 14 ships, captured two ships in an action against the 20-vessel fleet of French Admiral VILLENEUVE. After failing to engage Villeneuve the following day, he was COURT-MARTIALed at his own request and acquitted of cowardice. In 1810 he was promoted to FLAG RANK.

Caledonia Roman name of part of northern Britain, later applied poetically or rhetorically to Scotland or the Scottish Highlands.

calenture A tropical disease characterized by delirium in which the victim, it is said, believes the sea to be green fields and wants to leap overboard. Most commonly, any fever.

calipash The upper shell, or carapace, of the turtle. Also, the part of the turtle next to the upper shell, containing a dull green gelatinous substance.

calipee The lower shell, or plastron, of the turtle. Also, the part next to the lower shell, containing a light yellowish gelatinous substance.

callosity The condition of being callous; an abnormal hardness and thickness of the skin or other tissues. A callus.

calomel   Mercurous chloride, a tasteless medicinal white powder often used as a cathartic.

calor, rubor, dolor   Heat, redness, pain (the classic signs of inflamation), Latin.

calumba root   Columbo root, prescribed as a mild astringent tonic.

calvity   Baldness.

Calvinistical   Of the nature of or pertaining to the doctrines of John Calvin (1509–1564), the Protestant reformer.

Camaret *or* **Cameret-sur-Mer**   A village lying on the tip of a peninsula about ten miles south of Brest, at the northern extremity of the west coast of France.

camber   A slight convexity or curve so that the center is higher than the ends. To bend (a beam, etc.) upward in the middle, to arch it slightly.

cambric   A kind of fine white linen, originally made at Cambray in Flanders, usually used for handkerchiefs. Also applied to an imitation made of cotton.

cameloleopard   A giraffe.

Camperdown, Battle of   A British victory in the North Sea off the coast of Holland on October 11, 1797, in which Admiral Adam DUNCAN and a British fleet numbering 14 SHIPS OF THE LINE dealt a Dutch fleet of 11 ships of the line a crushing blow, taking nine ships of the line, two FRIGATES, and the Dutch commander-in-chief, Admiral Jon de Winter.

camphire   Same as CAMPHOR.

camphor-tree   *Cinnamomum camphora,* a tree indigenous to the Near and Far East, whose extract had many therapeutic applications, especially as a painkiller.

Canary Islands   Volcanic islands off the northwest coast of Africa, including Grand Canary and Tenerife, that belong to Spain.

Action off Camperdown. The Dutch fleet under Admiral de Winter faced a British fleet commanded by Adam, now Lord Viscount, Duncan, off Camperdown on October 11, 1797. The flagship of Admiral de Winter, the last to surrender, is seen nearly in the center, feebly returning the fire of the *Venerable*. The *Hercules*, a 64-gun Dutch ship, her stern on fire, is drifting across their bows. On the left in the background is the *Monarch* with her prize the *Jupiter*. (*Reproduced from* The Naval Chronicle, *vol. 4, courtesy of the Mariners' Museum, Newport News, Virginia*).

can-buoy   A navigational marker with a flat top, as opposed to a nun-buoy, which has a conical top, the underwater part being conical in both types.

Candlemas Day   A church festival celebrated with a great display of candles on February 2 to commemorate the feast of the purification of the Virgin Mary and the presentation of Christ in the Temple.

can-hook   A cask-length contrivance, consisting of a rope or chain with a flat hook at each end and TACKLE fastened to the middle, used for slinging a cask by the projecting ends of its STAVES.

canister shot *also* **canister** *or* **case-shot**   A precursor of the explosive shell made up of many small iron balls packed in a cylindrical tin case and fired from a cannon.

cannonade   A bombardment of artillery, or to attack with artillery.

canonical hours   Stated times of the day appointed by the canons of the Church of England for prayer and devotion. Also, the hours within which marriage can legally be performed in a parish church in England.

Canopus   The bright star in the southern constellation Argo, the ship, situated in its RUDDER.

cant   To pitch as by the sudden lurching of a ship; to tilt or turn over. Also, to swing around.

cantharides   *See* SPANISH FLY.

cant-purchase   A PURCHASE used in whaling for hoisting in blubber. It consists of a BLOCK suspended from the main-MASTHEAD and another block made fast to a cut made in the whale between the neck and fins, known as a cant.

cant-timbers   Frames at the BOW and STERN, which were placed radially, rather than perpendicular to the KEEL.

canty   Cheerful, lively, gladsome.

cap   A strong thick block of wood with two large holes through it, used to hold two MASTs together when one is erected at the head of the other in order to lengthen it.

caparison   To put trappings on, to deck, harness.

Cape Gris Nez   The closest part of the French coast to England, 15 miles southwest of Calais.

Capella   A double star of the first magnitude in the northern constellation Auriga, also known as Charioteer.

Cape of Storms   The original name given by the Portuguese explorer Bartholomew Diaz de Novaes in 1488 to the Cape of Good Hope, the promontory on the southwestern coast of South Africa.

Cape Peñas Cape on the northwest coast of Spain that projects into the Bay of Biscay, at the eastern base of which lies the seaport Gijón, where the Spanish Armada sought refuge following its defeat by the British in 1588.

Cape Prior Spanish cape, northeast of Corunna.

caper-bush A low, prickly shrub abundant on walls and rocky places in southern Europe, the flower bud of which is frequently pickled and served as a condiment.

Cape St. Vincent, Battle of Fought on February 14, 1797, by British Admiral Sir John JERVIS with 15 SHIPS OF THE LINE and Spanish Admiral Don José de Cordova with 27 ships of the line. It took place off Cape St. Vincent, a headland on the southwest coast of Portugal, and caught the Spanish fleet somewhat off guard as it was scurrying toward the harbor at CADIZ. Jervis managed to split the Spanish fleet, and NELSON, aboard the *Captain*, performed one of his legendary feats when he boarded the 112-gun *San Josef* via the 80-gun *San Nicolas*, which he captured first after the two ships, under heavy fire from H.M.S. *Prince George*, ran afoul of each other. Jervis could have pushed on for a potentially even greater victory but settled for the capture of four Spanish ships of the line. For their leadership in the victory, Jervis was made Earl St. Vincent and Nelson was knighted.

In *Post Captain*, Aubrey, who was on board the ORION at Cape St. Vincent, throws a ball at MELBURY LODGE in honor of the anniversary of the battle.

capitaine de vaisseau Post-captain (French).

caplin A small fish similar to a smelt, found on the coast of Newfoundland and used as bait for cod.

capot In the card game of PIQUET, the winning of all the tricks by one player.

cappabar *also* **capabarre, capperbar, Cap-a-Bar,** *and* **Cape Bar** A term in use in the early 19th century for the misappropriation of government supplies.

Capricorn   The zodiacal constellation of the He-Goat, lying between Sagittarius and Aquarius and used in navigation. Capricorn is the tenth of the 12 signs of the zodiac. It begins at the most southerly point of the ecliptic, or winter solstitial, point, which the sun enters around December 21.

capstan   A cylindrical revolving mechanism that works on the principle of the wheel and axle, arranged vertically, the power being supplied by the deck hands pushing moveable capstan-bars inserted into sockets around the top. As the capstan revolves, it winds up a CABLE around its BARREL. Used especially for weighing the anchor. A series of PAWLS, hinged in one direction, prevents any backward motion due to a heavy burden. *See* illustration, page 68.

Captain of the Fleet   An officer who is temporarily appointed as adjutant-general of a naval force and carries out all orders issued by the COMMANDER-IN-CHIEF but whose special duty it is to keep up the discipline of the fleet.

Capuchin   A friar belonging to an austere branch of the order of St. Francis that was dedicated to preaching and missionary work. So called from the sharp-pointed capuche, or hood, adopted first in 1525.

capybara   A large, tailless, mostly aquatic rodent reaching more than four feet in length and indigenous to tropical South America.

caracara   South American birds of an aberrant subfamily of the Falconidae, whose members have similarities to the vulture. The name caracara, originally from Brazil, derives from the caracara's strange hoarse cry.

Caracciolo, Francesco (*1752–1799*)   Neapolitan nobleman who served with distinction in the British Navy during the American Revolution and, in 1793, under Nelson at Toulon. When the French took Naples in 1798, Caracciolo returned and converted to French republicanism, only to be captured by the British when Naples was retaken a year later. On board Lord Nelson's FLAGSHIP the *FOUDROYANT*, a Neapolitan COURT-MARTIAL condemned him to die. Influenced by his infatuation for Lady Hamilton, a close friend of Queen Mary Caroline of Naples, Nelson granted the queen's wish for Caracciolo's swift execution. Wrongly in the eyes of many, Nelson ordered him hanged from the YARDARM of the *Minerva* without the usual 24 hours for confession and prayer.

caravanserai On trade routes in the lands from western Asia to the Far East, an inn where camel caravans put up, consisting of a large quadrangular building with a spacious court in the middle.

carbine A firearm, shorter and lighter than a musket, originally used by the cavalry.

Carbonari A secret political society that spread through Italy, Spain, and France early in the 19th century as a result of the turmoil brought on by the French Revolution and NAPOLEON. The Carbonari (literally, "charcoal-burners") sought to defend the rights of the people against all forms of absolutism, by any means, including assassination and armed revolt. It included army officers, government officials, and clergy and was tightly organized, with symbolic rituals and language, an oath of silence, and a rigid hierarchy. In 1814, the church issued an edict against secret societies, especially the FREEMASONs and the Carbonari. However, the Carbonari existed in some form until the middle of the century and were partially responsible for uprisings in Spain (1820), Naples (1820), and Piedmont (1821).

carboy A large roughly spherical bottle of green or blue glass covered with basket-work for protection, used chiefly for holding acids and other corrosive liquids.

carcharias Shark.

carcharodon Subspecies of shark.

card *or* **compass-card** The stiff circular piece of paper on which the 32 compass points are marked on a mariner's compass.

cardamom The true, or lesser, cardamom, *Eletteria cardamomum*. Because its aromatic seeds were thought to promote the expulsion of gas from the intestines, they were prescribed for dyspepsia, as well as to promote sweating.

Cardan, Jerome (*1501–1576*) An Italian physician, mathematician, and professor of medicine who developed a system for teaching the blind that foreshadowed Braille's. Cardan wrote on physiognomy (see PHYSIOGNOMIST), arguing that horoscopes could be drawn from the furrows in the forehead.

careen To HEEL a ship over on one side for cleaning, CAULKing, or repairing.

Carey's Warranted Arrowroot A proprietary brand of an edible powdered starch prepared from the roots of any of several South American plants and used to make a bland diet suitable for invalids.

carina A structure in the form of a KEEL or ridge; hence, the forward-projecting part of a bird's breastbone to which the flight muscles attach.

carious Decayed or rotten, said of bones and especially teeth.

carline *or* **carlingi** A piece of timber about five inches square, lying FORE-AND-AFT under the deck of a ship to support the deck planks near a HATCH or MAST.

Carrera, José Miguel (*1785–1821*) A leader in the independence movement and first president of Chile. By a coup d'état in 1811, Carrera took control of the national government and made himself dictator. However, strife within the independence movement soon led to the restoration of Spanish rule. In 1813, BERNARDO O'HIGGINS was made leader of the movement; however, early in 1814, Carrera regained control. During an invasion by Spanish forces from Peru, Carrera and O'Higgins were defeated in October 1814 at Rancagua, where Carrera failed to come to the assistance of O'Higgins. Carrera sought aid against his opponents, first in Buenos Aires and then, in 1815, in the United States. He returned to Argentina in 1816, but he was prevented from entering Chile and instead helped Argentine provincial chiefs in sporadic revolts against Buenos Aires. He was eventually betrayed by his own men, captured, and shot.

carronade *or* **smasher** A short-barreled lightweight gun with a chamber for the powder like a mortar and firing a heavy shot over a short distance. Taking its name from its place of manufacture, Carron Iron Works in Falkirk, Scotland, the carronade was first used on British ships in 1779.

cartel A commissioned ship sailing under a flag of truce in time of war to exchange prisoners or to carry a proposal from one enemy to another.

carotid pulse   Pulse felt in the carotid arteries on either side of the neck.

cartridge   A case made of paper, parchment, flannel, or metal that contains the charge of powder for a firearm.

caruncula   A small fleshy outgrowth, like the wattles of the turkey-cock. Also, an outgrowth on a seed.

carus   The various forms of profound sleep or insensibility; especially the fourth and most extreme degree of insensibility, the others being SOPOR, coma, and lethargy. Also means "dear" (Latin).

carvel-built   A vessel whose planks are all flush and smooth, the edges laid close to each other, in contrast to CLINKER-BUILT, where they overlap each other.

cascabel   The knob, or pommelion, at the rear end of a cannon. *See* illustration, page 214.

case-bottle   A bottle, often square, used for wine and medicines and made to fit into a case with others.

casemate   A bomb-proof chamber, generally under the ramparts of a fortress, used as a barrack or a battery.

case-shot   *See* CANISTER SHOT.

cashier   To dismiss from a position of command or authority with disgrace and permanent exclusion from the service.

cassia   A tree, *Cassia fistula,* whose bark is used as a cathartic. Also, any of various trees, shrubs, and plants of the genus *Cassia.*

Cassiopeia   The northern constellation (shaped like a *W*) between Cepheus and Andromeda, in which a brilliant new star appeared in 1572 but then disappeared.

cassowary   Any member of a genus (*Casuarius*) of large birds, related to the ostrich, that inhabit the islands in the East Indian Archipelago as far as New Guinea. They stand about five feet high and

The cassowary, *Casuarius galeatus*, a flightless bird of the East Indies

have wings that are of no use for flight but are furnished with stiff quills that serve for protection.

Castilian   Of or pertaining to the Spanish province of Castile, or a native of Castile. Also, the language of that province, which is considered to be standard Spanish, as distinct from provincial dialects.

Castle   In reference to Ireland, Dublin Castle, the seat of the English vice-regal court and administration. Thus, in politics, it refers to the authority based at Dublin Castle and Irish government officials.

castoreum   Castor, a reddish-brown liquid with a strong smell and nauseating bitter taste, obtained from two sacs in the body of the Russian beaver and used in medicine and in perfumery.

casus belli   Cause of or justification for war (Latin).

cat   A type of vessel based on a Norwegian model, distinguished by having a narrow stern, projecting QUARTERS, a deep WAIST, and no ornamental figure on the bow. Cats were often used in the coal and wood trade. Cats were sometimes bought into the service by the Admiralty, as was H.M.S. *Endeavour,* commanded by Captain COOK on his great voyage of 1768 to 1771. Also, short for CATHEAD. Also, to raise the anchor to the cathead and secure it. *See also* CAT-O'-NINE-TAILS.

Catalan   Of or pertaining to the Spanish province of CATALONIA, or a native of Catalonia. Also, the language of Catalonia, which is a dialect of Provençal and has affinities with Spanish.

catalepsy   A state of seizure or trance characterized by loss of sensation, voluntary motion, and consciousness.

Catalonia   The most northeasterly province of Spain, Catalonia is bordered by France to the north. Geographically, the Pyrenees Mountains form its northern and western boundaries and the Mediterranean, its eastern. Its wooded hills are a major source of cork, and the coastal plains, of grains, olives, and grapes. Formerly an independent principality, Catalonia's language is closer to Provençal than Castilian Spanish. From the 9th century, Catalonia was ruled by the counts of Barcelona, the port and principal city of the region. Catalonia's influence peaked during the 13th and 14th centuries, when it dominated Mediterranean trade, but declined during the 16th and 17th centuries. From 1640 to 1659, Catalonia joined France against Philip IV of Spain, and in 1714 it lost its autonomy. But the region has never lost its unique identity, and a separatist movement continues to the present day. *See also* CATALAN.

cataract   A waterfall, especially one falling headlong over a precipice; formerly also a waterspout. In medicine, a clouded eye lens, usually associated with aging.

catastrophié   Should be *catastrophé,* dismayed or dumbfounded (French).

catenary   The curve formed by a chain or rope of uniform density hanging freely from two fixed points not in the same vertical line.

caterwaul   To make the noise of cats at rutting time; to be in heat or lecherous. Also, to quarrel loudly.

cat-fall   In the cat-TACKLE, the rope between the cat-BLOCK and the sheaves in the cathead. *See also* CATHEAD.

cat-harpings   Small ropes that brace the SHROUDS of the lower MASTS under the TOP of SQUARE-RIGGED vessels. Until about 1820, the FUT-TOCK SHROUDS were secured to the lower shrouds and futtock-STAVES, rather than to the lower mast. To assist in securing the TOPMAST, ropes were snaked between the futtock-staves and FRAPped together to form the cat-harpin legs. Later, the cat-harpin legs were short lengths of heavy rope with an eye at each end and served through-out their length. Since the cat-harpins pulled the lower shrouds in a little, this facilitated the bracing up of the lower yard. In *Young Sea Officer's Sheet Anchor,* Darcy Lever illustrates a variation, in which the cat-harpings cross, forming an X. This is the source of O'Brian's cross cat-harpings.

cathead   A short, stout beam of timber projecting almost horizon-tally from the side of a ship's bow and used for hoisting the anchor to the deck without its touching the hull and for carrying the anchor when it is suspended outside the ship. The name may possibly derive from the custom, of unknown origin, of decorating these structures with carved or cast lions' heads, believed to bring good luck, or pos-sibly from the north German word *"kattenkopf,"* which is a square pin stuck in a hole of a WINDLASS, and to which the CABLE is secured. The anchor is catted, or raised and secured, to the cathead by means of the cat-TACKLE, or cat-PURCHASE, which consists of the cat-BLOCK, the CAT-FALL, and the SHEAVES in the cathead. The cat-block is furnished with a strong hook, the cat-hook, which is attached to the ring of the anchor by means of the cat-rope, or cat-back. When raised, the anchor is fastened by its ring to the cathead with the cathead-stopper, or cat-stopper.

catholicon   A panacea.

catlin *or* **catling**   A long, straight, narrow, double-edged knife used for performing amputations.

cat-o'-nine-tails *or* **cat**   Until 1881, an authorized instrument of pun-ishment in the British Navy, composed of nine pieces of cord about half a yard long fixed upon a piece of thick rope for a handle. Each length of cord had three knots at small intervals near the striking end. Sailors were flogged with the cat on the bare back for transgressing the ARTICLES OF WAR, the rules of the service. A "thieves' cat" had larger and harder knots than usual and was used only for punishing thieves.

cat's paw   A slight local breeze that shows itself by rippling the surface of the sea. Also, a hitch in a rope giving loops for hoisting.

catting the anchor   *See* CATHEAD.

caudle   A warm drink consisting of thin gruel mixed with wine or ale, sweetened and spiced. Given chiefly to sick people.

caulk   To seal a ship's seams and make it watertight by driving in OAKUM and pouring on melted PITCH or resin. Caulker's mallets and caulking-irons, which resembled chisels, are used to drive the oakum into the seams. Also, a small amount of liquor.

centaureum   A plant of a large genus (*Centaurea*) of herbs used in strengthening tonics.

Centurion, **H.M.S.**   The 60-gun, fourth-rate ship in which Admiral George ANSON circumnavigated the world, harassing Spanish merchants and taking a heavily laden MANILA galleon on June 20, 1743. Launched in 1732, she was broken up in 1769.

cephalopod   Any member of the class Cephalopoda, the most highly organized class of the phylum Mollusca. Cephalopods are characterized by a distinct head and highly developed eyes and tentacles. They include cuttlefish, octopuses, and squids.

ceruse   Lead acetate, used in many wound ointments. Also lead monoxide, largely used as a white pigment in paint.

cetacean   Of or pertaining to the order Cetacea of marine mammals, including the whale and the porpoise.

chaffinch   A common European bird with pretty plumage and a short, pleasant song.

chafing-dish   A small container to hold burning charcoal or other fuel, usually used for heating food at the table.

chain-pump   A machine for drawing up water that uses a chain attached to a number of buckets or cups to lift the water and pour it out.

chains The CHAIN-WALE, DEAD-EYES, and other hardware used to secure the lower SHROUDS of a MAST outside the ship's side. Usually the mast being reinforced is specified, as in forechains or mainchains. To stand "in the chains" means to stand upon the chain-wale between two shrouds, from where the LEADSMAN heaves the HAND-LEAD to measure water depth.

chain-shot *or* **chain** A kind of shot formed of two balls, or half-balls, connected by a chain, chiefly used in naval warfare to destroy MASTS, RIGGING, and sails. Also, a shot or discharge of this type.

chain-wale *or* **channel** A broad, thick plank that projects horizontally from each of a ship's sides abreast of a MAST, distinguished as the FORE, MAIN, or MIZZEN channel accordingly, serving to extend the base for the SHROUDS, which support the mast.

chaise *or* **shag** A light open two- or four-wheeled carriage for one or two people, often having a calash or top. Those with four wheels resemble the phaeton, those with two, the CURRICLE. Also loosely used for pleasure carts and light carriages. A carriage for traveling, having a closed body and seats for one to three people, the driver sitting on one of the horses; more distinctively called a post-chaise. A chaise and pair or four or six is a chaise drawn by a pair, four, or six horses.

chamade A signal by beat of drum or sound of trumpet inviting those involved to a parley.

Chamaeleon *or* **Chameleon** One of the southern circumpolar constellations, lying between Apus and Mensa.

Chambertin One of the finest red wines in the world, from the Côte de Nuits section of the Burgundy region of France.

Chambolle-Musigny A commune in France's Côte-d'Or department. Musigny, the name of a vineyard there, designates the red Burgundy the commune produces.

Chancery The court of the Lord Chancellor of England, the highest judicial court next to the House of Lords. It formerly consisted of two distinct tribunals. The system was radically altered in 1875.

chandler A dealer in provisions or equipment; a person who makes or sells candles.

'Change See ROYAL EXCHANGE.

channel   *See* CHAIN-WALE.

Channel fever   Much like spring fever, the euphoria felt by English seamen upon entering the English Channel on the homestretch.

Channel Fleet   The portion of the British fleet detailed for service in the English Channel.

chantery *also* **chanty** *or* **shanty**   A shipboard song, heard primarily on merchant ships during heavy work, such as turning the CAPSTAN or hoisting up a sail, to help coordinate the men's efforts and to pass the time. A designated chanteyman led the singing, and the crew joined in, the cadence varying according to the type of work being done. The custom dated from the 16th century. The word comes from the French *chanter*, "to sing."

charnel-house   A building, chamber, or vault for storing skeletons or cadavers.

chase-piece *or* **chaser**   *See* BOW-CHASER.

chasse-marée   The French name (literally, "chase-tide") for a three-masted coasting vessel, many of which were LUGGER-rigged during the Napoleonic wars and used for smuggling and PRIVATEERing. *See* illustration, page 62.

Château Lafite   The claret produced and bottled at Château-Lafite, in the Médoc district of the department of Gironde, France.

Chatham   An important base and dockyard of the Royal Navy on the River Medway in Kent.

check   A sharp stoppage of motion, an interruption in a course. To check a BOWLINE is to slacken it and BELAY it again. To check a BRACE is to ease it off when it is found to be too taut. To check a CABLE is to slow it when it is running out.

cheeks   The projections on each side of the MAST on which the TRESSLETREES rest. Pieces of timber on the ship's BOWS to secure the BEAKHEAD or CUTWATER. Also the sidepieces of a wooden gun-carriage and the two faces of a BLOCK.

cheek-block   A BLOCK fastened on one side to another object, such as a MAST.

chelengk *or* **chelengh**   Following the Battle of the NILE, a Turkish frigate was dispatched by the Grand Signor carrying for Nelson, as described by *Steel's Naval Chronologist of the War*, "a superb diamond aigrette, called a *Chelengh*, or plume of triumph, taken from one of the Imperial turbans, with a pelice of sable fur of the first quality (p. 18)." In the famous portrait by Lemuel Francis Abbott, Nelson wears the chelengh proudly in his hat. Aubrey's remarkable chelengk, awarded to him by the Grand Turk, is a diamond spray with a small mechanical heart that makes the sprays quiver.

chelonian   Of or belonging to the order of reptiles called Chelonia, distinguished by having the body enclosed in a double shell and comprising the various species of tortoises and turtles.

Cherbourg   An important port on France's Cotentin Peninsula, across the Channel from England's southern coast.

cheroot   A cigar open at both ends. Originally referred specifically to the ones made in Southern India or Manila.

Chesapeake, **U.S.S.**   One of the six original FRIGATES built for the U.S. Navy, she was commanded by Captain James Lawrence when she was captured in a bloody battle on June 1, 1813, in the Atlantic off Boston by Captain Philip BROKE in H.M.S. *SHANNON*. Lawrence was killed in the action, and 146 men were killed or wounded on the *Chesapeake* that day. Taken into the Royal Navy, she was sold in 1819.

chesstrees   Two pieces of wood bolted to the STEM of a ship perpendicular to the ship's center line, one on the STARBOARD and the other on the LARBOARD, and used to extend the CLEW, or lower corners of the MAINSAIL, to windward.

Chian   Of or pertaining to the island of Chios (now Scio) in the Aegean Sea, famed in ancient times for its wine.

chickadee   The black-cap titmouse of North America.

Chilon   A sixth-century B.C. politician of Sparta who was credited with helping to overthrow a tyranny.

chimaera   A fabled fire-breathing monster of Greek mythology, with a lion's head, a goat's body, and a serpent's tail (or according to some, with three heads, of a lion, a goat, and a serpent), killed by the Corinthian hero Bellerophon, who was helped by Pegasus, the winged horse. An unreal creature of the imagination, a mere wild fancy.

chirimoya *or* **cherimoya**   A small tree native to Peru, with sweet-scented greenish flowers. Also, the pulpy fruit of this tree, which is highly esteemed for its delicious flavor. It is large, irregularly heart-shaped, and has a scaly exterior.

chirurgical   Of or pertaining to surgery; skilled in or practicing surgery.

chit   Short for "chitty," a letter or note. Also, a certificate given to a servant, or the like. A pass.

chitinous   Of the nature of, or consisting of, chitin, the organic substance from which the elytra and integuments of insects and the carapaces of crustacea are made.

chivvy   To harry, harass, trouble, worry.

cholagogue   Any remedy that promotes the flow of bile from the liver in order to restore the balance among the four humors (see "Stephen Maturin and Naval Medicine in the Age of Sail," p. 31).

cholera morbus   Not true cholera but an illness that generally occurs in late summer and early autumn with symptoms that include diarrhea, vomiting, stomachache, and cramps. It is rarely fatal to adults.

chop-house   An eating-house where mutton-chops, beefsteaks, and the like are served.

chough   The red-legged crow, common to sea cliffs in Britain, particularly Cornwall. Also known as the Cornish chough.

chouse   To dupe, cheat, trick, swindle, or defraud.

chrestomathy   A collection of choice passages from an author or authors, especially one compiled to assist in the learning of a language.

chronometer   An instrument for measuring time, specifically one adjusted to keep accurate time in all variations of temperature. First successfully used for accurately determining longitude in 1736. To rate a chronometer is to compare its daily loss or gain with the true time.

chuff   Generally applied opprobriously, with a fitting epithet, to any person disliked; a rude, coarse, churlish fellow. Also, pleased, satisfied, happy.

Cimarosa, Domenico (*1749–1801*) Neapolitan composer of 65 operas. Worked in Rome and Naples and later at St. Petersburg and Vienna. Wrote *Le astuzie femminili* in 1794. In 1799 he was sentence to death in Naples for supporting the French republican army, but was reprieved and banished from Naples.

cinchona *See* BARK.

cingulum A girdlelike marking or stricture.

cinnabar Red mercuric sulphide, a MERCURY ore. Used as a pigment to create vermilion, a brilliant red to reddish orange. Used rarely in medicine.

Cintra *or* Sintra A town in western Portugal where a military convention was signed in 1808 between the British, Portuguese, and French. The agreement following England's defeat of the French was very lenient and a political disaster at home. The scenery here is celebrated in Lord Byron's *Childe Harold's Pilgrimage* (1812).

cirripede *or* cirriped A crustacean of the order Cirripedia, which includes acorn-shells, barnacles, and other organisms that attach themselves by flexible stalks to other bodies or become parasitic in the adult stage.

cistus A genus of shrubs known as rock-rose or gum cistus, with large spotted red or white flowers that seldom last more than a few hours after expansion. *See also* GUM-CISTUS.

civet *or* civet-cat A central African species of carnivorous quadrupeds, between a fox and a weasel in size and appearance.

civet du lapin Rabbit stew (French).

clack Din of speech, senseless chatter.

clamp One of the thick planks in a ship's side supporting the ends of the deckbeams. Also, a piece of timber applied to a MAST or YARD to prevent the wood from bursting.

clap on To add on, as in more sail or more hands on a line (possibly comes from the Old Norse *klappan,* "to act quickly"). To apply oneself with energy to a task.

Clarence, Duke of (*1765–1837*)   The third son of King George III, Prince William, entered the Navy in 1779 and saw active service. He was made Duke of Clarence and St. Andrews in 1789. He was promoted through the ranks, reaching Admiral of the Fleet in 1811. From 1790 to 1811 he lived with the Irish actress Dorothea (nee Bland) Jordan (1762–1816), who bore him ten children. In 1827–1828 he served as Lord High Admiral. In 1830, on the death of his eldest brother, George IV, he succeeded to the throne as King William IV. He was known as the "Sailor-King" and "Silly Billy."

clasp-knife   A knife with a blade that folds into the handle, especially one fixed open by means of a catch.

claw *or* **claw off**   To work a vessel to WINDWARD from a LEE shore in an effort to avoid shipwreck.

clear for action   To prepare a ship for battle by removing from the decks everything that is in the way.

clem   To starve or to suffer the pangs of hunger or thirst.

Clement XIV (*1705–1774*)   Pope from 1769 to 1774. Issued an apostolic brief suppressing the JESUITs in 1773.

Clementi, Muzio (*1752–1832*)   Born in Rome, Clementi, who some consider the father of the modern school of piano technique, studied in England from 1766 to 1770, where he became renowned as a pianist and composer. He settled in London and founded Clementi and Co., which traded in pianos and published music. During his career Clementi wrote 100 sonatas, many for the piano. He is buried at Westminster Abbey.

clench   To make a permanent joint, as with a bolt hammered over to prevent removal. A CLINCH.

clench-bolt   A bolt that is fixed securely, especially by bending or flattening the point.

clerk of cheque   An officer in royal dockyards who goes on board to MUSTER the ship's company, thereby checking false musters.

Clerk of the Hanaper   A clerk for a department of the CHANCERY into which fees were paid for the sealing and enrollment of charters and other documents.

clew *or* **clue**   A lower corner of a square sail or the aftermost corner of a FORE-AND-AFT sail, to which TACKs and SHEETs are made fast for extending the sail and for holding it to the lower YARD or BOOM. To clew up is to draw a sail's lower ends up to the yard or the MAST in preparation for furling. To clew down is to unfurl a sail or possibly to take in a TOPSAIL. Clew-garnets are TACKLE used to clew up the COURSEs when they are being furled, and clew-lines are the ropes used to haul up the clew of a topsail or TOPGALLANT.

climacteric   Constituting an important, critical, or fatal epoch. The period of life at which the vital forces start to decline.

clinch   A method of fastening large ropes by a half-hitch and stopping the end back to its own part by SEIZINGs. To fasten the planks of a small craft's HULL to the frame with CLENCHed copper nails.

clinker *or* **clinker-built**   Ships and boats in which the external planks overlap each other and are fastened together with CLENCHed copper nails.

Clive, Robert (1725–1774)   British soldier and colonialist. From humble origins in Shropshire, Clive rose to help found the empire of British India, became a member of Parliament and was created Baron Clive of Plassey in the Irish peerage. At the age of 18, Clive went to India as a clerk in the EAST INDIA COMPANY. He transfered to the company's military arm and rode a daring capture and defense of the town of Arcot against French and Indian forces in 1751 to great fame. Charismatic but unstable, Clive became governor of Madras, took control of Bengal, where he was eventually governor and commander-in-chief, and became very wealthy. But in 1774, following a parliamentary inquiry into his NABOB fortune, he committed suicide.

cloaths   Obsolete form of "clothes."

clock-calm   No wind whatsoever.

clog   An impediment attached to the leg or neck of a man or beast to prevent escape. Hence, an encumbrance, hindrance.

close-hauled   Sailing with sails HAULed in as tight as possible, which allows the ship to sail as CLOSE TO THE WIND as possible.

close-reefed   A TOPSAIL had three or four REEFBANDS, one or more of which could be taken in to REEF the sail. When the final reef is taken in, the sail is said to be close-reefed.

close to the wind   When a ship's BOW is pointing as far into the wind as possible without LUFFing the sails.

clouded yellow   A butterfly of the genus *Colias,* especially *C. edusa.*

club   A men's hairstyle fashionable in the second half of the 18th century in which the hair was worn in a club-shaped knot or tail at the back of the head.

club-haul   An emergency method of TACKing, which involved the sacrifice of an anchor. This maneuver, though much discussed by sea-men, was rarely used in practice. The splendid fictional account of club-hauling in Captain Frederick Marryat's novel *Peter Simple* was required reading for midshipmen.

Clusius, Carolus (1526–1609)   The French botanist Charles de L'Écluse, a professor at Leiden from 1593. He is said to have intro-duced the potato into Europe.

clutch   A brood of chickens, laying or sitting on eggs.

clyster   A medicine injected into the rectum with a syringe to cleanse the bowels. An enema, sometimes a suppository.

coach   A cabin on the HALF-DECK, foreward of the great cabin.

coak   A tabular projection left on the face of a SCARFed timber that fits into a notch in the face of another to which it will be joined. Used especially in the construction of a MAST from several pieces.

coal-scuttle   A receptacle for holding a supply of coal for a fire.

coaming   Raised border around HATCHes and SCUTTLEs that prevents water on deck from running below.

coaster   A vessel that keeps close to land, usually sailing in coastal waters between ports in the same country.

cob   A short-legged, stout type of horse, suitable for heavy riders. Also, a Naval punishment, to strike on the buttocks with a flat piece of wood called a cobbing-board.

coca The South American shrub *Erythroxylon coca* and its dried leaves, which contain cocaine. These leaves are chewed with powdered lime as an appeaser of hunger and as a stimulant. Coca first appeared as a patent medicine in the 1840s and as a local anaesthetic in 1884.

cochineal A powder made from the dried body of the insect *Dactylopius coccus*, found on cactus species in Mexico and elsewhere. The powder is used chiefly for making a brilliant red dye and was also used medicinally until around 1750.

Cochrane, Admiral Alexander *See* COCHRANE, THOMAS.

Cochrane, Thomas (1775–1860) A very successful fighting captain who captured many prizes, Cochrane entered the Royal Navy at age 17 as a MIDSHIPMAN on board H.M.S. *Hind,* commanded by his uncle, Captain Alexander Cochrane. In 1798 he served on board H.M.S. *Barfleur,* the FLAGSHIP of Admiral Lord KEITH, and in 1800, after taking the prize GÉNÉREUX into MINORCA, he was given command of the diminutive sloop *Speedy,* in which he would make his reputation. Although his boldness served him well at sea, on land it did not. A political radical, Cochrane was outspoken against naval abuses and corruption, damaging his career. He also accused Admiral GAMBIER of being timid at the Battle of Aix Roads (1809), in which Cochrane's bold attack won the day. The recriminations, however, marred the victory and further damaged Cochrane's career. In 1814 he was accused and perhaps wrongly convicted of taking part in a stock-exchange fraud. Dismissed from the Navy and removed from his seat in Parliament, he accepted a command in the Chilean navy, where he redeemed himself by defeating the Spanish. He was reinstated in the Royal Navy and promoted to Rear-Admiral in 1832.

Cochrane was a master of ruses de guerre. In his account of his 1800–1801 cruise of the *Speedy* (the inspiration for O'Brian's SOPHIE), he flies a Danish flag and claims to have the plague on board to escape a superior foe, he floats a raft with a light at night to deceive a pursuer, and before attempting to board the much stronger *El Gammo* (the Spanish XEBEC FRIGATE that is O'Brian's CACAFUEGO), he has his men blacken their faces to intimidate the enemy. Cochrane wrote in his *Autobiography of a Seaman* (1860), "In difficult or doubtful attacks by sea—and the odds of 50 men to 320 comes within this description—no device can be too minute, even if apparently

Thomas Cochrane striking a pose in 1807 (*from a portrait by Stroehling*)

absurd, provided it have the effect of diverting the enemy's attention whilst you are concentrating your own. In this, and other successes against odds, I have no hesitation in saying that success in no slight degree depended on out-of-the-way devices, which the enemy not suspecting, were in some measure thrown off their guard" (p. 51).

cock   A long, rambling story, especially one that is concocted or untrue, as in "cock-and-bull" story.

cockade   A ribbon, knot of ribbons, rosette, or the like, worn in the hat as a badge of office or party, or as part of a livery.

cock-a-hoop   In a state of elation or in a celebrating mode.

cockbill   *See* A-COCKBILL.

cocked hat   A hat with the brim permanently turned up, especially the three-cornered hat of this shape worn at the end of the 18th and beginning of the 19th centuries. On a chart, a triangle formed by lines of bearing created by some error in observation or plotting.

cockleshell   A small frail boat or vessel.

cockpit   The after part of the ORLOP deck of a MAN-OF-WAR, ordinarily the dark and stuffy quarters of the MIDSHIPMEN, the MASTER'S MATES, and others, but in action devoted to the care of the wounded. Also, in the BOWS of the ship, the quarters of the boatswain and the Carpenter were known as the fore cockpit.

cod-piece   A flap or bag concealing an opening in the front of the close-fitting hose or breeches worn by men from the 15th to the 17th centuries.

Codrington, Admiral Sir Edward (*1770–1851*)   Commanding the 74-gun H.M.S. *Orion,* Codrington captured the *Intrepide* and assisted in taking *Swiftsure* at TRAFALGAR. During the War of 1812, he organized army supplies for the attack on Washington, D.C. He was also victorious against the Turks and Egyptians in the Battle of Navarino in 1827.

Cogit amare jecur   The liver (for the Romans, the seat of emotions) knows how to love (Latin).

coign   In printing, a wedge.

coil   A selection, a choice.

coir   The prepared fiber of the husk of the coconut, used for making ropes, cordage, matting, etc.

Colchicum   A genus of plants of the lily family, including the meadow-saffron, found wild all over Europe. It blooms in autumn with a purplish mottled flower that contains colchicine, which is used to treat gout.

colcothar of vitriol   A powdery reddish or purple substance used as an emetic.

Coleoptera   A large, important order of insects—including beetles and weevils—with anterior wings converted into hard sheaths that cover the other pair when not in use.

Coleridge, Samuel Taylor (*1772–1834*)   English poet and critic, particularly known in the context of sea literature for his poem "Rime of the Ancient Mariner."

colic   Severe paroxysmal pains in the belly, usually caused by obstructions in the intestines, kidneys, or ureters.

collar   A rope formed into a wreath around a MAST to which STAYS are attached. An eye in the end of a SHROUD or stay that goes over the MASTHEAD.

coll' astuzia, coll' arguzia, col giudizio, col criterio . . . con un equivoco, con un sinonimo, qualche garbuglio si troverà   With cunning, with cleverness, with judgment, with discretion . . . with an ambiguity, with a well-chosen word, I'll find some way to create confusion (Italian; sung by Bartolo in act one of Mozart's *The Marriage of Figaro*).

collate   To confer a BENEFICE, or endowment of income or property, on a person. To appoint or institute a cleric.

collation   A light meal or snack, often consisting of light meats or delicacies such as fruit, sweets, and wine.

collier   A strong, BLUFF-BOWed ship used to transport coal. Many were bought by the ADMIRALTY for service.

Collingwood, Vice-Admiral Cuthbert (*1750–1810*)   Known for his strict but fair discipline and restrained use of the CAT-O'-NINE-TAILS, Collingwood distinguished himself at the GLORIOUS FIRST OF JUNE. Aboard H.M.S. *Royal Sovereign,* he was second in command at TRAFALGAR, leading the LEE column and earning NELSON's praise. Collingwood was COMMANDER-IN-CHIEF in the Mediterranean from 1805 to 1810.

Vice-Admiral Cuthbert Collingwood (*Reproduced from Alfred Mahan's* Life of Nelson, *1897 (courtesy of the Mariners Museum, Newport News, Virginia)*

collops   Bacon, when fried with eggs.

colocynth   The violently cathartic pulp of a gourd, *Citrullus colocynthus.*

colors   The flag, or ENSIGN, of a ship, indicating her nationality. While sailing under false colors was an accepted ruse of war, true colors were shown before an attack.

Colossus, **H.M.S.**   A 74-gun ship built at Deptford in 1803 that suffered heavy casualties (40 killed and 160 wounded) at TRAFALGAR in close fighting under the command of Captain James Morris. She was broken up in 1826. Also, an earlier 74-gun ship, loaded with a cargo of Greek and Roman antiquities collected by the diplomat and archaeologist Sir William Hamilton, was wrecked during a storm off the SCILLY ISLANDS in the English Channel on December 10, 1798.

combe   A deep, narrow valley.

commander   In the Royal Navy of this period, the rank above LIEU-TENANT and below Captain.

commander-in-chief   A naval officer in PENNANT command of a fleet, SQUADRON, or STATION.

commendatore   A knight of an order of chivalry in Italy.

commensal   One of a company who eat at the same table. A mess-mate.

comminatory   Conveying denunciation; vengeful, threatening, denunciatory.

comminuted   Of a bone, broken or crushed into several pieces.

commissariat   A department of the military service charged with the duty of providing food and other supplies for the army.

commission   The period of active service of a warship. Also, the order by virtue of which an officer takes command of a ship in active service.

commissioner   The official formerly in charge of each royal dock-yard.

Commissioner of the Navy   A member of the Navy Board, respon-sible for construction, repair, outfitting, and provisioning of ships.

commodore   A Captain appointed as COMMANDER-IN-CHIEF of a SQUADRON or station. Also, the senior Captain of a detached squadron or the senior master in a convoy of merchant ships.

Commons, House of   In the English constitution, the third estate: the body of people not ennobled who are represented by the Lower House of Parliament. Also, the representatives of the third estate in Parliament.

companion   An opening in a ship's deck leading to a cabin.

companion ladder *or* **companion way**   A ladder leading from the deck below to a cabin; also, the ladder by which the officers reach the QUARTERDECK.

compassé   Formal, stiff (French).

competence   A comfortable living or estate.

complement   The designated total number of officers and men to man a particular ship.

con   To give sailing directions to the steersman or to direct the steering from some commanding position on shipboard.

condor   Either of two large, now rare vultures, with black and white plumage and a remarkable caruncle over the bill, inhabiting the high Andes of South America (*Vultur gryphus*) and the coastal mountains of southern California (*Gymnogyps californianus*). Condors feed on dead animals and occasionally attack live prey. With a wingspan of 10 feet and weighing from 20 to 25 pounds, the predominantly black Andean condor is the heaviest flying bird of prey. The California condor is slightly smaller, lighter in color, and has an orange head.

coney   Formerly the common name for a rabbit but now superseded in general use by "rabbit," which originally was a name for the young only.

Confessions   The autobiography of Jean-Jacques Rousseau (1712–1778). Written in the tradition of other works of the same title, notably by St. Augustine in the fifth century, in which the author frankly reveals the mistakes he has made in his life.

Congreve, Sir William (*1772–1828*)   English inventor, producer of a military rocket fired from British ships in 1805 during an attack on the French at Boulogne and in the following year at the siege of COPEN-HAGEN.

consol   An abbreviation of Consolidated Annuities, the government securities of Great Britain.

Constantia   Originally, wine produced on the farm Groot Constantia near Cape Town in present-day South Africa. After 1778, any of several sweet dessert wines produced in the Constantia valley by Hendrick Cloete. Napoleon is said to have asked for a glass of Constantia wine on his deathbed on ST. HELENA.

CONSTITUTION, U.S.S.

The 44-gun FRIGATE launched at Boston in 1797 and nicknamed "Old Ironsides" for her heavy build and heavy arms. She captured the

British frigates *Guerrière* on August 19, 1812, and *Java* on October 26, 1812. She remains afloat as a commissioned ship in the U.S. Navy at Boston, Massachusetts.

The U.S.S. *Constitution* **defeats the H.M.S.** *Java:* The following report by H. D. Chads, Senior Lieutenant, and B. Robinson, Master, of the H.M.S. *Java,* accompanied this diagram of the action in an 1813 edition (volume 29) of *The Naval Chronicle.*

At 8 A.M. close in with the land, with the wind at N.E. discovered a sail to the S.S.W. and another off the entrance of St. Salvador, cast off the prize in tow, and made all sail in chase of the vessel to leeward. At 10 made the private signal, which was not answered. At 11 hauled up, bringing the wind on our larboard quarter, took in all studding sails, prepared for action, the stranger standing towards us under easy sail, and apparently a large frigate. At a little after noon, when about four miles distant, she made a signal, which was kept flying about 10 minutes, when she tacked and made sail from us under all plain sail, running just good full; hauled up the same as the chase, but the breeze freshening, could not carry our royals; we were going at least 10 knots, and gaining very fast on the chase. At 1.30 she hoisted American colours.

At 1.50, having closed with the enemy to about two miles, he shortened sail to his top-gallant sails, jib, and spanker, and luff'd up to the wind; hoisted our colours, and put ourselves under the same sail, and bore down on him, he being at this time about three points on our lee bow. At 2.10, when half a mile distant, he opened his fire from the larboard side, and gave us about two broadsides before we returned it, which was not done til within pistol shot, on his weather bow, with our starboard guns. On the smoke clearing away, found him under all sail before the wind; made sail after him.

At 2.25 engaged him with our larboard guns, received his starboard; at 2.35 wore, and raked him close under his stern, giving him the weather-gage, which he did not take advantage of, but made sail free on the larboard tack; luff'd up, and gave him our starboard guns, raking, but rather distant; made sail after him. At 2.40, enemy shortened sail; did the same, and engaged him close to windward. At 2.50, he wore in the smoke, and was not perceived till nearly round, having just lost the head of our bowsprit, jib-boom, &c.; hove in stays, in the hopes of getting round quick and preventing our being raked, but the ship hung a long time, and we received a heavy

TRACK OF THE ACTION,
Dec. 29, 1812.
H.M.S. Java mounted 46 guns, and had on board at the time of
the action 377 men.
The Constitution had 54 guns, and 485 men.
The Java had 22 killed and 102 wounded, 2 of whom died of their wounds.
The Constitution had 14 killed and 44 wounded.
Java's weight of metal . . . 1034   Tonnage 1000.
Constitution's   ———   . . . 1490   ——   1600.

raking broadside into our stern at about two cables' length distant; gave him our larboard guns on falling off; the enemy wore immediately; did the same.

At 2.55 I brought him to close action within pistol shot (at this time the master was wounded and carried below) till 3.5., when finding the day evidently gone, from all our rigging being cut to pieces, with our fore and main-mast badly wounded, Captain Lambert determined on boarding, as our only hope, bore up, and should have succeeded in laying him abreast of his main chains, but from the unfortunate fall of our fore-mast, the remains of our bowsprit passing over his stern and catching his mizen rigging, which was a great misfortune, as it brought us up to the wind, and prevented our raking him; whilst under the enemy's stern, attempting to board, there was not a soul to be seen on his decks, from which circumstance I am induced to believe there was a good prospect of success; this manoeuvre failing, we were left at the mercy of the enemy, which he availed himself of, wearing across our bows, raking us, when our main-top-mast went and wearing again at 3.2. under our stern.

At 3.30 our gallant captain was mortally wounded, and carried below; from this time till our mizen mast went at 4.15 he laid on our starboard quarter, pouring in a tremendous galling fire, whilst on our side we could never get more than two or three guns to bear, and frequently none at all. After this we fell off, and the enemy shot ahead, which again gave us the chance of renewing the action, which was done with good spirits broadside and broadside, *Java* very frequently on fire from firing through the wreck, which lay on the side; engaged till 4.35 when the *Constitution* made sail, and got out of gun shot, leaving us a perfect wreck, with out main-mast only standing, and main-yard gone in the slings; cleared the wreck, and endeavoured to get before the wind by setting a sail from the stump of the foremast and bowsprit; got the main tack forward, the weather yard-arm remaining aloft; cleared away the booms and got a top-gallant mast out, and commenced rigging it for a jury foremast, and a lower steering sail as a foresail, but before we could get this accomplished, we were obliged to cut away the main-mast to prevent its falling inboard, from the heavy rolling of the ships.

The enemy bore up to renew the action; made every preparation to receive him, reloaded the guns with round and grape; mustered at quarters, and found 110 men missing, six quarter-deck guns, four forecastle disabled, and many of the main deckers, with the wreck lying over them, the hull knocked to pieces, and the foremast, in falling, had passed through the forecastle and main decks, all our masts and bowsprit gone, the ship making water, with one pump shot away; consulted now with lieutenants Nerringham and Buchanan, when it was determined to engage him again, should he give us an opportunity of so doing, with a probability of disabling him, which was now our sole object, but that it would be wasting lives resisting longer, should he resume a raking position, which unfortunately was the case, and when close to us, and getting his broadside to bear, I struck, and hailed him, to say we had done so at 5.50.

At six she took possession of us, and proved to be the American frigate *Constitution;* the next day I found our loss was 22 killed and 102 wounded, two of whom are since dead. The Americans allowed they had 10 killed, but differed very much about their wounded, which I found to be 44 severely, and four mortally; the *slight* wounds I could not ascertain. [Paragraph breaks added.] *(Courtesy of the Mariners' Museum, Newport News, Virginia.)*

contre-coup Counterblow, repercussion (French). In medicine it usually refers to the injury sustained by one side of the brain when the opposite side of the head is struck, causing the brain to hit the inside of the skull.

contubernal   One who occupies the same tent; a tent-fellow, comrade.

cony   A dupe, a gull.

Cook, Captain James (*1728–1779*)   A legendary explorer who worked his way up from ORDINARY SEAMAN. During three voyages to the Pacific, Cook charted New Zealand and part of New Guinea and staked British claim to parts of Australia while establishing it as an island continent, explored the Pacific coast of North America, and circumnavigated Antarctica and discovered New Caledonia and South Georgia. He was killed by Hawaiian natives in 1779 while returning from an expedition to the North Pacific.

cooper   A craftsman who builds and repairs wooden vessels made of STAVES and hoops, such as casks, buckets, tubs.

cooperage   The coopering of casks, and the business or trade of a COOPER.

coot   Originally a generic name for various swimming and diving birds.

Copenhagen, Battle of *or* Battle of the Baltic   Battle of April 2, 1801, in which Admiral Sir Hyde Parker, with NELSON second in command, defeated a Danish force anchored off Copenhagen, Denmark's chief port. Despite heavy fire and Parker's signal to retreat—which prompted Nelson to utter his famous line, "You know, Foley, I have only one eye, I have a right to be blind sometimes"—Nelson carried on and won the day. In 1807, the British defeated forces at Copenhagen again, capturing the whole Danish fleet.

copepod   A minute crustacean with four or five pairs of feet chiefly used for swimming.

cop it   To "catch it," to be punished, get into trouble. Also, to die.

copper   A vessel made of copper, particularly a large boiler used for cooking or laundry.

copperas   Iron sulfate, also called green copperas or green vitriol, used in dyeing, tanning, the manufacture of ink, and, uncommonly, as a strengthening tonic medicine.

copper-bottomed Having the bottom covered or sheathed with copper to protect against the TEREDO (once known as shipworm) and the accumulation of shells and weeds. Introduced in the Royal Navy during the period 1779–1786. Also, figuratively, thoroughly sound, authentic, trustworthy.

copperplate A polished plate of copper on which a design is engraved or etched for printing. Also, a style of careful handwriting.

Copt A native Egyptian Christian belonging to the Jacobite sect of Monophysites, who believe that there was only a single divine nature in Christ.

Coquimbo A province in central Chile.

coracoid Literally, shaped like a crow's beak; a projection on the posterior surface of the shoulder blade.

corbel A strong stone, brick, timber, or iron projection from the face of a wall to support another weight.

cordage Cords or ropes, especially those in the RIGGING of a ship.

Corelli, Arcangelo (*1653–1713*) Italian violinist and composer who was born near Bologna and later lived in Rome. He was known in particular for his concerti grossi and violin sonatas, which influenced Bach's work.

corn To form into grains, specifically to form gunpowder into roundish particles by working it through sieves.

corn-chandler A retail dealer in corn and allied products.

corn-crake A bird with a harsh, grating call also called a landrail, found in the summer in Britain living in cornfields and hay fields.

cornelian A semitransparent quartz that is deep dull red, flesh-colored, or reddish-white in color.

Cornish Of or pertaining to Cornwall in southwestern England.

corn-powder Gunpowder that has been CORNed.

Corona Corona Australis or Corona Borealis. Constellations also known as the Southern or Northern Crown. They are formed by elliptical rings of stars, the former adjoining the constellation Sagittarius

on the south and the latter between the constellations Hercules and
Boötes.

coronal suture   The transverse line of junction of the skull between
the frontal and PARIETAL bones.

corpus vile   A living or dead body of so little value that it can be
used for experiment without regard to the outcome.

corrosive sublimate   Mercuric chloride, a strong poison that was
sometimes used in medicine.

corsair   A pirate, more particularly the PRIVATEERS of BARBARY, who
frequently attacked the ships and coasts of Christian countries.
Although largely regarded as pirates, corsairs were often authorized
and recognized by their own governments.

Corunna   A seaport on the northwest coast of Spain, called by
sailors "Groyne" or "the groin" (of Spain), an etymological perversion of the Spanish name, Coruna.

coruscation   A quivering flash or flashes of light. Originally the
term referred only to atmospheric phenomena.

corvette   A warship with a flush deck and a single tier of guns.

Corvisart des Marets, Jean-Nicolas (*1755–1821*)   Napoleon's favorite
physician. In 1808 he revived Leopold Auenbrugger's 1761 important
work on PERCUSSION and later wrote pioneering books in which he
classified the various kinds of heart disease.

cosset   A pet lamb, a pet. To treat as a pet, to fondle, indulge, pamper.

Cotopaxi   A 19,347-foot active volcano in what is today north-
central Ecuador.

counterpane   The outer ornamental covering of a bed, such as a
quilt or bedspread.

counter-timber *or* **counter**   The underside of the STERN overhang
down to the RUDDER.

country ship   A ship belonging to the EAST INDIA COMPANY and built
in India. Country trade was trade between ports of the EAST INDIES.

coup de main   A sudden attack (from French).

coup de tête   An impulsive act (French).

course The direction or point of the compass toward which a ship sails. The sails that hang from the lower YARDS of a SQUARE-RIGGED ship, now usually restricted to the FORESAIL (forecourse) and MAINSAIL (main-course).

courser A bird native to northern Africa noted for running swiftly, and related to the PLOVER.

court bouillon A stock for boiling fish and consisting of water, wine, vegetables, and seasonings.

court-martial A naval or military court made up of officers, usually superior in rank to the accused. In the Royal Navy, courts-martial were held for violations of the ARTICLES OF WAR and automatically occurred whenever a ship of the Royal Navy was lost.

According to *Falconer's Marine Dictionary* (1815), regulation held that "The courts-martial are to be assembled in the fore-noon, and held in the most convenient and public place of the ship, where all, who will, may be present; and the captains of all his Majesty's ships in company, which take post, have a right to assist there. It is required to set from day to day (Sunday always excepted) until the sentence be given; and no member shall absent himself from the court during the whole course of the trial. . . ."

When the sentence was death, continued *Falconer's*, "On the morning destined for the execution, the signal of death is displayed, and the boats of the squadron, manned and armed, surround the ship appointed for the execution. The crews of the respective ships are arranged on deck, and are acquainted with the crime for which the punishment is inflicted; after which a gun is fired; and, at the same time, the unhappy victim, who has violated the laws of his country, is run up by the neck, to the yard-arm, a terrible example to the surrounding spectators."

court-plaster An adhesive plaster used to cover superficial cuts and wounds.

cove A fellow, chap, or customer. Also, the master of a house or shop.

cover-point In cricket, a fielder (or the position of a fielder) a little in front of the batsman on the offside, one of the key fielding positions as walls are often deflected by the batsman to the side.

cow-leech A cattle doctor or veterinarian.

cowpat *or* **cow-flop**   Cow dung, often used dry as heating fuel.

Cowper, William *(1731–1800)*   Poet noted for his moving poem "On the Loss of the *Royal George*," which commemorated the sinking of that ship at SPITHEAD in 1782.

coxal   Pertaining to a coxa, the joint that connects an insect's leg to its body.

coxswain *or* **cox'n**   The helmsman of a boat; the person on board ship having permanent charge of a boat and its crew, of which he has command unless a superior officer is present. In a MAN-OF-WAR the Captain's coxswain, who has charge of the Captain's boat and attends him, ranks high among PETTY OFFICERS.

crack on   To CLAP ON full sail; to carry all sail.

crane   A large wading bird with very long legs, neck, and bill. Originally referred to the common European crane, once abundant in marshy places in Great Britain and prized as food, now extinct; about 15 closely allied species are found in other lands. Also, projecting pieces of iron or timber on board a ship to support a boat or SPAR. Pieces of iron or timber at a vessel's sides used to stow boats or spars on. Also, a bent tube used to draw liquor out of a vessel; a siphon.

crank   An unstable vessel, liable to lean to the side or capsize.

cravat   A scarf worn around the neck, chiefly by men.

creeping skerit *or* **skerret**   The water parsnip, *Sium nodiflorum*, which has edible white tubers, abandoned as a medicine by the mid-18th century. The Peruvian potato was sometimes called "skirret of Peru."

crepitation   A crackling noise. The sound and sensation caused by the entrance of air into the lungs in a certain stage of inflammation, or by the grating together of the ends of fractured bones. Also, the crackling noise sometimes observed when gangrenous parts are examined with the fingers.

creta alba   Literally, white chalk, calcium carbonate, prescribed for diarrhea.

crib-biting *or* **cribbing**   A harmful habit of some horses in which they seize a manger or other object with their teeth and at the same time noisily draw in breath.

criminal conversation   Adultery.

crimp   An agent whose business is to procure seamen or soldiers.

cringle   A loop of rope containing a THIMBLE, or ring, that is attached to the BOLTROPE of a sail and used for REEFing.

crinkum-crankum   Playful word for anything full of twists and turns or intricately or fancifully elaborated.

crocus   Various yellow or red metal ores.

Croesus   The last king of Lydia (560–546 B.C.), known for his wealth, as in the phrase "as rich as Croesus."

crofter   One who rents and cultivates a croft, or small holding. Especially in the Highlands and islands of Scotland, one of the joint tenants of a divided farm, who often tills a small croft and fishes.

cro'jack   *See* CROSSJACK.

croppy   One who has his hair cropped short, applied especially to the Irish rebels of 1798, who cut their hair short as a sign of sympathy for the French Revolution.

crossgrained tide *or* **cross-tide**   Water that flows in varying directions among shoals.

crossjack   The COURSE on the aftermost MAST of a SQUARE-RIGGED ship.

cross-sea   When two sets of waves cross each other, due to a change in wind direction.

crosstree   Horizontal cross-timbers that spread the SHROUDs, giving a better angle for supporting the MAST while also offering a standing place for seamen.

croup   An inflammatory disease of the larynx and trachea in children, marked by a peculiar sharp ringing cough and frequently fatal in a short time. "Croup" was the popular name for this affliction in the southeast of Scotland and was introduced into medical use by Professor Francis Home of Edinburgh in 1765.

crow A crowbar; a GRAPNEL.

crowbill Forceps used for extracting bullets or other foreign bodies from wounds.

crowdy A thick gruel made from meal and water. Any porridgelike food.

crowfoot A device consisting of a number of small cords passed through a long BLOCK or EUPHROE and used to suspend an awning.

crown A size of paper, 15 by 20 inches, originally watermarked with a crown. To crown a knot means to interweave the strands of the rope so as to prevent untwisting.

crow's nest A barrel or cylindrical box fixed to the MASTHEAD of an arctic, whaling, or other ship, as a shelter for the lookout.

crubeen The foot of an animal, especially a cooked pig's foot.

crudity Imperfectly digested or indigestible food. Also, indigestion.

cruiser A fast heavily armed ship, especially a warship commissioned to cruise for such purposes as protecting commerce, pursuing an enemy's ships, or capturing slave traders. During the 18th century, the word was commonly applied to PRIVATEERs.

crumpet A thin griddle cake made of buckwheat meal. A soft cake made of flour, beaten egg, milk, and barm, or baking powder, mixed into batter, and baked on an iron plate.

cryptogam A plant that reproduces by spores instead of by flowers or seed, including ferns, mosses, lichens, and fungi.

cuatro grupos, cinco minutos Four groups, five minutes (Spanish).

cuckold's neck A knot by which a rope is secured to a SPAR.

cuddy In a large sailing ship, a cabin under the POOP deck in which the officers took their meals. In the 18th century, also a sort of cabin or cook-room in a LIGHTER or BARGE. The small cabin of a boat, specifically the captain's cabin.

Cuirassier A mounted soldier wearing a cuirass, armor covering the body from neck to waist.

cullion A testicle. As a term of contempt, a base, despicable fellow.

cully One who is cheated or imposed upon, a dupe, gull, or simpleton. A man, a fellow, a companion, a mate.

cunning man A fortuneteller, conjurer, "wise man," wizard.

cunt-splice *or* **cut splice** A type of splice formed when two ropes are overlapped and joined in such a way as to form an EYE.

cupellation The process of assaying or refining precious metals by exposing them to high temperatures to cause the unwanted metals to oxidize and partly sink into the cupel, a small, shallow, porous cup. The separation of silver from argentiferous lead.

curate One entrusted with the cure of souls, a spiritual pastor. Any ecclesiastic who has the spiritual charge of a body of laymen. Also, the parson of a parish.

curculio Any of various WEEVILs, especially one that harms fruit.

curragh Marshy waste ground. Specifically, the proper name of the level stretch of open ground in County Kildare famous for its race-course and military camp. Also, in Ireland and Scotland, a wooden boat made of slats and covered with a watertight material, which in earlier times was usually hide and later was tarred canvas.

curricle A light two-wheeled carriage, usually drawn by two horses abreast.

custard apple The fruit of the tropical tree *Anona reticulata*. It has a dark brown rind and yellowish pulp resembling custard in appearance and flavor; it is native to South America and the WEST INDIES but was introduced into the EAST INDIES in the 16th century.

cutlass A short sword with a wide, flat, and slightly curved blade, more suited to cutting than thrusting. Especially, the sword with which a ship's company (but not the officers) are armed.

cutter A boat belonging to a ship of war, shorter and in proportion broader than the BARGE or PINNACE, that is fitted for rowing and sailing and is used for carrying light stores or passengers. Also, a swift single-masted scout ship first purchased by the Royal Navy in 1763 and known for being seaworthy. *See illustration,* page 72.

cutting-out   The capturing of a ship or ships at port usually by a surprise attack attempted in ships' boats at night.

cutwater   The forward edge of the STEM or PROW, which divides the water before it reaches the BOW.

Cuvier, Baron Georges (*1769–1832*)   A French naturalist and anatomist. Known as the "Magician of the Charnel House," Cuvier, who worked in a laboratory at the Museum of Natural History in Paris, could look at a bone fragment or a fossil and accurately name the animal it came from. He is considered the founder of comparative anatomy.

Cuzco   City in Peru founded in the 11th century and once the capital of the Inca empire. Taken by the Spanish under Pizarro in 1533, it is most famous for its ancient ruins. It is the site of a cathedral and a university, established in 1672.

cystotomy   Cutting into the bladder for extraction of a stone or other purpose.

dab   A species of small flatfish resembling the flounder and found in the waters of sandy parts of the British coast. Also, a common term for small, flat fish of any kind.

daedal   Skillful at fashioning and fabricating, like Daedalus; artistic. Also, intricate, mazelike.

Dalmatian   Pertaining to Dalmatia, a region on the eastern coast of the Adriatic Sea and formerly an Austrian province.

Dalrymple, Alexander (*1737–1808*)   Hydrographer and brother of the historian Sir David Dalrymple of Hailes. Born in Scotland, he became the first hydrographer to the EAST INDIA COMPANY in 1779, and then the first Hydrographer to the Admiralty in 1795. His privately printed book, *An Account of Discoveries Made in the South Pacific Ocean* (1767), was one of the few influential books mentioned by Captain James COOK and Sir Joseph BANKS during the voyage of H.M.S. *Endeavour*.

dame's school   An elementary school for children kept by a woman, usually in her home.

Damon   A fifth-century B.C. musician and philosopher of Athens who taught Socrates and Pericles, and was ostracized for his friendship with Pericles.

Dannebrog   The Danish national flag.

Dardanelles   The strategically important narrow strait that connects the Aegean Sea with the Sea of Marmara and, eventually, with the Black Sea via the Bosporus.

dark-lantern   A lantern with a slide or other fixture for hiding the light.

Darley Arabian   Sent by Thomas Darley from Aleppo to England in 1704 at the age of four, he was one of the three foundation sires (the others were the Godolphin Arabian and the Byerly Turk) from which all modern thoroughbred horses are descended. He was the great-great-grandsire of ECLIPSE.

Datura stramonium   Commonly known as thorn-apple, it was thought to induce sleep and diuresis, to strengthen the body, and to calm spasms (hence its promotion for the treatment of epilepsy). At high doses, it has marked side effects (attributable to various compounds in its berries), including dim vision, thirst, nausea, vomiting, and hallucinations.

davier   Dentists' forceps; also, DAVIT (French).

Davis Strait   Strait between Greenland and North America that connects Baffin Bay to the open Atlantic. Named after the British explorer Captain John Davis (1550–1605).

davit   A curved piece of timber or iron, with a roller, or SHEAVE, at the end, that projects from a ship's BOW and is used as a CRANE to HOIST the FLUKES of the anchor without injuring the side of the vessel. One of a pair of cranes on the side or stern of a ship fitted with sheaves and pulleys for suspending or lowering a boat. A line used to steady a davit GUY.

dead-eye   A flat round wooden BLOCK with three holes through which a LANYARD is ROVE, used for extending the SHROUDs. Also, the triangular blocks with one large hole, usually called hearts, used for extending the STAYs.

deadlight   A strong wooden or iron shutter fixed outside a SCUTTLE, or porthole, used to prevent light from escaping or entering or, in a storm, to prevent water from entering.

dead reckoning   The calculation of a ship's position based on the estimated speed, distance covered, and the courses steered by the compass, with corrections for known current, LEEWAY, etc., but without astronomical observations.

deal   A plank or board of pine or fir.

debellare superbos   To subdue the proud (Latin).

Decalogue   The Ten Commandments viewed collectively as a body of law.

decapod   A member of the highest order of the class Crustacea, those with ten feet or legs. The order includes the lobster, crab, crayfish, and shrimp.

decoction   A solution in which a substance, usually animal or vegetable, has been boiled, often to produce a medicine.

decree of nullity   The pronouncement that a marriage is invalid due to fraud, or legal, canonical, or physical incapacity.

deep   *See* MARK.

deglutination   The act of swallowing.

Deh vieni, non tardar   Come now, do not delay (Italian; sung by Susanna in act four of Mozart's *The Marriage of Figaro*).

de jure   By law (Latin).

delation   An accusation or denunciation. To delate is to inform against someone.

delf *or* **Delft ware**   Glazed earthenware made at Delf or Delft, Holland.

delirium tremens   Delirium characterized by trembling and delusions upon cessation of chronic drinking. The term was introduced in 1813 for a form of delirium that was believed to be aggravated by bleeding but relieved by opium. Subsequently it was applied to the syndrome that can occur when chronic alcoholics suddenly stop drinking.

demi-rep A woman whose character is only half reputable; a woman of doubtful chastity.

demy A size of paper (17½ by 22½ inches).

de non apparentibus et non existentibus eadem est ratio We make no distinction between that which is not visible and that which does not exist (Latin).

deperish To waste away.

depressed fracture Usually said of inwardly depressed fractures of the skull, requiring surgery with a TREPAN or TREPHINE to remove the fragments.

Derby Proper name of the most noted annual horserace in England, founded in 1780 by the twelfth Earl of Derby and run at Epsom Downs racecourse, usually on the Wednesday before or the second Wednesday after Whitsunday (the seventh Sunday after Easter).

derrick A CRANE that is made from a strong SPAR or BOOM equipped for hoisting and that pivots at the foot of a central post to work at various angles.

desman An aquatic insect-eating mammal related to the shrewmouse, but larger. Especially, the muskrat, which inhabits the rivers of Russia, chiefly the Volga and Don, and secretes musk. Another species is found in parts of the Pyrenees.

désolé Very sorry (French).

despatch To send off post-haste a messenger or message to an express destination, or the sending of such an official messenger or of troops, parcels, etc.

Deucalion's flood According to Greek mythology, a great deluge that occurred in Thessaly. Deucalion, the son of Prometheus, and his wife, Pyrrha, survived the flood—which was sent by Zeus to punish humans for their wickedness—in an ark. When the waters receded, they repopulated the earth by throwing stones behind them, Deucalion's becoming men and Pyrrha's, women.

Deus ex machina Literally, God from the machine (Latin). An unexpected and satisfactory conclusion to a problem. The term comes from the practice in ancient Greek drama in which a god was lowered by crane onto the stage to bring a happy resolution to the play.

devil   In the wooden deck of a vessel, a seam that adjoins a waterway. Also, the seam in the planking on the waterline. Both named for the difficulty involved in caulking the seam, as in the phrase, "The devil to pay!", meaning a tough, unenviable task.

dewlap   The fold of loose skin hanging from the throat of cattle and similar parts in other animals, such as the wattle of a turkey. A humorous reference to the pendulous folds of flesh about the human throat.

Dey   An adaptation of the Turkish word "Dāī," meaning maternal uncle, an honorary title bestowed on elderly men. In the 17th century, an elite force of soldiers in the Turkish army, the Janissaries, adopted the title for their commanding officers. When the Janissaries began to rule Algeria in the 17th century, it became the name of the ruler. The title also was used in Tunisia and in Tripoli.

dghaisa   A Maltese boat resembling a gondola.

dhow   A trading vessel used on the Arabian Sea, generally with a LATEEN sail on a single MAST, of 150 to 200 tons' burden. Also widely applied to all Arab vessels, especially those connected with the slave trade on the east coast of Africa.

Diamond Rock   A small, inaccessible, but strategically placed island less than a mile off the southwest end of the island of Martinique. In late 1803, Commodore Samuel Hood, on board the 74-gun *Centaur*, under Captain Murray Maxwell, decided to take the island and make it a stationary warship, as a depot for harassing the enemy's shipping. In January 1804, over the course of a month, the *Centaur* hoisted five guns (three long 24-pounders and two 18-pounders) to various positions on the 600-foot-high haystack-shaped island by means of a CABLE attached to one end of the ship and running up to the top of the island. Hood manned the island, dubbed a SLOOP of war, with a lieutenant and 120 men and boys.

Dianthus   The genus of flowering plants that includes the pinks and carnations. The July-flower (*D. caryophyllus*) was sometimes used medicinally for heartburn and as a flavoring.

diaphoretic   Causing or promoting perspiration.

dicotyledonous plant   A flowering plant embryo with two seed leaves, and sometimes more.

diddle   To cheat or swindle; to victimize.

Didus ineptis   *See* DODO.

Dies Irae   "Day of wrath," the first words, and thus the name, of a Latin hymn on the Last Judgment ascribed to Thomas of Celano (circa 1250) and sung as a part of Requiem Mass.

Digitalis purpurea   Purple foxglove. In 1785 Dr. William WITHERING introduced it as the first effective treatment for DROPSY. It removes EDEMA fluid by strengthening the heart, which secondarily produces diuresis and permits the pulse rate to slow. Its characteristic side effects include vomiting and abnormal yellow-green vision.

dimity   A cotton fabric woven with raised stripes or fancy figures, used for beds and bedroom hangings and sometimes for garments.

dingle-dangle   To hang loosely, swinging to and fro.

dingo   The wild or semidomesticated dog of Australia, *Canis dingo*.

Diocletian's palace   A magnificent palace built by Caius Aurelius Valerius Diocletianus (245–313). Proclaimed Roman emperor by the army in 284, Diocletian oversaw the restoration of Britain to the empire and the subjugation of the Persians during his reign. In 305, he retired to his hometown of Salona, a busy commercial port on the DALMATIAN coast of the ADRIATIC, where he built his palace outside of town. In the seventh century, Salona was sacked and a new city, Spalato (now Split, Croatia), sprang up around the palace.

Diogenes (400–325 B.C.)   A cynical Greek philosopher and ascetic who lived in a tub out of contempt for the comforts of civilization.

Diomedea exulans   *See* ALBATROSS.

dip   To lower and then raise a flag as a naval salute, an act of courtesy. To lower and raise a sail in TACKing. Also, a candle made by repeatedly dipping a wick into melted tallow.

dipping-needle   A magnetic needle mounted so that it can move in a vertical plane about its center of gravity and thus indicate by its dip the direction of the earth's magnetism.

directoire   Of, pertaining to, or resembling an extravagant style of dress, often imitative of Greek and Roman garb, prevalent at the time of the French Directory, the five-man executive body that governed France from 1795 to 1799, at which point it was overthrown by Napoleon Bonaparte.

dirk   A small sword or dagger worn mostly by MIDSHIPMEN but also by some commissioned officers and ADMIRALs.

discomfiture   Complete defeat in battle, overthrow, rout.

dish   To defeat, ruin, incapacitate; to cheat or circumvent.

dispart-sight   A gun sight mounted on top of the second REINFORCE-ring around the middle of a firing piece and used for point-blank or horizontal firing. It eliminates the difference of the diameters between the BREECH and the mouth of the cannon.

dispensary   A place where medicines are dispensed.

dispensation   The granting of license by a pope, archbishop, or bishop to a person to do something forbidden by ecclesiastical law.

displacency   The state of being displeased, the opposite of complacency.

disrate   To reduce to a lower rating or rank. To remove a ship from its RATE or class.

Dissent   A nonconformist who separates himself from the communion of the Established Church of England or, in Scotland, of the Church of Scotland.

distal   Away from the center of the body or from the point of origin, said of the extremity or distant part of a limb or organ; terminal.

distich   A couplet.

distraint   A legal term for the act of forcing one to satisfy an obligation by the seizure of his goods or property.

divisions   A ship's company in the Royal Navy is divided for purposes of discipline and welfare into divisions of various sizes, each with a divisional officer who is responsible for the work and care of his men. Also, the MUSTER or assembly for inspection and other purposes.

djerm *or* jerm   A small one- or two-masted vessel with large LATEEN sails used on the Egyptian coast. Formerly, larger trading vessels in the eastern Mediterranean.

Djezzar Pasha, Ahmed (c. *1722–1804*)   The Bey of Sidon and Damascus, with his seat of government at ACRE, Djezzar Pasha, whose name means, aptly, "the butcher," was the dominant political figure in southern Syria during the last quarter of the 18th century and the early 19th century. He was shrewd, savage, and extremely loyal to the Turkish Empire, for whom he acted as governor of the LEVANT littoral from the Nile to the Turkish border. His policy of ruthless repression and cruel punishment made him feared. The British, under Sir Sidney SMITH, assisted him in repelling France at Acre in 1799, ending NAPOLEON's eastward expansion and contributing to the ouster of the French from Egypt two years later.

docket   A warrant from a custom-house on entering goods that certifies payment of the duty.

Dodman Point   A cape on the south coast of Cornwall, between Plymouth and Falmouth.

dodo   A bird that once lived on the island of MAURITIUS, in the Indian Ocean. The dodo had a massive, clumsy body and small wings of no use for flight. Around 1600 trading ships began stopping at the island, and the sailors discovered that the dodo was both edible and easy prey. Also, rats and pigs brought to the island by these ships destroyed dodo nesting grounds. Three-quarters of a century later, the dodo was extinct.

dog-cart   A cart with a box under the seat for a sportsman's dogs. Subsequently, an open vehicle with two transverse seats back to back, the hind seat originally used as a dog kennel.

dogger   A two-masted fishing vessel with BLUFF BOWS, somewhat similar to a KETCH, used in the North Sea fisheries and often during the 17th and 18th centuries as PRIVATEERS. *See* illustration, page 61.

Dogger Banks   Extensive shallows in the North Sea between England and Denmark that cover an area more than 160 miles long and 60 miles wide and are known for their abundant populations of cod, haddock, mackerel, and other food fish.

Doggett's Coat and Badge   One of the world's oldest continuing rowing races, held annually (August 1) on the River Thames from London Bridge to Chelsea. Originally a sculling contest between the skiffs used to ferry passengers across the river, instituted in 1716 by the Irish actor Thomas Doggett (1670–1721) to commemorate the accession of George I in 1714. Doggett awarded a cash prize and "an Orange coloured Livery with a Badge representing Liberty" to the winner. At his death, he left funds so the race could be continued, and it still is, by the Company of Fishmongers.

dog-leg   Bent like a dog's hind leg.

dog's body   Sailors' name for dried peas boiled in a cloth.

dog's nose   A drink made of beer and gin or of ale and rum.

dog-vane   A small vane usually made of thread, cork, and feathers, placed on the WEATHER GUNWALE to show the direction of the wind.

dog-watch   The name given to each of the two short WATCHes (of two hours each instead of four) between 1600 and 2000 hours, one from 1600 to 1800 hours and the other from 1800 to 2000 hours. By this means, the day's 24 hours are divided into seven watches instead of six so that the watches that the crew stands every night are rotated. Maturin's classic dog-watch pun (*Post Captain*, p. 428, for all those who wish to return to the original scene of this oft-recurring crime) was, by the way, not original to O'Brian. SMYTH's *Sailor's Word-Book* (1867) notes: "Theodore Hook explains this as cur-tailed."

doldrums   A region of low pressure and very little wind around the equator. Above and below are the bands more favorable to ships where the TRADE WINDS blow. The word is likely derived from a combination of Old English *dol*, "dull," and *tantrum*.

Dolland *or* **Dollond**   Among other accomplishments John Dollond (1706–1761) and his eldest son Peter (1730–1820) used a combination of crown and flint glasses in constructing achromatic lenses, thus improving telescope lenses. In 1765 Peter invented an improved triple achromatic lens.

dollar   The English name for the peso or piece of eight (i.e., eight *reals*) once used in Spain and the Spanish American colonies and largely used in Britain's North American colonies at the time of the Revolutionary War.

dolphin   A mooring-post, or BOLLARD, on a dock or along a wharf or beach to make HAWSERS fast to. Also, a wreath of plaited CORDAGE fastened around a MAST or YARD to prevent the yard from falling in case the ropes or chains supporting it are shot away in action.

dolphin-striker   A short GAFF under the CAP of the BOWSPRIT for securing the JIB-BOOM. Also called a MARTINGALE, which refers to the ropes that connect it to the jib-boom.

domestique   A servant. When Aubrey is introduced to a Frenchman, he usually replies "Domestique, monsieur," his literal translation of, "Your servant, sir," but comparable to pronouncing himself a domestic servant.

Domett, Admiral Sir William (*1754–1828*)   ADMIRAL and Commissioner of the Navy who rose from humble West Country roots to command HOWE's FLAGSHIP at the GLORIOUS FIRST OF JUNE in 1794. Domett was Fleet Captain at the Battle of COPENHAGEN in 1801.

domino   A loose cloak with a small mask covering the upper part of the face, often worn at masquerades.

dona nobis pacem   Give us peace (Latin).

Doncaster   A market town in Yorkshire famous for its horse race, the ST. LEGER stakes.

dormouse   A small rodent of one of two families between squirrels and mice, the British species of which is noted for its hibernation.

dory   A small boat, especially a flat-bottomed one used by North American cod fishermen.

doss-house   A common lodging house, sometimes a brothel.

douanier   A custom-house officer (French).

double-bank   Having pairs of opposite oars pulled by rowers on the same bench, or having two rowers at each oar.

double-reef   To reduce sail by taking in two REEFS.

doubling   The act of sailing around or passing beyond a cape or point of land.

doubloon   A Spanish gold coin originally double the value of a pistole, or equal to 36 English SHILLINGS.

douceur A gift used as a tip or bribe, from the French word for sweetness.

Douglas, Admiral Sir Charles (1725–1789) Gunnery enthusiast and author of a manual on the subject, who experimented with steel springs and wedges behind TRUCK-wheels to lessen the impact of cannon recoil.

Dover Castle and port in Kent commanding the Straits of Dover, the narrowest part of the English Channel.

down-at-heel Having boot or shoe heels worn down; poor.

downhaul A rope passing up to the upper corner of the sail to pull it down when shortening sail. Specifically, a rope for hauling down the JIB. Also, a rope to the outer YARDARMS of STUDDINGSAILS used to take them in securely.

Downs, the The part of the sea within the GOODWIN SANDS, off Deal on the east coast of Kent, England, a famous rendezvous for ships. Also, the treeless chalk uplands along the south and southeast coast of England. The name derives from the Middle English word "doun," or hill, from which the word "dune" also derives.

doxy Floozy, prostitute.

drabbler An additional canvas laced to the bottom of the bonnet of a sail to give it greater depth.

drabble-tail *or* **draggle-tail** A slattern.

drachm The principal silver coin of the ancient Greeks, the drachma. Also, a weight approximately equivalent to that of the Greek coin. *See* DRAM.

dragoman A man who acts as guide and interpreter in countries where Arabic, Turkish, or Persian is spoken.

dragon's blood An expensive astringent made from the gum resin secreted by either of two East Indian climbing palms. It turns deep red in alcohol solution.

dragon-tree Any of various East Indian palms of several genera that were sources of dragon's blood, a deep red gum sometimes used medicinally as an astringent.

dragoon Originally dragoons were mounted infantry with firearms. Eventually they became horse soldiers, particularly cavalry regiments.

dram In apothecaries' weight, 60 grains, or ⅛ of an ounce. A fluid dram is ⅛ of a fluid ounce, or 60 MINIMs. Hence, a small draught of cordial, stimulant, or spirit.

draught The depth of water that a vessel DRAWS, or requires to float her. In medicine, a dose; a potion (*see also* BLACK DRAUGHT *and* SLIME-DRAUGHT). Also, a sketch or drawing.

draughts The game of checkers.

draw Of a sail, to swell out tightly with wind. Of a vessel, to require a specified depth of water in which to float.

dray A little cart or car on wheels. A low cart without sides used for carrying heavy loads, especially one used by brewers.

dreadnought screen *See* FEARNOUGHT.

drench A medicinal, soporific, or poisonous DRAUGHT; a potion.

driver Originally conceived of as a sort of STUDDINGSAIL, set at the peak of the MIZZEN GAFF. It could either be set SQUARE or FORE-AND-AFT. The driver-boom is the BOOM on which the driver is set.

Dr. Mead's Instant Invigorator A putative tonic probably promoted by a Dr. Mead, perhaps a quack, but certainly not the eminent early-18th-century physician Richard Mead of London.

drogue A contrivance, such as a wooden bucket, attached to the end of a harpoon line to check the progress of a whale when it is running or sounding. A submerged sail dragged to slow a sailing vessel.

droit A right; that to which one has a legal claim; perquisites due by legal right. Droits of Admiralty are certain rights or perquisites, such as a percentage of the proceeds arising from the capture of an enemy's ship (French).

dromedary A light and fleet breed of camel specially reared and trained for riding. Usually the Arabian, or one-humped, camel, but the two-humped Bactrian camel can also be improved into a dromedary.

dropsy   Abnormal accumulation of EDEMA fluid, most often in the chest, abdomen, or legs, produced by failure of the heart, kidneys, or liver. However, hydrocephalus was often called "dropsy of the brain," and large ovarian cysts were called "ovarian dropsy."

drowned baby   A sweet, suet pudding resembling SPOTTED DOG but cooked in a less tightly wrapped pudding cloth to give it a looser, more viscous consistency.

Druid   One of an order of men among the ancient Celts of Gaul and Britain who, according to Caesar, were priests or religious ministers and teachers, but who figure in native Irish and Welsh legend as magicians, sorcerers, and soothsayers.

Drury, William O'Bryen   COMMANDER-IN-CHIEF of the EAST INDIES STATION from 1808 until his death at Madras in March 1811.

dryad   A nymph of the woods; a sylvan beauty.

dry-dock   A dock from which the water is or may be let out, used for the repairing or building of a ship.

Dry Salvages   Also known as the Selvagens, a group of barren, uninhabited islets in the Canary Islands.

ducat   A gold coin of varying value, formerly in use in most European countries.

duces tecum *or* subpoena duces tecum   A writ that commands one to show documentary evidence in court or at a deposition (Latin).

duck   A strong, untwilled linen (or, later, cotton) fabric, lighter and finer than canvas, that was used for small sails and men's, especially sailors', trousers and outer clothing.

duck up   To raise with a jerk, HAUL up, for instance, to duck up a sail that obstructs the steersman's view.

duck-billed platypus   The duckmole (*Ornithorhynchus anatinus*) of Australia, an aquatic mammal that is the only species of its genus and family in the order Monotremata. It has glossy dark-brown or red-brown fur, webbed feet, and a flat bill like a duck's, which it uses for grubbing in sand or in muddy river bottoms. Burrowing in the river-bank, the duckbill lines its main chamber with dry grass, and here the

The duck-billed platypus, *Ornithorhynchus anatinus,* an aquatic mammal that lays eggs

female lays and hatches usually two eggs at a time. The male duckbill is larger than the female and possesses venemous spurs on its hind legs, the exact use of which is unknown. When it was discovered in New South Wales in 1797, the duckbill was considered the most unusual mammal in existence.

ducks and drakes   A pastime in which a flat stone is thrown along the surface of water, causing it to rebound or skip as many times as possible before sinking; skipping a stone.

ductus choledocus communis   Common bile duct, from which bile empties from the liver into the duodenum.

duff *or* **plum-duff**   Steamed suet pudding with currants.

dugong *or* **sea cow**   A large aquatic herbivorous mammal inhabiting the Indian sea, the male of which has upper incisors that form tusks. It is a relative of the manatee.

dulce loquentem, dulce ridentem   Speaking sweetly, laughing sweetly (Latin).

dulcify   To render sweet to the taste, sweeten; to neutralize the acidity of or wash the soluble salts out of a substance.

dumb-chalder   A metal cleat bolted to the back of a wooden STERN-POST for the end of a RUDDER-PINTLE to rest on and carry some of the rudder's weight.

dump-bolt   A short bolt driven into a plank and timber as a partial security prior to a more thorough fastening.

dum sola et cast fuerit   As long as she remains alone and chaste (Latin).

dun   An importunate creditor or an agent employed to collect debts.

Duncan, Admiral Adam, first Viscount (*1731–1804*)   Born in Dundee, Scotland, Duncan entered the Navy in 1764 and commanded the North Sea squadron from 1795. He faced a critical situation during the mutiny at the NORE in the spring of 1797. On October 11, 1797, he defeated the Dutch at the Battle of CAMPERDOWN capturing 11 ships, and was elevated to the peerage as Viscount Duncan of Camperdown and given an annual pension of £2,000.

Dundas, Henry, first Viscount Melville (*1742–1811*)   A Scottish lawyer and member of Parliament (1774–1802), Dundas served as lord advocate (the chief law officer of the Crown in Scotland) from 1775 to 1783 and was appointed to the Privy Council (a body of advisers appointed by the monarch) in 1782. A vocal supporter of the war in America and influential in Indian affairs, he became a PITT supporter and served as Secretary of War (1794–1801). The successful Egyptian campaign of 1801 was carried out under his auspices, against the wishes of Pitt and the king. He was raised to the peerage in 1802. He served as First Lord of the Admiralty from May 15, 1804, to May 2, 1805. However, he was removed from the Privy Council in 1805, then impeached and removed from all of his offices in 1806 for misuse of funds while serving as Treasurer of the Navy (1784–1800). He was acquitted of the charge but was found guilty of negligence. In 1807 he was restored to the Privy Council.

Dundas, Hon. George Heneage Lawrence (*d. 1834*)   Promoted to Lieutenant in 1797, Commander in 1800, and Captain in 1801, Dundas was made a Commander of Bath in 1815 and was promoted to Rear-Admiral in 1830. He served as an Admiralty Commissioner from 1830 to 1843 and as Controller of the Navy in 1831 and 1832.

Perhaps the inspiration for O'Brian's Heneage Dundas, the fictional younger son of HENRY DUNDAS. Heneage served as a MIDSHIP-MAN with Aubrey on board H.M.S. *Britannia*. In fact, the two were shipmates even before they were rated midshipmen and served "in half a dozen commissions together" (*Post Captain*, p. 333), which is not to say they always got along. In fact, they once fought a duel.

Nevertheless, the two remain friends despite the fact that Dundas, by virtue of his influence, eventually advances through the ranks much quicker than Aubrey.

Dundas, Robert Saunders, second Viscount Melville (*1771–1851*) The only son of HENRY DUNDAS. In 1796 he married Anne Saunders, great-niece of Admiral Sir Charles Saunders, whose name he took as his own. He became First Lord of the Admiralty in 1812 and remained in office for 15 years.

dunlin A small sandpiper, in color cinnamon to brown on top and white underneath, abundant in coastal regions.

dunnage Planks, timber, or light material, such as brushwood and mats, stowed among and beneath the cargo of a vessel to protect it from chafing and wetness. Also, a sailor's personal baggage.

Duns Scotus, John (*c. 1265 to 1308*) The Scottish philosopher and theologian also known as Doctor Subtilis. In theology, he is best known for his zealous defense of the doctrine of the Immaculate Conception, in opposition to Thomas Aquinas.

duodecimo The size of a book or of the page of a book in which each leaf is one twelfth of a whole sheet, or approximately 5 by 7½ inches.

duodenal Pertaining or relating to the duodenum, the first portion of the small intestine, immediately below the stomach.

Dupuytren, Guillaume, Baron (*1777–1835*) A French surgeon, anatomist, and, starting in 1812, professor at the HÔTEL DIEU, Paris, where he was a noted diagnostician and lecturer. He wrote on surgery, described a fracture of the fibula and a contraction of the hand that bear his name, and founded the chair of pathological anatomy at the University of Paris. He was made a baron in 1823.

dura mater The tough, outermost membranous envelope of the brain and spinal cord.

durian The oval fruit of a tree of Southeast Asia, with a hard, prickly rind and luscious cream-colored pulp. It is known for its very unpleasant odor.

durst Past tense of "dare."

Dutch William (*1650–1702*)   William III, son of Prince William II of Orange and Princess Mary, the eldest daughter of King Charles I of England. Stadholder of the Netherlands from 1672, he married his cousin, Princess Mary, the daughter of King James II of England. After the Catholic James fled England in 1688, Parliament declared the throne vacant and proclaimed the two Protestants, William III and Mary II, jointly king and queen of England in 1689. A few months later, the Convention did the same in Scotland.

Dyce! *or* **Thus!**   The command to maintain the ship in a constant relation to the wind. The intent was similar to the order "Steady!", which meant to keep the vessel on the same compass course.

Dynastes   The Hercules-beetle, growing to about five inches in length.

dyspepsia   Indigestion. Often used for various disorders of the digestive organs, especially the stomach, usually involving weakness and loss of appetite and accompanied by depression.

dysphony   Difficulty in speaking arising from disease of or injury to the vocal organs.

earing   One of a number of small ropes that fasten the upper corner of a sail to the YARD.

Earl Godwin's piece of bread   The Earl of Wessex and father of King Harold II of England, Godwin (d. 1053) gained control of England, but his acts, namely the blinding and death of Alfred, the brother of Edward the Confessor, also precipitated the Norman invasion. One story regarding the death of Godwin (or Godwine) purports that at a banquet, Godwin remonstrated that he was not responsible for the murder of Alfred and that if he lied, God should strike him dead, whereupon he promptly choked to death on a piece of bread. It is more likely that he died from excessive alcohol consumption.

Earnshaws   A chronometer made by the English watchmaker Thomas Earnshaws (1749–1829), who was the first to simplify and lower the cost of manufacturing chronometers, making them more affordable to the general public.

earwig   Any of various insects, all of the order Dermaptera, with pincerlike appendages protruding from the abdomen. So called from the notion that it penetrates into the head through the ear.

EAST INDIA COMPANY (ENGLISH)
Also known as the Honourable East India Company, H.E.I.C., The Honourable Company, or "John Company." Like its counterparts in other European nations (e.g., the Dutch East India Company), the English East India Company set up to trade in India, the East Indies, and the Far East. It was incorporated by Elizabeth I in 1600; along with a monopoly on trade in the region, it was eventually given the right to acquire territory, make treaties, and wage war. By 1757, the company controlled India, acting as the governmental authority for British possessions in the Far East. Following the 1774 Regulating Act and the 1784 India Act, it was a Board of Control responsible to Parliament. Its monopoly over British trade in the East was broken in 1813.

The Dutch East India Company, the H.E.I.C.'s chief rival for hegemony in the East, was successful during the 17th century and at one time controlled Batavia, Ceylon, Java, Malacca, AMBOYNA, and the Cape of Good Hope, among other places. It officially closed in 1799 after France invaded Holland.

East Indiaman   A large and heavily armed merchant ship built by the various East India companies and, in England, often commanded by a former Royal Navy officer. Considered the ultimate sea vessels of the age, the ships offered relatively luxurious quarters and were often adorned with gilding and ornamental carvings.

East Indies   Collective term for the islands off Southeast Asia, including Borneo, Celebes, Java, and Sumatra, along with India, at one point, and the MALAY Peninsula. The sources of much-valued spices and other products, they were subject to various colonial influences beginning with the Portuguese in 1511. In 1811, Java fell to Lord Minto and a British EAST INDIA COMPANY force, and Thomas Raffles was appointed lieutenant-governor.

easting   The distance gained to the eastward; a sloping or veering eastwards. Of a wind or ocean current, a shifting eastward of the point of origin.

Eccles cake   A pastry with a filling of dried fruit. Eccles is a town in Northwest England, in Greater Manchester.

Echidna   A genus of Australian toothless insectivorous mammals resembling hedgehogs, including the porcupine anteater.

echinoderm   A member of a phylum of animals (Echinodermata) that includes sea urchins and sea cucumbers. Most echinoderms have pointed spines that stud the skin.

Eclipse   Foaled in 1764, he was one of the three stallions (the others were Herod and Matchem) from which all true thoroughbred horses are descended, as registered in the English *General Stud Book*, first published in 1791. He was, in turn, descended from the DARLEY ARABIAN.

Eddystone   A dangerous reef 14 miles southwest of PLYMOUTH in southwest England that has been marked by a succession of lighthouses since 1696.

edema   Swelling, usually in the lower legs, abdomen, or chest, caused by abnormal accumulation of fluid, as in DROPSY.

edge away   To gradually change the course of a ship by sailing larger (more away) from BEFORE THE WIND.

égard   Regard, consideration, deference (French).

egret   Any of several white wading birds of related genera.

Egyptian pox   Probably syphilis; it was customary for its name in one country to include a pejorative attribution to another nation.

eider   Any one of several sea ducks of various genera abundant in northern regions that line their nests with their own down. The males have distinctive black and white plumage.

elbow   When a ship moored in a tideway crosses its HAWSER twice, entangling it.

electuary   A medicinal paste made with a powder or other ingredient mixed with honey, preserves, or syrup.

Eleonora's falcon   A falcon of the Aegean that winters around Madagascar and the South African coast and returns to Greece in April to forage for large insects. In August, colonies of Eleonora's falcon breed on remote rocky Aegean islands. This late breeding time enables them to hatch their young at the peak of the fall migration, when an abundancy of songbirds moving south provide food for the young.

elephantiasis   Various kinds of diseases caused by parasites indigenous to the tropics that cause the affected part, usually the legs and scrotum, to swell to enormous size.

Admiral Lord Keith
(*reproduced from Alfred Mahan's* Life of Nelson, *1897, courtesy of the Mariners' Museum, Newport News, Virginia*)

elevenses *or* **elevens**   Light refreshment eaten at about eleven A.M.

Elphinstone, George Keith, Viscount Keith (*1746–1823*)   Keith participated in the capture of Charleston, South Carolina, during the American Revolutionary War, and was made Rear Admiral at the beginning of the French Revolutionary War (1793–1801). As Admiral, he was primarily a gifted administrator. He helped resolve the naval mutinies of 1797 and in 1815 commanded the ship to which Napoleon surrendered, the BELLEROPHON. During Elphinstone's career, he commanded the India Squadron, the Mediterranean Fleet (conducting with General Sir Ralph Abercromby a successful amphibious action in Egypt against the reduced French forces in 1801), the North Sea Station, and the Channel Fleet. His second wife, Hester Thrale, was DR. JOHNSON's "Queeney" (*see* KEITH, LADY); in the Aubrey-Maturin novels she is Aubrey's dear friend and best influence with the ADMIRALTY.

embarras de choix   An overabundance of choices (French).

embay To lay a vessel within a bay. Also, of wind or tide, to force a vessel into or trap it within a bay.

embrasure In a fortress or parapet, an opening that is narrower outside than inside to allow a gun to be fired from a protected enclosure.

emu A flightless Australian bird discovered soon after the colonization of NEW SOUTH WALES in 1788 that was originally regarded as a species of CASSOWARY. The emu and cassowary are closely related, but the former is distinguished by the absence of the cassowary's horny "helmet" and the caruncles on the neck, and by the presence of a singular opening in the front of the windpipe.

en clair In ordinary language, as opposed to being in code or cipher (French).

enclosure The act of enclosing water or common land, involving the loss of common rights; the land thus enclosed.

Endeavour, H.M.S. Captain James COOK'S BARQUE, originally a COLLIER built in 1764 and called *Earl of Pembroke.* She is famous for her part in Cook's great discovery voyage from 1768 to 1771. She was purchased by the Navy in 1768 and sold in 1775.

Endymion, H.M.S. Modeled after the captured French frigate *La Pomme,* she was built in 1797 and became one of the Royal Navy's swiftest ships.

engouement Infatuation (French).

Ennius, Quintus (239–169 B.C.) Born in Calabria and made a Roman citizen in 184 B.C., Ennius hoped to become the Latin Homer and is indeed regarded as the father of Latin poetry. He translated Greek plays, especially those of Euripides, wrote comedies, satires, tragedies, and most notably his masterpiece epic poem, *Annales,* a literary history of Rome, which served as the national epic until superseded by Virgil's *Aeneid.* Only fragments survive from his work, including about 600 lines from *Annales.* Virgil, Lucretius, and Ovid borrowed freely from his work.

ensign The flag carried by a ship to indicate her nationality. In some navies, the lowest rank of commissioned officer.

eparterial On or over any artery.

epicene In Latin and Greek grammar, nouns having one form to denote both sexes. Also, partaking of the characteristics of both sexes.

epiphytic Disease caused by vegetable parasites.

episcopacy Government of the church by bishops; the system of church government with three distinct orders: bishops, presbyters or priests, and deacons. In the United States, the Church of England (Anglican Church) became the Protestant Episcopal Church in 1784.

Episcopal ring The ring worn by a bishop as an insignia of office.

epocha Something epochal or very significant.

equilibro Balanced.

equinoctial Happening at or near the time of the fall or spring equinox, when the length of night and day are equal. Said especially of the GALES prevailing about the time of the fall equinox.

Erastianism The theory of the Swiss theologian Thomas Erastus (1524–1583), who believed in the complete subordination of ecclesiastical powers to secular ones.

Erse The Gaelic dialect of the Scottish Highlands, which is in fact of Irish origin. Occasionally used to designate Irish Gaelic as well.

Erythroxylon coca Scientific name of COCA.

escheat In feudal law, when a fief reverted to the lord when the tenant died without leaving a successor qualified to inherit under the original grant. The lapsing of land to the Crown (in the U.S., to the state) or to the lord of the manor on the death of the owner.

escota *See* SHEET.

esculent Suitable as food, edible, used especially for vegetables.

espalier A latticework or frame of stakes upon which fruit trees or ornamental shrubs are trained against a wall. Also one such stake.

esquire A title originally applied to men who belonged to the higher order of English gentry, ranking immediately below a knight.

estovers The rights to wood for fuel, repairs, and other uses from land that one does not own, especially from land on which one is a tenant.

état d'âme   State of the soul (French).

Euphorbia   A genus of plants that secrete a viscid milky juice that may be astringent, sometimes poisonous, but always bitter.

Euphorbia praestans   A gum resin used chiefly to stimulate sneezing in order to remove unbalanced humors via the phlegm; in large doses it caused vomiting and catharsis.

euphory   Euphoria, good feeling.

euphroe   A long cylindrical BLOCK with a number of holes for receiving the legs, or lines, composing the CROWFOOT.

Euryalus, **H.M.S.**   The fifth-rate 36-gun FRIGATE nicknamed "Nelson's Watch Dog." Commanded by Captain Hon. Henry Blackwood, she provided advance notice to Nelson of the massing of French and Spanish ships that led to the Battle of TRAFALGAR. Built in 1803, she became a prison ship in 1826.

Eusebius of Caesarea (*c.260–c.339*)   A Palestinian theologian, church historian, and scholar who wrote *Life of Constantine* (c.338) and many other works.

evening gun   The warning gun that is fired to mark the time of day after which the sentries challenge.

evert   To turn the inner surface outward, for instance, to evert the eyelid.

ewer   A pitcher or jug with a wide spout used to carry water for washing the hands.

Ex Africa surgit semper aliquid novo,—novi   Something new is always rising up out of Africa (Aubrey's second guess—novi—is the correct one; Latin, from Pliny the Elder, Historia Naturalis 5).

Excellent, **H.M.S.**   A third rate of 74 guns built in 1787, she was commanded by Lord COLLINGWOOD at the GLORIOUS FIRST OF JUNE in 1794. She also fought at CAPE ST. VINCENT in 1797. She was later used as the Royal Navy gunnery training ship at PORTSMOUTH.

Exchequer bill   A bill of credit issued by authority of Parliament bearing interest at the current rate.

execrate   To pronounce a curse upon; to declare accursed.

Execution Dock   The dock at Wapping where criminal sailors were executed by being confined in a cage just over the low-tide mark so that they slowly drowned at high tide.

ex gratia   As a favor or gift; without compulsion (Latin).

exiguity   Scantiness, smallness in size or quantity.

extravasation   The escape of blood into surrounding tissues.

exulans   The great albatross, *Diomedea exulans*. *See* ALBATROSS.

eye   A loop of cord or rope, especially the circular loop of a SHROUD or STAY, where it goes over the MAST. Also, the loop at one end of a bowstring.

facies febris Literally, the face of fever, traditionally known as the "Hippocratic facies" seen in patients with advanced fevers and characterized by sunken eyes, hollow cheeks and temples, leaden complexion, and pinched expression of the entire face.

fadge To piece together, usually used with "up."

fag-end The last part or remnant; the end of a rope, especially a frayed end.

fairlead A strip of board or plank with holes for running RIGGING through. Also, a BLOCK or THIMBLE used for the same purpose.

fairway A navigable channel in a river or harbor.

fake One of the circles or windings of a CABLE or HAWSER in a coil. To fake is to lay a rope in fakes or coils; to coil.

Falconer, William (1744–1824) British physician who wrote on many medical subjects, including fevers. He should not be confused with the author of the same name who is famous for his *Falconer's Dictionary of the Marine.*

Falconer's Dictionary of the Marine A highly regarded lexicon of sea terms by William Falconer (1732–1769), a Scottish poet and sailor who drowned when the FRIGATE *Aurora* went down off Cape Town with all hands.

faldetta A cape with a hood worn by women in MALTA.

Falkland Islands A group of British islands 200 miles east of Patagonia in South America, named in 1693 for Lord Falkland, First Lord of the Admiralty (1693–1694). Spain claimed the islands in 1770 and gave them the name Malvinas Islands. This action caused a major international crisis that threatened to lead Britain to war against France and Spain.

fall The entire length of the rope in a TACKLE, of which the part of the rope attached to the BLOCK is called the standing part and the opposite end is called the hauling part. Thus, the part of a tackle to which power is applied.

falling damps Poisonous gases that are heavier than air, such as carbon dioxide. Humidity, condensed fog. Depression, unconsciousness.

falling-sickness Epilepsy, a disease of the nervous system characterized in its severer forms by convulsions.

Falmouth A port on the English Channel in southwestern Cornwall, England.

falsum in uno, falsum in omnibus False in one thing, false in all things (Latin).

fancy-line A rope used to overhaul the brails (*see* BRAIL UP) of some FORE-AND-AFT sails; a line threaded through a BLOCK at the jaws of a GAFF and used to lower the sail.

fanfaronade Boisterous, arrogant language; bragging.

fanlight A fan-shaped window over a door. Loosely, any window over a door.

"Farewell and Adieu" A traditional English sailors' drinking song that goes as follows:

Farewell and Adieu to you, gay Spanish ladies!
Farewell and Adieu to you, ladies of Spain!
For we've received orders for to sail for old England,
But we hope in a short time to see you again.

We'll rant and we'll roar like true British sailors,
We'll rant and we'll roar across the salt seas,
Until we strike soundings in the channel of old England;
From Ushant to Scilly is thirty-five leagues.

Then we hove our ship to, with the wind at sou'west, boys,
We hove our ship to, for to strike soundings clear;
Then we filled the main topsail and bore right away, boys,
Up the channel of old England our course we did steer.

The first land we made it was called the Deadman,
Next, Ramshead off Plymouth, Start, Portland, and Wight;
We sailed by Beachy, by Fairleigh, and Dungeness,
And hove our ship to, off the South Foreland light.

Then a signal was made for the grand fleet to anchor,
All in the downs, that night for to meet;
Then stand by your stoppers, let go your shank-painters,
Haul all your clew-garnets, stick out tacks and sheets.

Now let every man toss off his full bumper,
And let every man toss off his full bowl;
We'll drink and be jolly, and drown melancholy:
So here's a good health to all true-hearted souls.

farinaceous   Made of flour or meal or having a mealy texture.

farrier   A blacksmith. Also, someone who treats the diseases of horses.

farrow   A litter of pigs.

farthing   A quarter of a particular denomination of money or measure. Specifically, a coin worth a quarter of a penny, at one time of silver, later of copper or bronze.

fascine   A bundle of brush or sticks tightly bound at close intervals and used for such purposes as filling ditches or constructing batteries.

fashion-pieces   On a ship, the underwater timbers forming the shape of the STERN.

fatherlasher   The name used to refer to two species of sea fish, *Cottus bubalis* and *C. scorpius*.

Father Smith   An organ built by the German-born Bernhard Schmidt (c. 1630–1708), who moved to England in 1666 after the Restoration when organs were again in use in churches. Among the churches that he and his two nephews built organs for were St. Margaret's, Westminster (1675), St. Paul's Cathedral (1697), and Temple Church (1684).

fathom   Originally the length of the outstretched arms to the tips of the longest fingers but later standardized as six feet, the measure used in taking SOUNDINGS of the depth of water. Also, a measure of cord and anchor chain.

fatigue-party   A group of soldiers on fatigue-duty, which is extra work often assigned as punishment.

faute de mieux   For lack of a better alternative (French).

fearnought   A stout woolen cloth used as clothing in cold weather. Also, a thick felt used to cover the outside door of a powder MAGAZINE, portholes, and HATCHWAYS during battle. Also called "dreadnought screen."

febrifuge   Any drug that removes fever.

febrile   Affected by or suffering from fever; pertaining to fever.

fedai   One of the fidayoun, literally "men of self-sacrifice," a member of the ASSASSINS.

felucca   Italian word for a small Mediterranean vessel with LATEEN sails on two MASTS, sometimes also equipped with oars, used chiefly for coastal trading voyages. Similar to the *felouque* in France, *falua* in Spain, and *fallua* in Portugal. *See* illustration, page 63.

Fencibles   A part-time organization of fishermen and boatmen, commanded by naval officers for local defense against invasions.

fender   A bumper made of various materials, such as pieces of old CABLE or canvas bags of cork, and hung over a vessel's side to prevent chafing or collision with a wharf or another vessel.

fenum habent in cornu   They have hay on their horns (Latin). Figuratively: they are dangerous men. The term refers to the practice of padding the horns of menacing oxen with hay, both to soften the blow and to serve as a warning about the animals' nature. It was used in an ode by Horace to describe a dangerous man.

Fernando Poo   Known since 1979 as Bioko, an island off the coast of West Africa, 60 miles off Cameroon in the Bight of Biafra.

Ferrol   Seaport on the northwest coast of Spain and the site of a pre-TRAFALGAR skirmish between Admiral CALDER and Admiral VIL-LENEUVE.

fetor   An offensive smell; a stench.

fettle   Condition, state, or spirits, as when a person is said to be "in high fettle."

fib   To strike or beat, to deliver blows in quick succession.

Ficus religiosa   The BANYAN or Indian fig tree, a remarkable East Indian tree with branches that send shoots to the ground, which take root and support their parent branches. Extending in this way, one tree covers a great expanse of ground.

fid   A square bar of wood or iron with a shoulder at one end, used to support the weight of the TOPMAST and also the TOPGALLANT MAST. Also, a tapered hand tool for opening up the strands of a rope when splicing.

fiddle   A rack or rail or other contrivance to prevent dishes and cups from rolling off a ship's table in bad weather.

Fiddler's Green   A sailor's imagined paradise, free of the hardships of the sea and rich with wine, women, and song.

fiferail   The uppermost railing around the QUARTERDECK and POOP. Also, the rails around the MASTs holding BELAYING PINs for the running RIGGING.

figgy-dowdy   A West Country suet pudding with raisins, a favorite of Cornish and Devon men.

figure-head An ornamental carving, usually a bust or full-length figure, placed over the CUTWATER of a ship and a point of pride with seamen.

file An artful, cunning, or shrewd person; a fellow or COVE. In military use, a small column of men.

filibeg A kilt.

filioque Meaning "and from or to the Son" (Latin), the word "filioque" was inserted in the Western version of the Nicene creed to assert the doctrine that the Holy Ghost proceeds from the Son as well as from the Father, which is not admitted by the Eastern Church.

fin whale *also* **finner** *or* **finner-whale** Whale of the genus *Balaenoptera*, especially the rorqual, which has a dorsal fin and measures 60 to 90 feet in length.

finger-post A post at a crossroads with one or more arms (often ending in a pointing finger) to indicate directions; a guide-post.

Finisterre Cape on the northwest Atlantic coast of Spain, its westernmost point.

fire-bote The right of a tenant to take firewood from a landlord's estate.

fireman On board a warship, four men from each gun crew were detailed as boarders, and two of these acted as firemen in the event the ship caught fire during action. The ship's fire engine was manned by the second division of boarders, while the first division and carpenters cleared away obstacles.

fire-ship A vessel filled with combustibles and explosives and set to drift among enemy ships to destroy them. Also, one suffering from venereal disease; a prostitute.

firk To contrive to make a living. To get money from a person, especially by cheating or robbing.

firkin A small cask for liquids, fish, butter, etc., originally containing a quarter of a barrel or half a kilderkin. As a measure of capacity, half a kilderkin. (The barrel, kilderkin, and firkin varied in capacity according to the commodity.)

firman   An edict or order issued by an Oriental sovereign, especially the sultan of Turkey but also by the BASHAWs of North Africa; a grant, license, passport, permit.

First Lieutenant   The executive officer of a ship, usually the second in command.

First of June   *See* GLORIOUS FIRST OF JUNE.

first-rate   *See* RATE.

fish   A long piece of timber lashed to a MAST or YARD to strengthen it. To fish is to fasten a fish upon a BEAM, MAST, or YARD to strengthen it or to mend a broken SPAR with a fish or fishes. To "fish the anchor" is draw up the FLUKEs to the GUNWALE and secure the anchor there.

fish-fag   A female hawker of fish; a fishwife.

Fitzherbert, Mrs. (1756–1837)   Born Maria Anne Smythe, as a Roman Catholic widow, she secretly married the future King George IV, when he was the Prince of Wales, in 1785. Under the Royal Marriage Act of 1772, this marriage was invalid, since it was made without King George III's consent; the prince later denied that any marriage had taken place. When Prince George married the Princess Caroline in 1795, he temporarily stopped seeing Mrs. Fitzherbert, but resumed a connection with her with the Pope's consent. He finally broke off the relationship in 1803.

Flag-captain   The captain of a FLAGSHIP.

Flag-lieutenant   An officer acting as an aide-de-camp to an ADMIRAL.

flag officer   An ADMIRAL, Vice-Admiral, Rear-Admiral, or COMMODORE.

flag rank   The rank of ADMIRAL, Vice-Admiral, Rear-Admiral, or COMMODORE.

flag-share   An ADMIRAL's or COMMODORE's share of PRIZE-MONEY: one eighth.

flagship   A ship bearing an ADMIRAL's or COMMODORE's flag of command.

flambeau   A torch, especially one with several thick wicks dipped in wax; a lit torch.

The Fleet Prison as seen from Farringdon Street in 1830

flat   Of a sail, to make it flat or close against the MAST; to make it taut.

fleam   A surgical instrument for letting blood or for lancing the gums. Also, a lancet.

fleam-tooth   FLEAM-shaped tooth of a saw; that is, with the outline of a low Gothic arch.

Fleet Prison   Taking its name from the Fleet stream flowing into the Thames, a London prison infamous for the cruelties inflicted on its prisoners. Dating back to Norman times, it became notorious as the prison to which people sentenced by the Court of Star Chamber and, afterward, debtors, were sent. Burned down in the Great Fire of 1666, it was rebuilt, but was destroyed in the GORDON RIOTS in 1780, rebuilt in 1781–82, finally closed in 1842.

flemish   To coil in a FLEMISH FAKE.

Flemish fake   A method of coiling a rope into concentric circles that don't overlap so that the whole is rendered flat and solid to walk on and so that the rope will run freely when needed.

flense   To cut up and slice the fat from a whale or seal. To flay or skin.

flint-lock   A gunlock in which the hammer is struck against a flint to produce sparks that ignite the priming in the flash-pan.

flip   Beer and spirits, sweetened and heated with a hot iron.

flogging around the fleet   A severe form of punishment in which the convicted was rowed from ship to ship and lashed a dozen strokes beside each while the crew looked on and the drums on board beat the "Rogue's March."

flog the glass   To shake the WATCH-GLASS in order to speed up the passage of the sand inside and shorten the WATCH.

flotilla   A small fleet of ships or a fleet of boats or small vessels.

flowing sheet   When the lines, or SHEETS, controlling the sails are eased up or slackened off. When the wind is abeam.

fluke   One of the broad triangular plates on each arm of the anchor, which helps hold the anchor in place on the bottom. Seamen pronounced the word "flue."

flummery   A dish made of wheat flour or oatmeal, steeped in water and turned sour. Various custardlike sweet dishes made with milk, flour, and eggs. Also, empty flattery.

fluor albus   A mucous discharge from the uterus or vagina.

flush *or* slush   A seaman's name for grease collected from fat drippings.

flute   A distinctive ship design developed by the Dutch for an inexpensive and efficient cargo ship to carry bulky cargo with relatively few seamen and few, if any, guns. Also called a "fluit" or "flyboat."

flux   Diarrhea. *See also* BLOODY FLUX.

fly   Alert and aware, sharp. Also the length of a flag from the staff to the extreme end that waves in the breeze.

flying fox   A fruit-eating bat found in India, Madagascar, Southeast Asia, and Australia.

flying jib   A light sail set before the JIB, uppermost on the flying jib-BOOM.

flying squid   Also called the sea-arrow, a mollusk of the genus *Ommastrephes*.

fob   A small pocket in the waistband of breeches for a watch, money, or other valuable.

fo'c'sle *or* **forecastle**   A short raised DECK at the FORE end of a vessel, originally for archers to shoot arrows into enemy vessels. In a MAN-OF-WAR, the part of the upper deck forward of the FOREMAST. Also, a generic term for the crew, whose QUARTERS were beneath this deck, as in a "forecastle hand."

foeda est in coitu et brevis voluptas   There is a filthiness in sex and only brief pleasure (Latin).

foin   To thrust with a pointed weapon, to lunge, push.

folie circulaire   Literally, encircling madness. A form of insanity in which the patient has intervals of lucidity (French).

fons et origo   The source and origin (Latin).

foolscap   An image of a jester's pointed cap with bells used as a watermark for paper. Hence, a sheet of paper.

footpad   A highwayman who robs on foot.

foot-rope   A rope beneath a YARD for the sailors to stand on while FURLing or REEFing. *See also* HORSE.

fore   A part of a ship that lies near the BOW or in that direction; also, parts connected with the FOREMAST, as in fore ROYAL, the name of one of the upper sails on the foremast.

fore-and-aft   Placed or directed in the line of the vessel's length. Of sails: JIBS, STAYSAILS, and GAFF sails. A vessel rigged with such sails, as opposed to a SQUARE-RIGGED vessel.

forecastle   *See* FO'C'SLE.

forecourse   The largest and lowest square sail on a ship's FOREMAST. *See* illustration, page 64.

forefoot   The foremost piece of the KEEL or a timber that ends the keel in front and forms a rest for the STEM's lower end.

Foreign Office   From 1783 the department of the Secretary of State for Foreign Affairs. Also, the building that houses this department.

foremast   The forward lower-MAST in a vessel.

foremast man   A sailor below the rank of PETTY OFFICER.

forepeak   The extreme end of the forehold in the angle of the BOWS.

fore reach   The distance a ship's momentum will shoot her up into the wind when the BOW is swinging that way while TACKing. To fore reach is to shoot ahead or to draw ahead of another sailing vessel when CLOSE-HAULED.

foresail   In a SQUARE-RIGGED vessel, another name for the FORECOURSE, the principal sail set on the FOREMAST and the lowest on that mast. Above the foresail came the fore lower TOPSAIL, the fore upper topsail, the fore TOPGALLANT, the fore ROYAL, and the fore SKYSAIL. The triangular sail attached to the FORESTAY in a FORE-AND-AFT rigged vessel.

fore-tack   The rope securing the WEATHER corner of the FORESAIL.

foretop   The top of a FOREMAST and the small platform there. Also, one of the divisions of a ship's crew.

foretop man   One of the men stationed in the FORETOP.

fore topmast   The MAST above the FOREMAST.

foreyard   The lowest and largest YARD on the FOREMAST.

fork-tailed petrel   A small seabird with black and white plumage and long wings.

forlan   A lively Venetian dance, also its music.

forme   A body of type secured in a metal frame for printing at one impression.

Formidable, **H.M.S.**   The first ship in the Royal Navy by this name was captured from the French in 1759 at the battle of Quiberon Bay. In 1777, a second rate by the same name was launched at Chatham, and at the Battle of the SAINTS in 1782 she served as the FLAGSHIP of Admiral Sir George RODNEY.

forrarder   Farther forward.

fother   To seal a leak by lowering a sail over the side of the ship and positioning it to be sucked into the hole by the rushing sea.

Fouché, Joseph, Duc d'Otrante (1759–1820)   Napoleon's Minister of Police, who set up a feared police apparatus with an extensive network of informants, allowing him to ferret out real and imagined plots against the emperor, which he ruthlessly crushed.

***Foudroyant,* H.M.S.**   This name first entered the Royal Navy when the 80-gun *Foudroyant* was captured from the French in 1758. In 1798, the second *Foudroyant,* a second rate of 80 guns, was launched at PLY-MOUTH and later served as the FLAGSHIP of both Lord NELSON and Lord KEITH. She was wrecked in 1897. Following this, the 46-gun *Trincoma-lee,* built in 1817, was renamed FOUDROYANT and remains afloat today at Hartlepool.

foul   To entangle an anchor or a CABLE. To jam, block, or make incapable of working. To run afoul of, collide with.

four-in-hand   A vehicle with four horses driven by one person.

four-pounder   A gun that propels a four-pound shot.

fowling-piece   A light gun for shooting wild fowl.

fox   A strand formed by twisting several rope-yarns together and used as a SEIZING or to weave PAUNCHes, which were used around YARDS and RIGGING to prevent wear.

fragilis ratis   Fragile raft (Latin).

framework   Knitting or weaving done on a stocking-frame or knitting machine. Also, a knitting machine.

Franciscan   Of or belonging to the order of St. Francis. A friar of the order founded by St. Francis of Assisi in 1209.

francolin   A partridge of Southern Asia and Africa.

frank   The superscribed signature of a person, such as a member of Parliament, entitled to send letters free of charge. A letter or envelope bearing such a superscription.

Frank   A name given by the nations bordering on the LEVANT to a person of Western nationality, from the short-lived Frankish kingdoms established by French crusaders in the 11th and 12th centuries.

frap   To bind tightly.

freeholder   One who possesses a freehold estate, an estate held in fee or for life.

Freemason   Originally a skilled stoneworker. Later, an international society promoting brotherly feeling among its members.

freight-money   Payment for conveyance of freight.

freshen   Of the wind, to increase in strength. Also, to shift the place where a rope catches on something in order to relieve chafing. Thus, "to freshen the HAWSE" means to pay out more CABLE to relieve wear in one spot. Figuratively, to take a few nips of whisky or rum. "To freshen way" means to increase the speed.

Friar   A member of a mendicant order, such as the Franciscans, who originally lived a monastic life and generally did not believe in personal or communal property.

Friend   A member of the Society of Friends, a Quaker.

frieze   A kind of coarse woolen cloth, with a nap usually on one side only.

frigate   A fast three-masted fully RIGged ship of the fifth or sixth rate, carrying 20 to 50 guns on the MAIN deck, with a raised QUARTERDECK and FORECASTLE. Used for scouting and cruising. "FRIGATEs are the eyes of a fleet," said NELSON, who also stated in 1798, "Was I to die at this moment want of frigates would be found stamped on my heart."

The frigate bird, *Tachypetes aquilus*, also called the man-o'-war bird

frigate bird A large, swift predatory bird of the genus *Fregata*, found near land in the tropical and warmer temperate seas. It has long, pointed wings and the highest surface-area-to-body-weight ratio of any bird. Frigate birds are uniquely graceful flyers that hover and swoop to take food from the surface of the sea, rarely entering the water, and are known to rob other birds. Also called man-o'-war bird.

fritillary Any plant of the genus *Fritillaria* of the lily family, especially wild snake's head, which grows in damp meadows and has drooping purple or white bell-shaped flowers, and crown imperial.

frock A woolen GUERNSEY or JERSEY worn by sailors. Also, a coat cut long and similar in style to the civilian frock-coat, worn on semiformal occasions, such as Sundays and during WATCHes in harbor.

front-fish A PAUNCH, a wooden covering on the FORE side of a MAST to preserve it from chafing when masts or SPARs are lowered or raised.

froward Perverse, hard to deal with, ungovernable. Also, in a wider sense, bad or naughty.

frowsty Fusty, having an unpleasant smell.

frowzy Ill-smelling from being dirty, unwashed, or ill-ventilated. Untidy, soiled, unkempt.

fruit-bat A genus of tropical and subtropical bats having membranous wings, also known as FLYING FOXes.

frumenty A porridgelike dish made of wheat boiled in milk and seasoned with cinnamon, sugar, and sometimes dried fruits.

fuddle To intoxicate; to stupefy, muddle, or confuse, as with drink.

fug A close, stuffy atmosphere, especially in an overcrowded room with poor ventilation.

fui non sum non curo *See* NON FUI NON SUM NON CURO.

full toss In cricket, the delivery of a ball that doesn't touch the ground in its flight between the wickets.

fulmar A PETREL about the size of the common gull.

fulvous vulture The golden vulture, a very large bird of prey that feeds on carrion and has a featherless head and neck.

funnel   A cylindrical band of metal, especially one fitted onto the heads of the TOPGALLANT and ROYAL MASTs, over which the EYES of the RIGGING are placed.

furcula   A forked bone below the neck of a bird, the wishbone.

furl   To roll up and bind a sail neatly upon its YARD or BOOM. In *Post Captain*, Admiral Harte chastizes Aubrey for furling his sails in the bunt rather than in a body. At sea, sails were normally furled in a bunt, that is, hauled up under the yard and secured. In the late 18th century, a new system, furling in a body, was introduced to reduce windage aloft, to better protect the canvas, and for aesthetic reasons. For the TOPSAIL, for example, this involved gathering the loose part of the sail into the TOP. While many seamen criticized this as a "newfangled fashion," it became commonly used in harbor.

furlong   An eighth of an English mile, or 220 yards.

furze   A spiny evergreen shrub with yellow flowers that grows throughout Europe. Also called gorse or whins.

fusil   A light musket or firelock or a soldier armed with a fusil.

fustic   A yellow dye extracted from the wood of *Chlorophora tinctoria*, a tree native to America and the WEST INDIES.

futtock plate   An iron plate in the ship's TOP for securing the TOPMAST RIGGING.

futtock shrouds *or* puttocks   After about 1820, these ran from the futtock plates on the TOP to a band around the lower mast. In Aubrey's day, however, they were made fast to the futtock stave and the lower SHROUDs at the level of the lower YARD. This was inherently less sturdy than the later arrangement, since the LEE shrouds slackened off as the vessel rolled, and additional stiffening in the form of CAT-HARPINGS was needed.

futtock stave   A SPAR, iron rod, or stiff length of rope, placed where the futtock shrouds were made fast to the lower SHROUDs.

gabble   Voluble, noisy, confused, unintelligible talk.

gaby   A simpleton; a foolish fellow.

Gadarene Swine   A reference to the story in Matthew 8:28 of the swine that rushed down a steep cliff into the sea and drowned.

gaff   A wooden SPAR used to extend the heads of FORE-AND-AFT sails that are not set on STAYS.

gaff-topsail   A triangular or quadrilateral sail, the head of which is extended on a small GAFF that HOISTs on the TOPMAST.

gale   A wind of an intensity between that of a strong breeze and a storm. In the 19th century, it was more precisely defined as blowing at a speed of between 28 and 55 nautical miles per hour. In a gale, the waves are high with crests that break into SPINDRIFT, while in a strong gale the crests topple and roll and dense streaks of foam blow in the wind.

Gall, Franz Joseph (1758–1828)   Viennese physician who, with Johann Caspar Spurzheim (1776–1832), introduced the theory that the functions of the brain can be localized in the cerebral cortex, in four volumes published in 1810–1819. Although they made some important additions to cerebral anatomy, they were best known for introducing the pseudoscience of PHRENOLOGY.

galleon Originally a ship of war shorter in length but higher than the GALLEY and with a lower FORECASTLE than was previously common in large ships, making it more maneuverable. It became a principal trading ship for the Spaniards and a much valued PRIZE of English PRIVATEERS.

gallery A balcony built outside the body of a ship, at the STERN (stern-gallery) or at the QUARTERS (quarter-gallery), often ornately carved and highly decorated and protected from the weather by large glass windows.

gallery-ladder A rope ladder hung over each GALLERY and the STERN for boarding from a boat, primarily in foul weather.

galley A low sea-going vessel propelled by oars, once common in the Mediterranean and still used as a warship in the Baltic in the 1790s. A large open rowboat used on the Thames by custom-house officers and by PRESS-GANGS, as well as by the Captains of MEN-OF-WAR. Also, the kitchen on a ship.

gallinaceous Of or belonging to the order Gallinae, which includes domestic poultry and other birds such as pheasants and grouse. Resembling a cock, "cocky."

gallinule A wading bird of the RAIL family, typified by the moorhen.

galliot Originally, a small GALLEY or boat propelled by up to 20 rowers and with a single MAST and sail, often used to chase and board enemy vessels in the Mediterranean. Also, a one- or two-masted Dutch cargo boat or fishing vessel with a BLUFF and rounded BOW. *See* illustration, page 61.

gallipot A small earthen glazed pot often used by apothecaries for ointments and medicines.

gallows The wooden frame, consisting of cross-pieces on the small BITTS at the MAIN and FORE HATCHWAYS in flush-decked vessels, for stowing spare SPARS. The ship's boats were also stowed here.

gallows-bitt A wooden frame used by fishing boats under sail to rest their MASTs on when they stopped to work their nets.

Gambier, Admiral Lord James (*1756–1833*) As captain of H.M.S. *Defiance*, Gambier was the first to penetrate the French battle line at the GLORIOUS FIRST OF JUNE. Later served as one of the Lords Commissioners of the ADMIRALTY (1795–1801, 1804–1806, 1807–1808), as governor and COMMANDER-IN-CHIEF of NEWFOUNDLAND, and as commander of the CHANNEL FLEET. Well known for his evangelical activities in the Navy, in 1824, Gambier was one of the first major donors to establish Kenyon College in an Ohio village named after him.

game of fives A game that emerged in England in the 16th century in which a ball is hit by the hand against the front wall of a three-sided court.

gammon *or* gammoning To LASH the BOWSPRIT with ropes to the STEM or CUTWATER of a ship in order to secure the bowsprit in place, and the lashing itself. The ham of a swine. Also, talk, chatter, nonsense for deceiving simpletons only, humbug.

gang-board A plank—usually with cleats or steps nailed on it—for walking on, especially into or out of a boat. Also, the boards ending the HAMMOCK-NETTINGs at either side of the entrance from the ACCOMMODATION-LADDER to the deck.

ganglion A node in which many nerves are joined. Maturin wishes (in vain) to experiment with the giant ganglion of a squid, a laboratory preparation still used to study the physiology of nerves.

gangrene A visible mortification of part of the body due to infection or loss of blood supply.

gangway On deep-waisted ships, a narrow platform from the QUARTERDECK to the FORECASTLE for convenience in getting from one to the other. A gang plank connecting ship to shore or to another ship. A narrow passage left in a laden hold. "To bring to the gangway" means to punish a seaman by binding him to a GRATING for flogging.

gannet A large fish-eating seabird that breeds in colonies in northern coastal regions. The solan goose.

gantline *or* **girtline**   A rope passing through a single BLOCK on the head of the lower MASTS used to HOIST up the RIGGING. The gantline is the first rope employed to rig a ship.

gaol   British spelling of "jail."

gaol-fever   A virulent form of typhus occurring in crowded jails and often in ships and other confined places.

garboard strake *or* **garboard**   The first range of planks running along and outside a ship's bottom next to the KEEL. Also, the seam nearest the keel, the hardest to CAULK.

garçon manqué   Tomboy (French).

garland   A multipurpose word on shipboard. A collar of rope around a MAST that supports the standing RIGGING and prevents it from rubbing the mast. A carved wooden wreath surrounding a FORECASTLE or QUARTERDECK gun port. Also, a net hung above each MESS for the stowing of provisions safe from vermin. *See also* SHOT-GARLAND.

garnishee   A third party from whom money or property belonging to a debtor or defendant has been seized as a result of a suit brought by the creditor or plaintiff.

garstrake   *See* GARBOARD STRAKE.

Garter   The badge of the highest order of English knighthood; membership of this order; and the order itself. The founding of the Order of the Garter around 1340 is attributed to Edward III. It has been traditionally asserted that the garter was that of the Countess of Salisbury, which fell off while she was dancing with the King. He picked it up and tied it on his own leg, saying to those present, *Honi soit qui mal y pense* ("Shamed be he who thinks evil of it"). The garter, that is, the order's badge, is a dark-blue velvet ribbon, edged and buckled with gold and embroidered in gold with the above words. It is worn below the left knee. Garters also form part of the ornament of the collar worn by the knights of the order.

gaskets   Short lengths of plaited cord or SENNET used to secure a furled sail to its YARD.

gasteropod *or* **gastropod**   Mollusks of the class Gastropoda, including snails and slugs, characterized by the ventral position of the muscular locomotive organ.

gastrocnemius   Calf muscle.

gaucherie   Want of tact or grace, awkwardness.

Gazette   *The London Gazette*, the official government journal, published twice a week since 1665, listing government appointments, promotions, and other official public notices. It was particularly important to Naval officers, since all promotions, honors, and the mention of individuals in dispatches and reports of actions were announced, or "gazetted," in it.

gecko   A house lizard living in warm regions, most notable for its peculiar cry and climbing ability.

Généreux   A French 74, one of two that escaped capture or destruction at the Battle of the NILE in 1798. NELSON's squadron took her in 1800. At the time Second Lieutenant of the *FOUDROYANT*, the fictional Aubrey takes her into Port Mahon, MINORCA, just as the historical Thomas COCHRANE did. Cochrane was forced to go aloft himself in a gale to keep the damaged ship afloat, and was recommended by Lord Keith (*see* ELPHINSTONE) for promotion.

genet   A civet-cat native to southern Europe, western Asia, and Africa. The common species (*Genetta vulgaris*) is found in the south of France.

geneva   Dutch gin, a spirit distilled from grain and flavored with the juice of juniper berries. Made in Holland, it is also called Hollands, formerly Hollands geneva. It is often written with a capital *G* by confusion with Geneva, Switzerland. "Geneva" is actually the English form of the Dutch word *jenever*, which means "juniper."

gentian   Any plant belonging to the genus *Gentiana*, especially *G. lutea*, the source of a tonic often used to stimulate digestion and the circulation.

George III (*1738–1820*)   George William Frederick, grandson of George II, whom he succeeded in 1760 as King of Great Britain and Ireland and Elector of Hanover (King of Hanover from 1815). He ruled from 1760 until 1810, when his eldest son, George, Prince of Wales, was appointed regent for the remainder of his reign. He suffered periods of mental derangement at various times, but they did not become totally debilitating until after the death of his favorite daughter, Princess Amelia, in 1810.

German flute   A transverse flute, blown through an orifice on the side near the upper end, which in the 18th century replaced the flute that was blown through a mouthpiece at the end.

ghee   Butter made from buffalo's or cow's milk boiled to resemble oil in consistency.

gibbet   Originally, gallows. Later, an upright post with a projecting arm where the bodies of criminals were hung after execution.

gib cat   A name used in Northern England for a male cat. In later dialectal use, a cat that has been castrated.

gibbous   Convex, protuberant. Said of the moon or a planet when the illuminated portion exceeds a semicircle but is less than a circle.

GIBRALTAR
A strategic rocky promontory situated at the western end of the Mediterranean Sea and ideal for controlling the Strait of Gibraltar, the passage between the Mediterranean and the Atlantic Ocean. Captured by Dutch and British forces in 1704 during the War of the Spanish Succession and transferred to Britain by the Treaty of Utrecht in 1713, Gibraltar was continually under siege by the French and Spanish from 1779 to 1783. Gibraltar, which is three miles long and less than one wide, is connected to Spain by a sandy isthmus of about a mile. From the east, Gibraltar appears as a series of formidable cliffs. The limestone and shale ridge known as the Rock rises abruptly to 1,380 feet at Rock Gun, its northernmost summit, but is slightly higher at its southern end. The Rock shelves down to the sea at Europa Point, which faces Morocco, 20 miles to the south. Wild olive and pine trees grow on the Upper Rock, where the Barbary ape, the only wild monkey in Europe, lives. Gibraltar's Southport Gate, part of the town's old fortifications, was built in 1552, in the time of the Holy Roman Emperor Charles V, and was known as the Africa Gate.

   A sloop on duty near the Rock of Gibraltar, pictured on the next page. On the evening of November 6, 1799, His Majesty's Sloop *Speedy* (O'Brian's model for the *Sophie*), commanded by Captain Jahleel Brenton, and her convoy, a transport ship carrying wine for the fleet and a merchant BRIG bound for Trieste, were attacked in Gibraltar Bay by a French privateer XEBEC of eight guns and 12 Spanish GUNBOATS, two of which were SCHOONERS, carrying two 24-

pounders and 50 men each, while the others each carried a single 24-pounder and 40 men. The *Speedy* successfully fought off the attackers, and the transport worked around Europa Point through heavy fire, while the brig took advantage of a strong westerly wind after dark, carrying on to Trieste. The Spanish gunboats, which lost 11 men, fled to Fort Barbary, then to Malaga, leaving the trade unmolested in the Strait of Gibraltar for two months.

Captain Brenton, from an American Loyalist family that returned to England during the American Revolution, wrote this official letter to Admiral Duckworth concerning the event:

Speedy, Gibraltar, Nov. 21st, 1799

Sir,

I have the honour to inform you, that on the 6th instant coming into Gibraltar with two Vessels under Convoy, a Ship and a Brig, we were attacked by twelve of the Spanish Gun-boats from Algesiras; having a commanding breeze, we were soon enabled to rescue the Ship; the Gun-boats then united their efforts upon the Brig, but bearing up through their Line with a well-directed fire, we, in a short time, obliged them to relinquish that design also, and take shelter under the guns of Fort Barbary. The situation of the Speedy prevented my pursuing the advantage we had gained, having most of our running rigging cut away, our main-top-sail-yards shot through, and our fore-rigging much cut, besides the water being up to the lower-deck from shot received below the water-line. Not being able to carry sail upon the larboard tack, I was under the necessity of running for Tetuan Bay to stop the leaks, and arrived here the day following.

I cannot say too much in praise of Lieutenant Parker, Mr. Marshall, the Master, and the remainder of the Officers and men under my Command. From their spirited exertions, and strict attention to their duty, we were enabled to save our Convoy and His Majesty's Sloop.

I beg leave to enclose a return of our killed and wounded, and at the same time to add, that much praise is due to Mr. George Robinson, Master of the Transport Unity, for the manner he worked his Ship during a vary galling fire. I have the honour to be, Sir,

Your very obedient Servant,
Jah. Brenton.

Killed—Patrick Blake, and William Pring, Seamen.
Wounded—Thomas Rilay, Seaman.

From *The Naval Chronicle*, vol. 5. (*Reproduced courtesy of the Mariners' Museum*)

gig   A light, narrow, CLINKER-built ship's boat, adapted either for rowing or sailing and generally used by the COMMANDER. *See* illustration, page 73.

gigot   A leg of lamb, veal, or another meat, especially when cooked.

gimbal   An instrument usually consisting of a pair of rings moving on pivots that allows a ship's compass, chronometer, or other gauge to remain level while the ship PITCHes and rolls.

gingall   A heavy musket fired from a rest or a light gun mounted on a swivel, sometimes on a carriage. Used primarily in China and India.

gingerbread work   The carved and gilded decorations on the hulls of large ships.

glabrous   Smooth; hairless, bald.

glacis   A sloping bank, specifically one that extends in front of ramparts, allowing it to be swept by the defenders' fire.

gladwin   Variation of "gladdon," a popular name for the iris.

glass   Shipboard name for BAROMETER, sand-glass, and telescope. In the last case, short for long-glass or spy-glass.

glaucous   Of a pale green color passing into bluish white or grayish blue. In botany, covered with bloom.

glebe   The soil of the earth, the source of vegetable products. A cultivated land. A piece of land assigned to a clergyman as part of his BENEFICE.

gleet   White putrid discharge from the penis that is characteristic of gonorrhea.

glim   A light of any kind. A candle, a lantern.

glissando   A slurring or sliding effect produced by a musical instrument; portamento.

Glorious First of June   On June 1, 1794, in the first great fleet battle of the French Revolutionary War (1793–1801), a British force of 25 ships of the line commanded by Admiral Lord HOWE defeated a French force of 26 ships commanded by Villaret de Joyeuse in the North Atlantic about 400 miles from the coast of USHANT off Brittany. Howe's fleet captured six ships and destroyed one. Although it was a much-celebrated moral victory for the British, the French achieved their main goal, which was to protect a convoy of grain ships arriving from America.

glottis   The opening at the upper part of the trachea between the vocal chords, which by dilatation and contraction contributes to voice modulation.

glover   One who makes or sells gloves.

Gluck, Christoph Willibald (1714–1787)   Born in Bavaria, an opera composer who worked in various cities, including Prague, Vienna, Milan, London, Naples, and Paris. His dispute with Niccola Piccinni (1728–1800) divided Paris into Gluckists, who supported the French style of opera, and Piccinnists, who supported the Italian style. Gluck won over Parisians with his 1799 opera *Iphigénie en Tauride*.

glyconic   A lyrical epithet of three trochees and a dactyl; also a poem or stanza composed or consisting of such verses. This type of verse is most generally associated with Catullus and Horace.

Gmelin, Johann Georg (*1709–1755*)   A German botanist and professor who explored Siberia.

Gmelin, Leopold (*1788–1853*)   A nephew of Johann Gmelin, Leopold was a professor of medicine and chemistry and the discoverer of potassium ferricyanide, also known as Gmelin's salt. His *Handbuch der inorganischen Chemie* (1817–19) is still in use.

Gneisenau, August Wilhelm Anton (*1760–1831*)   A Prussian field marshal, who was BLÜCHER's chief of staff during the WATERLOO campaign. After Blücher was dismounted and briefly lost in the fray during the Battle of LIGNY, Gneisenau led a retreat 16 miles north to Wavre, parallel to WELLINGTON's line, not away from it, allowing the Prussians to play a crucial role at Waterloo two days later. Wellington called Gneisenau's decision "the decisive moment of the century."

gnosce teipsum   Know thyself (Latin, from the Greek *gnothi seauton*).

Gnostic   A member of certain heretical sects among the early Christians who believed that knowledge of spiritual truth was essential to salvation.

gob   Among its many meanings, mouth.

gobbet   A portion, piece, or fragment of something divided; a piece of raw flesh.

Godfrey's Cordial   Named after Thomas Godfrey of Hunsdon, Hertfordshire, this early 18th-century household panacea included sassafras and opium.

Godoy, Manuel de, "Prince of the Peace" (*1767–1851*)   After the Peace of AMIENS, Godoy succumbed to French bribes and blackmail and allied Spain with France against the Third Coalition (see page 25), hence Maturin's line, "remember Godoy has betrayed the kingdom to France," in trying to persuade BUSTAMENTE to surrender the Spanish treasure SQUADRON in 1804.

goffering-iron   An iron tool used for crimping, or goffering, lace, frills, and the like.

going large   *See* LARGE.

golden calf   The idol set up by Aaron and the similar images set up by Jeroboam in the Bible. In proverbs, a reference to the worship of wealth.

golden-eye   A sea duck of the genus *Clangula*.

Goliath, **H.M.S.**   The 74-gun ship in which Captain Thomas Foley spearheaded the British attack on the French at the Battle of the NILE on August 1, 1798. Leading four other ships, Foley managed to negotiate the shoals and penetrate between the shore batteries and the French fleet. Built in 1781, the *Goliath* was cut down to a 58-gun fourth RATE in 1812 and broken up in 1815.

Golovnin, Vasily Mikhailovich (1776–1831)   A Russian vice-admiral who circumnavigated the globe from 1817 to 1819 and wrote books about the voyages. Earlier, he served as a volunteer in the British Navy.

Goodwin Sands   A treacherous underwater bank of shifting sands in the entrance to the English Channel from the North Sea, about six miles off the east coast of Kent, that forms protection for the anchorage called the DOWNS off Deal, Kent.

gooseberry   The edible berry or fruit of any of the thorny shrubs of the saxifrage family. Also, a currant.

goose-wing   On a SQUARE-RIGGED ship, having the BUNTLINES and LEE-CLEW of a COURSE HAULed up and the WEATHER-CLEW down for SCUDding under, when the wind is too strong to set the entire sail.

Gordon Riots   Anti-Catholic riots in London causing a breakdown of law and order in London for several days in June 1780 in which troops were called out and 285 rioters were killed, 173 wounded, and 139 arrested. The riots occurred after Lord George Gordon (1751–1793), a member of Parliament and leader of the Protestant Association, led a procession of about 50,000 people to present a petition to Parliament asking to repeal the clauses in the 1778 Catholic Relief Act that had removed restrictions on the activities of Catholic priests. After the riots, Gordon—a graduate of Eton who had served as a Lieutenant in the Navy—was tried for high treason but acquitted. Later he became a Jew and took the name Israel Abraham George Gordon. In 1787 he was convicted of libel and sentenced to Newgate, where he often entertained, until his death.

Gorée   Island and town on the coast of West Africa (just south of the Cape Verde Peninsula in present-day Senegal). First occupied by the Dutch, it was captured by the French for the Senegal Company in

1677 and became an important slave-trading center. Taken by the British in the War of the French Revolution, it was restored to France by the Peace of AMIENS and retaken by the British in 1804. It was returned to France in 1817.

gores Sloping angles at one or both ends of a sail to widen it or increase its depth. Also, angular pieces of plank used to fill up a vessel's planking where needed.

goshawk A large short-winged hawk, *Accipiter gentilis,* and other species.

go snacks To have a share in something, to divide profits.

Gosport Municipal borough, Hampshire, on a peninsula between SPITHEAD and the west side of the entrance to Portsmouth harbor, directly opposite PORTSMOUTH. Gosport was the location of a number of facilities used by the Navy, including the ORDNANCE station at PRIDDY'S HARD, the Victualing Board's brewery and cooperage at Weevil Yard (from the 1830s, called the Royal Clarence Victualing Yard), and HASLAR Hospital.

gout A usually hereditary disease characterized by excruciatingly painful paroxysms of the joints, especially of the large toe. The pain is caused by deposits of uric acid within the joints.

gowk A fool, a half-witted person.

grains of paradise *or* **Guinea grains** The pungent seeds of *Amomum melegueta* of western Africa, used as a spice and to calm the stomach.

grallatores Long-legged wading birds, such as the CRANE or HERON.

gralloch The viscera of a dead deer. To gralloch is to disembowel a deer.

grampus The popular name of various CETACEANs having a high dorsal fin and a blunt rounded head and noted for their spouting and blowing. Frequently applied to the killer whale but also to an unaggressive cetacean resembling it in size and appearance but with fewer and smaller teeth, sometimes called cow-fish. The name has also been applied to the pilot whale.

Grand Banks *or* **Newfoundland Bank** Southeast of NEWFOUND-LAND, a large shallows and cod-breeding ground that once seemed inexhaustible and attracted fishing vessels from all over the world and especially from Maine and Massachusetts.

grape *short for* **grape-shot** Small cast-iron balls bound together by a canvas bag or other means to form a deadly charge for cannon that scattered like shotgun pellets when fired.

grapnel *or* **grappling hook** An iron-clawed instrument attached to a line and used to seize and hold an enemy's ship for boarding or to recover objects on the bottom of the sea; also used as an anchor for small vessels.

grass-comber A sailor's pejorative for a farm laborer.

grass-plat A plot of turf-covered ground, sometimes with ornamental flower beds.

grating The open woodwork cover for the HATCHWAY.

gratis pro Deo Free for the sake of God (Latin).

gravamen A grievance or a formal complaint or accusation.

Gravesend A port in the Thames estuary on the northern coast of Kent, England.

Great Belt The largest and the middle of the three entrances—the Sound, the Great Belt, and the Little Belt—to the Baltic through Denmark.

greatcoat A heavy overcoat.

great gun A firearm that must be mounted; a piece of ORDNANCE, a cannon. *See* illustration following page.

Great Mogul *or* **Grand Mogul** *or* **Mogul** The title of the ruler of the Mogul Empire, a Muslim dynasty that ruled most of India from 1526 to 1857.

grebe A diving bird of the family Podicipedidae with a short body, pointed bill, flattened and lobed feet set far back, and almost no tail.

green-fly An aphis, or plant-louse, green in color.

A Blomefield gun, showing the gun tackle with its blocks, and the breech tackle, with one end loose. Adapted from Serres's *Liber Nauticus*.

Parts (A) cascabel, (B) thimble, (C) flintlock and touchhole, (D) first reinforce ring, (E) trunnion, (F) second reinforce ring, (G) eyebolt, (H) block, (I) breech tackle, (J) carriage, (K) truck, (L) quoins.

greenheart   A tropical South American tree and its timber, used in shipbuilding.

Greenwich   A town on the south bank of the Thames adjoining London on the east, site of a Royal Palace and famed for the Royal Observatory, an astronomical observatory founded in 1675, through which passes the longitudinal meridian of 0°. Known as well for its hospital for Naval pensioners founded in 1694. Also, mean time for the meridian of Greenwich, used as a basis for calculating time throughout the world.

gregale   A squally northeast wind in the Mediterranean, affecting particularly Malta and Sicily.

grego *or* **griego**   A coarse jacket with a hood worn in the LEVANT. Also slang for a rough GREATCOAT.

Gregory's Patent Liquid   Probably a proprietary remedy with unknown properties, but not associated with the prominent James Gregory, a leading physician of late-18th-century Edinburgh.

gremial   Of or pertaining to the bosom or lap. Of a friend, intimate.

grenadier Originally, a soldier who threw grenades, round iron cases filled with powder. Though grenades went out of general use in the 18th century, the name "grenadiers" was retained for a company of the tallest and finest men in the regiment.

Gretna Green A village in the county of Dumfries, Scotland, three-quarters of a mile from the English border on the River Sark. Following the ban on FLEET marriages, English couples seeking a secret or quick marriage went to Gretna Green, where the local blacksmith often performed marriages under the relatively easy conditions of Scottish law, requiring the couples only to declare before witnesses their desire to marry. Many races between runaway couples and thwarted parents were decided on the level road leading to the little bridge over the Sark.

grey powder A rarely used panacea consisting of a mixture of elemental MERCURY and chalk.

griego *See* GREGO.

griffon vulture A vulture of the genus *Gyps,* especially *G. fulvus.*

grig A word having a variety of meanings, among them a wildly lively person, full of frolic and jest.

gripe A vessel is said to gripe when she tends to come up into the wind when sailing CLOSE-HAULED. Also, the LASHing used to secure a boat in its place on the deck of a ship. The piece of timber terminating the KEEL at the forward extremity, also called the "FOREFOOT."

groat The Scottish fourpenny piece, first struck in 1358. Its value was already only threepence English in 1373 and continued to fall. A very small sum.

grobian A clownish and slovenly person.

grog A mixture of rum and water served to a ship's crew twice daily. With the conquest of Jamaica in 1687, brandy was replaced by rum as the spirit offered in the Royal Navy, and, in 1740, in an effort to control alcoholic consumption, Admiral Vernon (whose nickname was "Old Grogram" for the cloak of grogram he wore) ordered that the ration—one pint for men and a half pint for boys—be diluted by the addition of water (for men, a half pint of rum with one quart of water) and served at noon and six P.M. The men called the mixture "grog." "Half-and-half grog" was equal parts of rum and water; "seven-water grog," was the sailor's derisive name for very weak grog. A sailor who drank too much grog was "groggy."

Groin *or* **Groyne**   *See* CORUNNA.

grommet   A ring of rope used to secure the upper edge of a sail to its STAY.

groom   A manservant.

grosso modo   Overall, roughly (Italian).

groundling   A frequenter of the "ground" or pit of a theater, hence, an uncritical or unrefined person.

ground-tier   The lowest tier of goods or casks of provisions stowed in a vessel's hold.

grouts   Dregs, grounds.

guacharo   A nocturnal bird of South America and Trinidad, valued for its oil, which is used for lighting and in cooking; the oil-bird.

guaiacum   Guiac, wood from *Guaiacum officinale,* a tree native to tropical America. Its bark was powdered for use in the treatment of syphilis and, occasionally, joint pains.

guanaco   A South American wild llama that produces a reddish brown wool.

Guards   By 1815, the Household troops of the English Army, which trace their origins to the personal bodyguards of medieval kings, consisting of the Foot Guards, the Horse Guards, the Grenadier Guards, and the Life Guards. Also applied, by extension, to the regiment of mounted infantry known as the DRAGOON Guards (as distinguished from Cavalry).

guard-ship   A vessel of war, usually the PORT ADMIRAL'S FLAGSHIP, that protects a harbor, superintends its marine affairs, and keeps seamen until they can join their ships.

gubbins   Anything of little value; a gadget.

gudgeon   A metal socket in which the PINTLE of a RUDDER turns freely in either direction.

Guernsey frock *or* **Guernsey**   A thick, tight-fitting vest or shirt, generally knitted of blue wool, worn by seamen.

Guerriere, **H.M.S.**   A fifth-rate 38-gun FRIGATE, captured from the French by H.M.S. *Blanche* in 1806 off the Faroes. As a British frigate, she was commanded by Captain Dacres and captured by the U.S.S. CONSTITUTION on August 19, 1812, in the western Atlantic and burned.

guerrillero   A guerrilla (Spanish).

Guildhall   Dating back to at least 1128 (though rebuilt), the hall of the Corporation of the City of London located on Gresham Street. The center of the civic government, it has often been the scene of state banquets and other formal occasions.

guillemot   A small sea bird of the genus *Cepphus.*

guinea   An English gold coin first struck in 1663 with the nominal value of 20 SHILLINGS but from 1717 until its recent disappearance circulating as legal tender at the rate of 21 shillings. In 1663 the Royal Mint was authorized to coin gold pieces for the use of the Company of Royal Adventurers of England trading with Africa. The 20-shilling pieces received the popular name of guineas because they were for use in the Guinea trade and made of gold from Guinea. The name was extended to later coins of the same value.

Guinea Coast   Named for an ancient kingdom, the term came into European use after 1500. It refers to the region on the west coast of Africa, between 15 degrees north and 15 degrees south latitude. Upper Guinea lies between present-day Gambia and Cameroon and Lower Guinea extends to southern Angola. Early European traders gave a number of separate names to sections of the Upper Guinea coast, for example, Slave Coast, Gold Coast, Ivory Coast, and Grain Coast.

guinea-fowl   A pheasantlike bird of the genus *Numida,* especially the domesticated species, *Numida meleagris,* which has slate-colored plumage with small white spots.

gule   Gluttony.

Gulf Stream   A great oceanic current of warm water that emerges from the Gulf of Mexico, flows parallel to the North American coast to NEWFOUNDLAND, and then flows across the Atlantic to northern Europe.

Gull Stream   A channel, leading northeast, through the GOODWIN SANDS from the anchorage off Deal in the DOWNS.

gum-cistus   A shrub, *Cistus ladanifer,* that yields the aromatic resin ladanum, used in perfume and to settle the stomach.

gumma   (pl. **gummata**) A gummy or rubbery tumor characteristic of advanced syphilis.

gummata   Used by Maturin to indicate raised scar tissue.

gunboat   A small vessel, usually of shallow DRAFT, fitted for carrying guns.

gunlayer   One who aims or lays a gun.

gun-money *or* **gunnage**   Money distributed among the captors of a ship, in proportion to the number of guns on the captured ship.

gunroom   In large ships of war, a compartment at the after end of the MAIN or lower deck, originally occupied by the gunner and his mates but later used as a MESS for junior officers. On board a ship of the line, the Chaplain, junior Marine officer, Gunner, and, perhaps, the Pilot, had small cabins around the gunroom, while the junior Midshipmen and volunteers messed in the central area. In a FRIGATE the gunroom was located below the Captain's cabin.

Gunter's scale   A marked-up flat rule used for solving surveying and navigation problems, named for the English mathematician Edmund Gunter (1581–1626). On one side are scales of equal parts, of chords, sines, tangents, etc., and on the other are scales of the logarithms of those parts.

gunwale   The upper edge of a vessel's side; in large vessels, the uppermost planking, which covers the timber-heads and reaches from the QUARTERDECK to the FORECASTLE on either side.

gurnard   A fish of the genus *Trigla* with a large spiny head, mailed cheeks, and three free pectoral rays.

gut   A general term for a narrow passage or strait between two bodies of water, as in the Gut of Gibraltar.

gutter   Of a candle, to melt away through the channel formed by a burning wick.

guy   A rope used to guide and steady something hoisted or lowered. Also, a rope, chain, or rod used to secure or steady anything liable to shift or be carried away, such as a MAST.

Guy Fawkes's night   November 5, the anniversary of the Gunpowder Plot, a failed scheme to blow up the English king, JAMES I, and the Houses of Parliament in 1605 to gain revenge for anti–Roman Catholic laws. Guy Fawkes (1570–1606) was the principal agent. An English Protestant who became a Catholic at an early age, Fawkes served in the Spanish Army in the Netherlands from 1593 to 1604. Robert Catesby, the leader of the Gunpowder Plot, invited him to return to England to help resist James I's new sanctions against Catholics following the end of the war with Spain. In preparation for a general Catholic uprising, Fawkes placed explosives in Parliament, but one of the other conspirators reported the plot. All the conspirators were seized and murdered or executed. The event was long used to justify the persecution of Catholics and the anniversary of Guy Fawkes's arrest has been celebrated since that time.

Guy's Hospital   On St. Thomas's Street in London, a private hospital founded in the early 18th century by Thomas Guy and ruled by the despotic Benjamin Harrison for 50 years beginning in 1793.

gybe *or* **jibe**   When sailing downwind, to cause a FORE-AND-AFT sail to swing from one side of the vessel to the other. To alter the course of a boat when there is a following wind so that her BOOM-sails gybe. When the wind crossed the stern of a square-rigger in this way and she ended up with wind on the previous LEE-side with her sails ABACK, she was said to have been "brought by the lee."

gymnosophist   One of a sect of ancient ascetic Hindu philosophers who wore little or no clothing, ate no meat, and devoted themselves to mystical contemplation. An ascetic or mystic.

gynandromorph   One who has both male and female characteristics; an insect that appears to have both male and female markings on the body.

hack A horse for ordinary riding, as distinguished from cross-country, military, or other special riding; a saddle-horse for the road. The word implies technically a half-bred horse with more bone and substance than a thoroughbred. Also, a person whose services may be hired for any kind of work required of him; a common drudge.

hackle The long shiny feathers on the neck of certain birds, such as the domestic cock, that rise when the bird is angry. "With the hackles up" means angry or ready to fight.

hackney-coach A four-wheeled coach with seats for six people, drawn by two horses and kept for hire.

hack-watch A watch used when taking observations so as not to disturb the standard chronometer.

haggis A traditional Scottish dish consisting of the heart, lungs, and liver (or sometimes the tripe and chitterlings) of a sheep or calf, minced with suet and oatmeal, seasoned with salt, pepper, onions, etc., and boiled like a large sausage in the stomach of the animal.

haglet A small species of seagull, the KITTIWAKE.

hake   An edible fish resembling or related to the common Atlantic cod; also called forkbeard, forked hake.

hakim   A Muslim or Indian doctor; a judge, ruler, or governor in a Muslim country or in India.

hale   Of a sail, to draw up, HOIST, set. Of a rope, to draw or pull.

half-deck   In old ships of war, a deck extending from the MAINMAST AFT, between the then smaller QUARTERDECK and the upper or MAIN DECK. When the two decks above the main deck were reduced to one quarterdeck, "half-deck" survived only in the expression "under the half-deck," the part of the main deck from the mainmast aft to the quarterdeck, formerly covered by the half-deck. The term was also applied to a deck-house placed aft of the mainmast. In the 19th and early 20th centuries, this was applied to a cabin on the deck of a merchant vessel, accommodating the apprentices.

half-galley   A GALLEY of about half the full size.

half-pay officer   An officer of the army or navy who receives a reduced allowance—usually half salary—when not in actual service or after retirement at a prescribed time.

halfpenny *or* **ha'penny**   A coin of either copper or bronze worth half the value of a penny; a sum equivalent to two FARTHINGS.

Haliaetus albicilla   The white-tailed eagle, a species of sea eagle.

Halifax   A major Canadian seaport and the capital of the province of NOVA SCOTIA, founded by the British in 1749 as a naval base and dockyard.

halliard   *See* HALYARD.

halloo   An exclamation to incite dogs to the chase, also to call attention at a distance or to express surprise.

Hallowell, Admiral Benjamin (*1760–1834*)   At the time a Captain, he commanded the *Swiftsure* at the Battle of the NILE (1798), after which he presented NELSON a coffin made from the MAINMAST of the French FLAGSHIP *L'ORIENT*. In 1806, Nelson was buried in it.

hallucinating cacti   Probably peyote (*Lophophora williamsii*), found in Mexico and the southwestern United States.

Halte là. Qui vive? . . . le docteur Ralphe Stop. Who goes there? . . . Doctor Ralph (French).

halyard *or* **halliard** Originally "haul yard," a rope or TACKLE used for raising or lowering a sail, YARD, SPAR, or flag.

Hamadryad, **H.M.S.** A 34-gun fifth-rate named for a tree nymph. Formerly the *Matilda,* taken from the Spanish in November 1804. Sold in 1815.

hammock A naval hammock usually consisted of a piece of hemp cloth, about six feet long and three feet wide, with several small lines supporting each end, gathered together in a CLEW and slung from the underside of the deck above. It often held a mattress made of flock or wool, but sometimes (and objectionably) of chopped, old clothes.

hammock-cloth A cloth used for covering the hammocks to protect them from wet when stowed in the nettings on the top of the BULWARKS.

hammock-netting Rope nettings along the sides of the upper deck and around the break of the POOP where rolled-up hammocks were stowed. They served as a shield against small arms fire or a flotation device when needed.

hamper A large basket or wickerwork used as a packing-case. Also, objects that are a necessary part of a vessel's equipment but that are in the way at certain times.

Hampstead Now a part of greater London, Hampstead, in 1810, was a village of about 900 houses and 5,500 inhabitants. During the reign of Henry VIII, the laundry of the nobility was washed in the village. Later its waters made it a spa destination, and eventually it attracted the idle doing the ill-advised. Its chief topographical feature is a large heath reaching nearly 450 feet above sea level. In *Post Captain,* Aubrey walks on the Heath after attending a ROUT at Lady KEITH's and is assaulted by a literary mugger.

hance A curved, often ornamentally carved rise of the FIFERAILS or BULWARKS from the WAIST to the QUARTERDECK.

hand Of a sail, to take in, to FURL. Also, a member of a ship's crew. A hand is also a linear measure, once equal to three inches but now to four. A palm, a hand-breadth.

hand-barrow   A flat, rectangular frame or litter with poles at each end for carrying it.

hand-mast   A round wooden pole between 24 inches (six hands) and 72 inches in circumference, suitable for making into a MAST. Those with a smaller circumference are called SPARS.

handspike   A wooden bar used as a lever or crow primarily in moving artillery pieces. Round at one end and square at the other and usually shod with iron, it also functioned as a lever for turning a WINDLASS.

hanger   A short sword that hung from the belt.

hangfire   A delay in the explosion of a gun's charge or of a blasting charge.

hanging knee   A wooden KNEE with one leg against a ship's side and the other on the underside of a BEAM.

hank   A small ring of rope, wood, or iron fastened to the LUFF of a FORE-AND-AFT sail or STAYSAIL to run on a STAY. Also, a coil of small line or twine used for small work.

Hannibal, **H.M.S.**   A 74-gun third rate (Captain Ferris) that surrendered beneath the batteries of Algeciras to a French SQUADRON commanded by Admiral Linois on July 5, 1801. Aubrey witnesses the taking of *Hannibal* in *Master and Commander.*

hapax   A word or form occurring only once in a body of literature.

hard   A firm beach or foreshore. Also, a sloping stone roadway or jetty at the water's edge for convenience in landing and putting out. In PORTSMOUTH, Hampshire, the street along the landing leading to the Dockyard Gate. On shipboard, to the fullest degree, as in "hard alee."

hard-tack   Ship-biscuit. Also, ordinary sea fare in general.

hare   To run or move speedily.

harness-cask   A cask or tub with a rimmed cover for keeping the salt meats currently being used.

harrier *or* **harrower**   Any of the hawks of the genus *Circus,* having long wings and slender bodies, such as the hen-harrier and the marsh-harrier. Harriers are indefatigable hunters of other birds and rabbits.

Harris's Guaranteed Unguent A proprietary topical remedy of unknown properties.

Harrogate A spa with mineral springs in West Yorkshire, 13 miles north of Leeds.

harrow A heavy frame of timber or iron with iron tines dragged over ploughed land to break clods, stir the soil, or bury seed.

harry To raid or ravage. To overrun with an army; to lay waste, sack, pillage, spoil.

hartebeest An antelope common in Africa.

hartshorn Calcium phosphates extracted from stag horns, used as a medicinal tonic. Ammonium chloride, often used medically as a diuretic. Smelling salts, a pungent mixture of ammonium bicarbonate and ammonium carbamate in water.

Harwich On the east coast of Essex, England, a port used by ships sailing between England and Holland or Scandinavia.

Haslar The largest naval hospital in the world in its time, built on Haslar Creek east of PORTSMOUTH, England, in 1746, and headed by the famous physician James LIND and later by Sir Gilbert BLANE.

hat *See* TRICORN.

hatchway A square or oblong opening in a ship's deck through which cargo is moved to the hold; a passage from one deck to another. Can be qualified, as after-, fore-, main-hatchway.

haud crede colori Do not trust outward show, or beauty (Latin).

haul To pull. To "haul her wind" or to "haul up" means to TRIM the sails of a ship so as to sail nearer to the direction from which the wind is blowing. To change or turn the ship's course. To sail in a certain course. Also, to sail along a coast.

hawse The BOWS of a ship where the HAWSE-HOLES are cut for the anchor CABLEs to pass through. The space between the STEM of a vessel at anchor and the anchors or a little beyond, as in "athwart the hawse."

hawse-holes Two cylindrical holes in the BOWS of a vessel for the anchor CABLE to run through. "To come in through the hawse-holes" means to enter the service at the lowest level.

hawser   A large rope or small CABLE, more than five inches in circumference, used in WARPing and MOORing.

hawser-laid   Of a rope, made of three or four strands laid up right-handed.

haysel   The hay season (proper to East Anglia).

head   A lavatory for seamen, found in the "head" or FORE part of the ship. Of a sail, the upper part.

head, down by the   Of a ship, drawing more water at the BOWs than the STERN.

headed by the wind   Of a ship, when the wind swings around to blow toward a ship's BOWs, causing a need to alter the ship's course.

headland   A point of land projecting into the sea; a cape or promontory.

head-money   A reward for prisoners taken, slaves recovered, or people brought in according to various prescriptions. In Britain, an allowance of £5 per head was paid for all persons captured who were on the enemy ship's books previous to the action.

head-piece   Person of intellect.

head-rope   One of the supporter STAYS for the head of a MAST. The part of the BOLT-ROPE along the upper edge of a square sail. Also, a small rope used to HOIST a flag.

headsail   Any of the sails set between the FOREMAST and BOWSPRIT.

healing by first intention   Facilitating the healing process by keeping the wound clean; healing by second intention implied that the appearance of pus was beneficial in that it demonstrated that the foul HUMOURS causing the inflammation were escaping from the wound site.

"Heart of Oak"   A patriotic song with references to victories at Minden, Quiberon Bay, and Quebec. Written in 1759 by David Garrick, with music by William Boyce, for the pantomime *Harlequin's Invasion.* A verse and the chorus:

> Come cheer up my lads, 'tis to Glory we steer, To
> add something more to this wonderful Year: To
> Honor we call you, not Press you like Slaves, For
> who are so free as the Sons of the waves?

chorus:
Heart of Oak are Our Ships, Heart of
Oak are our Men, We always are ready,
Steady Boys, steady, We'll fight and we'll conquer
again and again.

heath   An extensive area of level, uncultivated, open land without trees, usually of poor soil with a peaty surface in which heather and other low-growing plants naturally proliferate. There are several areas in London with this name, such as, Black Heath, west of the GREENWICH Observatory, and HAMSTEAD Heath. The term "one's native heath" means the place where one grew up.

heave   To pull or HAUL; to push, as at the CAPSTAN, to heave in the CABLE. To move the ship in some direction by these means. Of a ship, to move or turn.

heave to   To stop the vessel by shortening sail and throwing some of the canvas ABACK. A ship is also said to be "hove to" when lying ATRY (lying to) under storm canvas.

heave down   To turn a ship on its side for cleaning or repairing; to CAREEN. The part above the water is said to be "hove out."

hecatomb   In ancient Greece and Rome, a great public sacrifice of 100 oxen. Loosely, a large number or quantity, a "heap."

hedge-creeper   One that skulks under hedges for bad purposes; a sneaking rogue; a hedge-bird.

heel   To lean to one side; a ship normally heels in the wind. The usually squared lower end of a MAST or the lower end of a BOOM or SPAR. The point where the after end of the KEEL and the STERNPOST connect.

heel-piece   An angle-bar joining the HEELS of a frame across the KEEL. The piece forming the heel of a MAST or other SPAR.

heel-tap   Liquor left in the bottom of a glass after drinking; the dross of a bottle.

HEI Company   *See* EAST INDIA COMPANY.

Heligoland Bight   The area of water between the island of Heligoland in the North Sea and the German coast. The British captured the island in 1807 and retained it until 1890, after which it became a German naval base.

heliocentric   Having the sun as center. Also, considered as viewed from the center of the sun, as in heliocentric latitude and longitude.

hellebore   A drastic cathartic made from root of black hellebore or Christmas rose and containing several toxic compounds, including hyoscyamine, digitalislike compounds, and severe intestinal irritants. In classical times it was reputed to cure insanity. *Helleborus foetidus*, stinking hellebore; a green-flowered plant of the buttercup family found in calcareous woodlands.

Helleborus foetidus   *See* HELLEBORE.

Hellespont   The DARDANELLES, the strait that separates European Turkey from Asian Turkey and links the Aegean Sea with the Sea of Marmara.

helm   The handle or TILLER, in large ships the wheel, used to move the RUDDER and thus steer the vessel. Also, the entire steering apparatus. Orders to the helmsman were traditionally given in terms of the position of the TILLER, not the position of the RUDDER. Putting the tiller to STARBOARD made the vessel go to LARBOARD. Since sailing ships heel to leeward, the high side was to windward, thus, the order to put her helm up meant to push it to the windward side, while putting the helm down meant to turn the tiller toward the LEE side.

hemp   Rope made of the fibers of the hemp plant, *Cannabis sativa*. Where it is exposed to the weather, hemp rope needs to be tarred to prevent decay. Untarred hemp rope is called white rope. It is about three-quarters as strong as Manila hemp, a rope made from the leaves of the abaca plant, native to the Philippine Islands. Although mentioned by O'Brian, it was not imported for use in Europe or America until the 1820s.

hemp, vapour of   Known from antiquity, smoking marijuana seeds was reintroduced to European medicine by physicians who had accompanied Napoleon's army to Egypt in 1798. Used as an astringent, analgesic, and anticonvulsant.

henbane   Black henbane. Used medically as a sedative and an analgesic, it can also produce a wide range of poisonous effects, including death.

Hendaye   A town on the Atlantic coast of France, 13 miles southwest of Biarritz, on the Spanish frontier.

hepatic   Of or pertaining to the liver.

hepatica   Any of several plants of the genus *Hepatica*, whose tri-lobed leaves were thought to resemble the liver, hence its use in treating liver diseases. Sometimes called liverwort, but that name was more often applied to several species of moss.

hermaphrodite   A sailing vessel that combines the sails and RIGGING of two kinds of craft.

***HERMIONE*, H.M.S.**
A 32-gun fifth-rate ship built in Bristol in 1782 and handed over to the Spanish in 1797 by mutineers who murdered her Captain and nine officers in the WEST INDIES. In October of 1799, she returned to the Royal Navy when boats from H.M.S. SURPRISE under Captain Sir Edward Hamilton cut her out of the harbor at Puerto Cabello on Venezuela's Caribbean coast. She was renamed *Retaliation* and in 1800 was renamed again as *Retribution*. She was broken up in 1805.

Reproduced from *The Naval Chronicle*, vol. 5 (*courtesy of the Mariners' Museum, Newport News, Virginia*)

The H.M.S. *Surprise* **cuts out the** *Hermione. The Naval Chronicle,* on whose report of the attack the following account is based, called this event "one of the most singular, as well as the most gallant, which ever hitherto graced the naval annals of Britain." Pictured on the previous page is the *Hermione;* the crew of the *Surprise* is about to board her. Having received orders from Sir Hyde Parker, H.M.S. *Surprise,* under Captain Hamilton, had cruised between the island of Aruba and Cape St. Roman, near the gulf of Venezuela, to look for the *Hermione.* Hamilton found her at Puerta Cabello, moored between two strong batteries.

The *Surprise* prepared for the attack for two days. A speech by Captain Hamilton, along with the *Hermione's* well-known bloody history, so inspired the crew that "many instances occurred of pecuniary offers being made by those who were ordered to remain with the ship, on condition of their exchanging stations with such as had been selected to make the attack."

The *Surprise's* boats reached the *Hermione* under fire. Captain Hamilton and about ten men boarded at the forecastle and advanced to the starboard gangway, where they met a contingent of Spaniards. Hamilton left the Gunner in charge here and joined the Surgeon and his party, moving along the larboard gangway to the quarterdeck. Meanwhile, the black cutter, with a Lieutenant, the red cutter, under the Boatswain, and an Officer of the Marines and his party struggled to board. In the launch, the First Lieutenant and his crew were busy cutting the *Hermione's* bower cable, while in the jollyboat, the Carpenter and his men were cutting the stern cable. The crews of these boats were to immediately take the ship in tow.

On board the *Hermione,* the enemy was caught between the boarding parties. Many were killed and some jumped overboard. The cables were now cut, and the boats took the ship in tow. The boarding crew set sail while the battle raged on.

After the quarterdeck was taken, the Officer of the Marines and the Surgeon led an attack on the maindeck. Captain Hamilton and the Gunner had been too badly wounded to take part. Fortunately for the British, the Spanish shore batteries could not tell who possessed the ship. By the time it was clear that the British had won the bloody battle on board, the *Hermione* had traveled half a mile out. The shore batteries opened fire, but it was too late. The *Surprise* had pulled off one of the war's memorable achievements.

Hermitage   A French wine from near Valence in the north of the Rhône Valley, named for a ruin said to have been a hermit's cell.

heroic couplet   Poetry of iambic pentameter lines in rhymed pairs.

heron   Long-necked, long-legged wading birds of several genera.

herring-buss   The Dutch *haring-buis,* a round-bowed, two- or three-masted vessel used in herring fishing. *See also* BUSS.

Herschel, Sir William (*1738–1822*)   Noted English astronomer and mathematician who discovered the planet Uranus. His sister Caroline Lucretia (1750–1848) independently discovered eight comets.

Hessian boots   A high, tasseled boot, first worn by Hessian troops, that was fashionable in the early 19th century.

heuch   An exclamation of excitement. The cry of a dancer of the Highland fling, a Scottish folk dance.

hey-bote   A tenant's right to take wood or thorns for fence repair from a landlord's estate.

Heywood, Peter (*1773–1831*)   Joined the Navy at age 13. His first ship was H.M.S. *Bounty,* under the command of William BLIGH, on her infamous voyage to Tahiti to obtain breadfruit trees. When the mutiny broke out on April 28, 1789, the mutineers confined Heywood and apparently planned to put him into the *Bounty*'s launch with Bligh. However, there was not enough room and Heywood was left behind. In the *Bounty,* the mutineers reached Tahiti, and Heywood stayed there until H.M.S. *Pandora* arrived in 1791.

On the voyage home, Captain Edwards confined Heywood with the others in irons, caged on the QUARTERDECK. When the *Pandora* sank after hitting a reef in the Endeavour Strait, Heywood and a few of the others managed to escape in the boats. Edwards, as well as the officers of the Dutch merchant ship that took them from BATAVIA to England, treated the *Bounty*'s men severely.

Upon their return, the *Bounty*'s men were COURT-MARTIALed and all sentenced to death, but the court, presided over by Lord Hood, recommended mercy in Heywood's case. The First Lord, the Earl of Chatham, gave him an unconditional pardon. Hood advised Heywood to continue in the Navy. At the GLORIOUS FIRST OF JUNE, Heywood acted as captain's aide de camp on board the FLAGSHIP *Queen*

Charlotte, and on the ship's return was one of two Midshipmen attending the side when the King and Queen visited the ship. Promoted to temporary Lieutenant, his good behavior cleared his name for further promotion. Having served around the world and risen to the rank of Captain, he retired in 1816.

hiera picra   A cathartic made with aloes and canella bark, sometimes mixed with honey and other ingredients. Also, corrupted to hickery-pickery, hicra picra, higry-pigry.

hieratic   Pertaining to or used by the priestly class; used in connection with sacred subjects.

highland bonnet *or* **Scotch cap**   A man's hat made of thick, firm wool with no brim and decorated with two tails or streamers.

Highlander   A native or inhabitant of the Highlands of Scotland. Also, a soldier of a Highland regiment.

high road   A main road or highway.

hilum   Point at which one of the internal organs connects to the vascular system. Also, certain small apertures and depressions.

hip   Morbidly depressed, low-spirited.

hippogriff   A mythic creature with the foreparts of a griffin and the body and hindquarters of a horse.

hirundine   Of or pertaining to a swallow.

H.M.S.   The prefix to a ship's name, meaning "His/Her Majesty's Ship," used from 1789 on to indicate that a ship belongs to the Royal Navy.

Hoare's Bank   Originally a goldsmith business founded by Richard Hoare in 1672, it moved from Cheapside to Fleet Street in 1690 and became a bank around the turn of the century. Early customers were Samuel Pepys and John Dryden. The Hoare family still runs the privately held bank.

hobnail   Nails with large heads and short tangs, used for protecting the soles of heavy boots and shoes.

hoboy   An oboe.

hock A white wine from the Rhine Valley, originally from Hochheim, Germany.

hog Of a ship, to react to a strain by having the BOW and STERN droop and the KEEL and bottom arch upward. Also, a very stiff scrubbing brush made of birch twigs sandwiched between wooden planks and trimmed to make bristles.

hogget A young boar of the second year. A yearling sheep.

hogshead A large cask for liquids, especially one of a definite capacity that varied for different liquids and commodities and in different localities. For example, a hogshead of wine contained 63 old wine-gallons (52½ imperial gallons). The London hogshead of beer held 54 gallons, that of ale 48 gallons. In other places a hogshead of ale or beer held 51 gallons.

hoist To raise or HAUL up a flag, COLORS, sail, or anything else. The side of the flag on which the HALYARDs are attached. A group of flags that make a particular signal.

hola A form of "holla," a shout to draw attention.

holothurian An ECHINODERM with a tough, elongated body, and a ring of tentacles around the mouth. A sea slug, sea cucumber, or trepang.

holt A dwelling or refuge, an animal's den, especially an otter's.

holystone A soft sandstone used by sailors for scouring the decks of ships, after which the deck was hosed down with saltwater, creating a smooth, blanched appearance. Small HOLYSTONES were called prayer books and large ones BIBLES. The provenance of the terminology is unknown; the theories range from the possibility that the stones were first taken from the broken monuments of St. Nicholas Church in Great Yarmouth to the fact that sailors often scrubbed the deck on hands and knees.

Home Office In Great Britain after 1782, the department of the Secretary of State for Home Affairs, which deals with domestic administration and some of the matters dealt with by a ministry of justice in other countries.

hominy Ground corn boiled with water or milk.

Homo homini lupus Man is a wolf to man (Latin).

homoiousian   Of like essence or substance. A person who believes the Father and the Son, in the Godhead, to be of like, but not the same, essence or substance. *Compare* HOMOOUSIAN.

homologue   A counterpart, an equivalent in position, value, structure, or function.

homoousian   Of the same essence or substance. A person who believes in the doctrine of the Nicene Creed, that the Father and Son of the Trinity are of the same essence or substance. *Compare* HOMOIOU-SIAN.

honey-buzzard   A bird of prey of the genus *Pernis*, especially the European *P. apivorus*, which feeds on the contents of bees' and wasps' nests.

Honi soit qui mal y pense   *See* GARTER.

Honneur and Patier   *Honneur et Patrie* means Honor and Country (French).

hood-ends   The ends of the hull planks, which fit into slits, or RAB-BETS, in the STEM and STERN posts.

Hoogli *or* Hooghly River   The most westerly and most important channel of the Ganges River, leading to Calcutta, founded by the English in c.1690. Hooghly-Chinsura is a town on the river where the English first established a trading post in 1651. The Nawab of Bengal forced them out temporarily in 1685, and the Marathas sacked the town in 1742.

hooker   A variant of the KETCH employed primarily by the Dutch as a fishing vessel. An irreverent reference to a ship past its prime.

hoopoe *or* hoop   *Upupa epops*, a southern European bird with variegated plumage and a large standing crest, occasionally seen in England.

hop-pillow   A pillow made to induce sleep by being stuffed with hops, the ripened cones of the female hop plant, considered to be soporific.

horchata   A sweet white drink made from either the juice of almonds or from chufa (also called nut grass or earth almond), popular in Spain and Latin America.

horn-book   A kind of primer for children, often covered by a thin plate of animal horn and mounted on a wooden tablet with a handle, consisting of a leaf of paper containing the alphabet and sometimes the ten digits, rules for spelling, and the Lord's Prayer.

hornpipe   A wind instrument possibly so called from once having the bell and mouthpiece made of horn. Also a lively English country dance, usually to the tune of a wind instrument, and especially associated with the revelry of sailors.

Horsburgh, James (*1762–1836*)   The cartographer who succeeded DALRYMPLE as Hydrographer of the EAST INDIA COMPANY. He is often remembered as the compiler of *Directions for Sailing to and from the East Indies, China, New Holland, Cape of Good Hope and Interjacent Ports* (1809–1811).

horse   A FOOTROPE stretched under a yard and supported by STIR-RUPS, which is used by sailors to stand on while REEFing or FURLing sails. Also, various other ropes used to support or to guide. A Flemish horse is a short footrope used by the man at the YARDARM when furling or reefing.

horse-coper   A horse-dealer.

Horse-Guard   Cavalry picked for special service as a guard. Also the cavalry brigade of the English Household troops, specifically the third regiment of this body. The guard house at Whitehall, home of the British Army's mounted troops. Nearby is the Horse Guard Parade, a broad plaza bordering ST. JAMES'S PARK. It is the site of military exercises, medal presentation ceremonies, and other processions.

horse-leach *or* **horse-leech**   A horse doctor or veterinary surgeon.

horse-pistol   A large pistol carried by a horseman beside the pommel.

horseshoe-bat   Any species of bat having a horseshoe-shaped nose.

horse-tail   In Turkey, an ornament used as a military standard, as a symbol of war, and as an ENSIGN denoting the rank of a pasha.

hortus siccus   A collection of dried plants (Latin); also, a set of boring facts, minutiae, etc.

Hoste, Sir William (*1780–1828*)   An officer who served under NELSON in H.M.S. AGAMEMNON and later was Captain of the *Mutine*. Hoste commanded a SQUADRON of British FRIGATEs in the Adriatic from 1808 to 1814, regularly defeating the French in land raids and sea battles.

hostler   A man who attends to horses at an inn; a groom.

Hôtel Dieu   Said to have been founded in the late seventh century, it was one of the great teaching hospitals of early-19th-century Paris. Maturin tells Aubrey he had "walked the wards" there, meaning that he had purchased a ticket that allowed him to further his professional training by following a professor of medicine on his regular daily patient rounds for a given period, usually an academic term.

houario   A French lug-rigged boat of the CHASSE-MARÉE type.

houbara bustard   A game bird, *Chlamydotis undulata*, found in North Africa and in Asia as far east as India and Persia.

hounds   Projections attached to either side of the MAST just below the MASTHEAD to support the TRESTLETREES. The hounds of the lower masts are called CHEEKS.

house-bote   The right of a tenant to cut wood for house repairs from a landlord's estate.

House of Commons   The elected, lower chamber of Parliament.

hoveller   An unlicensed pilot or boatman, especially on the coast of Kent. A boatman who goes out to wrecks to render aid or sometimes to plunder. Also, the craft used by these boatmen.

howdah   A seat usually with a railing and a canopy erected on the back of an elephant for two or more people.

Howe, Admiral Lord Richard (*1726–1799*)   Called "Black Dick" for his dark complexion, Admiral Howe—brother of General Sir William Howe, who commanded British troops during the American Revolution—was one of the Royal Navy's great tacticians. He won his greatest victory when he defeated the French fleet under Villaret de Joyeuse at the GLORIOUS FIRST OF JUNE, 1794. Howe sank one French warship and captured six more without losing a British ship, but he allowed the convoy they were protecting to reach port safely. Nelson believed he should have pushed his advantage more and later referred to an unfinished victory as a "Lord Howe victory." For reasons of health, Howe retired from the Navy soon after the battle, in 1797. He served as First Lord of the ADMIRALTY from 1783 to 1788.

howitzer A short piece of ORDNANCE, usually of light weight, specially designed for firing shells with small charges and adapted for use in a mountainous country.

howker *See* HOOKER.

hoy A small COASTING vessel often with a large MAIN hatch for moving goods and supplies in and out quickly.

hoyden A rude or dumb fellow; a rude or rambunctious girl or woman.

hubble-bubble A rudimentary form of the oriental hookah, or smoking pipe, in which the smoke bubbles through a coconut shell half filled with water. Also, similar pipes, made of clay, glass, silver, or other materials.

Hugli *See* HOOGLI.

huitième Eighth (French).

hull-down So far away that only the MASTs and sails are showing and the hull is not visible, being below the horizon.

hull-up When the hull of a ship on the horizon is visible.

Humane Society The Royal Humane Society, for the rescue of drowning people. It was founded in England in 1774. The Society once awarded Aubrey, the savior of some two dozen sailors, a gold medal, which he hocked in Gibraltar.

humble pie A pie made of the "umbles," or innards, of a deer or other animal.

Humboldt, Baron Alexander von (*1769–1859*) Prussian naturalist and explorer who traveled in South America from 1799 to 1803 and spent two decades analyzing his scientific findings. The northward-flowing Pacific current from Antarctica along South America is named the Humboldt Current after him. Humboldt's work *Kosmos* detailed his beliefs on the physical laws of the universe.

Hummel, Johann Nepomuk (*1778–1837*) Born in Pressburg, Bratislava, the son of the director of the Imperial School of Military Music, Hummel studied piano with Mozart for two years in Vienna. He toured Europe as a child prodigy pianist. He was the concertmaster to Prince Esterházy from 1804 to 1811. He composed about 130 works, primarily for the piano, but also wrote nine operas and three masses.

hummum A Turkish bath; a hammam. A bathing place called "the Hummums" was opened in Covent Garden in London in 1631 and later became a hotel.

humour In ancient and medieval physiology, any fluid or juice of an animal or plant, either natural or caused by disease. One of the four chief fluids of the body—blood, phlegm, choler, and melancholy or black choler—whose relative proportions, it was believed, determined a person's physical and mental qualities and disposition. For more on the humours, see "The Disease Burden of the Royal Navy," page 37.

hundredweight A unit of weight equal, in Britain, to 112 pounds, but originally and in the United States, equal to 100 pounds and so the name. Abbreviated as CWT.

Hunter, John (*1728–1793*) Famous teacher of surgery and anatomy in London, regarded as the founder of experimental pathology and a pioneer in physiology. After accidentally infecting himself with syphilis, he used the opportunity to study the disease in himself. An expert on gunshot wounds, he developed a number of improvements in trauma surgery along with his copious anatomical discoveries.

Huron A confederation of five Iroquoian peoples formerly living near Lake Huron in North America. Also, a member of the Huron, or their language.

hurricano Hurricane.

hussar A member of a military unit based on the light horsemen organized in Hungary in the 15th century and subsequently introduced in most European armies. The bright, elaborate uniforms of the Hungarian force set the dress standard for hussars of other nations.

hussif A small case for sewing gear, such as needles, pins, thread, and scissors. The word is a corruption of "housewife."

hydatic cyst   The encysted larva of the tapeworm *Echinococcus granulosus,* found in the livers of afflicted patients. The word "hydatid" is now used.

hydrography   The scientific description and study of the waters of the earth's surface, including rivers, lakes, and seas. It includes the charting of bodies of water and physical features, such as shallows, winds, tides, and currents. Earlier, it included the principles of navigation. Also, a treatise on or a scientific description of the waters of the earth. The Admiralty Hydrographic Office was established in 1795.

hydropericardium   Abnormal accumulation of water in the PERICARDIUM.

Hygeia   Goddess of health.

hygrometer   Instrument for measuring the humidity of the air.

hylobate   A long-armed ape or gibbon.

hyoid bone   The U-shaped tongue-bone, or os linguae, between the chin and the thyroid cartilage. In most mammals it is comparatively larger, more complicated, and more important than in humans.

hyperaemia   An excess of blood.

hyperborean   Of or relating to the extreme north of the earth.

hypnotic   A sleeping medicine.

I

Ibadite In Arabic, "Ibadiyyah," originally part of the puritanical Kharijite Islamic sect that rebelled against Muhammad's son Ali when he showed willingness to negotiate the succession to the caliphate. The Kharijites felt that the caliphate was turning into a purely political Arab kingdom and were angry that converts to Islam were not being welcomed into full brotherhood. Some Kharijite sects still survive, notably the Ibadites of northern Oman, East Africa, southern Algeria, and Libya.

ibis A member of a genus of large wading birds with long legs and long slender curved bills, related to the stork and heron and inhabiting lakes and swamps in warm climates. Especially the sacred ibis of Egypt with white and black plumage, much revered by ancient Egyptians.

Ibn Haukal *or* **Hawqul** An Arab geographer of Nisibis and Upper Mesopotamia, who traveled extensively throughout the Mediterranean region and recorded his observations. His chief work was *Configuration of the Earth* (10th c.).

Ibn Khaldun (*1332–1406*) Born in Tunis, he is considered the greatest of the Arab historical thinkers. In his masterpiece, the *Kitab al-Ibar* ("universal history"), he attempted to treat history as a science and outlined a philosophy of history, setting forth principles of sociology and political economy. He completed an autobiography in 1394 and expanded it a few months before his death.

ice-bird   The little AUK, or sea-dove. Also, the Indian NIGHTJAR.

ice fender   A guard to protect a vessel from damage by ice.

ice-pudding   A frozen, puddinglike confection.

ichu   An alpine grass growing on the uplands of the Andes and useful for fodder and thatching.

Idelfonso Treaty   The name of two treaties in this period. The first, signed August 19, 1796, was the treaty of alliance between France and Spain. As a result of the treaty, British leaders thought it prudent to withdraw from Toulon, relinquish Corsica, and evacuate the Royal Navy from the western Mediterranean, moving to Gibraltar. By the second treaty, signed October 7, 1800, Spain transferred the Louisiana Territory to France.

idler   Anyone on a ship-of-war who is on constant day duty and so not required to keep the night-WATCH, usually the Carpenter, Cook, Sailmaker, and BOATSWAIN.

Île de France   *See* MAURITIUS.

Il faut que le prêtre vive de l'autel   The priest must make a living within the Church (French). A variation of the saying *Qui sert a l'autel doit vivre de l'autel:* Every man must live by his profession.

iliac *also* **iliac passion** *or* **ileus**   Painful obstruction of the longest segment of the small intestine, the ileum.

iliac crest   The relatively sharp anterior prominence of the pelvic bone.

***Illustrious,* H.M.S.**   A third-rate 74-gun ship built at BUCKLER'S HARD, the shipbuilding port in Hampshire, in 1789. In 1795, she suffered great damage and was captured in a battle known as Hotham's Action against an inferior French fleet. In tow, the *Illustrious* broke loose during a GALE, ran aground, and was lost.

Illyrian   Of or pertaining to the Illyrians or to ancient Illyria (or Illyricum), located on what is now the Adriatic coast of Croatia. The breed of dog that originated here.

imago The last and perfect form of an insect after all metamorphoses.

Imam In Islam, a recognized leader or a religious teacher. The Twelve-Imam Shiite doctrine presents the Imams as infallible intermediaries between the human and the divine. The continuous presence of the Imams is a prerequisite for human salvation. Al-MAHDI, the last Imam, is considered hidden from humanity since 874 and is expected to return near the end of creation as a messiah-like figure.

Imperial Guard One of the most celebrated military units in history, the Imperial Guard was so named in 1804, the year of NAPOLEON's coronation. His beloved highly disciplined and decorated corps evolved during the Napoleonic wars from a small regiment to a complete army, peaking in 1814 at 112,500 but consisting of just 25,900 at WATERLOO. The Guard was formed of three main sections: the Old Guard (the élite, consisting of the GRENADIERs and chasseurs of the Guard), the Middle Guard (formed in 1806 but so named later, eventually two regiments of fusiliers and two of flankers, or marksmen), and the Young Guard (formed in 1809, mainly regiments of light infantry, the cream of the conscripts). "When the eagles of the Old Guard were seen advancing through the smoke of the conflict, the result was no longer doubtful," wrote one mid-19th-century historian. "When its columns were ordered to move to the attack, every soldier knew it was to march where the struggle was deadliest, and the fate of the army was to be decided. He knew, too, that over the dead and dying, over flaming batteries, and through ranks of steel, the steady battalions were to go. The bugle was never to sound a retreat for him and no reserve help him sustain the shock."

Implacable, **H.M.S.** Originally the French 74-gun *Duguay-Trouin*, taken after TRAFALGAR in November 1805. In the novel *Blue at the Mizzen*, this third-rate is the fictional Lord Barmouth's FLAGSHIP.

imposthume *or* **impostume** A purulent cyst, an abscess.

Impregnable, **H.M.S.** A 98-gun second rate built in 1789 that fought in the GLORIOUS FIRST OF JUNE in 1794. She was wrecked near Chichester in 1799. In *Post Captain* O'Brian has the *"Impregnable's* libertymen . . . staggering by with a troop of whores" (p. 203) in Portsmouth, circa 1804; in reality, there was no ship by that name in the Royal Navy between 1799 and 1810.

IMPRESS *OR* IMPRESSMENT
Forced service in the British Army or Navy during wartime. It became an important instrument of recruiting during the War of the French Revolution and the Napoleonic War. While no completely reliable figures on the numbers of men forced into the service through impressment have been published, estimates suggest that for the period up to 1802, about half the men in the Royal Navy were pressed. For the period after 1803, the proportion may be as high as 75 percent pressed and 25 percent volunteer.

Certain groups of people were protected from impressment, including those under age 18 or above 55, foreigners serving in British merchant ships or PRIVATEERS, watermen on the Thames belonging to insurance companies (up to 30 per office), certain designated seamen aboard ships in the coal trade, and certain fishermen and whalers, including the "harpooner, line manager, or boat-steerer belonging to any vessel fitted out for the Southern Whale Fishery."

In 1797, the Impress Service was relatively large, headed by an ADMIRAL with 47 Captains and Commanders under him, and 80 LIEU-TENANTS. The war demanded huge numbers to man British ships as the table on page 7 shows, and impressment was unable to meet the Navy's needs. The government then resorted to the Quota System, or the "Quod," which required various counties to produce certain numbers of seamen each year for service, in addition to those who volunteered or were impressed.

Local authorities generally passed over the healthy and capable men, choosing instead to send misfits and criminals. Once chosen, a QUOTA-MAN was allowed to find a substitute or buy himself out, but the latter happened only rarely because it was expensive; the price in 1811 was 80 pounds. There is some evidence that suggests it was Quota-men who were the leaders behind the mutinies of 1797.

Another source of recruitment was to cull men from foreign ships and foreign ports. Some of these were British merchant seamen or deserters and others were foreign nationals from merchant vessels or from PRIZES. (Forcing foreigners to serve in the Royal Navy enraged Americans and became one of the causes of the War of 1812.) In 1808 the H.M.S. *Implacable* carried 563 men, of whom 86 percent were British and 14 percent foreign. Of the 80 foreigners, the largest single group (28) were Americans. One historian estimated that in a typical ship of 1812, 8 percent were boy volunteers, 15 percent were men volunteers,

50 percent were British pressed men, 12 percent were Quota-men, and 15 percent were foreigners. Impressment ended in Britain in 1815.

Impress Service   The official name for the press gang. *See also* IMPRESS.

inanition   Malnutrition. Also, lack of social or moral will.

Indefatigable, **H.M.S.**   A third-rate 64-gun FRIGATE built in 1784 and commanded by Sir Edward PELLEW, one of the greatest British frigate Captains. Reduced to 38 guns in 1795, she fought in the famous action with the *Droits de l'Homme* in 1797, when that French ship was driven ashore after an all-night battle. In October of 1804, *Indefatigable* led the capture of four Spanish treasure ships. She was broken up in 1816.

Indiaman   A ship engaged in the trade with India, especially a ship of large tonnage belonging to the EAST INDIA COMPANY. *See also* EAST INDIAMAN.

indisposée   Indisposed; menstruating (French).

indraught   An inward flow or current of water or air, especially one toward land or up an inlet or estuary.

infusion   A medicine prepared by steeping medicinal plant parts, such as leaves, in hot water (as in making tea).

inguinal   Of or in the groin.

ink-horn   A vessel fashioned from a horn to hold writing-ink.

innominate artery   A large artery branching off from the arch of the aorta.

in omnium   In all (Latin).

Inquisition   An ecclesiastical tribunal for the suppression of heresy and punishment of heretics, formed in the 13th century under Pope Innocent III and governed by the Congregation of the Holy Office. The Inquisition existed in Italy, France, the Netherlands, Spain, Portugal, and the Spanish and Portuguese colonies. The Spanish Inquisition was notorious in the 16th century for its brutality. The Inquisition lasted in France until 1772 and in Spain until 1834.

in soundings   To be relatively close to the shore or in shallows, where the depth is 100 FATHOMS or less, as opposed to "off soundings," where the water depth is greater than 100 fathoms.

inspissate   To thicken, condense.

intension   The action of stretching. Tension, straining.

Intermissa, Venus, diu rursus bella moves   Venus, you would renew battles long suspended (Latin, from an ode by Horace).

intermittence du coeur   An intermission of the heart (French).

interregnum   The interval between the end of one king's reign and the start of his successor's. Any period where a state has a provisional government or no ruler at all.

in terrorem   Literally, into a state of terror (Latin). To warn, done as a deterrent.

intromittent organ   A penis.

invalid   Of a sailor, to go on the sick-list or to leave the service because of illness or injury.

Invincible, **H.M.S.**   This 74-gun ship was captured from the French by Vice Admiral Sir George ANSON off Cape FINISTERRE in May of 1747 and was taken under the same name into the British Navy. Because of her superior design, she was used as a model for many British 74-gun ships, and after being wrecked at St. Helen's in 1758 was followed by four other *Invincible*s. The second was launched in 1765 and took part in the battle of the GLORIOUS FIRST OF JUNE in 1794. Commanded by Thomas Pakenham, she was severely damaged. In 1801, after a navigational error by the pilots guiding her through the narrow channels of Great Yarmouth, the *Invincible* was wrecked on Harborough Sands. The crew dismasted her to reduce topweight, but she drifted into deep water and sank, taking down her Captain, John Rennie, and about 400 of her crew.

Io triumphe   Hurrah for the triumph! (Latin).

ipecacuanha   The dried root of the ipecac plant, ground and used as an emetic.

Iphigenia   In Greek mythology, the daughter of Agamemnon and Clytemnestra and the sister of Orestes and Electra. In an early account she was sacrificed to the goddess Artemis after Greek hunters killed one of Artemis's wild animals. The fifth-century tragic poet Euripides wrote, instead, that Iphigenia was saved at the altar and transported to the land of the fierce Tuaurians, where she was kept as the priestess of the temple of Artemis and made to consecrate her fellow Greeks before they were sacrificed to Artemis by these enemies of the Greeks. She was saved by her brother Orestes after he and his friend Pylades were captured and arrived at the temple. The reunion was a surprise to both. They discovered each other when Iphigenia promised Pylades she would save him if he would return and deliver a letter to her brother Orestes.

iris   A member of a genus (*Iris*) of herbaceous plants native to Europe, North Africa, and the temperate parts of Asia and America, most species having tuberous roots, sword-shaped leaves, and showy flowers. Also called fleur-de-lis or flower-de-luce.

iron-bound   Rock-bound, inhospitable.

Ironmonger   A dealer in ironware; a hardware merchant.

iron-sick   When the iron bolts and nails of a wooden ship become loose due to corrosion. Acid in the wood rusts the metal, creating rot in the wood.

Iroquois   A confederacy of North American Indians also known as the Five Nations, primarily in New York State and Ontario.

isabella-coloured   Grayish yellow or light buff.

jabot   A ruffled or pleated fall of cloth or lace, worn by men, attached to the front of a neckband and descending along the front and center of a shirt. Also, a similar fall in drapery.

jack   A ship's flag, consisting only of the canton (upper left-hand quarter) of the national flag, sometimes used at sea as a signal or mark of distinction. Specifically, the small flag flown from the JACK-STAFF on the BOWSPRIT of a vessel, as in the British Union Jack, Dutch Jack, French Jack. Also, a British naval seaman (originally, only ABLE SEAMEN and men whose station was on the MASTS and YARDS of SQUARE-RIGGED warships).

jackass   A kind of heavy rough boat used in NEWFOUNDLAND. Also, U.S. Navy name for a HAWSE-bag, a canvas bag filled with OAKUM used to plug the HAWSE-HOLES to keep seawater out.

jackass rig   Any RIG of a sailing ship that substantially differs from the one normally associated with that type of ship.

jack-crosstree   The CROSSTREE at the head of the TOPGALLANT MAST.

jackeen   Contemptuous term for an obnoxious, self-assertive person of little talent or knowledge.

Jack-in-the-dust *or* **Jack of the dust**   Slang term for the PURSER's Assistant, who worked in the BREADROOM, where the flour was stored.

Jack-in-the-green   In May Day dances and the like, a man or boy who participates in the festivities, enclosed in a wooden or wicker pyramidal framework covered with leaves.

Jack-pudding   A buffoon, clown, or MERRY-ANDREW.

jack-staff   A short staff, usually set on the BOWSPRIT or at the BOW of a ship, on which the flag called the JACK is HOISTED when the ship is at anchor.

Jacobin   A friar of the order of St. Dominic, a Dominican. Originally, the term referred to the French members of the order, so called for the church of Saint Jacques, which was near their first convent, in Paris. A member of a French political society founded in 1789 in the old convent of the Jacobins to support the principles of extreme democracy and absolute equality. A sympathizer with the Jacobins of the French Revolution; a radical. About 1800, a nickname for any political reformer.

Jacobite   A supporter of James II (1633–1701), who left the English throne in 1688; a supporter of the Stuart pretenders to the English throne.

jactitation   Extreme restlessness; tossing from side to side.

J'ai failli attendre   I almost had to wait (French).

Jain   A member of a non-Brahminical East Indian sect, established about the sixth century B.C., whose main doctrines are similar to those of Buddhism.

jakes   A privy.

jalap   A mild cathartic.

James I (*1566–1625*)   Successor to Elizabeth I and the first Stuart King, James I is often considered to have had a negative effect on the Navy. He made peace with Spain soon after he ascended the throne and allowed Elizabeth's fleet to fall into decay. However, this fleet began to revive after 1618, and James's 64-gun *Prince Royal* of 1610, the largest ship of its time, pointed the way toward the three-decker.

James's powder   Invented by Dr. Robert James (1703–1776), a diaphoretic and cathartic mixture of ANTIMONY and calcium phosphate that was a popular fever reducer in the late 18th and early 19th centuries.

janissary   A soldier of an elite Turkish infantry that formed the Sultan's guard and was the most potent part of the standing army. First organized in the 14th century, its ranks were filled mainly with Christian slaves, who remained unmarried and lived in barracks. After a long decline in the corps's viability, it was finally abolished by Mahmud II after he massacred many of its members in 1826. By extension, any Turkish soldier, especially one involved in escorting travelers in the East.

J'arrive, mon capitaine ... qu'est-ce que ce remue-ménage? ... Vous êtes un officier anglais, monsieur? ... Chez le colonel.   I'm coming, captain ... what is this hullabaloo? ... Are you an English officer, sir? ... With the colonel (French).

jaunting-car   In Ireland, a light two-wheeled carriage pulled by a single horse, usually having back-to-back seats hung over the two wheels.

jeer *or* **jear**   Heavy TACKLE for hoisting and lowering the lower YARDS, the former a procedure known as "swaying up the yards." The "jeer CAPSTAN," between the FOREMAST and MAINMAST, was used by the sailors to assist in hoisting the yards.

jelly-bag   A bag used for straining the fruit when making jelly.

Jersey   The largest of the Channel Islands, on the south side of the English Channel. Also, the stockings, sweaters, and other knitted articles that the islanders produced.

Jersey, Frances, Countess of (*1753–1821*)   Mistress of the Prince of Wales, later GEORGE IV, c.1795–96, until the return of Mrs. FITZHERBERT. She continued to make difficulties for Prince George, who later referred to her as that "infernal Jezabel."

Jervis, Admiral Sir John (*1735–1823*)   First Earl St. Vincent. Born at Meaford, Staffordshire, Jervis ran away from home and entered the Navy at age 13. He served with distinction in the American Revolutionary War and afterward became a Member of Parliament. He commanded an expedition to the WEST INDIES, capturing Martinique and

Admiral Sir John Jervis, Earl of St. Vincent (*reproduced from Alfred Mahan's* Life of Nelson, *courtesy of the Mariners' Museum, Newport News, Virginia*)

Guadeloupe from the French in 1793 and 1794. At the Battle of CAPE ST. VINCENT in 1797, Jervis, with the help of NELSON, captured four Spanish ships and disabled many others off the southwest tip of Portugal, for which he was made an earl. Nicknamed Hanging Jervis for his strict disciplinarian nature, he was deeply religious and known to be of high integrity and sound judgment. He served as First Lord of the ADMIRALTY from 1801 to 1804. Kindhearted and generous in his personal relations, Jervis was given to vehement reproofs for unprofessional conduct and was often undiplomatic in his approach; nevertheless, he made substantial improvements to the administration and organization of the Navy.

Jesuit A member of the Society of Jesus, a Roman Catholic order founded by Ignatius Loyola in 1533 and sanctioned by Paul IV in 1540. The object of the society was to support the Roman Church in its struggle with the 16th-century reformers and to propagate the faith among the heathen. Hated and feared by Protestants, the order, with its authoritarian constitution and its principle of total obedience to papal commands, became suspect to many in Roman Catholic countries, too, as Jesuit schools and confessionals came to exercise great influence on rulers and high society. Enemies accused the Jesuits of teaching that the end justifies the means, and the lax principles of casuistry put forward by a few Jesuit moralists were ascribed to the Society as a whole, giving rise to the second sense, a dissembling person; a prevaricator.

Jesuits' bark *or* **Peruvian bark**   *See* BARK.

jew's ear   An edible, cup-shaped fungus that grows on the roots and trunks of trees.

jib   A triangular HEADSAIL that stretches from the outer end of the JIB-BOOM to the FORE TOPMAST head in large ships, and from the BOWSPRIT to the MASTHEAD in smaller craft. Introduced in smaller craft around 1705, the jib became standard in larger ships by 1719. As a verb, a variant of GYBE. Also, of a horse or other animal in harness, to stop and refuse to proceed, to balk stubbornly.

jib-boom   A SPAR run out from the end of the BOWSPRIT, to which the TACK of the JIB is LASHed, and beyond which is sometimes extended the flying jib-boom.

jib of jibs   In a clipper ship, a sixth JIB on the BOWSPRIT, the sequence being storm, inner, outer, flying, SPINDLE, jib of jibs. A light-weather sail only set in a gentle breeze. In the Royal Navy, the single jib was the rule, and rarely would anything have been set outside the FLYING JIB.

jinn   In Muslim demonology, an order of spirits lower than the angels and said to have the power of appearing in human and animal forms and of exercising supernatural influence over men.

jobber   One who does odd jobs, a HACK. One employed and paid by the job, rather than continuously engaged and paid wages.

job captain   An officer temporarily in command of a ship while its Captain was otherwise employed. The situation occurred not infrequently during the 18th and 19th centuries, particularly with naval officers, including RODNEY, JERVIS, PELLEW, and HOWE, among others, who were also Members of Parliament.

joe *or* **johanne,** *also* **jo**   The name in the British American Colonies for a Portuguese gold coin worth 6,400 reis, or about 36 SHILLINGS sterling.

John Company   *See* EAST INDIA COMPANY.

John o' Groats   Point on the north coast of Scotland, often considered the most northerly point in Great Britain. However, the most northerly point is actually Dunnet's Head, some miles to the west.

Johnson, Samuel *(1709–1784)*   Born at Lichfield and educated at Pembroke College, Oxford, Dr. Johnson was the leading literary scholar and critic of his day, making a profound contribution to English letters. He is remembered as the compiler of the first comprehensive lexicon in English, *The Dictionary of the English Language* (1755). His brilliant conversation, wit, and aphorisms were documented by his friend and biographer, James Boswell. Maturin's opinion of Dr. Johnson is expressed in *Master and Commander* (p. 147): " 'The most respectable, the most amiable of the moderns. I disagree with all he says, except when he speaks of Ireland, yet I honour him; and for his life of Savage [*Life of Savage,* 1744] I love him.' " About Ireland, Boswell records Johnson: " 'There is no instance, even in ten persecutions, of such severity as that which the Protestants of Ireland have exercised against the Catholicks. Did we tell them we have conquered them, it would be above board: to punish them by confiscation and other penalties, as rebels, was monstrous injustice. King William was not their lawful sovereign: he had not been acknowledged by the Parliament of Ireland, when they appeared in arms against him.' "

joiner   A craftsman who constructs things by joining pieces of wood and does finer work than a carpenter, such as the furniture and fittings of a ship.

jolly   A Navy nickname for a Royal MARINE.

jolly boat   A ship's boat, smaller than a CUTTER, with a BLUFF BOW and a wide STERN, used chiefly for small work and usually HOISTED at the STERN of the vessel. *See* illustration, page 72.

Jonah   The name of a Hebrew prophet, the subject of the Book of Jonah. A person who brings bad luck.

Jones, John Paul *(1747–1792)*   The "Paul Jones" taunt of the British by the Americans refers to John Paul Jones, the American naval hero of the Revolutionary War. Jones's raids on British warships earned him the French Merité Militaire, making him the only officer in the American armed services to be so decorated. Born in Scotland as John Paul, he apprenticed in ships sailing to America and adopted it as his new home, where he changed his name to John Paul Jones. He was loathed in Britain for attacking the ships of his native country and considered a pirate.

Jones, Tom The boisterous hero of Henry Fielding's novel *The History of Tom Jones* (1749).

judas A small lattice or aperture in a door found in some old houses and in prison cells, through which a person can look without being noticed from the other side. A peep-hole.

Judas-coloured Of the hair or beard, red, from the medieval belief that Judas Iscariot had red hair and a red beard.

judas-hole See JUDAS.

judicial combat A duel.

judy A woman or girl, from the female character in Punch and Judy shows.

jug To stew or boil in a jug or jar, especially a hare or rabbit.

jumped-up Something of new and sudden self-importance, implying conceit or arrogance.

junk An old or inferior CABLE or rope or old cable or rope material cut up into short lengths and used for making such things as FENDERs, REEF-POINTS, GASKETS, and OAKUM. Also, junk or jonk, a flat-bottomed native sailing vessel in China and the EAST INDIES having a square PROW, prominent STEM, and a full STERN, carrying LUG-SAILs frequently made of cane or bamboo mats, and using wooden anchors.

***Juno*, H.M.S.** The 32-gun FRIGATE, built on the Thames in 1780 and named for the goddess Juno, the wife of Jupiter, is probably best known for its amazing escape in the winter of 1794 when, her Captain, Samuel Hood, unaware that the British had left TOULON, sailed her into the French Republican–held port. The French did their best to conceal their identity and even caused the ship to run hard aground. However, the crew soon caught on to the deception and managed to maneuver into clear water. Although guns from the surrounding ships and the forts battled her, the *Juno* managed to gain the open sea and escape without a man lost.

Jupiter, **H.M.S.**   Named after the Roman supreme god of heaven and earth, this 50-gun fourth-rate ship was launched in 1778 and saw action at the Cape of Good Hope (*see* CAPE OF STORMS) in 1795. She was wrecked in 1808 at Vigo Bay on the Atlantic coast of Spain.

jury-mast   A temporary MAST put up in place of one that has been broken or carried away. Thus, jury FOREMAST, jury MAINMAST, etc.

kampong A MALAY village, consisting primarily of bamboo and wooden houses with thatched roofs.

kapok A large tropical tree, *Ceiba casearia*. Silky, cottonlike fiber produced from the soft seed covering found within the tree's fruit, used as stuffing for mattresses, cushions, and the like.

kava An intoxicating drink made from the macerated (chewed, grated, or pounded) roots of the Polynesian shrub *Piper methysticum*.

kedge *or* **kedge anchor** A small anchor with an iron or wooden stock used in MOORing to keep a ship steady and clear from her BOWER anchor while she rides in a harbor or river, particularly at the turn of the tide, when she might ride over her principal anchor, entangle the stock or FLUKEs with her slack CABLE, and loosen the anchor from the ground. Also used in WARPing, a way of moving a ship from one part of a harbor to another by dropping the kedge anchor and pulling on the HAWSER, thus "kedging off."

kedgeree An Indian dish of rice boiled with split pulse (edible leguminous seeds such as peas, beans, or lentils), onions, eggs, butter, and condiments. Also, in Europe, a dish made of fish, boiled rice, eggs, and condiments.

keel The principal piece of timber in a ship, usually first laid on the blocks in building, to which the STEM, STERNPOST, and ribs are attached. "By comparing the carcass of a ship to the skeleton of a human body," explains *Falconer's*, "the keel appears as the backbone, and the timbers as the ribs. Accordingly, the keel supports and unites the whole fabric." Also, a prominent ridge along the breastbone of birds of the class Carinatae, at first cartilaginous but afterward becoming ossified.

keelhaul To HAUL a person under the keel of a ship, either by lowering him on one side and pulling him across to the other side, or, in smaller vessels, lowering him at the BOWS and drawing him along under the keel to the STERN. *Falconer's* describes it as "a punishment inflicted by the Dutch navy," which suspends "the culprit by a rope from one YARDARM, with a weight of lead or iron upon his legs, to sink him to a competent depth, and having another rope fastened to him, leading under the ship's bottom, and through a block at its opposite yardarm; he is then repeatedly and suddenly let fall into the sea, where, passing under the ship's bottom, he is hoisted up, on the opposite side of the vessel, to the yardarm. As this extraordinary sentence is executed with a serenity of temper peculiar to the Dutch, the culprit is allowed sufficient intervals to recover the sense of pain. . . . This punishment is supposed to have peculiar propriety in the depth of winter, whilst the flakes of ice are floating on the stream; and . . . is continued till the culprit is almost suffocated for want of air, benumbed with the cold of the water, or stunned with the blows his head receives by striking the ship's bottom." The practice was largely abandoned in favor of punishment by the CAT-O'-NINE-TAILS at the beginning of the 18th century.

keelson (*pronounced* "**kelson**") A BAULK forming a sort of inner keel, placed inside the floor-timbers and bolted through the keel, which lay below them. Sister-keelsons were placed on the BILGEs on either side of the keelson.

Keith, Admiral George *See* ELPHINSTONE.

Keith, Lady Hester Maria *or* **Queeney (1762–1857)** The eldest daughter of the 12 children born to Henry Thrale, a prosperous brewer, and the famous Mrs. THRALE. SAMUEL JOHNSON took on a great affection for the Thrales and, for some 16 years, was a regular visitor to their house, Streatham Park (about five miles south of London), where he wrote rhymes about Queeney as a child. Queeney married George ELPHINSTONE, Baron Keith, at Ramsgate on January 10, 1808.

As the wife of the wealthy and prestigious Keith, she became prominent in London society. In the Aubrey-Maturin novels, Queeney
plays the role of adoptive older sister to Aubrey. She helps raise him
after his mother dies and then serves as one of his chief benefactors
via her husband's powerful influence.

Kenites   In the Bible, a nomadic tribe in the wilderness friendly to
the Hebrews. Some scholars believe that they may have introduced
the Israelites to the worship of Yahweh. The words Cain and Kenite
share the same Hebrew root consonants, leading some to link the
Kenites to the genealogy of Cain in the book of Genesis.

Kerguelen Islands   A group of desolate sub-Antarctic islands discovered and claimed for France by Yves Joseph Kerguélen-Trémarec
in 1772. Kerguelen Island, the largest in the archipelago, is also
known as Desolation Island. Although it appears that this is where
the *Leopard* repairs in the novel *Desolation Island*, Aubrey denies it in
The Thirteen Gun Salute.

Kerr, Lord Mark (1776–1840)   A naval officer who is best remembered for his pre-TRAFALGAR actions. While his FRIGATE H.M.S. *Fisgard*
was refitting at GIBRALTAR in April 1805, he saw VILLENEUVE's fleet of 11
warships leaving the Mediterranean and sailing out to the Atlantic.
Taking quick action, he hired a BRIG and sent a LIEUTENANT to warn
NELSON. Then he rushed *Fisgard* to sea and was able to warn CALDER's
SQUADRON as well as to get the information to Ireland and to London.

kerseymere *also* **"karsimir"**   A twilled, fine woolen cloth of a peculiar texture, one third of the warp being always above, and two thirds
below each shoot of the weft.

ketch   A strongly built two-masted vessel, originally used primarily
for coastal trading and adapted by the English, French, and Dutch
navies during the Napoleonic wars to tend the fleets. Also, with the
forward section largely open, the KETCH was perfect for the mounting
of a large MORTAR and thus was much used by the English as a BOMB-
vessel, or bomb-ketch. *See* illustration, page 58.

kevel *or* **range**   A frame made of two pieces of timber nailed to a
ship's side with two arms, or horns, to which certain ropes—the
TACKS and SHEETS, or great ropes, which extend the bottoms of the
MAINSAIL and FORESAIL—are secured.

khat   *See* QAT.

kickshaw A fancy food dish. The term was primarily used contemptuously by the British for, say, dainty French cooking, as opposed to a hearty English dish. Something dainty or elegant but unsubstantial, a trifle or gewgaw.

kid A small wooden tub used domestically, especially a sailor's MESS-tub.

killick An anchor once used by small craft consisting of a stone tied to a rope. Sailors' slang for anchor.

kingfisher A small European diving bird with a long cleft beak, bright plumage, and crested headfeathers, that feeds on fish and aquatic animals. Also, various birds of the same family.

King Log A reference to the log that Jupiter, according to fable, made king over the frogs. Often used to signify inertness on the part of rulers.

King's Bench In full, King's Bench Prison. A jail for debtors and criminals confined by authority of the supreme court at Westminster and other such courts.

King's hard bargain A worthless or incorrigible person.

King's malady, the A reference to the bouts of insanity suffered by King GEORGE III, now thought to have been caused by porphyria, an inborn error of the metabolism of hemoglobin.

The kingfisher, of the family *Alcedinidae* (*from* Encyclopaedia Britannica, *1771*)

kip A common lodging-house or a bed in such a house. A bed in general.

kipper To cure by cleaning, rubbing repeatedly with salt and pepper or other spice, and drying in the open air or in smoke. A kippered fish, as salmon or herring.

kipping-ken A lodging-house.

kite *or* **flying kite** A general name for sails above the TOPGALLANT sails, STUDDING-SAILS, and JIB-TOPSAILS set only in a light wind blowing on the STERN to maximize speed. Also, a bird of prey, a member of the hawk family, with long wings and usually a forked tail. About 30 species of kites are widely distributed over the warmer regions of the Old and New Worlds and are most commonly found near water or wetlands.

kittiwake Any seagull of the genus *Rissa,* but refers primarily to the common species of the North Atlantic and Arctic Oceans, which is a small gull with white plumage, black markings, and very long wings.

klipspringer A small African antelope, *Oreotragus oreotragus.*

knacker One who by profession buys old and useless horses and slaughters them for their hides and hoofs and for making dogfood. A "knacker's yard" in seamen's slang is a shipbreaker's yard.

knee A piece of timber shaped in a right angle, often naturally so, that is used to secure parts of a ship together, especially to connect the BEAMs and the timbers. A HANGING KNEE lies beneath and supports the ends of the deck beams; a lodging knee fastens the forward side of a ship's beam to the ship's side; and a bosom knee the afterside of the beam to the ship's side. In smaller vessels, knees support the THWARTS.

knighthead One of two large timbers in a vessel on each side of the upper STEM that support the BOWSPRIT, which is fixed between them. Formerly they were carved with a man's head.

Knights of Malta Members of the military religious order of the Hospital of St. John of Jerusalem, also called the Knights of St. John, of Jerusalem, of Rhodes, or of MALTA. The order grew out of an 11th-century pilgrim's hospital in the Holy Land, where it grew rich and powerful. The order took Rhodes in 1310. Emperor Charles V gave the Knights the island of Malta in 1530, which they defended against the Turks. After the battle of LEPANTO (1571), the Knights ruled the island and engaged in hospital work until Napoleon took the island in 1798. The British took it from the French in 1800.

knittel   A small line made of yarn, used on board ship for various purposes.

knob   Slang for "head."

knocking-shop   A brothel.

knot   A piece of knotted string fastened to the LOG-LINE, one of a series fixed at such intervals (every 47 feet 3 inches) that the number of them that run out while a 28-second sand-glass is running indicates the ship's speed in nautical miles per hour, or "knots." Hence, each of the divisions so marked on the log-line, as a measure of the rate of motion of the ship (or of a current).

koala *or* **koala bear**   An Australian arboreal marsupial mammal (*Phascolarctos cinereus*). Ashen-gray in color, small, clumsy, and somewhat similar in shape to a sloth, the koala feeds on eucalyptus leaves.

koekje   Cookie, from the Dutch *koek*, "cake."

Korah   The third son of Esau by his wife Aholibamah. Born in Canaan, Korah became a chief of an Edomite tribe (Gen. 36:18).

Kraken   A mythical sea monster of enormous size, sometimes represented as a giant octopus or squid, said to have been seen at times off the coasts of Norway and Sweden.

kree   A MALAY dagger.

kris   A MALAY dagger with a wavy blade.

Krishna   The name of a Hindu deity or hero. The worship of or belief in Krishna.

Kyrie eleison   In Latin, from Greek, "Lord, have mercy." The words of a short petition used in various offices of the Eastern and Roman churches, especially at the start of the Mass; in the Anglican service, represented by the words "Lord, have mercy upon us" in the Response to the Commandments during Communion Service. These words set to music, especially as the first movement of a Mass.

La bêtise c'est de vouloir conclure   The absurd thing is the desire to come to a conclusion (French).

lachrymation   The shedding of tears, weeping.

Laconical helot   In ancient Sparta a serf, originally from the town of Helos, ranking in social status between an ordinary slave and a free citizen.

lacuna   In a text, a hiatus, a blank or missing portion. In physical science, a gap, an empty space, a cavity.

Lady-Day   A day given to celebrating an event in the life of the Virgin Mary.

Lady Jersey   *See* JERSEY, FRANCES.

lady's bedstraw   A genus (*Galium*) of plants containing many species, with slender ascending stems, whorled or cruciate leaves, and small, clustered flowers.

Laënnec, René-Théophile-Hyacinthe (*1781–1826*)   Parisian physician who made extensive studies in which he correlated clinical findings with postmortem observations. He invented the stethoscope in 1816, although he did not publish its usefulness for another three years.

La Forte   Launched at Rochefort in 1795, she was, at the time, the largest FRIGATE ever built originally as a frigate. She was taken in the Indian Ocean by H.M.S. *Sybille* in 1799.

la garce   The bitch (French).

La Hogue *or* **La Hougue**   A bay on the east side of the Cotentin Peninsula on the northwest coast of France. Following the Battle of Barfleur in May 1692 during the Nine Years' War (1689–1697), the main French fleet sought refuge here. Entering the bay on June 3, Vice-Admiral Sir George Rooke attacked the anchored fleet, destroying 12 French battleships. The actions at Barfleur and La Hogue were the most spectacular English victories at sea in the period.

lakh   One hundred thousand. Also, many.

lambdoid suture   Line of union between the occipital bone, over the back of the skull, and the two parietal bones, which lie over the major upper portion of the skull.

Lammas   Loaf Mass, August 1, which was celebrated in the early English Church with a harvest festival, involving the consecration of bread made from the first harvest of corn; also, the time of year in which Lammas occurs.

lamprey   A fish elongated like an eel, with no scales, a mouth like a sucker, pouchlike gills, seven spiracles or apertures on each side of the head, and a fistula or opening on the top of the head.

Lancaster, Duchy of   Refers to the estates throughout England owned by the Crown since the Middle Ages and which are private property, not part of the Crown Estate. Part of this land is in London. *See* SAVOY, LIBERTIES OF THE.

lancet   A medical tool, usually having two sharp edges and a point like a lance, used for such purposes as letting blood and opening abscesses.

landsman *or* **landman**   In the Royal Navy, the RATE of a sailor with no naval training who performed basic tasks on board ship, chiefly

HAULing and HOISTing. A landsman was paid less than an ABLE SEA-MAN or ORDINARY SEAMAN.

langouste   The edible spiny lobster of Europe, which lacks the large pincers of the American lobster.

langrage *also* **langrel, langrace,** *or* **langridge**   A type of CASE-SHOT with jagged pieces of irregularly shaped iron and a wide pattern, favored by PRIVATEERs and especially useful in damaging RIGGING and sails and killing men on deck.

lanyard   A short piece of rope made fast to anything to secure it or to use as a handle. Used to secure SHROUDS and STAYS and for firing flintlock guns.

lap   To enwrap or swathe; to clothe; to bind up or tie around.

lapis lazuli *or* **lapis**   A semiprecious stone that is a complex silicate containing a bright azure sulphur. Also, the color of this mineral.

lapsus calami   A slip of the pen (Latin).

lapsus linguae   A slip of the tongue (Latin).

larboard *or* **larbowlin**   The lefthand, or port, side of a ship when looking toward the BOW, as opposed to STARBOARD. The term was later replaced by "port" to avoid confusion with "starboard."

larbolins *also* **larbowlines, larbolines,** *and* **larbowlins**   The part of the ship's crew who formed the LARBOARD, or port, WATCH.

larder   A room or closet in which meat and other provisions are stored.

large   Said of a wind that crosses the line of a ship's course in a favorable direction, especially on the BEAM or QUARTER. In a SQUARE-RIGGED ship, the point where STUDDINGSAILs would draw. To sail large (going large) means to sail with the wind blowing on the stern and the SHEETs eased.

lark   A name used to refer generally to any bird of the family Alaudidae, but usually to the skylark. The lark has sandy-brown plumage and very long hind-claws.

lascar   An Indian or East Indian sailor.

lash To secure or bind something with a rope or cord. Also, a stroke of the CAT-O'-NINE-TAILS.

lashing-eye Fittings formed from loops made in the ends of ropes, for a lashing (a rope used to secure something) to be ROVE through.

lask To sail LARGE, with the wind on the QUARTER.

La Sybille Taken in 1794 by H.M.S. *Romney*, Captain Hon. W. Paget, *La Sybille* (40 guns) became the British fifth rate *Sybille*. She took the larger LA FORTE in 1799 but lost her captain, Cooke, who was mortally wounded during the battle.

lateen sail *or* **lateen** Of ancient origin, the word derives from "Latin," meaning "Mediterranean," where the sail was commonly used. A triangular sail suspended by a long YARD (made from two or more timbers and often longer than the boat itself) at an angle of about 45 degrees to the MAST. Frequently used by XEBECs, polacres (*see* POLACRE RIG), SETTEES, FELUCCAS, DHOWS and other vessels in the Mediterranean. Also, a vessel with a lateen RIG.

Latham, John (*1740–1837*) An English ornithologist who, between 1821 and 1828, published the 12-volume *A General History of Birds*, which he illustrated himself.

latibule A hiding-place.

laudanum Alcoholic TINCTURE of OPIUM. The 16th-century German alchemist and physician Bombast von Hohenheim (also known as PARACELSUS) introduced the medicinal use of opium in an expensive mixture he called laudanum.

Lauds A religious office of solemn praise to God that follows Matins and forms with it the first of the seven canonical hours.

launch The largest boat of a MAN-OF-WAR, longer, lower, and more flat-bottomed than a merchantman's LONG-BOAT, often carrying one FORE-AND-AFT sail and capable of short autonomous cruises. Also, a somewhat larger, flat-bottomed boat used in the Mediterranean as a GUNBOAT, and a similar but smaller rowboat used in shallow waters. In 1789, Captain BLIGH sailed the Bounty's launch for 41 days from the site of the mutiny to Timor. *See* illustration, page 71.

laurel   The bay-laurel, a southern European tree, the foliage of which was used by the ancient Greeks to crown the winners at the Pythian games. Used occasionally as a medicine.

lavender   A small shrub with purple flowers and thin oblong leaves, native to southern Europe and northern Africa but cultivated in other countries for its perfume. Sometimes used as a tonic remedy.

Lawrence, James (*1731–1813*)   American naval officer who, commanding the 18-gun SLOOP *Hornet,* on January 25, 1813, sank the British 16-gun BRIG H.M.S. *Peacock* off British Guiana (now Guyana). Considered very capable, he was promoted to Captain. But Lawrence made a fatal miscalculation as commander of the *Chesapeake* in 1813, when, with an inexperienced crew and short of officers, he nonetheless attacked the British FRIGATE H.M.S. *Shannon* off Boston. Almost immediately, he was mortally wounded and the *Chesapeake* was seriously damaged, with 146 men killed and wounded. The *Chesapeake* was captured and sailed to England. Lawrence's dying words became an American battle cry: "Don't give up the ship."

lay   To twist the strands of a rope together. Also, to direct the course of a vessel.

lay by   *See* LIE TO. Also, a wide section of a river or canal where a vessel can tie up and allow another to pass. To "lay by the heels" means to put in irons or the stocks, to arrest; also, to overthrow, disgrace.

lay lord   A peer who is not a lawyer, as opposed to a "law lord."

lay up in ordinary   Said of a ship when out of commission.

lazaretto *or* **lazarette**   A hospital where seamen or others with contagious or infectious diseases were isolated and quarantined. Often called "Lazaretto's island," though a lazarette was not necessarily an island. Also, a compartment in smaller ships used for storing provisions, usually regulated by the Master to prevent pilfering.

lead (*pronounced* "led")   A device for determining the depth of water consisting of a large piece of lead weighing from seven to 14 pounds attached to a long rope, called the LEAD-LINE, about 25 FATHOMS in length for shallow water and more than 100 fathoms for deep water. The lead was HOVE into the water by the LEADSMAN, who called out the depth by sighting the MARK on the line at the surface of the water.

leading mark   An object, such as a tree, spire, or buoy, that when aligned with another object guides the pilot safely into port.

lead-line   A sounding line or plumb line (*plumbum* is Latin for "lead," the metal), usually 25 FATHOMS long for relatively shallow water and 100 fathoms for deep-sea SOUNDINGS. *See also* LEAD.

leadsman   The man who, standing in the CHAINS, heaves the LEAD to take SOUNDINGS.

league   A distance of three nautical miles, or 3,041 FATHOMS (one fathom equals six feet). Before the SEA MILE came into use, navigators measured distance traveled in leagues. This was not a very precise measurement but was about three land miles.

Leander, H.M.S.   A fourth-rate 52-gun ship launched in 1780. In *Post Captain,* Aubrey reveals that he was on board her at the Battle of the NILE (1798). Following the battle, she carried Captain Edward Berry with NELSON's dispatches to Admiral St. Vincent (*See* JERVIS) and was captured by the 74-gun *GÉNERÉUX,* a French survivor of the battle. The *Leander,* commanded by Captain Thomas Boulder Thompson, fought against overwhelming odds for six and a half hours and was severely battered before striking colors. Afterward the crew was treated very harshly by its captors. The ship was recaptured from the French by the Russians at Corfu in 1799 and returned to the Royal Navy. Renamed *Hygeia* in 1813, she served as a medical depot ship before being sold in 1817. A second *Leander* of 58 guns was launched in 1813 and served until 1830.

leather stock   A stiff, tight neckcloth once worn by men.

lee   The side sheltered from the wind; the side of a ship, the land, a rock, or any other object that is away from the wind. Used also to indicate that an object is on the lee side of a vessel, as in "lee shore," a shore that is downwind of a ship. A lee shore is dangerous to a ship that has not provided itself with enough "leeway," the lateral distance a ship is displaced from its course in the direction of the wind, as the ship is in danger of being driven onto the shore.

leech   The free vertical edges of a sail, for example, the vertical edge of a square sail (called the LARBOARD or STARBOARD leech) and the aft edge of a FORE-AND-AFT sail.

leeches   Aquatic, blood-sucking worms. The species *Hirudo medici-nalis* was used in therapeutic bleeding (for its rationale, see "Stephen Maturin and Naval Medicine in the Age of Sail," p. 31). Leeches, each of which could remove up to an ounce of blood before becoming fully engorged and falling off, were placed over parts of the body in which an inflammation was assumed to be causing the patient's symptoms; for instance, for severe headaches, one or two leeches would be induced to suck blood through the skin over one or both temples, or four or five might be placed over the chest of a pneumonia patient.

legation   The sending of a representative, as a papal legate. A group, such as a diplomatic minister and his suite, dispatched on a mission.

Leghorn   The English name for Livorno, a major Tuscan seaport, free and neutral and used by the merchants of many nations until 1796, when Napoleon seized all the hostile ships in the port. After a brief time, the port returned to its free and neutral status until 1867, when it was incorporated into the newly formed nation of Italy.

Leguat, François (*1637–1733*)   A Frenchman who published a description of his voyage to Rodriguez, MAURITIUS, Java, and the Cape of Good Hope from 1690 to 1698. It was translated into English in 1708. There is doubt as to whether this was an authentic voyage.

lemon rob   A conserve made from lemon juice that is reduced by boiling and preserved with sugar. Sometimes used to prevent or treat SCURVY.

Le monsieur est touché. . . . Sais pas, commandant. Il parle plus: je crois bien que c'est un macchabée à présent. Y à du sang partout. Vous voulez pas me faire passer une élingue? . . . Parlez   The gentleman is hit. . . . Don't know, commander. He ain't talking: I really believe he's a corpse now. 'S blood everywhere. You mind handing round a sling? . . . Speak (French).

lemur   A family of nocturnal mammals found mainly in Madagascar, allied to the monkey but with a pointed, foxlike muzzle.

lenitive   A soothing or softening medicine, usually laxative.

Lenten   Pertaining or appropriate to Lent. Of provisions or diet, meager. Of clothing or disposition, gloomy or sorrowful.

lentisk Wood of the mastic tree, *Pistachia lentiscus,* used in some medicines. Also, its gum, mastic, also used medically.

Leopard, **H.M.S.** A fourth-rate ship of 50 guns launched in 1790, which was involved in a confrontation with the U.S. FRIGATE CHESA-PEAKE on June 22, 1807, off Norfolk Roads, Virginia. During a search for British seamen, the *Leopard* fired on the *Chesapeake,* boarded her, and seized four seamen said to be deserters from the British Navy. The *Chesapeake* was not fully armed at the time, and the incident created an outcry for war against Britain. But President Thomas Jefferson preferred to use other means to gain reparation, and a trade embargo resulted. In Patrick O'Brian's *Desolation Island,* it is aboard the *Leopard* that Captain Aubrey duels with the Dutch 74-gun *Waakzaamheid.* Later, at an inopportune moment, he feels the bitter scorn of the crew of an American whaler because of the earlier event involving the *Leopard.*

leopard's bane A remedy made from the leaves of *Arnica montana* that was introduced as a substitute for the BARK in 1712, and later promoted for the treatment of paralysis and fever.

Lepanto A naval battle fought on October 7, 1571, between a fleet from Christian nations in the Holy League and the Ottoman fleet and named for the site of the confrontation, the Lepanto strait, which separates the northern Peloponnesus from the Greek mainland. The battle was viewed as a major Christian triumph and demonstrated the ultimate development in Mediterranean GALLEY warfare. Some 30,000 Turks died in the battle, about half of whom were experienced seamen.

Lepidoptera A large order of insects having four membranous wings covered with scales, including butterflies and moths.

les agissements néfastes . . . le perfide The evil doings . . . the treacherous (French).

lese-majesty An offense against a sovereign authority; treason.

Les hommes: c'est difficile de s'endormir sans Men: it's difficult to fall asleep without them (French).

Letter to the Ephesians A letter addressed to the residents of Ephesus, a Greek city in what is now Turkey. This letter is a portion of the

New Testament, attributed to Paul writing in prison, but it was probably written by one of Paul's disciples before A.D. 90.

letter of marque (and reprisal)   A license granted by a sovereign authorizing the Captain of a privately owned and armed ship to make reprisals on the subjects of a hostile state for injuries allegedly committed against the holder of the letter. In the 18th century, the PRIVATEERS, as they were known, were basically profiteers attempting to make money by capturing enemy merchant ships. The holders of letters of marque were entitled by international law to commit acts that might otherwise have constituted piracy. Ships captured in this way were dealt with as PRIZE cases and adjudicated in Admiralty Court.

Levant   Name for the eastern shores of the Mediterranean Sea, lying between Greece and Egypt.

Levanter   A strong, often humid, easterly or northeasterly wind blowing in the Mediterranean from its eastern shore, the LEVANT.

Levantine   Of or pertaining to the LEVANT. A ship trading to the Levant. In the manner of the Levantines. Also, a twilled black silk material, very soft, of excellent wear and having a face and back of different shades.

levator   A muscle that raises the part to which it is attached.

levee   A formal reception of visitors just after rising from bed, a morning assembly held by a king, prince, or person of distinction.

Leviathan   An enormous sea creature first mentioned in Scripture, similar to either a crocodile or a sea serpent. Also, a whale or an exceptionally large ship.

levin   Lightning or a flash of lightning. Also, a bright light or flame.

Leviticus   The third book of the PENTATEUCH, containing details of Levitical law relating to priests and rituals. It also contains an account of events in the final month of the second year of the exodus from Egypt.

le voilà   Here he is (French).

liana   Various climbing and twining plants that proliferate in tropical forests.

libeccio   In Italian, the southwest wind.

liberty man   A sailor with leave to go ashore.

lickerous   Pleasing or tempting to the palate, delightful. Of a person, having an appetite for delicious food, a keen desire for something pleasant. Also, lecherous, lustful, wanton.

lictor   An ancient Roman officer who attended upon a magistrate, bearing the fasces, a symbol of authority, before him, and who executed sentences on offenders. A dictator had 24 lictors to attend him, a consul, 12.

lie to *or* **try, lie-a-try, lie by**   In a gale, where the ship could not run before the wind, sufficient canvas was set to keep her head about six points from the wind, coming up and falling off, and maintaining enough way to maintain steerage.

lie (or lay) on one's oars   To cease rowing. To lean on the handles of one's oars and raise the oar blades out of the water. To halt one's efforts.

Lieutenant   The most junior of the traditional sea officers' ranks in the Navy. *See also* page 15.

life-line   A line or rope running along the decks of a ship for the sailors to hang on to in heavy seas.

ligature   Something used in binding or tying, a bandage. In surgery, a thread used for many purposes, especially to tie off a bleeding artery.

light along   Lend assistance in HAULing CABLES, HAWSERs, or large ropes.

light-ball   A combustible fired from a mortar at night to light up the enemy's operations.

light diet   One without meat, especially red meat, or strong drink, so as not to further fuel the internal fires of a feverish inflammation.

lighter   A vessel, usually a BARGE, used in ferrying cargo to or from ships that cannot be discharged or loaded at a wharf and for moving goods of any kind in a harbor.

lights An ancient word for the lungs.

lightship A vessel with a small crew moored in dangerous waters and serving the same purpose as a lighthouse. Lightships were first employed in British waters in 1732.

lignum vitae Literally, wood of life, *Guaiacum officinale*. It was introduced in 1519, in the form of a powder made from its bark that was taken in wine or water, as the antisyphilitic remedy called guaiac, but it had come to be used chiefly as a DIAPHORETIC by the late 18th century. (However, Maturin uses it, or the thick gum extracted from the wood, to repair his viola.)

Ligny, Battle of While attempting to drive a wedge between the allied armies of WELLINGTON and BLÜCHER in Belgium, NAPOLEON (with 80,000 men) encountered the Prussians (84,000 men) on June 16, 1815. In fierce fighting, the Prussians suffered 25,000 casualties (and deserters, mostly recent recruits), while the French lost 11,000. Blücher himself was dismounted in a cavalry charge while attempting unsuccessfully to turn the tide. The French failed to deliver a knockout blow, however, and the Prussians' retreat to Wavre under GNEISENAU, made possible by Blücher's brave counterattack, put them in a position to determine the outcome of the Battle of WATERLOO, two days later.

Liguria An ancient geographical region in northwestern Italy. In 1797 the strip of coast surrounding Genoa was made the Ligurian Republic. It was annexed by France in 1805.

limber The detachable fore part of a gun-carriage, consisting of two wheels and an axle, a pole for the horses, and a frame that holds one or two ammunition chests. It is attached to the trail of the gun-carriage proper by a hook. Also, one of a series of square holes cut through the floor-timbers on each side of the KEELSON allowing BILGE water to pass to the PUMP-well.

limicole An earth-dwelling worm lacking a specialized head.

limmer A rogue or scoundrel; a strumpet; a hussy or minx.

limpet A gastropod mollusk with a flat conical shell and a wide opening at one end where it clings to wood and rocks. Hence, one who clings to someone or something, especially superfluous officials who cling to their offices.

linctus   A solid medicine ingested by licking it like a lollipop.

Lind, James (*1716–1794*)   An Edinburgh University–trained naval surgeon whose chief place in medical history lies in his verification that oranges and lemons counteract SCURVY. Although he published these findings in *Treatise of the Scurvy* in 1753, it wasn't until 1795 that Sir Gilbert BLANE managed to have lemon juice issued regularly in the Royal Navy. Lind, who was in charge of the naval hospital HASLAR from 1758 to 1783, also wrote books on hygiene and the first handbook on tropical medicine.

line-of-battle ship   A RATED ship; a ship of sufficient size to take part in the battle line during a major fleet action.

lingua franca   A mixed language used in the LEVANT, chiefly Italian without its inflections. Any mixed language used as a common language by people who speak different languages.

linhay   A shed or farm building with an open front and usually a lean-to roof.

link   A torch made of tow, or yarn, and pitch, wax, or tallow and used to light one's way through the streets.

Linnaeus, or Linné, Carl von (*1707–1778*)   Swedish botanist and founder of the modern study of botany. Professor of medicine (1741) and botany (1742) at Uppsala University. He established a system of plant classification based on sexual characteristics.

Linois, Charles Alexandre Leon Durand, comte de (*1761–1848*)   French admiral who fought COCHRANE at the battle of Algeciras in 1804. Taken prisoner in the EAST INDIES in 1806, he was brought to England, where he remained until 1811. At the restoration in 1814, he became governor of Guadeloupe.

linseed   Seeds and oil of common flax, *Linum usitatissimum*, used as an emollient in enemas and poultices.

linstock   A staff with a forked tip used to hold a lit match for the firing of a cannon.

lint   A soft, absorbent material made by scraping or unraveling linen cloth that was used for dressing wounds.

lintel   A horizontal piece of timber, stone, or other material over a door, window, or other opening that bears the weight above it.

Li Po (*701–762*)   One of the most acclaimed Chinese lyric poets, the author of nearly 2,000 poems.

liquor ammoniae acetatis   Solution of ammonium acetate prescribed as a DIAPHORETIC FEBRIFUGE.

Litera scripta manet   The written word endures (Latin).

lithotomy   Surgical incision into the bladder to remove stones. The English surgeon William Cheselden (1688–1752), who wrote *The Anatomy of the Human Body* (1713), originated the operation of lateral lithotomy, entering the bladder from the side. A suprapubic lithotomy entered through the area of the lower abdomen overlying the bladder just above the pubic area.

***Lively*, H.M.S.**   A 32-gun fifth rate built in 1794 and wrecked near Cadiz in 1798. Another fifth rate (38 guns) built in 1804 and wrecked near Malta in 1810.

liver, palpable state of   When the liver is enlarged by disease, such as yellow fever or hepatitis, it can be palpated, or felt, through the anterior abdominal wall.

livery   Provisions or an allowance allotted to servants. A distinctive uniform dress or a badge worn by servants or by an official. The uniform of a soldier or sailor.

livre   A book; also, a (monetary) pound (both French). In this period, a unit of French currency divided into 20 *sols* (or *sous*).

Livy (*59* B.C.–A.D. *17*)   A Roman historian (Latin name, Titus Livius) who, under the patronage of Emporer Augustus, wrote *The Annals of the Roman People* (142 books). Books I to X and XXI to XLV still exist; the rest have been fully or partially destroyed.

lixiviation   The separation of a soluble substance from an insoluble one by the percolation of water, for example, the extracting of salts from wood ash.

lizard   A short rope with an EYE at one end by which means it runs along another rope or STAY.

Lizard Point *or* **The Lizard**   The southern-most point of Cornwall, a formidable headland where many wrecks have occurred.

Lloyd's   International insurance market founded in 1680s by a group of underwriters who met at a coffeehouse operated by Edward Lloyd (1688–1713) in Tower Street, London. From 1760 it issued an annual list of merchant vessels and their owners. From 1774 to 1838, Lloyd's operated in space rented at the ROYAL EXCHANGE.

Lloyd's presentation sword   It was common for corporate or patriotic bodies to give swords as a reward. Among the best known were those given by Lloyd's Patriotic Fund, established in 1803.

lobcock   A bumpkin, a blundering fool.

loblolly boy   An assistant who helps a ship's surgeon and his mates, so called after loblolly, the gruel commonly served in the sickbay.

lobscouse   A common sailor's dish consisting of salted meat stewed with vegetables, spices, and crumbled ship's biscuit.

lobster   Derogatory term for a British soldier. Originally it was applied to a regiment that wore complete suits of armor, and then was easily transferred to red-coated soldiers.

log   A device for measuring the speed of a ship (*see* LOG-LINE and LOG-SHIP); also, short for LOG BOOK.

logarithm   A type of mathematical function invented in 1614 and used to abridge calculation.

log-board *or* **log-slate**   A hinged pair of boards divided into several columns, containing the hours of the day and night. In it were recorded the direction of the winds, the ship's course, latitude by observation, and all the material occurrences that happen during the 24 hours, or from noon to noon. From this table the officers worked the ship's course and compiled their journals and the LOG-BOOK, where the contents of the log-board were recorded daily. Written with chalk, the log-board was rubbed out every day at noon.

log-book *or* **log**   The daily record of a ship's journey, a book ruled in columns like a LOG-BOARD, into which the account of the log-board was transcribed every day along with other information such as maneuvers, weather, crew activity, actions, and encounters. The intermediate divisions, or WATCHes, of a log-book, containing four hours each, were usually signed by the commanding officer in ships of war and EAST INDIAMEN. In the Royal Navy, separate logs kept by the captain, LIEUTENANT, and MASTER were required to be turned in at the end of each cruise. Part of a MIDSHIPMAN's training was to keep a log, which an officer frequently checked for legibility and accuracy.

loggia   A roofed gallery or arcade open to the air on one or more sides and often overlooking a court.

log-glass   A half-minute sandglass used on a vessel to time sailing speed by comparing the length of line run out to a fixed interval of time.

log-line   A line of 100 FATHOMS or more attached at one end to the LOG-SHIP, which was released overboard (the act called "heaving the log"). KNOTs tied in the log-line were counted as sand ran out of a LOG-GLASS. By comparing the amount of time passed to the number of knots released, the speed of the vessel was calculated in nautical miles per hour, or "knots." With a 28-second glass, the line was divided into lengths of 47.33 feet; with a 30-second glass, 50.75 feet.

log-ship *also* **log** *or* **log-chip**   A wooden apparatus in the shape of a piece of pie attached to the LOG-LINE and used for calculating a ship's speed. Weighted with lead along the arc, it floated point up in the water.

Loligo   A genus of cephalopods, including squids.

London's Change   *See* ROYAL EXCHANGE.

London Gazette   *See* GAZETTE.

London River   A common term for the River Thames, including its docks, pools, reaches, and shipping outlets.

long-boat   Similar to a Navy LAUNCH, the largest boat belonging to a sailing ship, CARVEL-BUILT with high sides, capable of carrying a ship's gun in the BOWs and fitted with a MAST and sails for short journeys.

Used primarily for provisioning, for transporting water casks for refilling, and as a lifeboat.

longicorn   Pertaining to a family of beetles that includes those with long horns.

long nine   A nine-pounder gun (one that fires nine-pound balls) with a long barrel for greater range.

longshoreman *or* **stevedore**   A worker who is employed along the shore to perform such tasks as loading and unloading cargoes.

long-stop   In cricket, a fielder positioned behind the wicket-keeper to stop balls that get past him.

long tackles   BLOCKs used in hoisting up TOPSAILs from the deck to the YARD.

looby   A clumsy, hulking person, a lout, a LUBBER.

loom   The shaft of an oar, between the blade and the handle. When in use, the shaft of the oar between the rowlock and the hand; also, the handle. Also, the glow of a light visible over the horizon before the source of the light can be seen.

loose-box   A box stall in which a horse can move around freely.

Lord Mayor's men   At the time of the Quota Acts of 1795, Lord Mayor's men were those who entered the Navy "to relieve themselves of public disgrace, and who were sent on board by any of the city magistrates for a street frolic or a night charge." Within a few years the term was applied to any landsman who volunteered for the Navy and was distinguished by the fashionable cut of his civilian clothing.

Lords   The higher of the two bodies that formed the legislative branch of the governments of England, Scotland, and Ireland when they were separate kingdoms, and then of Great Britain.

Lord Warden   Title of the Governor of the CINQUE PORTS, who was also Constable of Dover Castle.

Lorient   The major merchant and naval shipbuilding center at the mouth of the rivers Scorff and Blavet on the BAY OF BISCAY in western France, where the French East India Company (Compagnie des Indes Orientales) was based.

L' Orient The 120-gun French flagship of Vice-Admiral de Brueys that, after dismasting and setting on fire H.M.S. *Bellerophon* at the Battle of the Nile in 1798, was engaged by both the *Swiftsure* and the *Alexander*. Paint buckets left on the deck of *L' Orient* caught fire. The ship was engulfed in flames, and eventually her MAGAZINE exploded. Most of the crew, including de Brueys and Captain Casabianca and his ten-year-old son, perished in the horrific eruption. This is the explosion Aubrey is referring to in *Post Captain* (not the *Orion*) when he tells that he served on board the LEANDER at the NILE.

lorikeet A small, brightly plumed parrot of the MALAY Archipelago.

louis d'or *or* **Louis** A French gold coin, first issued in 1640, carrying the portrait of Louis XIII and his successors. Valued at 24 LIVRES.

Louis XVIII (1755–1824). The brother of King Louis XVI and the king of France from 1814 to 1824, Louis XVIII had his reign briefly interrupted by the return of NAPOLEON from Elba in 1815, but returned to power after Napoleon's defeat at WATERLOO. Known as the comte de Provence, he fled France during the revolution (1791) and passed his exile on the Continent and in England. He was recognized as king by French émigrés after the death of Louis XVII in 1795, and with the assistance of Charles de TALLEYRAND was placed on the throne after the allies entered Paris. Although he adopted a conciliatory policy toward the former revolutionists and granted a constitutional charter, ultra-royalists, led by his brother, the comte d'Artois (later Charles X), rose to power, and Louis, then old and infirm, allowed them to take control. The wealthy classes increased their power, curbing civil liberties, and this process intensified under Louis's successor, Charles X.

Low Countries A political and historic term rather than a strictly geographic concept, the Low Countries are the region of Europe now comprising the Netherlands, Belgium, and the Grand Duchy of Luxembourg. The northern parts of the Netherlands and Belgium form a low plain along the North Sea, but southern Belgium and Luxembourg are part of the Ardennes plateau.

Low Dutch The Germanic peoples of the sea coast and the Low Countries. Also, the Dutch and Flemish languages.

lower deck The deck above the ORLOP deck where seamen lived and the ship's heaviest guns were located. Also, all the men who were not officers, those quartered on the lower deck.

lowering   Frowning, sullen; gloomy, threatening weather.

loyalist   One who adheres to his sovereign or constituted governmental authority in times of upheaval. More specifically, when capitalized, an American supporter of the British Crown during the American Revolution.

lubber *or* **landlubber**   A derogatory term used by sailors for those unacquainted with the duties of seamen or for particularly clumsy seaman, probably deriving from "lob," a clumsy, ignorant person.

lubber's hole   A hole in the ship's TOP by the MAST offering an easier and less risky way to ascend or descend than by climbing the FUTTOCK SHROUDS, the route taken by seasoned sailors.

Lucatellus's balsam   An expensive softening unguent made with yellow wax, olive oil, turpentine, and DRAGON'S BLOOD or red sanders, two exotic ingredients from trees that are indigenous to the EAST INDIES.

Lucullus, Lucius Licinius (*117–58* B.C.)   A wealthy Roman who was a patron of the arts and was famous for his lavish banquets.

lucus a non lucendo   Literally, a grove from the lack of light (Latin). This expression is used to refer to things that are the opposite of what they are billed to be. Thus, when O'Brian uses it to characterize "what Jack called the rose-garden," the reader can be pretty sure that it was nearly devoid of roses.

Ludolphus's palsy   A form of PALSY that Maturin associates with the German physician Hiobe Ludolph (d. 1720), but no description of its special features is known.

lues venerea   Syphilis (Latin).

luff   Of a sail, the FORE, or WEATHER, part. In some seamanship manuals this was called the weather leech. To luff means to steer or sail more toward the direction from which the wind is blowing. "Luff!" is an order to the helmsman to put the TILLER toward the LEE side, so the ship will sail closer to the wind.

lugger   A swift and weatherly craft used for coastal trading and fishing, usually with two MASTs carrying LUGSAILS. When employed for smuggling or as a PRIVATEER, primarily by the French, a third mast was often added. *See also* CHASSE-MARÉE. *See* illustration, page 58.

lugsail   A four-sided sail secured to a YARD that is normally two-thirds the length of the foot of the sail, so that the sail hangs obliquely.

lump   A barge or LIGHTER used in dockyards; also, a load from one.

lumpers   Laborers hired to load and unload a merchant ship in harbor. So called because they worked in gangs and were paid a lump sum.

lunar observation   At sea, a way of calculating lunar distances—the distance between the moon and a planet or a fixed star in the moon's path—used in finding longitude. Sometimes known as "Maskeleyne's method" because Nevil Maskeleyne, the Astronomer Royal from 1765 to 1811, advocated it in his *New Mariner's Guide* (1763).

lunarian   One who studies the moon or employs the lunar method in finding longitude.

lupus   Any of several skin diseases.

lurcher   A petty thief, swindler, rogue; someone who loiters suspiciously; a spy.

lustra decem   Ten five-year periods, or 50 years (Latin).

lustration   A ceremonial purification, usually spiritual or moral, as by sacrifice or by washing with water.

lutestring   A glossy fabric made of silk. A dress or ribbon of this material.

lycopod   A club-moss, such as ground pine.

Macao   A Portuguese territory and port city on the south coast of China. From 1717 until the 19th century, Macao and Canton were the only ports in China open to European trade. Burial place of St. Francis Xavier and residence of the poet Camoëns.

Macassar oil   A hair unguent flamboyantly advertised in the early part of the 19th century by its producers, Rowland and Son, who claimed it consisted of ingredients obtained from Macassar, a district of the island Celebes. The name was subsequently given commercially to various other natural products imported from the East.

Macchiavel   Anglicized form of the name of Niccolò Machiavelli (1469–1527), the Florentine statesman who advocated in his 1513 treatise *Il principe* (*The Prince*) the pursuit of statecraft at the expense of morality. Also, one who acts on Machiavelli's principles; an intriguer, an unscrupulous schemer.

mace   A scepter or staff of office once carried by some officials, including the judges of ADMIRALTY Courts. A spice made from the outer covering of the nutmeg, found in both the EAST and WEST INDIES.

***Macedonian*, H.M.S.**   A 38-gun fifth rate built in 1810 and taken in a one-sided battle by the more powerful U.S.S. *United States* (44 guns) on October 25, 1812. While the *Macedonian,* commanded by Captain John Surman Carden, suffered around 104 killed and wounded, the *United States,* Commodore Stephen Decatur, had only a dozen killed or wounded. Decatur had fought well, and his much sturdier ship had protected her crew. Along with the losses of the *Guerriere* (August 19, 1812) and the *Java* (December 29, 1812) to the U.S.S. *Constitution,* the capture of the *Macedonian* was shocking news to the British.

madder A Eurasian herbaceous climbing plant, *Rubia tinctorum,* cultivated in Holland and France for the red dye, alizarin, obtained from it. The root, which was occasionally used medicinally to calm overexcited patients, turns urine red.

mad-doctor A physician specializing in mental disorders.

Madeira A fortified wine, amber in color and full-bodied, produced on the Portuguese island of Madeira, in the Atlantic about 400 miles off the northwest coast of Africa. The British occupied the island for a short time in 1801 and again from 1807 to 1814.

Madras A port on the east coast of India founded by the English EAST INDIA COMPANY, which built Fort St. George there in 1639 and turned the town into one of the company's chief outposts. During the War of Austrian Succession, Madras was captured by the French but was restored to the British two years later in 1784 by the Treaty of Aix-la-Chapelle. In the American Revolution, Madras was again threatened by a French force under the command of Admiral Suffren, but Admiral Sir Edward Hughes was able to fend it off until the war ended.

magazine *See* POWDER-ROOM.

Magellan, Ferdinand The English name for the Portuguese navigator Fernão de Magalhães *(c. 1480–1521),* who orchestrated the first circumnavigation of the earth but was killed while making it. He was the first European discoverer to pass into the Pacific Ocean through the channel named in his honor, the MAGELLAN STRAITS, at the southern tip of South America. Magellan was killed in a native war on the island of Mactan in the Philippines.

Magellan jacket Hooded coat first worn on WATCH, it is said, by Captain COOK's seamen.

Magellan Straits *or* **Strait of Magellan**   A winding, 320-mile channel that connects the Atlantic and the Pacific Oceans at the southern tip of South America and separates Tierra del Fuego from the mainland. Treacherous and stormy, the narrow straits were much feared by seamen, who often preferred to sail farther south around Cape Horn.

maggots   Mayfly larvae were sometimes, although rarely, introduced into deep wounds in order to clean them, as the maggots ate the necrotic tissue.

Magicienne, **H.M.S.**   A fifth rate of 32 guns that was captured from the French in 1781 and fought at San Domingo in the WEST INDIES. Burned after running aground at MAURITIUS in 1810 to avoid capture by the French.

maharaj *or* **maharaja**   The title of certain Indian princes.

Mahdi   In Arabic, "he who is divinely guided." In Sunni Islam, the restorer of the faith, who will appear at the end of time to restore justice on earth and establish universal Islam. Among the Shiites, the concept of the Mahdi takes a different form (*see* IMAM).

Mahomet   Alternative spelling of the Arabic name Mohammed or Muhammad, the founder of Islam (died 632).

Mahommedan   A follower of Mohammed, the founder of Islam.

main   A much-used adjective on board ship, meaning "principal," as in the MAINMAST. The "main top" is the platform at the head of the lower portion of the mainmast. The "main YARD" is the yard on which the MAINSAIL (or main COURSE, as it is also called) is bent (*see* BEND). Also, short for mainland.

Main, the   *See* SPANISH MAIN.

main deck   In a MAN-OF-WAR, the deck below the SPAR DECK. The principal deck in a ship with several decks.

main forte   Assistance in executing something, generally in difficult or dangerous circumstances (French).

mainmast   A ship's principal MAST; in a three-masted ship, the center mast.

mainsail (*pronounced* **mains'l**) A vessel's principal sail. On a SQUARE-RIGGED ship, the lowest and largest sail on the MAINMAST, the main COURSE.

maintack The lower WEATHER corner of a square MAINSAIL and, on a FORE-AND-AFT MAINSAIL, the forward lower corner.

main works The principal fortifications of a place.

Mais qu'est-ce qui se passe? What's going on here? (French)

make a leg To bow in a gesture of obeisance by drawing back one leg and bending the other.

make and mend A time designated for seamen to repair their clothes, a period of relative leisure.

make sail To spread a sail or sails; to begin a voyage.

Malaga A seaport and province on the Mediterranean coast of Spain. The only fleet action of the War of Spanish Succession was fought off Malaga in 1704 between an Anglo-Dutch fleet, commanded by Admiral Sir George Rooke, and a Franco-Spanish fleet. While tactically indecisive, it prevented the French from retaking GIBRALTAR. Malaga was sacked by the French under General Sebastiani in 1811.

Malay A peninsula and archipelago in Southeast Asia, the location of the Straits (of Malacca) Settlements of Penang (Prince of Wales Island), Malacca, and Singapore, and such islands as Sumatra, Java, Borneo, Celebes, Moluccas, and Timor. The sea surrounding the archipelago. A person or language from the region.

malleolus Either of the two bony protrusions at the ankle, the internal belonging to the tibia, the external to the fibula.

malmsey A strong, sweet wine, originally from the area around the Greek city of Monemvasia (Napoli di Malvasia) in the Morea and later also from Spain, the AZORES, MADEIRA, and the CANARY ISLANDS, as well as Greece.

Malta A small, strategically placed island south of Sicily in the central Mediterranean, with a very fine and well-defended deep-water port at Valletta. Because of its prime position in a relatively narrow channel between Europe and Africa, the island has been a trading center and a naval base and has a long history of war and capture, including by Napoleon in 1798. In 1800, after two years of blockades and sieges, the island was surrendered to the British. Britain's refusal to evacuate the island in accordance with the Treaty of Amiens was the immediate spark that led to renewed hostilities with France in 1803.

malt-horse A heavy kind of workhorse used by makers of malt. The term is sometimes used derogatorily.

malversation Corruption committed while in office or a position of trust; the corrupt use of public money.

Mamelukes Originally a military body of non-Arab slaves who served various Muslim rulers in the Middle East. The Mamelukes seized Egypt's throne in 1254 and formed the ruling class there into the 19th century. Reigning from 1254 to 1517, the Mameluke sultans used powerful cavalry forces to defend themselves against invasions by the Mongols and the Crusaders, but in 1517 they were conquered by the Ottoman Sultan Selim I. Under Ottoman sovereignty, Egypt was governed, via a Turkish viceroy, by 24 Mameluke beys, and the Mamelukes, now the long-established ruling class, continued to thrive. Following the French invasion (1798) and occupation, however, the Mamelukes were massacred in 1811 by Mohammed Ali, PASHA of Egypt.

mammothrept A nursling or pampered child.

Mandeville, Sir John A pseudonym for a French physician, usually identified as Jehan de Bourgogne (died 1372). In 1371 he published a famous book of travels, partly invented and partly compiled from true accounts of adventures and encounters with strange natural phenomena by other writers. Published in England in 1499, Mandeville's book received great praise, and he was proclaimed the "father of English prose"—a status that changed when the French origin of the manuscript was established in 1725.

mandragora *also* **mandragore** The root of the Mediterranean herb mandrake, of the nightshade family, which was reported to be a powerful sedative and aphrodisiac in medieval lore. However, it has little, if any, discernible effect. The forked root, believed by some to resemble the human form, was said throughout the Middle Ages to utter a deadly shriek when plucked from the ground.

mandrill   The largest and most ferocious of the baboons; native to western Africa.

mangabey   A monkey, native to Africa, of the genus *Cercocebus*, especially the sooty mangabey.

manger   A small triangular area in the BOW of a ship-of-war set off by a movable BULKHEAD and used to prevent water that enters through the HAWSE-HOLES from flooding the deck. Also, the same space used for keeping a ship's animals.

mangonel   An apparatus for catapulting stones and other missiles at an enemy.

mangosteen   An East Indian fruit with a hard, reddish-brown rind and a sweet, juicy flesh.

mangrove   A tropical tree or shrub that grows on the seashore and issues masses of interlacing above-ground roots that catch and retain mud and weeds and cause the land to build toward the sea.

Manichaean   A believer of a religious system popular from the third to the fifth century A.D. that mixed Gnostic Christian, Mazdean, and pagan elements. The system is best known for its acceptance of dualistic theology, whereby Satan is held to be coeternal with God.

Manila   In the Philippine Islands, the capital and main port, which was established as a Spanish base in 1571 and belonged to the Spanish empire for over three centuries. From Manila, Spanish ships known as Manila (or Acapulco) galleons carried great treasure across the Pacific to Acapulco, Mexico, en route to Spain. Manila was captured by the British in 1762 during the Seven Years' War but was returned to Spain following a peace treaty the next year.

man-of-war *or* **man-o'-war**   A vessel armed for war and carrying between 20 and 120 guns. An armed ship of a national navy.

man-of-war bird   *See* FRIGATE BIRD.

manropes   The ropes on each side of a GANGWAY or ladder, used like a bannister.

Mansion House   The official residence of the Lord Mayor of London.

mantilla   A veil worn over a woman's head and shoulders, especially in Spain. A small, light cape.

Manton, Joe (*1766–1835*)   A noted gunsmith and the maker of the Manton, his signature FOWLING-PIECE.

man-trap   A trap for catching trespassers on private grounds.

mantua   A loose gown, or manteau, worn by women in the 17th and 18th centuries.

Manx shearwater   Any of several large migratory sea birds, related to the PETREL and the FULMAR, that have long, narrow wings and fly very close to the water when feeding.

maravedi   A Spanish copper coin valued at a fraction of a penny sterling.

marchpane *or* marzipan   A confectionery of almond paste and sugar, often molded into small decorative forms.

marelle   An English game nearly identical to hopscotch.

Maremma   A low marshy region near the sea in the southwest of Tuscany, Italy.

Maremma sheepdog   Common in central Italy, an ancient breed of sheepdog used by Tuscan farmers for herding livestock.

Margaux   A Bordeaux wine (or claret in England) manufactured in the commune of Margaux, in the department of Gironde, France.

Mariae duodecies sacrum   Dedicated 12 times over to Mary (Latin).

Mariae lembi nostri duci et magistrae do dedico   I present and dedicate this to Mary, the master and commander of our yacht (Latin).

mariage blanc   An unconsummated marriage (French).

Marial   Pertaining to the Virgin Mary or showing special devotion to her.

Maria Theresa dollar   Austrian silver coin. A thaler.

mari complaisant   Obliging husband (French).

marine *or* Royal Marine   A specialized soldier who serves on a MAN-OF-WAR and at dockyards, or on shore in certain cases. In Britain, a radical reorganization of the marines brought them under the control of the ADMIRALTY in 1755. During the Napoleonic War, the COMPLEMENT of a large ship of the line often consisted of over 20 percent marines, who served in gun crews and boarding parties and as sharpshooters and sentries. They became known as the Royal Marines in 1802.

marine glue   Glue used in ship carpentry.

Marine Society   Founded by Jonas Hanway (1712–1786) to raise recruits, mostly the poor and orphaned, for the Royal Navy. It was the first secular and imperial charity in the English-speaking world. By 1805 it had raised 55,000 recruits.

mark   The intervals of a LEAD-LINE, indicated by attachments that could be seen easily or felt by the LEADSMAN. Two FATHOMS was marked by 2 strips of leather, 3 fathoms by 3 strips of leather, 5 fathoms by a strip of white DUCK, 7 fathoms by a piece of red bunting, 10 by a leather square with a hole, 13 by a piece of blue serge, 15 by a piece of white duck, 17 by a piece of red bunting, and 20 fathoms by a piece of cord with two knots. All other depths were unmarked and were known as "deeps." The leadsman estimated these by looking at the nearest visible mark. The calls "by the mark" or "by the deep" indicated to the navigator the degree of accuracy of the depth the leadsman was calling out.

Markham's sick-berth   Admiral Markham, when captain of H.M.S. *Centaur* in 1801, set apart a space 19 feet to accommodate 22 swinging cradles for the sick; attached to it was a dispensary, where drugs were prepared and dispensed to sick patients and where men came to have their wounds dressed. The area, designed for maximum efficiency, was situated between two forward guns on the starboard side; it had access to the heads, but also had its own "necessary house." This arrangement was copied in other ships in the Home Fleet, under prompting by Dr. Thomas Trotter, as PHYSICIAN OF THE FLEET. Further implementing Markham's recommendations, in 1801 Admiral JERVIS ordered that the sick not be kept below the upper deck of any line-of-battle ship, and that all sick-berths were to be on the starboard side, under the forecastle.

mark twain   On a LEAD-LINE, the two-FATHOM mark.

Marlbrouk s'en va-t-en guerre, mironton mironton mirontaine . . . Marlbrouk ne revient plus   Marlbrouk is going away to war, rat-a-tat, rat-a-tat, rat-a-tat tat tat . . . Marlbrouk is never coming back. From a famous French song about John, Duke of Marlborough, one of England's most victorious warriors.

marline   Small line of two strands, sometimes tarred, used for SEIZINGS.

marline-spike   A pointed iron tool used to part strands of rope so they can be spliced. Also, a nickname for the BOSUN-BIRD.

marmoset   Any of a variety of tropical American monkeys with claws instead of nails, except on the big toe. In general, they have bushy tails, long eartufts, and soft, dense fur. They were considered playful pets.

Maronite   A sect of Syrian Christians loyal to the Pope, found chiefly in Lebanon.

maroon   A firework making the sound of a cannon, used as a warning, as in foggy weather.

Marrano   A christianized Jew or MOOR of medieval Spain, especially one who converted in order to avoid persecution.

Marrano. Herético pálido   Swine. Pale-skinned brute (Spanish).

Mars, **H.M.S.**   A second-rate 74-gun ship, built in 1794, that fought at TRAFALGAR in 1805 under Captain George Duff. Her 98 casualties included Captain Duff. The French commander-in-chief and his staff were received on board *Mars* at their surrender. She was at COPEN-HAGEN in 1807, in the Channel from 1808 to 1813, and was broken up in 1823.

Marsala   A fortified white wine that resembles a light sherry and is exported from Marsala, Sicily.

Marseilles   A southeastern French city and the largest seaport on the Mediterranean. The battle hymn of the French Revolution, "La Marseillaise," was written by Claude Joseph Rouget de Lisle at Strasbourg in 1792, and it was named for the volunteers from Marseilles who entered Paris singing it on July 30, 1792.

Marshalsea   In London's Southwark section, a debtor's prison notorious for its squalid conditions.

marthambles   No such diagnosis was used in regular 18th-century medical practice. O'Brian discovered the colorful term in a quack's pamphlet of the late 17th or early 18th century advertising a curative product for a variety of diseases. Thus, marthambles was a nonexistent disease invented to help advertise the virtues of a probably useless medicine. Maturin uses the term in the sense of a contagious affliction that causes gripping abdominal pain.

martingale   In a SQUARE-RIGGED ship, a lower STAY for securing the JIB-BOOM or FLYING JIB against the upward pull of the fore-TOPGALLANT stays. Sometimes applied to the DOLPHIN-STRIKER itself.

Martinique   A volcanic island in the Windward Islands of the WEST INDIES. Like many Caribbean islands, Martinique passed back and forth from British to French hands several times during the Seven Years' War, the French Revolution, and the Napoleonic War. It was finally returned to France in 1814.

Marwari   An inhabitant of Marwar, an area in the Indian state Rajasthan. The dialect of Hindi used there.

marzipane   *See* MARCHPANE.

mast   A vertical pole to carry a vessel's sails that descends to the KEELSON, where its squared HEEL is stepped. Originally the mast was built from the trunk of a single fir tree. As ships grew in size during the 17th and 18th centuries, masts had to be extended and broadened to carry more sail. To add girth and strength, the lower mast was fashioned from more than one timber (known as a made mast), while TOPMASTs and TOPGALLANT masts (usually single-trunk or -pole masts) were added above.

master   An officer with the same rank as a LIEUTENANT but subordinate to him in command. He was responsible for the navigation and sailing of a ship of war and was appointed by the NAVY BOARD. Also, the captain of a merchant vessel, who qualified for the position by passing an examination to earn his "master's ticket."

master and commander   Before 1794, the title of an officer in the Royal Navy who had the same rank as a LIEUTENANT but was treated like an intermediate between a Captain and a Lieutenant. From 1794, this position was filled by the newly created rank of COMMANDER. An officer of this rank usually commanded a ship-of-war smaller than a post-ship (under 20 guns), such as a SLOOP-of-war or BOMB-vessel, but larger than the little vessels commanded by a Lieutenant. As with post-rank, an officer could obtain the rank of Commander only by receiving such a command. It was not until 1827 that an officer could have the rank of Commander without commanding such a vessel. At that time, the position of FIRST LIEUTENANT in a SHIP OF THE LINE was made a Commander's job.

master's mate   A PETTY OFFICER subordinate to but working with the MASTER of a ship-of-war. More highly paid than other petty officers, Master's Mates were the only ratings allowed to command any sort of vessel.

masthead   The highest reach of a MAST. More specifically, the head of the lower mast frequently used for observation or as a place of solitary confinement for serving a punishment. Also, the top of the whole mast where flags were flown.

mastic   *See* LENTISK.

match-board   A board with a tongue cut along one edge and a groove in the opposite that was joined with similar boards to form one larger piece.

match-tub   A tub with a perforated cover, where SLOW-MATCHes, lit end down, were hung to be ready for use.

maté   A mildy stimulating drink made of the leaves of the South American evergreen bush *Ilex paraguayensis,* a member of the holly family; the active ingredient is caffeine. It is drunk like tea or coffee all over South America.

Matthew Walker knot   An end knot on a multistranded rope to prevent it from slipping through an EYE. Probably named for its inventor.

Mauritius   Called Île de France by the French, an island in the Indian Ocean about 500 miles east of Madagascar originally colonized by the Dutch in the 17th century. It later became a key base for the French in their rivalry with the English EAST INDIA COMPANY, especially during the FRENCH REVOLUTION and the NAPOLEONIC WAR, when French PRIVATEERs captured and destroyed many EAST INDIAMEN. A

British blockade of the island failed, but in 1810 the British finally captured the island, albeit with heavy ship losses, and made it a British Crown Colony. This campaign served as the historical basis for Patrick O'Brian's *The Mauritius Command*.

maxilla   The upper jaw.

mazed   Dazed, cowed, and confused; terrified.

meal   Finely ground gunpowder. To meal is to grind into fine powder.

medico   A medical practitioner or student.

Medusa, **H.M.S.**   A 50-gun fifth rate wrecked near Lisbon in 1798. Another fifth rate built in 1801 and broken up in 1816.

Medway   A river in Kent on whose banks lies the Naval dockyard at CHATHAM and at whose mouth lies the refitting port SHEERNESS.

megrim   A severe headache usually on one side of the head. A headache resulting from nervousness or sickness.

Melampus, **H.M.S.**   A fifth rate of 36 guns built in 1785 that fought in battles at Donegal in 1798 and Guadeloupe in 1810. The name is taken from a celebrated prophet and physician in Greek mythology. She was sold to the Dutch in 1815.

melancholia   A mental illness characterized by paranoia, depression, physical pains, and sometimes hallucinations and delusion.

Melbury Lodge   The dwelling that Aubrey and Maturin lease on the South Downs in Sussex, within a day's ride of London.

ménage   Household, domestic arrangement (from French).

menarche   The onset of menstruation.

Mennonites   A sect of Christians founded in Friesland, a region in Holland, by Menno Simons (1492–1559), that opposed infant baptism, oath taking, and civil and military service.

mens rea   Literally, guilty mind (Latin). Criminal intent.

menus plaisirs   Small pleasures (French).

mephitis   A release of noxious or pestilential gases, especially from the earth. A foul smell.

Mercator projection   A map that represents the world with MERIDI-ANs of longitude and parallels of latitude that cross each other at right angles, such that a constant compass bearing is represented by a straight line, known as a rhumb-line. A major breakthrough in map-making, it was developed by the Flemish geographer and cartographer Gerhardus Kremer (1512–1594), who used the Latinized form of his name, Mercator. First published in 1569, Mercator's projection came into standard use in the mid-17th century.

mercurial   Any medicinal drug preparation containing MERCURY.

mercury   Also known as quicksilver, a silver-white liquid metallic element. Preparations made with the raw metal, or one of its various compounds, were applied topically or given by mouth in the treatment of syphilis. (For its reputed efficacy against syphilis, see "Stephen Maturin and Naval Medicine in the Age of Sail," p. 31.) Doctors assumed that the desired effect had been achieved when the patient began to complain of a metallic taste in his mouth, and of excessive salivation. The most widely prescribed mercury compound was CALOMEL, used as a cathartic and diuretic into the early 20th century.

merde d'oie   Literally, goose shit. Used to describe something contemptible or without value (French).

mere   A pond or marsh.

meridian   Either a line of latitude, which parallels the equator, or one of longitude, which runs perpendicular to the equator.

Merino   A breed of white sheep that has very fine wool and is native to Spain. It was introduced to England at the close of the 18th century, where it was interbred to improve the fleece-bearing sheep of Britain and her colonies.

mermaid   A term sometimes applied to the manatee, a tropical herbivorous mammal, and similar animals, which reminded observers of the mermaid of fable.

Merry-Andrew   One who entertains with antics and buffoonery; a clown. Originally, a MOUNTEBANK's assistant.

mésalliance   A marriage with a person of inferior social standing, from the French word for misalliance.

mess   Each one of the several groups into which a ship's company was separated whose members dined together. Also, where meals were served.

mess-kid   A small wooden tub used domestically, especially a sailor's mess-tub.

messenger   Because the anchor CABLE was too thick and heavy to be taken round the CAPSTAN (that in H.M.S. *VICTORY* was 24 inches around, for instance), the turns were taken instead by a smaller HAWSER called the messenger, whose ends were seized together to make an endless loop. The cable was temporarily secured to this at the bow with NIPPERS, and as the messenger was hove in, the men holding the nippers walked back to the main hatchway, where the nipper was cast off, and the cable dropped down into the CABLE-TIER on the ORLOP to be stowed by the tierers. An earlier version of this was the voyal, which was particularly useful at the juncture when the heaviest heave was needed to break the anchor out of the ground. In this case, the cable was itself taken round the main capstan, but the effort was aided by employing the JEER-capstan and voyal. This was an endless loop similar to the messenger and, like it, secured to the cable by nippers. It passed through the VOYAL-BLOCK, which was secured to the MAINMAST, and ran forward where turns were taken on the jeer-capstan.

Messieurs les Anglais, tirez les premiers.   My English friends, take the first shot (French).

metacarpal   Of or belonging to the metacarpus, the part of the hand between the wrist and the fingers; a metacarpal bone.

Methody   A perversion of the word "Methodist."

metopic   Of or pertaining to the forehead; frontal.

Metrodorus   Fifth-century B.C. Greek philosopher of Lampsacus who wrote an allegorical interpretation of Homer's *Iliad* and of the Olympian pantheon.

mew up   To shut up or confine; to hide.

mias   The orangutan, a long-armed ape of BORNEO and Sumatra with brown skin and long reddish-brown hair.

miasmas *or* **miasmata** One of the putative sources of some diseases; see "Stephen Maturin and Naval Medicine in the Age of Sail," p. 31.

micaceous schist Metamorphic crystalline rock containing mica.

Michaelmas The feast of St. Michael the Archangel, September 29. In the English business year, a quarter-day (a day that begins a new quarter).

mid *See* MIDSHIPMAN.

mid off In cricket, a fielder on the off-side in front of the batter and near the bowler. Also, the spot this player occupies.

mid on In cricket, a fielder on the on-side in front of the batter and close to the bowler. Also, the spot this player occupies.

middle deck The deck above the ORLOP and LOWER DECK; site of medium-size artillery.

middle In cricket, the position occupied by a batter so that his bat defends the middle stump.

middle watch The WATCH from midnight to four A.M., and the crew on deck duty at that time.

midshipman Originally, a senior PETTY OFFICER. Beginning in 1677, all candidates for commissioned rank had to serve one year as a midshipman; from 1703, the time was at least two years. From 1794, all newly rated midshipmen were considered as candidates for a commission. The number of midshipmen in each ship was determined by the rating of the ship. *See also* page 15.

midshipman's hitch A hitch used to secure a rope temporarily to a hook.

mill-pond The water retained by a mill-dam for driving the mill-wheel.

mill-race A current that drives a mill-wheel; the water's channel to the mill-wheel.

minim The smallest unit of fluid measure, one drop of liquid.

Minorca One of the Balearic Islands in the western Mediterranean off the coast of Spain. In 1708, during the War of the Spanish Succession, the British took Minorca for the allies and eventually received it through the Treaty of Utrecht, but they lost it to the French in 1756 at the beginning of the Seven Years' War. Dispatched to relieve the beleaguered garrison at PORT MAHON, the island's principal town and harbor, Admiral John BYNG fought with the French fleet off Minorca but failed to disrupt the French invasion of the island, instead returning to GIBRALTAR to await reinforcements. In his absence, the French captured Port Mahon. As a result, Byng was COURT-MARTIALed, found guilty of neglect of duty, and shot. Britain regained Minorca with the advent of peace in 1763, only to lose it to the Spanish during the American Revolutionary War. During the Napoleonic War, Vice-Admiral COLLINGWOOD controlled the island and used it as a base for the blockade of TOULON. After Napoleon's defeat in 1815, Minorca returned once again to Spain.

Minotaur, **H.M.S.**   A 74-gun third rate built in 1793 and commanded by Captain Thomas Louis. Although her crew was implicated in the 1797 mutiny at SPITHEAD, they fought heroically under Louis at the Battle of the NILE in 1798, with 23 killed and 64 wounded. She also fought at TRAFALGAR in 1805 under Captain Charles Mansfield. The *Minotaur* was wrecked in 1810 in a severe GALE off TEXEL in the North Sea and went down with all 370 hands. A picture of the wreck was painted by J. M. W. Turner.

minute   An official memorandum authorizing or recommending the pursuit of a certain course.

minute-gun   The firing of a gun at one-minute intervals to signify mourning or distress.

Mirdites *or* **Mirdita**   A region on the river Drin in Albania and the tribal people living there.

mistral   A strong, even violent, cold northwest wind that blows down France's Rhône Valley into the Mediterranean sea. It is said that murderers have been found innocent due to temporary insanity caused by the howling of this wind in winter.

mitre   A headdress that is part of the insignia of a bishop and that is also worn by certain abbots and other ecclesiastics as an emblem of exceptional dignity.

Mitre, the   A tavern at Mitre Court on Fleet Street, popular among members of the Royal Society, which once held its anniversary dinner there. It was also Samuel JOHNSON's favorite watering hole and the meeting place of Johnson and James Boswell, author of the *Life of Samuel Johnson*. The Mitre ceased to be a tavern in 1788.

mizzenmast *or* **mizzen**   The aftermost MAST of a three-masted ship.

Moahu   A fictional volcanic island in the South Pacific, to the south of the Sandwich group and about a three days' sail north-northeast of Christmas Island.

mohur *or* **gold mohur**   A Persian gold coin, also used in India beginning in the 16th century. The chief gold coin of British India, which contained 165 grains of pure gold and was valued at 15 rupees.

moil   To wallow in mud or mire. To toil.

mole   A massive earthen, masonry, or stone pier, breakwater, or junction between two places separated by water. Also, the harbor created by such a structure. *See* illustration below.

The new mole at Gibraltar, one of the three landing places there, and in the background Europa Point, the southern tip of Gibraltar, and the Barbary Coast. (*Reproduced from* The Naval Chronicle, *vol. 18, courtesy of the Mariners' Museum, Newport News, Virginia*)

Molina, Tirso de (*c. 1580–1648*) Pseudonym for Gabriel Téllez, a great dramatist of the Spanish Golden Age. In 1634 he introduced Don Juan into literature in the tragedy *El burlador de Sevilla.*

mollymawk *also* **mollie, mollymauk,** *or* **mollyhawk** Sailors' name for a species of small ALBATROSS common to the Cape of Good Hope and known for its greedy and skillful fishing. Also, the FULMAR and similar or related birds of the southern seas.

mome A blockhead, dolt, or fool.

***Monarch*, H.M.S.** The first *Monarch* was a third rate that was captured from the French in 1747 and later was the site of the notorious execution of Admiral John BYNG. (In *Post Captain*, O'Brian has a laugh by placing Aubrey's COURT-MARTIAL for losing the *Polychrest* on a later ship of this name.) The second, a third rate of 74 guns, was constructed at Deptford in 1765 and went on to become one of the Royal Navy's most battle-hardened and glorious ships. She took part in actions at USHANT in 1778, St. Vincent in 1780, and in the WEST INDIES in 1781. In 1795, she served as the FLAGSHIP of Vice Admiral Sir G. ELPHINSTONE (later Lord Keith) in his expedition to capture the Cape of Good Hope. In 1797, the *Monarch* led the British fleet at CAMPER-DOWN, where her crew had 36 killed and 100 wounded. She lost her Captain, James Robert Mosse, at the first Battle of COPENHAGEN in 1801, while her company suffered 56 killed and 164 wounded. She was condemned and broken up in 1813.

monkey's blood A WARDROOM nickname for red wine.

monk's bane Also known as monk's hood, wolfsbane, and aconite (*Aconitum napellum*). Its powdered root had long been used for homicidal purposes because its bitter taste could be disguised by adding it to wine. It was promoted in the 18th century for diseases characterized by swollen glands or painful joints. Said to be narcotic, tonic, and diuretic, its lethal effect was on the heart.

monk-seal A white-bellied seal of the Caribbean and Mediterranean seas that was hunted nearly to extinction for its fur.

Monmouth cap A flat round cap worn by soldiers and sailors, named after a town in Wales.

***Monodon monoceros or* narwhal** A dolphinlike whale of the Arctic seas, also known as the sea-unicorn. The male has a remarkable spiraled tusk.

monoglot   A person who speaks only one language.

monophysite   A heretic who believes that there is only one divine— not human—nature in the person of Jesus Christ, even though he was on earth. Christians who profess this belief include those in the Coptic, Armenian, Abyssinian, and Syrian Orthodox churches.

monotreme   A member of the order Monotremata of egg-laying mammals, which includes the DUCK-BILLED PLATYPUS and several species of spiny anteaters, native to Australia and New Guinea.

Monsieur, j'ai l'honneur de introduire une amie . . . l'espagnol capitaine . . . vino, chocolato, aguardiente?   Aubrey's pidgin French for, "Sir, I have the honor of presenting a friend . . . the Spanish captain," and his pidgin Spanish for, "wine, chocolate, brandy?"

monsignor   An honorific title bestowed upon Roman Catholic prelates, officers of the papal court and household, and others, usually by the Pope.

Montagu, Lady Mary Wortley (*1689–1762*)   A writer and English society figure chiefly remembered for her published *Letters from the East* and who attempted to create support for smallpox inoculation in England, which she discovered in Turkey when her husband served there as ambassador from 1716 to 1718.

Monte Video *or* Montevideo   A fortified seaport city on the northern bank of the Rio de la Plata estuary, in what is today Uruguay, South America.

Montrachet   A wine-growing district in the Côte d'Or region of France and the white wine produced there.

Montserrat   A famous ninth-century monastery and ecclesiastical center on a mountain near Barcelona.

mooncalf   An abortive fleshy mass in the womb, once regarded as a product of the moon's influence. A false conception. Also, a born fool.

moonsail *or* moonraker   A small sail sometimes set in light winds above a SKYSAIL. When triangular, called a SKYSCRAPER.

moor   To secure a ship or boat in a particular place, using an anchor or ropes. A ship lying in harbor or at anchorage between two anchors is said to be moored.

Moor   Originally, a native of Mauretania, an area of northern Africa now forming parts of Morocco and Algeria. Later, a Muslim of mixed Berber and Arab race from northwestern Africa. The Moors conquered Spain in the 8th century.

Moor's head   In heraldry, a profile of the head of a MOOR, wreathed around the temples and wearing a pearl earring.

Mornington, Earl of, and Marquis of Wellesley (*1760–1842*) Richard Colley Wellesley, older brother of the Duke of WELLINGTON and a British statesman who, as governor of Madras and governor general of Bengal (both 1797–1805), greatly enlarged the British Empire in India and who, as lord lieutenant of Ireland (1821–28, 1833–34), attempted to reconcile Protestants and Catholics in a bitterly divided country.

mortar   A short piece of ORDNANCE with a large bore and with TRUNNIONS on its BREECH for throwing shells at high angles, especially useful for bombarding a town and taking out enemy artillery, barracks, and magazines.

mortification   Gangrene.

Moses   A broad boat with a flat bottom and powered by oars. They were used in the WEST INDIES for moving HOGSHEADS (large barrels) of sugar from the beach to waiting ships.

Mother Cary's chicken   A sailors' name for the STORM PETREL, whose presence near a ship was believed to presage a storm. The term Mother Cary is believed to have derived from the Latin *mater cara,* "dear mother," referring to the Virgin Mary. Also, in the plural, a slang term for falling snow.

Mother Shipton   A renowned 16th-century seer.

mountebank   An itinerant quack who appealed to his audience from a raised platform by means of stories and tricks, often assisted by a professional clown or fool. A charlatan.

mourning-dove   A wild blue-gray North American dove that has a plaintive call.

mourning-ring   A ring worn in memory of a dead loved one.

mouse   Used in the RIGGING, a small collar of SPUNYARN for holding something in place.

mousebirds   Birds native to Africa of the genus *Colius,* also called colies. Mousebirds are brown or gray in color, live in brush or by forests, and eat primarily fruit.

mousing   The fastening of SPUNYARN or rope across the opening of a hook to prevent it from clearing itself. Rope or yarn fastened this way, or a latch.

muck-sweat   Profuse sweat.

muchwhat   A word of many uses, at different times meaning greatly, almost, just, pretty much, or pretty well.

mud-scow   A barge used to carry away dredged mud.

Muggletonian   A member of the sect founded around 1651 by Lodowicke Muggleton and John Reeve and based on the belief that its founders were the two witnesses of Revelations 11:3–6.

mulct   A fine levied for an offense. To punish a person with a fine.

mullet   Any of various fish of the family Mugilidae, found worldwide. Especially the red or gray mullet.

mumchance   Silent (mum) or tongue-tied.

mumping   Begging; mumbling and toothless; grimacing.

mundungus   Stinking tobacco.

munera navium saevos inlaqueant duces   Gifts may ensnare the savage leaders of ships (Latin; Horace, *Odes* III, 16).

Mungo's Cordial   A proprietary remedy designed to raise one's spirits.

munnions   The pieces that part the lights in the STERN and QUARTER GALLERY.

Murano   An island near Venice where Venetian glass is manufactured.

murrain   Plague, pestilence.

murre   Any of several species of GUILLEMOT, diving birds of the AUK family.

musk   A strong-smelling, reddish-brown secretion in a gland or sac of the male Asian musk-deer, used as the basis of many perfumes and in medicine as a stimulant and antispasmodic. Also, similar substances secreted by certain other animals.

musketoon A short musket with a large bore.

muster To assemble a ship's company for inspection, verification of numbers, introduction into service, exercise, or for other activities; also, a list of ship's company present.

muster-book The official log of a ship's company, including the name, rating, date of entry and discharge for each member, used to determine the issue of food and pay. The names of dead men and deserters were often fraudulently retained to the gain of unscrupulous officers.

muster-roll An official list of the officers and men in a ship's company (*see* MUSTER-BOOK). The reading of the muster-roll; roll-call.

mutatis mutandis After making the appropriate changes (Latin).

mutton-bird Either of two species of the genus *Puffinus*, in New Zealand the sooty SHEARWATER and in Australia the short-tailed shearwater. An Antarctic PETREL.

muzzle astragal A ring or molding encircling a cannon about six inches from the mouth.

Myrmidon One of a bellicose people of ancient Thessaly, who followed Achilles, their king, to the siege of Troy. A faithful bodyguard, follower, or servant. Also, a hired ruffian or one who executes unscrupulous commands.

myrrh A gum resin produced by several species of trees of the genus *Commiphora*, especially *C. abyssinica*, used in perfume and incense. Also, the TINCTURE made from this and used medicinally as a stimulant and antiseptic.

Mzab A stony, barren valley in the northern Sahara of Algeria. It was settled c.1000 by members of an austere Muslim sect, the Kharijites. The inhabitants, called Mzabites, dug wells, created date-palm oases, and built seven towns, united in a confederation. As traders, they made the area a caravan junction. A subgroup of the ZENATA, the tough, horse-riding Beni Marin, occupied the area and formed the great Merinide dynasty.

nabob The title for the deputy governors of provinces in the Mogul Empire of India; a governor of a town or district in India. Also, a person returning from India having made a large fortune there; thus, a wealthy, prominent, and luxurious person. A wealthy passenger in an EAST INDIAMAN.

naevus *or* **nevus** A purplish, often raised, congenital skin growth or birthmark; a mole.

Naiad, **H.M.S.** A 38-gun fifth rate, built in 1797, that had a distinguished career and fought under Captain Thomas Dundas in the battle at TRAFALGAR, where she served as the eyes of the fleet. Broken up in 1898, she was the longest-lived of the TRAFALGAR ships except for *VICTORY.*

Namur, **H.M.S.** A 1697 second rate that was wrecked in 1749. Another second rate by the same name, with 90 guns, was built in 1756 and fought in many battles, including Louisbourg in 1758, Havana in 1762, the Saintes in 1782, and St. Vincent in 1797. Cut down to a 74-gun third rate in 1805, she was placed in harbor service in 1807 and was eventually broken up in 1833.

Nancy Dawson   A popular ship name that came from a dancer in John Gay's *The Beggar's Opera*. The tune she danced to was popular with seamen during the 18th century, and tradition holds that the song was played to summon sailors for their daily issue of GROG, which was itself then sometimes called Nancy Dawson by sailors.

nankeen   A kind of cotton cloth, originally made at Nanking, the chief city of the province of Kiangsu in China, from a yellow variety of cotton.

Nantz *or* Nantes   The seaport of Nantes in western France near the mouth of the Loire River was a center of the slave trade. Also known for its brandy.

Napier's bones   Thin pieces of bone, ivory, or wood marked with numbers and used as a mathematical aid according to the method of John Napier of Merchiston (1550–1617), the inventor of LOGARITHMs.

napoleon   A 20-franc gold coin issued by NAPOLEON I (1769–1821).

NAPOLEON I (Napoleon Bonaparte *or* Napoleone Buonaparte) (*1769–1821*)   Born at Ajaccio, Corsica, Napoleon was sent with his older brother, Joseph, to school in France in 1778. In 1784 he moved to Paris, where he studied at the Ecole Militaire for a year before being commissioned into an artillery regiment. At various garrison stations, Napoleon, who excelled at science and mathematics and possessed a remarkable memory, continued his studies in military history and theory. An ardent Corsican nationalist despite his French education, he supported Paoli until a bitter dispute with that leader forced Napoleon to flee with his widowed mother and siblings to southern France in 1793.

Napoleon welcomed the French Revolution in 1789. In 1793 he commanded the artillery at Toulon and received deserved credit for defeating British troops occupying that key port. This led to his promotion to Brigadier General, igniting a meteoric rise to power. After defeating a Royalist mob in Paris in 1795, Napoleon was appointed commander of the Army of the Interior, from whence he was appointed to the command of the Army of Italy in 1796. His Italian Campaign was highly successful, forcing the Austrians to seek peace and ingratiating him with leaders in Paris by providing a stream of booty. *Le Petit Caporal*, as he was affectionately known, also became the hero of his soldiers.

Napoleon Bonaparte, emperor of France, known fondly as *le Petit Caporal* and contemptuously as Puss-in-Boots (*mezzotint by G. W. H. Ritchie, after a painting by Jacques-Louis David*)

Following a campaign in and around Egypt, where he was dogged by NELSON (at the Battle of the NILE) and by Sir William Sidney SMITH, Napoleon secretly left his stalled army and returned to Paris. In 1799 the opportunistic general emerged from the coup d'état of Brumaire— along with the Abbé Sieyès and Roger Ducos as co-Consuls. He then forced his fellow conspirators out of power and became the de facto supreme ruler of France. To consolidate his popularity, and thus his rule, Napoleon moved quickly. With victories over the Austrians and on the German front, he crumbled the Second Coalition, causing the downfall of Prime Minister William PITT in England and bringing on the Peace of AMIENS. Napoleon had ended a decade of bloodshed and secured his own preeminence in France as a peacemaker.

In 1803–4, Napoleon established his Civil Code, retooling the economy and governance of France. In 1804 the Consul for Life proclaimed himself Emperor of France. The Pope attended the coronation, but Napoleon insisted on placing the crown on his own head and on the head of his wife Josephine, whom he had married in 1796.

(He eventually divorced Josephine after she failed to produce a child; the Emperor would have a son by the Austrian Archduchess Maria Luisa in 1811.) War had broken out again in 1803, and Napoleon's Grand Armée knifed into central Germany, winning a major victory over the Austro-Russian Army at Austerlitz in 1805. In a costly campaign, Napoleon subdued Russia in 1807, marking the height of his power (though not the size of his empire, which would not peak until 1810 with his marriage to Archduchess Maria Luisa). Soon France was at war in Portugal and Spain, and, with his forces spread too thin, Napoleon began losing control of his realm. England gained footholds on the Peninsula, tying down great numbers of French troops. Napoleon's disastrous invasion of Russia in 1812 sealed his fate. Prussia and Sweden joined Russia in a counteroffensive in the east, and Wellington attacked from the west, as the Allies overwhelmed the weakened French conscripts. Paris fell on March 30, 1814. Napoleon adbicated at Fontainebleau and was exiled to the island of Elba. On March 1, 1815, he returned to Paris with popular support. With war imminent, he marched into Belgium, and on June 18, 1815, at Waterloo, his army fell to the Duke of Wellington's. Napoleon was condemned to live out his final years on the remote island of ST. HELENA.

narwhal   *See MONODON MONOCEROS.*

nata mecum consule Buteo   Born with me at the time of Bute's consulship (i.e., prime ministership), Latin. (Romans often referred to years past by the name of the Consul who was then serving his one-year term. John Stuart, third Earl of Bute, was Prime Minister of Britain from May 1762 to April 1763.)

Nautical Almanac and Astronomical Ephemeris   Founded by Nevil Maskelyne (1732–1811), who held the office of Astronomer Royal for 46 years from 1765. In that year, the Board of Longitude authorized publication of the *Almanac*. The first volume was issued in 1765 for use in 1767. Published annually since that time, it provides astronomical data to seamen for use in finding a ship's position when out of sight of land. The main table gives angular distances between the moon's center and certain fixed stars and the sun, at intervals in Greenwich time. The *Almanac*, along with the sextant, made the use of lunar distances at sea a practical method of finding longitude.

nautical mile *See* SEA MILE.

Naval Chronicle, The A monthly journal published from 1799 to 1818 that detailed actions involving the Royal Navy during the two Napoleonic wars and the War of 1812, along with other naval and maritime topics. Naval officers, including NELSON and COLLINGWOOD, contributed accounts or biographical sketches. Illustrative prints and detailed maps accompanied many stories. In O'Brian's *Post Captain*, both Sophia and Diana visit Admiral Haddock to brush up on nautical matters after Aubrey moves into Melbury Lodge. The Admiral refers them to the 1801 edition of *The Naval Chronicle,* probably meaning one of the biannually collected volumes.

nave-line A line used to support the TRUSS when it has been overhauled.

naveta *or* **navetta** A chambered, megalithic tomb from the Bronze Age (4000–3000 B.C.) in the shape of an upturned boat, found on the island of MINORCA (Catalan).

Navy Board Established under Henry VIII in the mid-16th century, a commission under the Lord High Admiral that supplied and administered the British Navy until 1832, when it was merged into the Board of ADMIRALTY.

Navy List An official publication issued by the London publisher Steele from 1780 to 1815 containing a list of the officers of the Navy and other information.

Navy Office The headquarters of the NAVY BOARD at Somerset House, the Strand.

neap *or* **neap tide** A tide occurring shortly after the first and third quarters of the moon, when the moon and sun are at a right angle to each other, in which the difference between the high- and low-water levels is least. To be neaped is to run aground at the height of a SPRING TIDE, which is the opposite of the neap tide, the difference between the high- and low-water levels being greatest, and be forced to await the next spring tide to get afloat again.

neat's leather Leather made from the hides of neat cattle, the common domestic bovine.

necessary-bottle   Urinal.

neep   A turnip.

negus   A drink invented by Colonel Francis Negus (d. 1732), consisting of wine, especially port or sherry, hot water, sugar, lemon juice, and spices.

NELSON, HORATIO, FIRST VISCOUNT (1758–1805)
Few people, wrote Alfred Mahan in his great biography of Nelson, "are those whose departure is as well timed as their appearance, who do not survive the instant of perfected success, to linger on subjected to the searching tests of common life, but pass from our ken in a blaze of glory which thenceforth forever encircles their names." Nelson was born at a time when great military leadership was of crucial importance to Great Britain, and he was clearly driven to achieve that "blaze of glory."

England's legendary naval hero was born at Burnham Thorpe in Norfolk on September 29, 1758. At age 12, he went to sea aboard H.M.S. *Raisonnable*. By the age of 20, he was made POST-CAPTAIN while serving in the WEST INDIES. In 1793, after five years on half-pay, Nelson returned to sea as Captain of the *AGAMEMNON*. At the siege of Calvi in 1794, he lost his right eye, but the aggressive Captain was promoted to COMMODORE and given the larger 74-gun *Captain*. On February 14, 1797, at the battle of CAPE ST. VINCENT, 15 British SHIPS OF THE LINE, including Nelson's, under the command of Sir John JERVIS, defeated a fleet of 27 Spanish ships of the line. Nelson was instrumental in the taking of four PRIZES, boarding two of them himself. Less than a week after the battle, he became Rear-Admiral of the Blue by seniority. In July of that year, Nelson lost his right arm during a failed attempt to take a Spanish treasure ship at Santa Cruz, Tenerife, in the CANARY ISLANDS.

After he recovered from the wound, Nelson's next major feat occurred in the Mediterranean, where he hunted down and devastated a French fleet under Admiral François Brueys at the battle of the NILE in ABOUKIR Bay, on August 1, 1798. Nelson was again the hero at

Vice-Admiral Lord Nelson. (*Reproduced from Alfred Mahan's* Life of Nelson, *1897, courtesy of the Mariners' Museum, Newport News, Virginia*)

the battle of COPENHAGEN, in April of 1801, where he disregarded orders from the fleet commander, Admiral Sir Hyde Parker, to end the engagement and instead pressed on to victory. Subsequently, Parker was recalled by the ADMIRALTY while Nelson was made COM-MANDER-IN-CHIEF and a viscount.

After blockading TOULON for two years and shadowing the French fleet across the Atlantic, Nelson, aboard the *VICTORY,* finally had his ultimate showdown near Cape TRAFALGAR, on the southwest coast of Spain, on October 21, 1805. Inspired by his famous flag signal, "England expects that every man will do his duty," Nelson's force crushed a Franco-Spanish fleet under Admiral VILLENEUVE. It was the last great fleet battle of the age, and it was the fearless admiral's last fight. He was mortally wounded by a marksman aboard the French *Redoubtable.* Nelson's last words were reportedly, "Thank God I have done my duty."

"It is the appointed lot of some of History's chosen few to come upon the scene at the moment when a great tendency is nearing its crisis and culmination," wrote Mahan. "Specially gifted with quali-ties needed to realize the fulness of its possibilities, they so identify themselves with it by their deeds that they thenceforth personify to the world the movement which brought them forth, and of which their own achievements are at once the climax and the most dazzling illustration."

Nelson chequer   A famous pattern for the painting of ships that was favored by NELSON. The sides and port-lids were black, and yellow streaks marked each deck of guns, the black port-lids creating a checkered pattern.

nepenthe   A drink or drug used by the ancients to bring forgetful-ness of trouble or grief, possibly containing OPIUM as its active ingre-dient. A drug possessing such sedative properties.

***Nereide,* H.M.S.**   A 36-gun fifth-rate ship captured from the French in 1797 by H.M.S. *PHOEBE* off the SCILLIES. Recaptured by the French in August 1810 at MAURITIUS and four months later once again captured from the French, still at Mauritius. She laid up there until she was sold in 1816. In O'Brian's *The Mauritius Command,* Jack Aubrey is the COMMODORE of the British forces who retake the ship. (She was named for the Nereides, who in Greek legend were the 50 daughters of Nereus and Doris and were all nymphs of the sea.)

nescio, sed fieri sentio et excrucior   I don't know, but I feel it happening and I am tormented (Latin; from a poem by Catullus).

Nessus   The centaur slain by Hercules and whose blood soaked the tunic that consumed Hercules with fire. Nessus's shirt is a destructive or purifying force or influence.

nestle-cock   The last-hatched bird or weakling of a brood; a mother's pet or spoiled child.

neume   Any of various signs used in the notation of plainsong during the Middle Ages.

nevvy   Short for nephew.

New Bedford   The leading whaling port in New England, located on Buzzard's Bay in Massachusetts.

Newcastle   A port on the Tyne River on the northeast coast of England that delivered much coal to southern England.

Newfoundland   A large island lying off Canada's Atlantic coast, known for its prime fishing grounds and the object of much rivalry between the English, French, Basque, and Portuguese. The British obtained sovereignty of Newfoundland in 1713 at the end of the War of Spanish Succession.

New Holland   The original name of Australia.

Newmarket   An English town still famous for its racetrack.

New South Wales   The first area in NEW HOLLAND to be colonized, named by Captain COOK in 1770 on his first voyage. It is the location of Port Jackson, now Sydney, Australia.

night-ape *also* **night-monkey** *or* **owl-monkey**   Any of several South and Central American monkeys of the genus *Aotus*, having large eyes, long nonprehensile tails, and nocturnal habits.

night-glass   A short refracting telescope constructed for night use.

nightjar   A common nocturnal bird that feeds on insects and is named for the odd whirring noise, similar to that of a large spinning wheel, made by the male during the incubation period.

Nile, Battle of the, *or* **Battle of Aboukir Bay**   Occurring on August 1, 1798, in the bay of Aboukir off Egypt's Mediterranean coast, this was NELSON's first command of a fleet action, and his aggressive tactics produced a decisive victory, including two vessels sunk and nine prizes, and ended in the spectacular and horrifying explosion of the French ship *L'ORIENT*. In a classic case of understatement, Nelson reported, "To do nothing was disgraceful; therefore I made use of my understanding." The British victory isolated NAPOLEON's forces in Egypt, making their position tenuous.

nimbus   A large, uniformly gray rain cloud.

ninepins   A bowling game in which nine wooden club-shaped pins are the targets.

nipper   A piece of plaited SENNET, about five FATHOMS long, used to secure the MESSENGER to the anchor CABLE when hauling in the anchor.

nitrous oxide   Commonly known as laughing gas, its anesthetic properties were discovered by Sir Humphry Davy in 1799. However, that effect was overlooked at the time, and for some years afterward it was used only to induce exhilarating "frolics" as a party amusement. It was first introduced into medical usage, for the painless extraction of teeth, in 1844, but did not gain widespread acceptance until two or three years later.

nob   A person of wealth or social distinction.

nobble   To tamper with a horse, usually by drugging or laming it, in order to prevent it from winning a race.

nobbut   Only, merely, just.

nocturn   In the Roman Catholic Church, one of the three canonical divisions of the office of Matins.

nocturna versate manu, versate diurna   Page through by night and day (Latin; from Horace's *Art of Poetry*).

noddy   A dark, tropical seabird with the body of a tern but with shorter wings and less of a fork to the tail.

non amo te, Sabidi   I do not love you, Sabidius (Latin; from the 33rd Epigram of Martial).

Non fui non sum non curo   I was not, I am not, I care not (Latin).

non olet It doesn't stink (Latin).

non omnia possumus omnes We cannot all do everything (Latin; from Virgil's *Aeneid*).

Non sum qualis eram I am not what I used to be (Latin; Horace's *Odes* VI, 1).

Nootka Sound Inlet on the west coast of VANCOUVER Island, Canada, that was visited by Captain COOK in 1778. Spain's seizure of it in 1789 led to a breach with England that was settled by the Nootka Convention of October 28, 1790.

nordcaper A North Atlantic species of baleen whale, variously identified with *Balaena mysticetus* and *B. biscayensis*.

Nore, The A sandbank and naval anchorage about two miles northeast of Sheerness at the confluence of the Thames and the Medway rivers. Locating the Nore bank was the key to finding the main channels of both rivers. For many years, two buoys were moored on either side of the long bank, and in 1731 the world's first light ship, the Nore Light, was moored at the easterly, seaward end of the Nore bank. The bank is located about 48 miles downstream from London Bridge and is generally used as the dividing point between the Thames River and the broad Thames estuary. The Nore was the site of a failed mutiny in 1797. Concessions in pay, food, and shore leave had previously been gained at a mutiny in SPITHEAD, and much of the North Sea Fleet at Yarmouth initially joined Richard Parker of the H.M.S. *Sandwich* and his cohorts before enthusiasm for the plot crumbled. Parker and 24 conspirators were tried and hanged at the YARDARM.

Nore Light *See* NORE, THE.

Norman Cross A prisoner-of-war camp in Cambridgeshire where some 1,800 French soldiers and sailors died in captivity.

North Foreland The 100-foot-high cliff on the northeast coast of Kent, off which the Royal Navy fought one of its most difficult battles in 1666, during the Second Dutch War, defeating the Dutch while suffering heavy losses.

Nostradamus (1503–1566) French physician and astrologer (French name, Michel de Nostredame) who became known as a prophet after he accurately predicted the death of Henry II of France.

nostrum   A medicine with unrevealed ingredients; a quack remedy. A patent medicine—although securing a patent necessitated revealing the ingredients.

N'oubliez pas l'ours, messieurs-dames   Don't forget the bear, ladies and gents (French).

Nova Scotia   A maritime province on the eastern coast of Canada first settled by the French in 1605. Called Acadia, it was the first permanent North American settlement north of Florida. Possession alternated between the French and English until 1713, when the entire area became British. In 1749, Halifax was settled as a naval dockyard and base for ships on the North America station. During and after the American Revolution, many LOYALISTS moved to Nova Scotia.

novena   In the Roman Catholic Church, a devotion of special prayers or services on nine successive days.

nunc dimittis   The first words of the Song of Simeon in Luke 2:29–32, *nunc dimittis servum tuum, Domine* (Latin): "Let thy servant depart now, Lord." To sing one's *nunc dimittis* is to declare oneself willing or delighted to depart from life or from some occupation.

nunc est bibendum   Now is the time for drinking (Latin; Horace, *Odes* I, 37).

nunc et in hora mortis nostrae   Now and at the hour of our death (Latin).

nutation   A slight oscillation of the earth's axis.

nympholept   One who is in an emotional frenzy as a result of a violent enthusiasm, especially for an unattainable ideal.

O

Oaks, the   A classic race for three-year-old fillies, dating to 1779, and run at Epsom, England, on the Friday after the DERBY.

oakum   Old pieces of rope untwisted, picked into shreds, and tarred, for use in caulking ships' seams, stopping up leaks, and sometimes in dressing wounds. The making of oakum, a tedious process, often served as a naval punishment.

objective glass   In a telescope or other optical instrument, the lens or lenses nearest to the object viewed and so receiving rays of light directly from it.

obnubilate   To obscure, dim, or hide with or as with a cloud.

obsidian   A dark-colored volcanic glass.

occultation   The concealment of one heavenly body by another that passes between it and the observer, as of a star or planet by the moon. Also, the concealment of a heavenly body behind the body of the earth.

octavo   The size of a book or the page of a book when the sheets are folded so that each leaf is one-eighth of a whole sheet.

off the reel   Without halting, in an uninterrupted course or succession. Also, immediately.

off the wind   Said of a ship sailing with the wind blowing between the BEAM and the STERN.

offing   The part of the distant sea visible from the shore or beyond the anchoring ground. Also, the distance a vessel keeps from land or other navigational hazards.

O fortunatos nimium, sua si bona norint, agricolas   How exceedingly happy farmers would be if only they knew their good fortune (Latin; from Virgil's *Georgics* II).

Ohé, du bateau. . . . Ohé. . . . La Diane, où ce qu'elle se trouve à présent? . . . Au quai toujours, nom de Dieu. T'es Guillaume? . . . Non. Etienne. . . . Ben. Je m'en vais. Qu'est-ce que tu as là? . . . Des galériens. . . . Ah, les bougres. Bon. Au plaisir, eh? . . . Au plaisir, et je te souhaite merde, eh?   Ship ahoy! . . . Ahoy. . . . Where's the *Diane* now? . . . Still at the quay, for God's sake. Is it William? . . . No. Stephen. . . . Okay. I'm off. What do you have there? . . . Some convicts. . . . Oh, the scoundrels. Good. See you later, huh? . . . See you later, and break a leg, huh? (French).

O'Higgins, Bernado (1778–1842)   The Chilean-born son of an Irish father and a Chilean mother, O'Higgins was educated in England. He returned to Chile in 1802 and took an active part in liberal politics favoring independence. Inspired by Napoleon's invasion of Spain and the fall of King Ferdinand VII in 1808, he took part in a revolt in Chile led by Juan Martinez de Rozas in 1810. He was made Commander of the rebel army in 1813 and suffered a major defeat at Rancagua in 1814. But after joining forces with the Argentinian liberator San Martín, he won a decisive battle against the Spanish at Chacabuco in 1817 and led his country to independence, serving as a liberal dictator until 1823 when he was deposed by revolution. Known as "Liberator of Chile."

oilskin   A cloth or garment made waterproof by treatment with oil.

Old Harry   A familiar name for the Devil. To play Old Harry with someone or something means to play mischief with or to ruin.

Old Ironsides   Nickname for H.M.S. *Britannia*, a first rate built in 1762 and renamed *St. George* in 1812. Also the nickname for the sturdy FRIGATE U.S.S. *Constitution*.

oldster   A MIDSHIPMAN with experience, one of four years' standing.

olla podrida   A highly seasoned meat-and-vegetable stew traditional in Spain and Latin America.

Omnia perdidimus, tantummodo vita relicta est,/Praebeat ut sensum materiamque mali   We have lost everything, only life is left/Offering the sense and substance of misfortune (Latin; Ovid, *Epistulae ex Ponto*).

omnium   On the British Stock Exchange, the total value of the stocks and considerations offered by the government in raising a loan for each unit of capital (i.e., every £100) subscribed.

omnium gatherum   Coming together (Latin).

on a bowline   Said of a ship when CLOSE-HAULED, sailing as close as possible in the direction from which the wind is blowing.

on the beam   Abeam, at a right angle to a vessel's FORE-AND-AFT line. *See also* BEAM-ENDS.

onion-fly   A winged insect, *Delia cepetorum*, whose larvae are destructive to onions.

on the wind   Said of a vessel when she is sailing with her SHEETs HAULed as far aft as possible, as close as possible to the direction from which the wind is blowing.

opisthotonos   A spasm of the neck, back, and leg muscles in which the body arches backward, as in severe tetanus.

opium   The dried latex exudate of seed pods of the opium poppy. Used in medicine to control diarrhea, induce sleep, and alleviate pain, it was often highly addictive. Commonly prescribed as LAUDANUM.

opium-eating   The behavior of opium addicts, who usually drank LAUDANUM.

orange-peel   Used chiefly as a flavoring, but sometimes as a cooling tonic or for dyspepsia.

orbicular   Various organs or structures of circular or ringlike form, especially muscles, known as sphincters, that surround and close natural apertures of the body, especially those of the mouth, eyes, anus, and vagina.

orchitis   Inflammation of the testes.

ordinary   Of a ship, "in ordinary" means not fully manned and ready to sail, usually in some form of storage or disrepair in a harbor or dockyard. Also said of the men left on a ship laid up in ordinary. A tavern or eating house where meals are offered to the public at a fixed price; a dining room in such an establishment.

ordinary seaman   A RATE of sailors who can make themselves useful on board a ship but who are not expert sailors; one of the latter is known as an ABLE SEAMAN.

ordnance   Military materials, stores, or supplies in general. More specifically, artillery—cannons, MORTARs, and the like.

***Orion*, H.M.S.**   The most famous ship by this name was a 74-gun third rate built on the Thames in 1787. At the GLORIOUS FIRST OF JUNE in 1794, she was commanded by Captain John Thomas Duckworth and suffered many casualties. She also played significant roles at the Battles of CAPE ST. VINCENT in 1797, the NILE in 1798, and TRAFALGAR in 1805 under Captain Edward CODRINGTON. She also fought at COPENHAGEN in 1807 with GAMBIER and in the Baltic in 1808 with SAUMAREZ, who had commanded her in 1795.

   Commanded by Sir James SAUMAREZ at the Battle of Cape St. Vincent, she and the *Irresistable* were the first to engage the Spanish flagship *Santissima-Trinidad.* In *Post Captain* (p. 38), Aubrey informs Mrs. Williams, " 'I was third of the *Orion,*' " at the Battle of Cape St. Vincent. Later (p. 426) he mistakenly identifies her as the ship that blew up at the Nile, when he should have said *L'ORIENT.*

Orkneyman   A native or inhabitant of the Orkney Islands, off the north coast of Scotland.

orlop deck   The lowest deck of a ship, lying on the BEAMS of the hold and named from the Dutch words *overloop* and *overlopen.* The ship's CABLES and supplies were stored on the orlop deck, and the PURSER and carpenter often had offices here, near their supplies. Below the waterline, this was also the site of the POWDER MAGAZINE, and sometimes the stuffy quarters for gunners, BOATSWAINS, carpenters, and MIDSHIPMEN. Originally, the orlop deck was the single floor or deck covering the hold of a ship; with the additions of decks above, the orlop became the lowest deck of a SHIP OF THE LINE and was not usually called a "deck." When a ship had two complete levels these were called orlop and deck; when three levels, they were orlop, lower, and upper deck; when four levels, orlop, lower, middle, and upper deck.

ornithologist   One who studies birds.

Ornithorhynchus   The genus of an aquatic mammal of Australia, the duck-billed platypus, or duck-mole (*O. paradoxus* or *anatinus*), the only species of its genus and family in the order Monotremata. It has glossy dark-brown fur, webbed feet, and a bill like a duck's, and it lays eggs like a bird.

orris-root   The rhizome of *Iris florentina*, which has a fragrant smell like violets. In powdered form it was used as a perfume and medically as a strong cathartic. It was also applied to the skin to stimulate the circulation.

Ortegal   Cape Ortegal projects into the Bay of Biscay at its most southwestern point, on the northwest coast of Spain.

Orthoptera   An order of insects that includes the cockroaches, walking-stick insects, leaf-insects, crickets, and grasshoppers.

osprey *also* **sea-eagle, fishing-eagle,** *or* **fish-hawk**   A large dark-brown-and-white bird of prey that frequents rocky sea coasts and lake borders and eats fish.

Ossian *or* **Osian**   In one of the more bizarre episodes of literary history, James McPherson (1736–1796), a Scottish poet, created a series of literary forgeries, which he claimed to have translated from Gaelic manuscripts. He attributed the authorship namely to a third-century poet named Ossian. In 1775 Dr. JOHNSON charged McPherson with having written the work himself and demanded to see the originals, which were never produced. McPherson's sham works, *Fragments of Ancient Poetry collected in the Highlands of Scotland* (1760) and the epics *Fingal* (1762) and *Temora* (1763), were acclaimed by Napoleon and Goethe and influenced Blake, Burns, and most of the poets of the age. McPherson was granted a position with a salary for life and at his death was buried in Westminster Abbey.

ostler   One who attends to horses at an inn; a stable hand or groom.

otary   Any of a variety of seals with small external ears; fur seals and sea lions.

over   In cricket, the umpire's call for the players to switch to the opposite places in the field on a change of the bowling to the other end of the wicket after a certain number of balls have been bowled from one end.

overfall   Turbulent water with short breaking waves, caused by a strong current or tide setting over a submarine ridge or shoal or by the meeting of contrary currents.

oxer   Fox-hunting slang for an ox-fence, a sturdy fence used for cattle, especially one bordered by a hedge on one side and a ditch on the other.

oyster-catcher   A wading bird of the genus *Haematopus* with black-and-white or black plumage and a bright red bill. The common European species was once known as sea pie.

packet *or* **packet-boat**   A passenger boat plying at regular intervals between two ports for the conveyance of mail and goods; a mail boat.

paduasoy   A strong corded or grosgrain silk fabric, worn in the 18th century by both sexes. Also, a garment made of this material.

Paganini, Niccolò (*1782–1840*)   Born in Genoa, the son of a dockyard worker, Paganini was a violin prodigy who toured Italy in his teens (1798–1801) to great success, but he developed a weakness for gambling and heavy drinking, which nearly killed him. Paganini's innovative violin playing emphasized pizzicato effects and new methods of fingering. He composed six violin concertos, 24 caprices, 12 sonatas for violin and guitar, and many sets of variations for the violin.

Paget, General Sir Henry William (*1768–1854*)   The "fire-eating" and "influential" general on the *Charwell* in *Post Captain*, Paget was a member of Parliament for Carnarvon (1790–1796) and Milborne Port (1796–1810). He raised an infantry regiment (80th Foot) in 1793 and fought in Flanders in 1794 and Holland in 1799. Later he was instrumental in the British retreat to Corunna (1808–1809), following which, despite already being married, he eloped with the Duke of Wellington's sister-in-law, Charlotte. He commanded the Household Brigade at Waterloo, where he lost a leg in action. For his services at Waterloo, he was raised to the peerage as first Marquis of Anglesey.

pagoda A gold or sometimes silver coin once used in Southern India, worth about seven SHILLINGS.

pagoda-tree Any of several tree species found or cultivated in India, China, and other parts of the East: *Sophora japonica,* an ornamental leguminous tree with white or cream-colored flowers, cultivated in China and Japan; *Plumeria acutifolia,* with fragrant flowers, a native of the WEST INDIES and cultivated in India; and the BANYAN tree of India.

painter A rope attached to the BOW of a boat for securing or towing it. The STOPPER securing the shank and FLUKEs of an anchor was called the shank-painter.

Paita A seaport town on the northwest coast of Peru.

pake *or* **pack** A person of low or worthless character; almost always used with "naughty."

Pakenham's rudder Designed by Edward Pakenham as a JURY RUDDER for use in an emergency, it used various parts readily available on board ship, including a TOPMAST, a spare lower CAP, an anchor stock, and a mast CHEEK, BIB, or other light planking.

palanquin A covered litter or conveyance, usually for one person, used in India and other Eastern countries, consisting of a large box with wooden shutters like Venetian blinds and carried via projecting poles on the shoulders of usually four or six men.

Palestrina, Giovanni Pierluigi da (*c. 1525–1594***)** An Italian composer known for his motets, hymns, and Masses.

paling Wood prepared for or made into pales, or stakes; pales collectively; fencing.

palings A fence of pales (pointed boards).

Palladian Of or pertaining to Pallas Athena, the Greek goddess of wisdom; hence, pertaining to wisdom, knowledge, or study. Also, of or according to the school of the Italian architect Andrea Palladio (1518–1580), whose style, based on ancient Roman architecture, was made popular in England by Inigo Jones and spread to America in the mid-18th century.

***Pallas*, H.M.S.**   A 32-gun fifth rate built in 1793 and wrecked in PLYMOUTH Sound in 1798. Another 32-gun fifth rate built (of fir instead of oak) in 1804 and given to COCHRANE in 1804 when HENRY DUNDAS became First Lord of the Admiralty. In 1805 she ruturned to Plymouth with three five-foot-long candlesticks displayed from her masts following a successful cruise raiding Spanish shipping off the AZORES. In 1806 Cochrane engaged the much-heavier 40-gun French FRIGATE *Minerve,* and might have taken her had not his ship been made of the lighter wood, which took substantial injury when the two collided. The *Pallas* was wrecked off the Firth of Forth in 1810.

Pallas, Peter Simon (1741–1811)   A German naturalist who made an extensive scientific exploration of Russia and Siberia. Pallas made important contributions to botany, zoology, geography, astronomy, and other sciences.

pallet   A straw-filled mattress; a narrow, hard, or temporary bed.

Pallière, Christie   Captain of the *Desaix,* which took COCHRANE prisoner after the capture of the *Speedy* by LINOIS's SQUADRON in the GUT of GIBRALTAR. He treated Cochrane kindly. Cochrane later wrote: "On going aboard the *Desaix,* and presenting my sword to the captain, Christie Pallière, he politely declined it, with the complimentary remark that 'he would not accept the sword of an officer who had for so many hours struggled against impossibility,' at the same time paying me the compliment of requesting that 'I would continue to wear my sword, though a prisoner' " (*Autobigraphy of a Seaman,* p. 60). In *Post Captain,* Pallière is described as "a bear-like man, not as tall as Jack, but stouter, and he could stand his drink." Aubrey discovers from his English Christy cousins that Christy-Pallière (as he is called in the Aubrey-Maturin novels) is not fully sympathetic to the revolution.

Pall Mall   The name of a fashionable street in London that was built on an abandoned mall and that became a site for stylish residences.

palm   Worn by sailmakers to protect their hands, a canvas or leather shield with a piece of iron covering the palm to catch the needle as it is forced through heavy canvas. "Palm and picket men" are those who sew and work on canvas.

palmar   Of, pertaining to, or involving the palm of the hand (or the paw of an animal).

palmar aponeurosis   The network of tendons, and their fibrous sheath, that cross the palm of the hand.

palmate   Resembling a hand with the fingers spread; of a plant, having leaflets or lobes radiating from a common point.

Palmer, Nathaniel Brown (*1799–1877*)   A sealer from Stonington, Connecticut, who in 1820 explored the Antarctic Penninsula. Land later called the Palmer Coast was one of the early recorded sightings of the Antarctic mainland. Jointly with the British sealer George Powell he also discovered the South Orkney Islands in 1821.

palmetto   Any of several smaller species of palms with fan-shaped leaves, especially the dwarf fan-palm of southern Europe and North Africa and the cabbage palmetto of the southeastern United States.

palpate   To examine or explore by touch, especially as a method of medical examination.

palsy   A disease of the nervous system characterized by the loss of power to feel or control body movement; paralysis.

Panama   A narrow isthmus and country in Central America. Early Spanish explorers saw the possibility of cutting a waterway to link the Caribbean and Pacific Oceans, but it was nearly 400 years before a canal was built.

pandit   A Hindu who knows Sanskrit and is learned in Indian philosophy, law, and religion; a wise or learned man—often used as an honorific in India.

panegyric   A public speech or piece of writing in praise of some person, thing, or achievement; a formal or elaborate encomium or eulogy; elaborate praise.

pangolin   A toothless mammal of the genus *Manis*, of tropical Asia and Africa, whose body is covered with horny scales and whose protruding snout and sticky tongue are ideal for catching ants, which it eats. A scaly anteater.

Pantaloon   A character in the commedia dell'arte portrayed as a lean and foolish old man wearing spectacles, slippers, and tight trousers. In modern pantomime, a character represented as a foolish and vicious old man, the butt of the clown's jokes and his abettor in pranks and tricks. A dotard, an old fool.

Pantelleria   A small island in the Mediterranean Sea between Tunisia and Sicily. During Roman times it was a place of banishment.

Papenburg *or* **Pappenburg**   A shipbuilding city in the Grand Duchy of Arensburg (today part of Germany), near the Ems River and the Dutch border.

paper nautilus   A marine mollusk with a papery, thin, single-chambered, detached shell. Also called an argonaut.

Papin's digester   A strong vessel in which bones or other substances can be dissolved by subjecting them to the action of water or another liquid at a temperature and pressure above the boiling point.

papist *or* **papisher**   A Roman Catholic, usually used disparagingly.

Paracelsus (1493–1541)   The professional name of Philippus Aureolus Theophrastus Bombast von Hohenheim, a major forerunner of chemical pharmacology. The name Paracelsus refers to Celsus, who, although not a physician himself, wrote the first major work on medicine in Latin in the first century A.D. Discarding ancient humoral notions (see "The Disease Burden of the Royal Navy," page 37), Paracelsus's own medical theories, based on alchemical and astrological concepts, were fantastic and incomprehensible. Nevertheless, he introduced many chemical—that is, nonbotanical—drugs that remained in common use well into the 19th century.

paradise-bird   Any of various birds found chiefly in New Guinea, remarkable for the striking beauty of their plumage.

parallel   Each of the imaginary circles on the earth's surface, or actually drawn on a globe or map (usually at intervals of 5° or 10°), that parallel the equator and mark the degrees of latitude. Short for "parallel of latitude."

parasol   A species of mushroom with a broad reddish-brown pileus, or cap.

parbuckle A rope whose middle is looped around a post and whose two ends are passed around a cask or other cylindrical object and that is hauled in or paid out to move the object up or down an inclined plane. To raise or lower by means of a parbuckle.

parce, precor, precor Spare me, I beg you, I beg you (Latin).

pardi Of course! (French).

parietal Belonging or connected to the wall of the body or any of its cavities. Applied especially to a pair of bones forming part of the sides and top of the skull, between the frontal and occipital bones, and to structures connected with these or situated in the same region.

parky Cold, chilly.

parley An informal conference, especially between enemies for the discussion of terms or the arrangement of such matters as the exchange of prisoners. A discussion of terms.

Parliament The supreme legislative body of the United Kingdom, consisting of the three Estates, namely the Lords Spiritual and the Lords Temporal (together forming the House of Lords), and the House of Commons, made up of representatives of the counties, cities, boroughs, and universities.

parole Word of honor given or pledged, especially the pledge made by a prisoner of war that he will not try to escape, or that, if released, he will abide by stated conditions.

parrel A band of rope, a chain, or an iron collar that holds a YARD to a MAST in such a way that it may be hoisted or lowered and trimmed to the best position for the wind.

parthenogenic Organisms born in the absence of a sexual union; because the Greek goddess Athena was born from her father's forehead, her great temple in Athens was called the Parthenon.

partie A match in a game; a game.

partita In music, a set of related instrumental pieces, as an air with variations, or a suite.

partner A wooden frame used to strengthen a ship's deck where a MAST, CAPSTAN, PUMP, or other device or structure passes through.

parturition   Childbirth.

Pascal, Blaise (*1623–1662*)   The French scientist and religious philosopher credited with founding the modern theory of probability, Pascal also contributed to the advance of differential calculus and to the understanding of atmospheric pressure. Beginning in 1654, he turned his attention to religion. His influential *Lettres écrites à un provincial* (1656–57) circulated throughout Europe. His *Pensées* (1670), which argue that reason alone is inadequate to solve man's difficulties or to satisfy his hopes, is considered a religious and philosophical classic.

pasha   A former title of honor used in the Ottoman Empire for officers of high rank, such as rulers of tributary states, military commanders, and provincial governors.

passade   A brief love affair; a passing romance.

passaree *also* **pazaree** *or* **placery**   A rope or TACKLE used to spread taut the foot of a square FORESAIL when sailing BEFORE THE WIND.

passerine   Of or pertaining to the largest order of birds (Passeriformes), which includes more than half of all known birds and consists of songbirds and perching birds such as jays, blackbirds, finches, warblers, and sparrows.

passing note   In music, a note not belonging to the harmony but interposed between two notes essential to it, in order to provide a smooth transition from one to the other.

pasty   A pie, usually consisting of seasoned venison or another meat enclosed in a crust of pastry and baked without a dish; a meat pie.

patarero *or* **pedrero**   A piece of ORDNANCE originally used for discharging stones. Also used to discharge broken iron, partridge shot, and other scattershot and for firing salutes.

patchouli   A shrubby mint, native to Silhat, Penang, and the MALAY Peninsula, that yields a fragrant essential oil; a penetrating and lasting perfume made from this oil.

pater classis   Father of the fleet (Latin).

patristic   Of or pertaining to the early fathers of the Christian church or their writings.

patten   An overshoe or sandal with a wooden sole mounted on an iron ring, or any similar device, whose purpose is to raise the ordinary shoes out of mud or wetness.

patty   A little pie; a PASTY baked in a small pan.

patty-pan   A small tin pan or shape in which PATTIES are baked.

paunch   A thick, strong mat woven of yarn or strands of rope, used on a ship to prevent chafing. A rubbing paunch is a wooden covering or shield mounted on the FORE side of a MAST to preserve it from chafing when the masts or SPARS are lowered or raised.

Pavo   A constellation in the Southern Hemisphere, from the Latin word for peacock.

pawl   Various forms of ratchet were used to prevent the WINDLASS or CAPSTAN from running backward when they were being used to HEAVE in the CABLE. To pawl is to stop a capstan's backward motion.

pay   To smear or cover with waterproof material, such as PITCH, TAR, resin, or tallow.

pay off   Of a ship, to cause to fall to LEEWARD, or away from the wind.

peach   To give incriminating evidence against, to inform against, to betray. To turn informer. To blab, divulge.

Pearl River   Flows from Canton to the South China Sea, divided by the narrow channel called the Bocca Tigris into the upper and lower Pearl rivers. The lower river is the large bay that separates MACAO and present-day Hong Kong.

pease   Peas. Pease pudding is a dish of boiled, mashed peas.

peccary   A piglike nocturnal mammal native to the Americas, of which there are two species, the collared peccary, extending north to Texas, and the white-lipped peccary of South America.

peccatum illud horribile inter Christianos non nominandum   That terrible sin that has no name among Christians (Latin).

peccavi   An acknowledgment or confession of sin, from the Latin for "I have sinned."

peccavi nimis cogitatione, verbo, et opere I have sinned greatly in thought, word, and deed (Latin).

peculation The appropriation of public money or property by one in an official position; the embezzlement of money or goods entrusted to one's care.

pediculus A louse, a parasitic insect that infests the hair and skin of humans and other warm-blooded animals, causing irritation. Also, other kinds of parasitic insects. Degraded crustaceans that infest fish.

peepul-tree *or* **pipal-tree** An Indian species of fig tree, regarded as sacred by Buddhists.

peerage The body of peers in the United Kingdom; the nobility, aristocracy. The rank or dignity of a peer, including the five titles: duke, marquess, earl, viscount, and baron. A book listing peers and their families.

Pelagian Of or pertaining to Pelagius (*c.* 354–418), a heretical British monk who denied the Catholic doctrine of original sin and maintained that the human will is of itself capable of good without the assistance of divine grace.

pelagic Of or pertaining to the open or high sea, as distinguished from shallow coastal water; oceanic. Now especially, living on or near the surface of the open sea or ocean, as distinguished from its depths.

pelisse A long mantle or cloak lined with fur. A long, lightweight cloak worn by women, often with openings for the arms.

Pellew, Sir Edward, Viscount Exmouth (*1757–1833*) A daring and highly regarded FRIGATE captain and ADMIRAL, who went to sea at age 13 and quickly showed a talent for standing on his head on the YARDARMS. Pellew, commanding the frigate *Nymphe*, captured the French frigate *Cléopâtre*, the first frigate taken in the War of the French Revolution (1793–1801), and with it the enemy's signal code. In 1797, Pellew, commanding the frigate INDEFATIGABLE, in company with the *Amazon*, commanded by Captain R. C. Reynolds, destroyed *Droits de l'Homme*, a 74-gun French SHIP OF THE LINE off the coast of France in a famous all-night duel. Pellew later served as COMMANDER-IN-CHIEF in the EAST INDIES and the Mediterranean, commanding at the bombardment of Algiers in 1816.

Peloponnese The Peloponnesus, the large peninsula south of the Gulf of Corinth that forms the southernmost part of the Greek mainland.

Penang Prince of Wales Island, which lies off the west coast of the MALAY Peninsula and served as a base for the EAST INDIES STATION.

pendants Short, heavy ropes secured to the lower MASTS, just under the SHROUDS. They had an EYE in the lower end to which were hooked the fore and main TACKLES.

pénétré Moved, affected, impressed (French).

Penlee Point *or* Head Cape southwest of PLYMOUTH.

pennant A tapered flag, longer in the fly than in the hoist, specifically one flown at the MASTHEAD of a vessel in commission, unless it is distinguished by a flag (making it a FLAGSHIP) or a broad pendant. The flying of the pendant at half-mast denotes the death of the Captain, its absence, that the vessel is out of commission. A broad pendant is a short, swallow-tailed pendant indicating a COMMODORE's ship in a SQUADRON.

Penny-Post A post established for the benefit of London and the adjacent parts by which any letter or parcel weighing no more than 16 ounces could be quickly sent to and from all parts within ten miles of London.

pennyweight A measure of weight equal to 24 grains, .05 of a troy ounce, or approximately 1.55 grams (formerly equal to 22.5 grains, which was the actual weight of a silver penny).

pentamerous Having five parts or divisions. In botany, having flower parts in sets of five. In zoology, consisting of five joints, as the segmented tarsi of insects' legs. Also applied to such insects themselves, as the beetles of the group Pentamera.

Pentateuch The first five books of the Old Testament (Genesis, Exodus, Leviticus, Numbers, and Deuteronomy), traditionally ascribed to Moses.

penteconter A ship of burden with 50 oars.

perch A pole, rod, stick, or stake used as a weapon, a prop, or for various other purposes.

percussion   The technique, introduced by Leopold Auenbrugger of Vienna in 1751, of tapping, with the fingers, various areas of the body to determine by their resonance the condition of organs within the body cavities, and for ascertaining the location and amount of EDEMA fluid in the chest or abdomen. Auenbrugger based his technique on that used by innkeepers to determine how much beer or wine remained in wooden storage casks. *See also* CORVISART.

peregrine   A widely distributed falcon, with gray and white plumage, often used for falconry.

Pergolesi, Giovanni Battista (*1710–1736*)   Italian composer. Born in Jesi, Italy, Pergolesi entered the Conservatorium dei Poveri di Gesù Cristo in Naples at the age of 15. He composed 16 operas, in addition to many cantatas, sonatas, symphonies, and concertos, before dying of tuberculosis.

pericardium   The membranous sac that encloses the heart and roots of the great blood vessels of vertebrates and certain invertebrates.

peritoneum   The bilayered membrane that lines the cavity of the abdomen of mammals.

Pernis apivorus   The honey-buzzard, a bird of prey that feeds on the contents of bees' and wasps' nests.

perspective-glass   A telescope.

Peruvian Bark   *See* BARK.

pervenche   A shade of light blue, the color of periwinkle flowers, from the French word for periwinkle, with the same spelling.

petechia   A small red or purple spot on the skin caused by a minute hemorrhage, occurring with SCURVY and certain fevers, especially typhus and GAOL FEVER.

peter-boat   Name used on the Thames and adjacent coasts for a decked fishing boat smaller than a YAWL. Also, a double-ended boat used for dredging.

petit-four   A small iced cake, usually decorated.

petrel   A seabird with black to gray or brown plumage and a hooked bill. Petrels breed on land but spend most of their lives at sea, primarily in the Southern Hemisphere but also along northern shores, including the Mediterranean. Related to ALBATROSSes, the petrel species are found in three families: the large petrels; including the FULMAR; the prions and the SHEARWATERS; and the smaller STORM PETRELs and diving petrels. All have long wings and short, wide tails and are strong fliers. Storm petrels and diving petrels usually reach up to ten inches in length while large petrels can grow to three times that size. The name "petrel" probably derives from St. Peter, because, like the saint, the smooth-gliding petrel seems to walk on water.

pettichaps   The garden warbler and other species of warblers. The name was common in Yorkshire and Lancashire and entered into ornithological nomenclature in 1670, but never gained general usage.

petticoat-trousers   A wide outer garment of oilskins or rough canvas worn by fishermen in warm weather. They reach below the knee and are often undivided.

pettifog   To act as a pettifogger, a petty, squabbling, disreputable lawyer. To practice legal chicanery. To plead or conduct a petty case in a minor court of law. Also, to quibble about trifles.

Petty Bag   A clerk of the Court of Chancery, whose records were kept in *petit* (French for "little") leather bags.

petty officer   A naval officer corresponding in rank to a noncommissioned officer in the army.

Pezophaps solitarius   The solitaire, a large flightless bird formerly inhabiting the island of Rodriguez, near MAURITIUS.

Phaeacian   An inhabitant of the island of Scheria (the name in ancient legend for Corfu), known for luxury; a gourmand.

phalanger   Any of various tree-dwelling marsupials of Australia, ranging in size from a mouse to a large cat, with thick woolly fur and long tails.

phalarope   Any of several small wading birds of the family Phalaropodidae, resembling sandpipers but with lobed toes that allow them to swim. They include the gray or red phalarope, noted for its spectacular seasonal changes of plumage.

phanerogam   A plant that has obvious reproductive organs, such as stamens and pistils.

pharaoh's hen The Egyptian vulture (*Neophron perchopterus*), also called pharaoh's chicken.

pharaonic Pertaining to the nature or character of a pharaoh, a ruler of ancient Egypt.

pharmacopoeia A volume specifying the ingredients of a medicine in any one city or country, so that all apothecaries there would make up a given remedy in exactly the same way. The major British pharmacopoeias of the late 18th century were written and published by the physicians of London, Edinburgh, and Dublin; no national pharmacopoeias would be published before that of the United States, in 1820.

Pherecratean A poetic measure, named for a fifth-century B.C. Greek poet, consisting of three feet, typically spondee, dactyl, and spondee (or trochee).

philoprogenitive Inclined to produce offspring; prolific. Also, of or pertaining to love of offspring.

philosophers' stone A hypothetical substance or preparation believed to have the power of changing other metals into gold or silver, the discovery of which was an objective of alchemy. Some also believed it to prolong life indefinitely and to cure wounds and diseases.

Philosophical Transactions One of the earliest learned journals, published since 1665 by the ROYAL SOCIETY of London, the oldest scientific society in Great Britain (established in 1660).

Phoca Any aquatic mammal of the *Phocidae,* or seal and walrus family.

Phoebe, **H.M.S.** A 36-gun fifth rate built on the Thames in 1795. In the Mediterranean in 1801, the *Phoebe,* under Captain Robert Barlow, captured the 40-gun *L'Africaine,* which was packed with 400 troops. During the two-hour action, *L'Africaine* lost 200 men killed and 143 wounded, while the *Phoebe* suffered only one killed and 12 wounded. The *Phoebe* fought at TRAFALGAR in 1805 under Captain Hon. Thomas Capel and helped capture Java and MAURITIUS in 1811, earning three single-ship action medal awards in the process. In 1814, under Captain Hillyar, she and the *Cherub* (20 guns) fought a famous battle with the U.S.S. *Essex* at VALPARAISO.

phrenology The notion, developed after 1810 by GALL, that an individual's moral, sexual, and intellectual traits, which he assumed to be located in specific areas of the brain, can be measured by palpating irregularities on the surfaces of the skull overlying those areas. Although it had a veneer of scientific respectability, phrenology was exploited by quacks and ridiculed by physicians.

phthisis A progressive wasting disease, in most cases tuberculosis.

physic Medicine, especially a cathartic or purgative. The profession of medicine.

Physician of the Fleet In the British Navy, the highest ranking medical officer assigned to a fleet.

physiognomist One skilled in physiognomy, the art of reading character, temperament, and even the soul or the future, from the face, invented by the Swiss poet and mystic Johann Kaspar Lavater (1741–1801).

pianissimo Very softly, a direction in music.

pianoforte A piano (from the Italian *piano e forte,* "soft and loud").

piastre *or* piaster A PIECE OF EIGHT, or Spanish dollar. Also, a small Turkish coin.

piazza A public square or marketplace, especially in an Italian town. From the 16th to 18th centuries, an open space surrounded by buildings, such as the parade ground in a fort; also, a colonnade or covered walkway.

pice *or* paisa A small Indian copper coin equal in value to ⅟₁₀₀ of a rupee.

piece of eight A Spanish dollar or PIASTRE, made of silver and worth eight reals, or four British SHILLINGS.

pier glass A large, tall mirror, especially one designed to fit a pier, or space between two windows.

pig An oblong mass of metal, usually iron or lead, poured from a smelting furnace; an ingot. Also, short for "pig-iron," crude iron cast in pigs. A "pig of ballast" was a pig of iron (rarely of lead) used as ballast.

Pigot, Hugh (*1769–1797*) A Royal Navy Captain remembered primarily for his cruelty while commanding the H.M.S. *HERMIONE*. The crew mutinied, killed most of the officers, including Pigot, and delivered the ship to the Spaniards. Dudley Pope's book *The Black Ship* (1963) expertly recounts the event and its aftermath.

pig's trotters Pig's feet, as food.

pilau *or* pilaf A dish of seasoned rice with meat and vegetables.

pilchard A small sea fish related to the herring but smaller and rounder, especially an edible species found abundantly off the coasts of Cornwall and Devon.

piles Hemorrhoids.

pillory A punishment device consisting of a wooden framework on a post with holes for the head and hands in which an offender was locked in order to be exposed to public ridicule, insult, and molestation. In Great Britain the pillory was abolished for everything but perjury in 1815, and entirely in 1837.

pilot An experienced seaman who is specially qualified with local knowledge to bring a ship into port.

pilot-cutter A CUTTER used by PILOTs to guide ships into port.

pilot-jacket A pea jacket, a short double-breasted overcoat of heavy wool, now commonly worn by sailors.

pilot-water A piece of water in which the service of a PILOT is necessary.

pimping Insignificant, paltry, petty. In poor health or condition, sickly.

pin The projecting bone of the hip, especially in horses and cattle.

pinchbeck An alloy of about five parts copper to one part zinc used to imitate gold in jewelry, clock-making, etc. A cheap imitation. Counterfeit, spurious.

Pindaric Of or pertaining to Pindar, a fifth century B.C. Greek poet; written in a style resembling that of Pindar. A Pindaric ode.

pinion   To prevent a bird from flying, especially by cutting off the pinion, or outer rear edge, of its wing. To disable by binding the arms; to shackle.

pink   Used at various times and with various meanings for a small narrow-STERNed and SQUARE-RIGGED ship employed primarily for COASTING, fishing, and as a warship, differing considerably among the Dutch, Danish, and Mediterranean types.

pinnace   A boat, usually with eight oars, carried on a MAN-OF-WAR; a small ship or ship's boat, especially one used as a TENDER.

pinny   Colloquial name for "pinafore," a sleeveless dress or apron fastened in the back.

pintado   A species of PETREL, also called cape pigeon.

pintail   A common species of duck with white, gray, and brown plumage and a sharply pointed tail.

pintle   A pin forming part of the hinge of a RUDDER, usually attached to the rudder and fitting into a ring or GUDGEON on the STERNPOST.

pip   One of the dots on playing cards, dice, or dominoes. Also, a fruit seed or pit.

pipe   The BOATSWAIN's whistle, a silver pipe used by the boatswain to convey orders to the crew. Most orders had their own particular cadences by which they were identified. Also, the sounding of the boatswain's pipe to call the crew. To escort to the accompaniment of a pipe; to convey orders by sounding the boatswain's pipe.

pipe clay   A fine white clay that forms a ductile paste when mixed with water, used for making tobacco pipes, whitening leather, and, especially by soldiers, for cleaning white clothes; given to excessive attention to dress or appearance.

pipe one's eye   In nautical slang, to shed tears, cry.

pipistrelle   A small bat common in Britain and Europe.

pippin   Any of numerous varieties of apple, usually yellow flushed with red. A fruit seed or pip. A person or thing very much admired.

pipit   A ground-dwelling bird, brown above and lighter underneath, of the family Motacillidae, resembling the lark and common in most parts of the world.

piquet *or* **picquet**   A card game played with a deck of 32 cards (sevens through aces only) and in which points are scored on various combinations of cards and on tricks.

pis aller   Last resort (French).

piscary   The right of fishing.

pitch   Of a ship's motion, the FORE-AND-AFT rocking created when a wave lifts first the BOW and then the STERN. A mixture of TAR and other substances used in CAULKing a ship's deck or side seams to coat and seal the OAKUM.

Pitt, William, the Younger (*1759–1806*)   Son of William Pitt, first Earl of Chatham, the Elder Pitt, who had been the great prime minister during the SEVEN YEARS' WAR. In 1781 the Younger Pitt entered PARLIAMENT at the age of 22. His reputation rose rapidly. He became Chancellor of the Exchequer in 1782 and First Lord of the Treasury in December 1783. Fighting tremendous opposition in Parliament, Pitt skillfully won the election of 1784. This and following elections made him one of the most powerful prime ministers in English history, keeping him in office without a break until February 1801. At that point he resigned in favor of his follower, Henry ADDINGTON, but resumed office in 1804. He remained in office until his death in 1806 and, after TRAFALGAR, was hailed as "the savior of Europe."

pixy-led   Led astray by pixies, or elfin creatures. Lost; bewildered, confused.

pizzicato   In music, played by plucking the string of an instrument with the finger instead of using a bow.

pizzle   The penis of an animal. A whip made from a bull's penis.

plaice   A European or American flatfish, popular for eating.

plaid   A long piece of twilled woolen cloth, in a cross-barred pattern, worn instead of a cloak or mantle in Scotland and northern England.

plain-chant   Early Christian vocal music, also called plainsong, consisting of melodies composed in the limited Gregorian scale and in free rhythm, and sung in unison.

plane   A lofty spreading tree with broad PALMATE leaves and bark that scales off in irregular patches, especially the Oriental plane, a native of Iran and the LEVANT, common in European parks and squares and along avenues.

planksheer A continuous planking that covers the timber-heads of a wooden ship, in MEN-OF-WAR forming a shelf below the GUNWALE. Covering-board. Also, loosely, the gunwale.

plantain-eater, *also* **Turaco** *or* **Touraco** *or* **Lourie** Any of the African birds of the family Musophagidae, placed with the cuckoos or separated as a distinct order. Some of the grayish species are known as go-away birds, in imitation of their calls. Some are gray, brown, and white, but the ten species of the genus *Tauraco* and the two of *Musophaga* have a remarkably beautiful red-and-green coloring. Long tailed and short winged, they spend their time entirely in trees in search of fruit, taking a few invertebrates. Ironically, they do not eat plantains.

plash Shallow standing water, a pool made by rain; a puddle.

pleat Strands of rope twisted into FOXes, or braided into SENNET.

pledget A small compress, sometimes steeped in medicine, used to dress a wound or sore.

Pleiades A cluster of small stars in the constellation Taurus representing the seven daughters of Atlas and Pleione, figures in Greek mythology. Six of the stars are visible to the naked eye; the seventh represents the oldest daughter, Electra, the "lost Pleiad."

plethoric Overloaded; swollen, inflated.

plover Any of several gregarious wading or shore birds with long wings, a short tail, and a short, stout beak.

pluck Courage and daring; boldness, fortitude, spirit; determination to keep fighting in the face of difficulty. To want pluck means to be a coward.

plum-cake A cake made with raisins, currants, and often preserved fruits.

plum-duff A boiled suet pudding containing raisins or currants.

plummet A plumb; a SOUNDING-LEAD.

plusher's Rum remaining in the barrel after it has been served out.

Plymouth A historic and strategic English seaport and naval base in South Devon at the western end of the English Channel that served as the starting point for numerous sea explorations and enterprises as early as 1311. A naval dockyard was developed there in 1689.

Plymouth How *or* **Hoe** The famous coastal vantage point located at PLYMOUTH, England.

pocket-borough A borough in Great Britain whose parliamentary representation was under the control of one person or family.

Pocock, Nicholas (*1741–1821*) A British marine painter, whose eye for the fine detail of MASTS and RIGGINGS was trained while he was a merchant ship Commander. He is especially noted for his paintings of naval battles, many of which can still be seen at the National Maritime Museum in GREENWICH, England.

point Each of the equidistant divisions on the circumference of the mariner's compass, indicated by one of the 32 rays drawn from the center and used to identify the part of the horizon from which the wind blows or in which an object lies; the four "cardinal points" are North, South, East, and West, and the four "half cardinal points" are Northeast, Southeast, Southwest, and Northwest. Also, the angular interval between two successive points (one eighth of a right angle). *See* illustration, next page.

point-device Perfectly correct; neat or nice to the extreme; precise or scrupulous.

poke A bag; a small sack. Also, a pocket.

polacca A two- or three-masted merchant vessel of the LEVANT and Mediterranean, the two-masted, or BRIG, version having square sails on both MASTS and the three-masted, or ship, version—also known as a polacre-settee—having a LATEEN sail on the FOREMAST and sometimes on the MIZZEN.

polacre rig A square rig of the eastern Mediterranean in which the lower MAST, TOPMAST, and TOPGALLANT are made of a single SPAR, the upper YARDS being lowered all the way to the deck for FURLing.

poldavy A coarse canvas or sacking, originally woven in Brittany and often used for sailcloth.

Points of sailing. The arrow pointing down at the top of the illustration shows the direction of the wind. The ship *m* is sailing before the wind, or with the wind right aft; *n* and *l* have the wind one point on the quarter; *o* and *k* have the wind two points on the quarter; *p* and *i* have the wind three points on the quarter; *q* and *h* have the wind on the quarter, or six points large; *f* and *s* have the wind four points large, or two points abaft the beam; *g* and *r* have the wind five points large; *e* and *t* have the wind one point abaft the beam, or three points large; *u* and *d* have the wind on the beam, or two points large; *c* and *x* have the wind one point large; *B* and *y* are sailing close-hauled.

The vessels shown on the right-hand side of the diagram are on the larboard tack, while those on the left-hand side are on the starboard tack. Those in the range from *s* to *n* and *l* to *f* are "quartering." Those in the range from *u* to *s* and *d* to *f* are "sailing large," or "going free." The area at the top of the diagram into which a ship cannot sail is "dead." (*Illustration from* Burney's Dictionary).

pole   A ship's MAST; also, the upper end of a mast, rising above the RIGGING. "Under bare poles" means with no sail set, with FURLed sails.

poleax *or* **poleaxe**   A battle-ax used until the end of the 18th century in naval warfare for such things as boarding, resisting boarders, and cutting ropes. In naval use it usually had a handle of about 15 inches and a spike at the back of the ax head that could be driven into the side of an enemy ship and used with other poleaxes as a ladder for boarding.

pollack   A saltwater fish of the cod family with a protruding lower jaw, popular as food in Europe and the United States.

poll-parrot   A parrot. From Polly, a popular nickname for a parrot.

poltroon   A spiritless coward; a mean-spirited wretch.

Polychrest, **H.M.S.**   An experimental craft with sliding keels and rudders and designed to carry a secret weapon: a missile that could destroy a first rate from a mile away, the testing of which cost the inventor, Mr. Eldon, his life. Equipped with twenty-four 32-pound carronades, she is rated a SLOOP instead of a post-ship by First Lord Melville in order to let Aubrey take command of her. The *Polychrest* is fictional.

polyp   Any of various coelenterates that have a cylindrical body and a mouth fringed with many small tentacles bearing stinging cells, as a sea anemone, jellyfish, or hydra.

polypody of oak   A widely distributed fern that grows on moist rocks, old walls, and trees.

pommel   The round knob on the hilt of a sword, dagger, or the like.

pommelion   A CASCABEL, or knob, on the BREECH of a muzzle-loading cannon.

Pompey   A nickname used by sailors for PORTSMOUTH, the English Channel port, the exact derivation of which is unknown.

poop   A short, raised aftermost deck of a ship, above the QUARTER-DECK, found only in very large sailing ships. Also a ship is said to be "pooped" when a heavy sea breaks over a vessel's STERN, a potentially hazardous situation in a GALE.

poor fist   A poor attempt.

poor-rate   A tax for the relief or support of the poor.

popinjay   An early name for a parrot. A woodpecker, usually the green woodpecker. Also, used contemptuously for a vain person who engages in empty chatter, an allusion to the parrot's gaudy plumage or to its mechanical repetition of words and phrases.

poppet   A small or dainty person. A term of endearment for a pretty child, girl, or young woman; darling, pet. Also, one of the timbers used to support a ship at launching; a small block of wood that fits inside and supports the GUNWALE or WASHBOARD.

poppy   An annual or perennial flower with showy red, white, pink, yellow, or orange petals and capsules containing numerous small, round seeds. Some varieties contain OPIUM.

porphyria   In *Blue at the Mizzen* (p. 110), should be "porphyrio," from *Porphyrio porphyrio*, the Latin name of the purple gallinule, a large RAIL with blue plumage, a red bill, and red legs.

porphyry   A very hard, fine red or purple stone with red or white feldspar crystals.

portable soup   A soup made from cattle offal, flavored with salt and vegetables and cooked down to hard, gluey cakes. With water added, it was used to make green vegetables boiled in it more palatable and to protect against scurvy.

Port Admiral   An ADMIRAL in command of a naval port and chiefly concerned with dockyard repairs, supplies, and administrative duties. Often the target of derision from the seamen under his authority as any commander would be who sent men to war while remaining behind in a comfortable and often corrupt town, yet was entitled to a portion of their spoils.

Porte   *See* SUBLIME PORTE.

porter   A dark-brown slightly bitter beer brewed from malt partly charred or browned from being dried at a high temperature.

porter's chair   A leather armchair with a high back and an arched hood that protected a porter from drafts, used in the entrance halls of well-furnished houses, especially during the Georgian period.

portion   The part of an estate received by an heir. Also, a dowry.

portlast   The GUNWALE of a vessel; a YARD is said to be a-portlast when it lies on the deck.

port-lid   A cover for a porthole, or SCUTTLE.

Port Mahon   On the east side of MINORCA, the chief town and port of this strategic western Mediterranean island and the object of many battles during the 18th century. Taken by the British in 1708 during the War of Spanish Succession, the port was captured in turn by the French in 1756, when Admiral John BYNG failed to relieve it. In 1762 it was restored to the British, who lost it again during the American

Revolutionary War. Admiral COLLINGWOOD used the port as a base for his blockade of TOULON during the Napoleonic wars. With the demise of Napoleon, Spain regained hegemony in 1815.

Port of Spain   The chief port and capital of Trinidad in the WEST INDIES, with a sheltered harbor offering access to the island's natural riches. Following the decline of Spanish power in the Caribbean, the port was the source of much rancor between the Dutch, French, and English.

Ports Down Hill   An open down approximately 600 feet high, it runs for seven miles along the coast opposite the islands of Portsea and Hayling and the harbor of PORTSMOUTH in southern England.

port-sill   The timbers that line the top and bottom of a gunport on a MAN-OF-WAR.

Portsmouth   In Hampshire, England, on the English Channel, the chief dockyard of the Royal Navy, with an ideal harbor and an anchorage nearby at SPITHEAD that is sheltered from the Channel by the Isle of WIGHT.

posada   An inn in Spanish-speaking countries.

po'shay   Contraction of "pony-shay." *See* POST CHAISE.

posset   A drink made of hot milk curdled with ale, wine, or other liquor and sugar and spices, used as both a delicacy and a remedy for colds and other illnesses.

possibile è la cosa, e naturale. . . . E se Susanna vuol, possibilissima   It's possible, and natural. . . . And if Susanna is willing, most possible (Italian; sung by Figaro in act two of Mozart's *The Marriage of Figaro*).

post   The upright timber on which the RUDDER is hung; the STERN-POST. Also, the mode of travel by POST CHAISE.

post-boy   *See* POSTILLION.

post-captain *or* **post**   The rank in the Royal Navy indicating the receipt of a COMMISSION as officer in command of a POST SHIP. This commission entitled a full-grade Captain (officially called a Post-Captain) to a MASTER, who was responsible for the navigation of the ship, as well as to position in the order of seniority on the list of Captains. The Post-Captain was distinguished from a MASTER AND COM-

MANDER, an officer of inferior rank who was given the courtesy title of Captain while serving as an acting Captain, and from a LIEUTENANT commanding an unRATEd vessel (a ship of fewer than 20 guns). Officially, the term "Post Captain" was used until 1824, at which time it was replaced with "Captain." Officers appointed to command post ships and up were technically the only ones to be called Captains. But, unofficially, the courtesy use of "Captain" for a Master and Commander or Lieutenant commanding a smaller vessel continued.

post chaise   A four-wheeled horse-drawn carriage with a closed body, used to carry mail and passengers.

postern   A back or private door or gate, not the main entrance.

postillion   One who rides a post-horse; a swift messenger. One who rides the left, leading horse when four or more are used to pull a carriage or POST CHAISE, especially one who rides the near horse when one pair only is used and there is no driver on the box. Also called a post-boy.

post ship   In the Royal Navy, a RATEd ship (one having no less than 20 guns), the command of which was held by a POST-CAPTAIN.

potable gold   A supposed solution of gold in vinegar (a notion derived from alchemy), but by the 18th century, an aquaeous solution of LENTISK, used occasionally as medicine.

pot-boy   An assistant to a publican, or keeper of a pub.

poteen   Bootleg whisky distilled in Ireland.

potentate   A person of independent power, such as a prince or monarch.

pot-hooks and hangers   A children's name for the strokes—resembling the hooks and chains used to hang kitchen pots—used in writing cursive letters.

pot-house   A small, unpretentious, or low tavern or public house, or characteristic of one. Low, vulgar.

pouffe   An old form of "puff," an effeminate or homosexual man.

poulterer   A person who sells poultry and often hares and other game.

poultice   A soft mixture of bread, meal, bran, linseed, herbs, or the like, usually boiled in water, spread on muslin or linen, and applied to the skin for warmth or moisture, as a counterirritant or as an emollient for a soreness or inflammation.

pound   An English unit of currency. Originally, the basic unit of currency was a sterling, equal to ½₄₀ of a pound of silver, and 240 sterlings became known as a pound sterling. The pound remained convertible into silver until 1717, when Britain changed to the gold standard. The gold sovereign, a coin, represented the pound at 113.001 grains of fine gold or 7.32238 grams. Britain abandoned the gold standard between 1797 and 1816.

pourparler   An informal conference prior to a negotiation.

powder-hoy   An ORDNANCE vessel specially equipped to carry powder from a land magazine to a ship and signified by a red flag.

powder of Algaroth   Antimony oxychloride, used rarely as an EMETIC; also known as "mercury of life."

powder-room *also* **powder-magazine** *or* **magazine**   A dry room below deck, often in the ORLOP, where the gunpowder and ammunition is stored on board a ship.

pox   Pocks or eruptive pustules on the skin. The term usually referred to syphilis, also known as the "great pox," and was only rarely applied to SMALLPOX.

praecordia   The area over the heart.

pram   A flat-bottomed boat, or LIGHTER, used primarily in Baltic and North Sea ports to transport cargo between ship and shore. A small flat-bottomed ship with two or three MASTS and mounted with 10 to 20 guns, used by the French as a floating battery in coastal defense. A small ship's boat.

pratique   Permission granted to a ship to proceed into port after being cleared by the health authority (from French).

prayer-books   Blocks of sandstone, smaller than HOLYSTONES or BIBLES, and used by sailors to scrub in among the crevices and hard-to-get places.

presbytery   Part of a church or cathedral reserved for the clergy. The set of three seats, or sedilia, on the south side of the eastern part of the chancel. The eastern part of the chancel beyond the choir, where the altar is. The sanctuary.

Pressburg, Treaty of   In 1491, the treaty by which the Habsburgs secured rights to the Hungarian succession. In 1805 the harsh treaty NAPOLEON imposed on Austria after his victories at Ulm and Auster-litz, in effect ending the Holy Roman Empire and creating a ring of French client states.

press-gang   A group of men, commanded by an officer, who IMPRESS men for service in the navy or army.

press-tender   *See* TENDER.

preventer   Any rope used as an additional security to aid the stand-ing RIGGING in supporting SPARS during a strong GALE or to prevent further damage caused by their breaking.

Prévost d'Exiles, Antoine-François (*1697–1763*)   Known as Abbé Prévost, he was a French novelist and adventurer. Prévost entered the Benedictine order in 1721 but left it in 1728 to travel and write. Among his notable works are *Les Mémoires d'un homme de qualité* (1728), *Histoire du Chevalier des Grieux et de Manon Lescaut* (1731), and *Mémoires d'un honnête homme* (1745). He translated many works into French, including Richardson's *Pamela* and *Clarissa*. His 20-volume *Histoire Générale des Voyages* (a translation from English), first published in 1745, contains many maps and illustrations. It serves as one of Patrick O'Brian's most valued sources for geography and natural history.

Priapean   A poetic meter associated with poems celebrating PRIAPUS. Extraordinarily sexually active.

Priapus   The Greek and Roman god of procreation and also of gar-dens and vineyards, where his statues, always with a prominent erec-tion, were often placed. A representation of the phallus.

prick the chart   To locate one's position on a chart.

Priddy's Hard   An Ordnance Board station located in the north sec-tion of GOSPORT, directly across the harbor from PORTSMOUTH dockyard.

priming   The gunpowder in the pan of a firearm to be sparked in fir-ing. Also, the train of powder that connects a fuse with a charge in blasting.

priming-iron *or* **priming-wire** A sharp-pointed wire at the end of a wooden handle used in gunnery to clear the touchhole, or vent, and pierce the cartridge before firing.

Primula A genus of herbaceous, mostly hardy, perennial plants, with yellow, white, pink, or purple flowers, especially the primrose. It is found chiefly in Europe and Asia.

primum mobile Literally, first moving thing (Latin). The prime mover.

Prince of Wales A title given to the eldest son of a British sovereign. Originally, the Prince of Wales was the only prince in England, but in the reign of JAMES I, the title "prince" was extended to all the sons of the sovereign, and under Victoria, all children of royal sons became princes and princesses. The Prince of Wales during the reign of GEORGE III was his eldest son and successor, GEORGE IV.

Prince Regent *See* GEORGE IV.

prion A small saw-billed PETREL found in southern seas.

prior In an abbey, the officer immediately beneath the abbot, appointed by him to oversee certain offices, maintain discipline, and preside in his absence. In a smaller or daughter monastery, the resident superior. In monastic cathedrals, where the bishop took the place of the abbot, the prior was the working head of the abbey.

Priorato A fortified wine of Catalonia, dark in color and naturally very sweet, formerly known as Tarragona Port.

privateer A privately owned vessel of war, furnished with a commission or commissions from the state, called LETTERS OF MARQUE, authorizing it to cruise against the enemy, taking, sinking, or burning their ships. These vessels were generally governed on the same plan as His Majesty's ships. The commission empowered them to appropriate for their own use whatever PRIZES they took after the prizes vessel had been legally condemned by the ADMIRALTY Court and named a sum to be paid for every man on board an enemy ship taken or destroyed. In case of war with more than one country, the ship had to have a commission authorizing action against each enemy. If a captain carrying a letter of marque only naming the Spanish took a French ship, the prize could not be condemned for him. NELSON, like many in the ROYAL NAVY, had a very low opinion of privateers and once wrote: "The conduct of all privateering is, as far as I have seen, so near piracy that I only wonder any civilized nation can allow them. The lawful as well as the unlawful commerce of the neutral flag is subject to every violation and spoliation." While a privateer by definition had to carry a letter of marque, some people thought that the term "privateer" implied a pirate and *not* a legally commissioned vessel. Those who made this distinction preferred to use the term "letter of marque" instead of "privateer."

privity   Private or secret knowledge; participation in something private or secret; personal affairs.

Privy Council   In England, the traditional King's Council. In the 18th century, most of its functions were taken over by the cabinet and it ceased to act as a deliberative body, although it retained authority in areas relating to the powers of the sovereign, for example, in judicial appeals.

prize   An enemy vessel and its cargo captured at sea by a warship or a PRIVATEER, later to be condemned by a Court of the ADMIRALTY, or PRIZE COURT. Technically and legally, the prize belonged to the Crown, but as a gift to the captors, the Crown allowed it to be sold after official condemnation and its worth to be shared by a ship's crew according to a prescribed formula in the case of ships of the Royal Navy or, in the case of PRIVATEERS, as agreed by the owners and crew. *See also* PRIZE MONEY.

prize-agent   An agent hired to sell prizes taken in maritime war and condemned by a Court of the ADMIRALTY, or PRIZE COURT.

prize court   A department of the ADMIRALTY court that adjudicated all matters concerning PRIZE.

PRIZE MONEY
The profits accruing from the sale of a PRIZE. Among PRIVATEERS, it was divided according to the agreement between the owners and the crew. According to *Falconer's Marine Dictionary* (1815), in the Royal Navy's ships of war, the prize money was to be divided among the officers and crew according to this proclamation:

The following is the Distribution of Prize-Money for Captures from France, Spain, Holland, and the Italian and Ligurian

Republics, and Ships bearing the Flags of Prussia and Pappen-
burgh, pursuant to the King's Proclamations of the 7th of July,
1803, 31st of January, 1805, and 5th of June, 1806.

The distribution shall be made as follows: the whole of the nett
produce being first divided into eight equal parts:

To captains actually on board at the taking of any prize, three
eighth parts: but in case any such prize shall be taken by any ships
of war under the command of a flag or flags, the flag officer or officers being actually on board, or directing and assisting in the capture shall have one of the three eighth parts; the said one eighth
part to be paid to such flag or flag officers, in such proportions,
and subject to such regulations, as are hereinafter mentioned.

Captains of marines and land-forces, sea-lieutenants, and master on board, shall have one eighth part, to be equally divided
amongst them; but that every physician appointed to a fleet or
squadron of ships of war, shall, in the distribution of prizes taken
by the ships in which he shall serve, or in which such ship's company shall be entitled to share, be classed with the sea-lieutenants
with respect to the said one eighth part, and be allowed to share
equally with them; provided such physician be actually on board
at the time of taking such prizes.

The lieutenants and quarter-masters of marines, and lieutenants, ensigns, and quarter-masters of land forces, secretaries
of admirals or commodores, with captains under them, second
masters of line of battle ships, boatswains, gunners, pursers, carpenters, master's mates, chirurgeons, pilots, and chaplains, on
board, shall have one eighth part, to be equally divided amongst
them.

The midshipmen, captain's clerks, master sailmakers, carpenter's mates, boatswain's mates, gunner's mates, masters at arms,
corporals, yeomen of the sheets, coxswains, quarter masters, quarter master's mates, chirurgeon's mates, yeomen of the powder-
room, serjeants of marines and land forces on board, shall have
one eighth part, to be equally divided amongst them.

The trumpeters, quarter gunners, carpenter's crew, steward's
cook, armourers, steward's mate, cook's mates, gunsmiths, coop-
ers, swabbers, ordinary trumpeters, barbers, able seamen, ordinary seamen, and marines, and other soldiers, and all other
persons doing duty and assisting on board, shall have two eighth
parts, to be equally divided amongst them. (pp. 353–54)

Malay proas in Coupang Bay. In the background is the south side of Coupang Bay and the island of Timor. Fast sailers either by or from the wind, proas had two masts fixed to their sides meeting in a point at the top. They frequently made voyages of 1,000 miles and more and were used throughout the Malacca Islands. Reproduced from *The Naval Chronicle,* vol. 20. (*courtesy of the Mariners' Museum, Newport News, Virginia*).

proa   A MALAY boat powered by sails or oars; specifically, a Malay sailing boat, used frequently by pirates, about 30 feet long with a large LATEEN sail, a sharp STEM and STERN, and an outrigger for steadiness. *See* illustration, page 347.

Procellaria pelagica   *See* STORM PETREL.

proctor   Someone who manages the affairs of another, such as an agent, deputy, proxy, or an attorney; an agent for the collection of tithes and other church dues; a supervisor or an administrator.

procuress   A madame.

Proddy   Slang for Protestant.

prodromus   A premonitory symptom of disease.

pro hac vice   For this occasion (Latin).

projector A person who plans or designs some project, enterprise, or undertaking; a founder.

protea An evergreen shrub or small tree usually native to southern Africa or Australia and bearing conelike heads of small flowers with prominent bracts.

protection A document guaranteeing protection, exemption, or immunity to a specified person; a safe-conduct, passport, pass. A document from the King granting immunity from arrest or lawsuit to one engaged in his service or venturing abroad with his cognizance. A certificate granting immunity from impressment to certain people, such as masters and mates of merchant ships, those building light-houses, men over 55, apprentices under 18, harpooners in the Greenland fishery, employees of the Royal Dockyards, and others already strategically employed.

prow The part of the BOW above water. The fore-part of a boat or ship, from where the BOW-CHASERs fire. A type of sailing BARGE found in Bombay.

ptarmigan Also called the white or rock grouse, a bird of the genus *Lagopus* that inhabits high altitudes in Scotland and Northern Europe. Its plumage changes from dark in summer to white in winter.

Ptolemy *or* **Claudius Ptolemaeus (*c.* A.D. *90–168*)** An Egyptian-born mathematician and astronomer of Greek origin who spent most of his life in Alexandria. A pioneer of cartography, he created a system of projections to represent the curved surface of the earth on a flat surface. Ptolemy's most famous work was the eight-volume *Geographical Treatise*, which included an atlas of the world and a list of latitudes and longitudes for eight thousand locations.

public schools, England's great A group of independent secondary schools, typically evolving from charitable institutions founded by benefactors during the late Middle Ages or the Renaissance to prepare local boys from humble backgrounds for Oxford and Cambridge and then public service. From about the 17th century, boys of the upper classes began to attend these schools, where the curriculum placed heavy emphasis on the Greek and Roman classics. But the schools' impact went beyond the academic: they instilled in their students a class-conscious code of behavior, speech, and appearance that set the standard for conduct in the life of officialdom. The concept of the Old Boy Network is based on these schools; their alumni, "old boys," were supposed to look out for one another in civil service, in the City, or in the Armed Forces.

The so-called great English public schools, in the order of their founding, include: Winchester College, chartered 1382; Eton College, founded by King Henry VI, 1440; St. Paul's School, 1509; Shrewsbury School, founded by King Edward VI, 1552; Westminster School, probably a cathedral school, reestablished by Queen Elizabeth I, 1560; Merchant Taylors' School, 1560; Rugby School, 1567; Harrow School, 1571; Charterhouse School, 1611.

puddening (*in the United States*, **pudding**)   A thick mat of OAKUM used to prevent chafing. A wreath of cordage around the MAINMAST and FOREMAST of a ship to prevent their YARDS from falling down in case the ropes by which they were suspended were shot away in battle and to prevent unnecessary chafing. Puddening was also used in other areas to prevent chafing.

puffin   Seabirds of the genera *Fratercula* and *Lunda*, especially the common *F. arctica*, abundant on the coasts of the North Atlantic, that have a large oddly shaped furrowed and multicolored bill. Once erroneously thought to be wingless, and by some to be a fish.

pule   To cry in a thin or weak voice, like a child; the cry of the KITE.

pulmony   An affliction of the lungs, usually pneumonia.

Pulo Prabang   An equatorial volcanic island in the vicinity of the Lingga Archipelago, east of Sumatra in the South China Sea. The island is fictional.

pulvis Doveri   Dover's powder, introduced by Thomas Dover of Bristol and London in 1732 as a DIAPHORETIC for the treatment of DROPSY and upper respiratory diseases. Its major ingredients were OPIUM and ipecac, an emetic that also stimulates sweating. Used as a FEBRIFUGE.

puma   A cougar.

pump   On a sailing vessel, an apparatus for removing water that collects in the BILGE. A common hand-pump near the MAINMAST was used for small jobs, while a "burr-pump," or "bilge-pump," consisting of a leather SPAR and a scoop lifted by a rope, was used for more serious jobs, as was the preferable "chain-pump," one similar to a bilge-pump but with a continuous motion. Also, a low-cut light-weight shoe with no fastening; a slipper or a more substantial low-heeled shoe, worn by dancers, couriers, duelists, or others who required freedom of movement.

pump-dale A wooden tube or trough that carries away water, especially from a ship's PUMP.

pump ship Literally, to pump out bilge water, but also a slang term, to urinate.

puna Any high, cold, arid plateau in the Peruvian Andes. Puna is also the name of the plateau that lies between the two great chains of the Cordilleras at an elevation of more than 10,500 feet.

puncheon An instrument used for perforating, piercing, or stamping.

punctilio A fine point or minute detail of conduct, procedure, or ceremony; a petty formality; also, a fastidious objection, a scruple.

punk Dry, decayed wood or a fungus growing on wood used for tinder. Touchwood, amadou.

punkah A large cloth or palmyra-leaf fan controlled by a cord; a servant who works such a fan.

punt A flat-bottomed craft with a shallow draft sometimes used in the CAULKing of a ship's waterline seam and for various other maintenance functions. A flat-bottomed craft with square ends poled along rivers.

Purbeck A peninsula on the Dorsetshire coast of England. A stone quarried there or an object made of this stone. The geological formation typical of that region.

purchase A means of applying or increasing power; leverage. A device that provides mechanical advantage or power in moving or raising a heavy object. Any contrivance for increasing applied power, especially, in nautical use, a rope, pulley, WINDLASS, or other TACKLE.

purdah A curtain, screen, or veil used to hide Hindu or Muslim women from men or strangers. The practice of such seclusion.

purpura Any condition characterized by PETECHIAe, purplish spots scattered over the skin, caused by intracutaneous hemorrhage; usually accompanies SCURVY.

purse-net   A bag-shaped net whose mouth can be drawn together with cords, used for catching fish and especially rabbits. A "purse seine" is a fishing net with its upper edge buoyed and its lower edge weighted.

purser (*commonly pronounced* **"pusser"**)   An officer responsible for keeping a ship's accounts and issuing provisions and clothing. He was appointed by ADMIRALTY warrant but had no professional examination. Pursers played a dual role. On one hand, they were responsible for government-owned supplies, and on the other, they were private contractors who could make a profit on supplies. Pursers were considered to have WARDROOM rank after 1808.

pusser's shirt on a handspike   A descriptive phrase meaning ill-fitting.

puss-in-the-corner *or* **puss**   A children's game in which one player stands in the center and tries to capture one of the "dens" or "bases" of the others as they change places. Also, in a more elaborate form, a game played by sailors in the British Navy.

putain   A whore (French).

puya   A herbaceous or woody plant, sometimes as large as a small tree, native to dry regions of the Andes and distinguished by rosettes of spiny leaves and blue or yellow flowers.

Pym, Admiral Sir Samuel (*1778–1855*)   As a young Lieutenant in 1799, he served on H.M.S. *Ethalion,* 36, one of the ships that captured the Spanish treasure ships *Thetis* and *Santa Brigida* near Cape Finnisterre, earning for himself more than £5,000 in prize money. In command of H.M.S. *Atlas,* he was with Duckworth at Santo Domingo in 1806. Later he took part in the attack on MAURITIUS in 1810. In attempting to enter Grand Port, his ship H.M.S. *Sirius* went aground and had to be abandoned. Pym was taken and remained a prisoner of war on the island until it was taken by Sir Albermarle Bertie in 1811. Cleared of all blame, Pym commanded H.M.S. *Niemen* in the WEST INDIES between 1812 and 1815. He became an Admiral after the war.

pyrites   Various sulfides with a metallic appearance of which pyrite, or fool's gold, an iron disulfide with a brassy yellow color, is the most common.

Pythagoras (*c. 580–c. 500* B.C.)   Greek philosopher and mathematician who was famous chiefly for his theorem stating that for a right triangle, the square of the hypotenuse equals the sum of the squares of the two sides. His numerical ideas were incorporated into the theory of the four humors (*see* "The Disease Burden of the Royal Navy," page 37).

qat *also* **kat** *or* **khat**   The buds and leaves of a large shrub, *Catha edulis,* indigenous to Ethiopia and the Arabian Peninsula; when eaten they produce excitation and increase energy, while reducing the need for sleep and food, somewhat as COCA does, but in this case the active chemical is not known.

quacksalver   A charlatan, a quack.

quadrant   In the late 18th century, this was an instrument in the form of a graduated eighth-circle (actually an octant, although called' a quadrant because it could measure a quarter of a circle by using reflective mirrors). It was used for measuring angles in navigation, especially altitudes of heavenly bodies above the horizon or angles between two terrestrial objects in coastal surveying. The seaman's quadrant was invented by John Hadley in 1731. It superseded Davis' Quadrant, invented by John Davis in 1594. *See also* SEXTANT.

quadrille   A French form of square dance, usually involving four couples in five stages, each a complete dance in itself.

quaere   Ask, inquire; a question (Latin). Used chiefly in the imperative to introduce a question.

quartan A type of malaria in which a paroxysm of fever occurs every 72 hours. *Compare* TERTIAN.

quarter The upper after parts of a ship's side (between the after part of the MAIN CHAINS and the STERN), as in STARBOARD quarter. Of a YARD, the part between the SLINGS and the YARDARM. The distance between the slings and the yardarm on each side is divided into the first, second, and third quarters, and yardarm. "To sail with the wind on the quarter" is to sail with the wind blowing between BEAM and STERN. A sea is said to quarter when it strikes a vessel on the quarter. Quarter also means mercy, clemency, especially toward a defeated opponent.

quarter-bill A list of the ship's officers and men and their appointed battle stations.

quarterdeck The part of the ship from which the Captain, MASTER, or officer of the WATCH commands the sailing activities and that is used as a promenade by the officers. Originally, a smaller deck above the HALFDECK, covering about a quarter of the vessel. The tradition of saluting the quarterdeck when entering or leaving a ship or reporting there to an officer dates from early times. There is a historical debate about the origins of this custom. Some argue that the practice developed in ancient times when a pagan altar was located on board a GALLEY and others say it comes from an independent English practice. Officers on the quarterdeck traditionally lifted their hats in return to those who saluted in this way. By the late 18th century, the quarterdeck itself was considered virtually sacred and treated with great respect by all seamen and officers.

quarter-gunner A PETTY OFFICER subordinate to the Gunner, whom he assists in keeping all guns and carriages in working order. The number of quarter-gunners allowed per ship is one for every four guns.

quartermaster A PETTY OFFICER who assists with numerous tasks, including attending to the BINNACLE, steering the ship, signaling, and navigational duties.

quarter-netting Netting extended along the rails on the upper part of a ship's QUARTER for the stowage of hammocks.

quarters Living accommodations or battle stations. "To beat to quarters" meant to play the drummer's tune—in British ships frequently "Heart of Oak"—that called men to their battle stations.

quart major In cards, the sequence of ace, king, queen, knave.

quarto The size of paper obtained by folding a whole sheet twice to form four leaves. A book printed on quarto pages.

quasi pannus menstruate Like a menstrual cloth (Latin).

quay An artificial bank or landing place, usually built of stone, alongside or parallel to a navigable water for loading and unloading ships. When projecting into the water as a breakwater and a landing place, it is also known as a MOLE. In later American usage, this is also called a pier, but in England in the late 18th century, a pier was normally a quay protecting the entrance of a river, harbor, etc.

Queen Anne's Free Gift A sum of money granted annually to ships' Surgeons to boost their modest monthly income. Queen Anne's Bounty was first instituted in 1704 to supplement the income of clergymen who had inadequate stipends.

Queen Charlotte, **H.M.S.** Named after King George III's consort, this 100-gun first rate built in 1790 fought in the GLORIOUS FIRST OF JUNE in 1794. She was blown up in an accident off LEGHORN in 1800. A well-known painting by Henry Briggs depicts George III presenting a sword to Lord HOWE on board his FLAGSHIP, H.M.S. *Queen Charlotte*, on June 26, 1794. Also, a second rate of 1810.

Queeney *or* Queenie *See* KEITH, LADY.

Queen of May A girl chosen to be "queen" of the games on May Day and crowned with flowers.

queue A long plait of hair that hangs down behind from the head or from a wig; a pigtail.

Quichua An Indian people of Peru and neighboring parts of Bolivia, Chile, Colombia, and Ecuador. The group of related languages that these people speak.

quicksilver The metal MERCURY, so called for its liquid state at normal temperatures.

quid   One POUND sterling.

qui ferox bello tamen inter arma/sive iactatam religarat udo/litore navim . . . et Lycum nigris oculis nigroque/crine decorum   He who had fought boldly in war, after mooring his ship ashore . . . [he sang of the Muses . . .] and of Lycus with black eyes and black hair adorned (Latin, Horace's *Odes*, I, 32).

quillon   One of the two arms that form a sword's cross-guard, the device that protects the swordsman's hand.

quinoa   A plant, *Chenopodium quinoa*, found on the western slopes of the Andes, cultivated for its edible wheatlike seeds.

quire   A set of four sheets of parchment or paper doubled to form eight leaves, a unit common in medieval manuscripts. Any collection of leaves, one within another, in a manuscript or book. Also, 24 or 25 sheets of writing paper.

quittance   A release from a debt or obligation; a receipt, repayment, or reprisal.

qui venit   Who has come (Latin).

Quixote   An eager visionary similar to Cervantes's fictional character Don Quixote, who was inspired by lofty, unattainable ideals.

quizz   An odd or eccentric person in character or look.

quod volunt credere   What they wish to believe (Latin).

quoin   A wooden wedge with a handle at the thick end used to adjust the elevation of a gun.

Quo me rapis?   Where are you carrying me off to? (Latin)

Quoniam tu solus sanctus, tu solus Dominus, tu solus altissimus   Because you alone are holy, you alone are the Lord, you alone are the most high (Latin).

quota-men *or* **Lord Mayor's Men**   Recruits raised for the Navy after the passage of Pitt's quota-bill in 1795, requiring each county to provide a certain number of recruits. Payments to these recruits, often outcasts and ne'er-do-wells, ranged from 20 to 70 pounds, far surpassing the sums previously paid to volunteers, which angered Navy seamen.

rabbet A groove or slot cut along a board's edge, made to receive the tongue of another board cut to fit the groove.

râble de lièvre Saddle of hare (French).

rachitic Having rickets or pertaining to rickets, a disease of the young caused by a lack of sunlight or vitamin D and resulting in deformed bones.

rack-rent A very high rent, often approaching the annual income that a tenant can earn by working the property.

radix serpentaria Virginia snakeroot (*Aristolochia serpentaria*), prescribed as a tonic, diuretic, and diaphoretic for fever patients.

Raffles, Sir Thomas Stamford (*1781–1826*) The son of an impoverished sea captain, Raffles was born at sea off Jamaica. He was hired as an office boy by the East India Company in 1795, and in 1805, he was sent out to PENANG as assistant secretary to the first governor. As secretary to Lord Minto, Governor-General of the Malay States, he accompanied the expedition that took Java from the French and was appointed Lieutenant Governor, reforming its internal administration, befriending the Javanese, and greatly increasing the company profits there. He returned home in 1816 and was knighted. Appointed Lieutenant Governor of Fort Marlborough on Sumatra in 1818, he established, without other authority, Singapore in 1819, where he remained until 1824. He founded and was first president of the London Zoo.

ragabash An idle, worthless person; rabble or riffraff.

ragot Malicious gossip (French).

rail A wading bird of the family Rallidae, structurally similar to the crane but smaller, with short, round wings and long toes for running on mud. On a ship, any of the narrow ornamental planks on the upper works, such as the FIFE-RAIL.

Rainier, Peter (*c. 1741–1808*) A British ADMIRAL who was COMMANDER-IN-CHIEF in the EAST INDIES from 1794 to 1804, during which time AMBOYNA, Trincomalee, and Banda Beira came under British control. Promoted to Rear-Admiral in 1795, he subsequently became Vice-Admiral in 1799 and Admiral in 1805.

Rainier, Peter (*1784–1836*) The son of Admiral Peter Rainier, he served under his father from 1803 to 1804. Commanding H.M.S. *Caroline* in October of 1806, he captured the Dutch 32-gun FRIGATE *Maria Reigersbergen*.

raison d'état For reasons of the State, State policy (French).

rake The projection or slope of the upper part of a ship's hull at STEM and STERN beyond the KEEL. The slant of a ship's MASTs, usually but not always AFT to increase speed. To fire a deadly and destructive BROADSIDE at a ship's BOW or stern, the weakest points of a ship and those that provide the longest destructive path for a well-aimed shot.

râle An abnormal rattling sound heard in diseased or congested lungs (French). "Rale" in English.

Ramadan The ninth month of the Muslim year, observed strictly with 30 days of fasting during daylight hours. The lunar reckoning of the Muslim calendar brings the fast 11 days earlier each year.

Ramillies, H.M.S. A name used three times in the 18th-century Royal Navy. The first was a rebuilt ship that served as Admiral John BYNG'S FLAGSHIP at MINORCA in 1756 and was wrecked in 1760, taking down 700 hands. The second was a third rate of 74 guns launched in 1763 and taking part in the action against the French off USHANT in 1778. In 1782, under the command of Rear-Admiral Thomas Graves, she burned in a hurricane off NEWFOUNDLAND in the Atlantic, but her crew was rescued. The third, also a third rate of 74 guns, was built in 1785. She fought in the GLORIOUS FIRST OF JUNE in 1794 and joined in action at Quiberon Bay and the Battle of COPENHAGEN. She was also engaged in the War of 1812, where the Americans, using a diving boat, attempted but failed to blow her up with a mine. She was finally broken up in 1850.

ramus   A projecting part or branch of a plant, vein, or bone.

rapparee   An Irish pikeman or irregular soldier of the Nine Years' War (1689–1797). An Irish bandit, robber, or freebooter, or the same in other countries.

raptor   A member of an order of birds of prey that includes the eagle, hawk, buzzard, and owl.

rara avis in mara, maro   A rare seabird, at sea (Latin).

RATE
A seaman's station, according to his skills and duties, as marked in the ship's MUSTER-BOOK. The chief grades in the Royal Navy included ORDINARY SEAMEN, ABLE SEAMEN, and PETTY OFFICERS; below them were the LANDSMEN and boys. Also, of naval SHIPs commanded by POST-CAPTAINs, their classification based on size and armament. The rating system was introduced by Admiral Lord ANSON in the 1750s. The British Navy like most large navies had six different rates.

Ships of the first three rates were powerful enough to fight in a line of battle in a major fleet action. CARRONADES were not counted in the rating. The rates (in 1810 the number of guns shifted up by about ten in each):

Rate	Number of Guns
1st	100+
2nd	90–98
3rd	64–80
4th	50–60
5th	32–48
6th	20–32

See also "Rated Ships of the Line," page 9.

Ratitae   Flightless birds having a flat, keelless sternum, as do the ostrich, EMU, and CASSOWARY.

Ratite   Of or belonging to the RATITAE.

ratline   One of the small lines made of tarred rope and fastened horizontally to the SHROUDS of a vessel, forming steps by which seamen climb up and down the RIGGING.

ratsbane   Rat poison, usually arsenic trioxide.

rattan   One of several species of climbing palms that grow mainly in the EAST INDIES, and also in Africa and Australia, with long thin jointed and pliable stems. Also, a switch or stick of rattan, used for beating a person or thing.

rattle   To furnish with RATLINEs, usually used with "down."

raveline *or* **ravelin**   In fortification, an outwork with two faces that form a protruding angle, constructed beyond the main ditch and in front of the main wall.

razee   A ship of the line reduced in height by the removal of her upper deck or decks, making a heavy FRIGATE.

receiving ship   Old and often decrepit and filthy ships employed at ports to house and process new recruits or pressed men for the Royal Navy.

reculing pour mew sauter   Aubrey's pidgin French for drawing back in order to spring.

redbreast   A robin.

Redemptorist   A member of the Roman Catholic Congregation of the Most Holy Redeemer, founded in Naples in 1732 by St. Alphonsus Liguori and devoted chiefly to work among the poor, often through missionaries.

red gum   An irregular rash occurring usually in children who are cutting their teeth.

Red Sea   A long, narrow sea bordered to the east by Saudi Arabia and to the west by Egypt, Sudan, and Ethiopia and so named for its reddish tint, caused by floating algae.

reef   A horizontal portion of a sail that can be rolled or folded up in order to reduce the amount of canvas exposed to the wind. In SQUARE-

RIGGED ships, the sails up to the TOPSAILS usually have two reefs, and sails above the topsail have none. To take in a reef (or to reef) means to reduce the amount of exposed sail by rolling up a part and securing it with the REEF-POINTS. (*See also* CLOSE-REEFED.) Also, a ridge of rock or coral in water shallow enough to be a hazard to vessels.

reefband A long piece of canvas sewed horizontally across the sail to strengthen it along the REEF-POINTS, where the stress lies when a sail is REEFED.

reefed Of MASTS, shortened. Of sails, having a REEF or reefs taken in, decreasing the amount of canvas exposed to the wind.

reefer One who reefs. A familiar name for MIDSHIPMEN who were sent aloft to the TOPS to supervise the operation of REEFing.

reef-point A short length of plaited SENNET, attached to a sail along the REEFBANDS and used to secure the canvas when REEFED. *See* illustration, p. 359.

reeve To pass a rope through a hole, ring, eye, THIMBLE, or the throat of a BLOCK. Afterward the rope is said to be rove through it.

regimentals The dress of any particular regiment; military uniform.

regrediar I shall return (Latin).

regulator A clock or watch that keeps accurate time, by which other timepieces may be regulated.

Regulus A bright star in the northern constellation Leo, called also Cor Leonis.

reinforce The part of a gun next to the BREECH, and specially strengthened to withstand the explosive force of the powder.

Reis Captain (Arabic).

relict A widow.

relieving tackle A set of two powerful TACKLES used when a ship was CAREENed on a beach for cleaning or repairs. They allowed her to be HEELed over at an angle sufficient for the work to be performed but kept her from overturning and also aided in righting her again when the work was finished. Also, a tackle hooked to the TILLER in bad

Topmen working on the yard as they reef a sail. They are hauling up the REEF-POINTS to secure bundles of sail to the yard (*from Darcy Lever's* Young Sea Officer's Sheet Anchor).

weather to help in steering when the pressure was too great to steer with the wheel, or in action when the wheel or TILLER-ROPE was broken or shot away.

relievo Relief; the projection or apparent projection of a figure or form from a flat background; a work of art that contains such a projection.

remigium alarum Winged oars (Latin).

remittents   Fevers characterized by temporary abatements of symptoms.

remora   The sucking-fish, which clings to other fish and to ships, believed by the ancients and some sailors to have the power to halt a ship to which it is attached.

remove   The act of taking away a dish or dishes at a meal in order to put others in their place; a course of a meal.

remue-ménage   A commotion, disturbance, hubbub (French).

rencontre   An encounter (French).

rencounter   A hostile meeting or encounter. A duel, sometimes specifically an unpremeditated one.

Rendez vous. . . . Jé mé rendre . . . Parola. . . . Capitaine, cessez effusion sang. Rendez-vous. Hommes desertés. . . . Jamais, monsieur. . . . Capitaine, en bas, dessous, s'il vous plait. Toutes officiers dessous. Surrender. . . . I surrender. . . . Word of honor. . . . Captain, stop the bloodshed. . . . Surrender. . . . Men deserting. . . . Never, sir. . . . Captain, below, beneath, please. All officers beneath. (French—more or less—except *parola,* Italian.)

rent-roll   A list of lands and tenements and the rents paid on them. The income shown by such a list.

repique   In the game of PIQUET, the winning of 30 points on cards alone before play begins (and before the adversary begins to count), entitling the player to begin his score at 90.

requies Nicholai   Literally, Nicholai's rest (Latin); a sleeping medicine made with OPIUM, MANDRAGORA, and hyoscyamus (black hellebore), invented in the 13th century but archaic by the 18th century.

Requisite Tables   A volume used in conjunction with the NAUTICAL ALMANAC to aid a sailor in fixing his position at sea, devised by English astronomer Nevil Maskelyne in 1766. A second and improved edition appeared in 1781, adding several useful tables, among which were logarithmic solar tables and a table of latitudes and longitudes of places around the world. A third edition was published in 1802, and an appendix was added to that in 1809, containing tables of natural sines and cosines and an extended table of logarithms.

res angusta   Straitened circumstances (Latin).

resection   The operation of cutting out or paring away part of a bone or organ.

Resolution, **H.M.S.**   The most famous vessel by this name was a 562-ton COLLIER launched as the *Marquis of Granby* in 1770 that was bought by the Royal Navy, renamed the *Drake,* and then renamed again in 1771 the *Resolution.* Captain COOK sailed her on his second and third voyages around the world, from 1772 to 1775 and from 1776 to 1779. In 1781, she became an armed TRANSPORT, serving under Admiral de Suffren in the EAST INDIES, until she was captured by the French ship *Sphinx* in June 1782.

resurrector   An exhumer and thief of corpses.

reticule   A small ladies' bag, usually woven, carried on the arm or in the hand.

retractor   A bandage or other appliance used in various operations to pull back parts that would otherwise impede the operator.

retsina   A Greek resinated wine.

Revenge, **H.M.S.**   The most famous ship by this name was Sir Francis Drake's FLAGSHIP, which battled in 1588 against the Spanish Armada and was later immortalized in Lord Tennyson's poem "The Revenge," which tells of her last fight in 1591, when, under Sir Richard Grenville, she fought a hopeless battle with a Spanish SQUADRON in the AZORES in which she held out for 15 hours. The ninth ship of the name was a third rate of 74 guns built in 1805 that fought at TRAFALGAR under the command of Captain Robert Moorsom. She served until 1842 and was finally broken up in 1849. She was one of the first vessels to be painted with Nelson's checker pattern, which later became standard for British warships.

revenue cutter   A single-masted CUTTER carrying up to ten LONG NINEs and employed by the customs authorities for the prevention of smuggling.

Rhadamanthine   An inflexible judge or a rigorous or severe master who resembles Rhadamanthus, in Greek mythology the son of Zeus and Europa and one of the judges in the lower world.

Rhazes (*860–932*)   Persian physician and philosopher, and encyclo-
pedist of medicine whose work was based on the sixth-century B.C.
writings of Hippocrates. He is remembered chiefly for the first clinical descriptions of measles and smallpox.

Rhea   A genus of birds that includes the South American or three-
toed ostrich. Also, the bird itself.

rhubarb   The root of various species of the genus *Rheum*, used in
medicine as a mild cathartic. Although the best grade was thought to
come from China, trade barriers encouraged the substitution of European varieties.

rick-yard   A farmyard or enclosure containing stacks of hay, wood,
or other commodities.

ride   A rope is said to ride when one of the turns by which it is
wound around the CAPSTAN or WINDLASS lies over another, thus inter-
rupting HAULing.

riding-bitts   Usually two sets of two upright oak timbers in the FORE
of the ship forming BITTS to which the CABLE is hitched by the STOPPERS
when the vessel rides at anchor. Each unit was composed of two
posts, two KNEES, a cross-piece, and bolster.

rifle   To form spiral grooves in the barrel of a gun or the bore of a
cannon.

rig   The general way in which the MASTS and sails of a vessel are
arranged, with the two main categories being SQUARE-RIGGED and
FORE-AND-AFT rigged. These can be subdivided into specific types of
vessels, such as CUTTERS, BARQUES, or BRIGS. Sometimes used in slang
to refer to a uniform.

Riga   Seaport and city in the Hanseatic League in Livonia, modern-
day Latvia. It was held by Sweden from 1621 to 1710; then taken by
Russia after the Battle of Poltava. It was a major trading source for
timber and naval stores.

Rigel Kent *or* Rigil Kentaurus   One of the bright, first-magnitude
stars visible in the Southern Hemisphere. It is located to the east of
the Southern Cross. A line drawn eastward from the star CRUX, then
curving slightly to the south, leads first to Hadar, then to Rigel Kent,
and continues on to the southern triangle, Triangulum Australe.

rigger   One who rigs ships, fitting and repairing the standing and running RIGGING of a ship.

rigging   The general term for the lines used on a vessel. Standing rigging are the lines that support the masts and yards and the BOWSPRIT. Running rigging are the lines used to move and control sails.

right sailing   Sailing a course along one of the four cardinal POINTS, so as to alter only the latitude or longitude of the ship.

right whale *or* **baleen whale**   A whalebone whale, especially of the genus *Balaena,* having instead of teeth plates of whalebone developed from the palate that aid in filtering plankton from the water.

rigor   Rigor mortis, the stiffening of muscles after death.

ring-bolt   A bolt with an EYE at one end to which a rope or TACKLE is secured.

ringtail   A small triangular sail extended on a short MAST on top of a ship's STERN in light, favorable winds. An extension for a FORE-AND-AFT MAINSAIL, hoisted beyond the after-edge of the sail to provide more canvas.

riot   During a hunt, a hound's indiscriminate chasing of scents other than that of the quarry.

risus sardonicus   An involuntary or spasmodic grin caused by disease.

River Plate   The English name for Río de la Plata, the estuary formed by the Paraná and Uruguay rivers at the Atlantic Ocean and lying between Uruguay and Argentina. Its name in Spanish means river of silver, and it was named by the explorer Sebastian Cabot for a legendary mountain of silver believed to exist somewhere upstream. On the river's southern shore lies Buenos Aires, Argentina.

rivière   A necklace of diamonds or other precious stones, from the French *rivière de diamants* (literally, river of diamonds).

roadstead   A convenient or safe anchorage near the shore but outside a harbor, for example, SPITHEAD in England.

roast beef dress   Full uniform, probably from its resemblance to that of the beefeaters, yeomen of the royal guard in England.

roban *or* **rope-bands**   A piece of small rope ROVE through an eyelet-hole in the HEAD of a square sail and used to secure it to the YARD above.

Robinson, William   A LANDSMAN who volunteered and fought at TRAFALGAR before deserting the Royal Navy and writing a critical book about his years in the service, life on the lower deck, and conditions in the British Navy. Published in 1836 and entitled *Nautical Economy, or Forecastle Recollections of Events during the last War, dedicated to the Brave Tars of Old England, by a Sailor politely called by the Officers of the Navy, Jack Nasty-face*, the book depicts Navy officers negatively. The name "Jack Nasty-face" became used as an epithet for someone with a constant grievance.

roborate   To strengthen, invigorate, or fortify.

roc   An enormous, powerful bird of Eastern myth.

Rochefort   An important French naval dockyard and base on the west coast of France at the mouth of the Charente River that was involved in many struggles between the British and French in the 18th century. Following Napoleon's defeat at Waterloo and his abdication, he surrendered to the commander of the H.M.S. *Bellerophon* at Rochefort on July 15, 1815.

rock-dove *or* **rock-pigeon**   A species of dove (*Columba livia*) that inhabits rocks and is believed to be the source of the domestic pigeon.

rod   A measure of length equal to 5½ yards, or 16½ feet. A perch or pole.

Rodgers, Commodore John (1773–1838)   The dominant figure in the U.S. Navy for the quarter century that included the War of 1812. In 1811 Rodgers, in U.S.S. *President*, defeated H.M.S. *Little Belt*.

Rodney, George Brydges (1718–1792)   The first Baron Rodney was a daring but controversial ADMIRAL who won inspiring victories for the Royal Navy while keeping one step ahead of his creditors. In 1749 he was made governor of NEWFOUNDLAND. As COMMANDER-IN-CHIEF of the Leeward Islands station, he battered MARTINIQUE and took from the French the islands of St. Lucia, Grenada, and St. Vincent. He was made governor of GREENWICH Hospital in 1765 but gave up the post for a command in Jamaica. For a period of time he lived in Paris to escape creditors, but in 1780 he returned to the Navy, intercepting a

SQUADRON of Spanish ships near Cape St. Vincent in an engagement called the Moonlight Battle, in which one Spanish ship was sunk and six captured without British loss. This achievement was rewarded with a knighthood. The crowning moment of his career was the 1782 victory with his second in command, Samuel Hood, over Admiral de Grasse off Dominica when, in the Battle of the SAINTES, his fleet broke through the French line and captured four enemy ships, garnering a much-needed moral victory for the British.

rodomontade   Arrogant boasting or bragging.

Rogue's March   The tune drummed in the Royal Navy to signal the ceremony for dismissal from the Navy of a person guilty of some offense committed on board the ship or for a FLOGGING AROUND THE FLEET. Originally the tune was used in the Army for drumming out of the regiment a soldier guilty of a serious crime.

roi des trente-six parapluies, et très illustre seigneur de mille éléphants   King of 36 umbrellas and very illustrious lord of a thousand elephants (French).

rolling-tackle   A PURCHASE set up between the YARDARM and the MAST to steady a YARD in heavy weather and to relieve strain.

roly-poly pudding   A pudding made of a sheet of pastry covered with jam or preserves, rolled, and boiled or steamed.

Roman fish   A reddish-skinned marine fish, *Chrysoblephus laticeps*, found chiefly in tropical and subtropical waters.

Romanist   A member of the Church of Rome, a Roman Catholic.

Romish   Belonging, pertaining, or adhering to Rome with regard to religion. Roman Catholic (usually with negative connotations).

rood   A unit for measuring land, properly containing 40 square RODS, or about a quarter of an acre, but varying locally. A plot of land of this size. A length varying from 5½ to 8 yards.

ropewalk   A very long shed or stretch of ground where a ropemaker makes ropes by means of a spinning machine that twists the fibers (usually HEMP) into strands and the strands into ropes.

rostrum   A beak or snout.

Rothschild, Nathan (1777–1836)   A German-born British banker of the famous Rothschild family. He opened a business house in London in 1805 and acted as a vital agent of the British government in supplying subsidies to the powers opposing NAPOLEON. He was aided in his transactions by a very efficient information service. Notified of the allied victory at WATERLOO by carrier pigeons, he made a fortune in a single day and prevented the collapse of the London stock exchange by buying up all the shares sold by frightened investors.

rough-tree One of the stanchions supporting a ROUGH-TREE RAIL. Also, an unfinished SPAR.

rough-tree rail Any spare SPAR used as a rail or fence along the ship's WAIST.

rouleau A number of gold coins secured in a cylindrical packet. One 1796 dictionary gives the number as from 20 to 50 or more.

round-house A square cabin or set of cabins on the afterpart of the QUARTERDECK of an EAST INDIAMAN, the roof of which is formed by the POOP deck. Lavatories or a privy.

round jacket A short jacket cut circularly at the bottom and worn by MIDSHIPMEN.

round shot Balls of cast iron or steel for firing from smooth-bore cannon.

rouse in To HAUL in the slack part of a CABLE to keep it from FOULing the anchor.

rout A large and fashionable evening party or reception in vogue in the 18th and early 19th centuries. Also, rabble.

rout-cake A rich cake originally served at ROUTs.

rove Past tense of REEVE.

rowed of all The order for the rowers to stop rowing and boat their oars simultaneously, in naval style.

row-port Ports cut through the side of a small vessel for the use of SWEEPs during calm weather.

royal A small sail hoisted above the TOPGALLANT sail, originally called the topgallant royal, and used in light and favorable winds.

Royal Exchange Located near the intersection of Threadneedle Street and Cornhill in the CITY, London's chief marketplace was opened in 1570 by Queen Elizabeth I. It remained a bustling center of commerce until 1939.

***Royal George*, H.M.S.**   The most famous ship of this name was the 100-gun first rate launched at Woolwich in 1756. She had the tallest MASTS (114 feet, 3 inches) of any ship yet built in England, and she participated in the Battle of Quiberon Bay in 1759. In disrepair, she foundered at SPITHEAD in 1782. Over 900 men, women, and children, including Admiral Kempenfelt, went down with the ship. The loss was commemorated in William Cowper's poem "The Loss of the Royal George." Another *Royal George*, launched in 1788, took part in the Battles of the GLORIOUS FIRST OF JUNE, in 1794, and of Groix Island, in 1795. Three ships named *Royal George* also sailed for the EAST INDIA COMPANY between 1737 and 1825.

A first-rate ship of the line, H.M.S. *Royal George* (*from Serres's* Liber Nauticus)

royal pole   A tapered extension of the ROYAL MAST rising above the highest part of the RIGGING.

Royal Society   An organization incorporated by Charles II (1630–1685) in 1662 for the pursuit and advancement of the physical sciences, including those important to navigation. Sir Joseph BANKS served as President of the Royal Society from 1778 to 1820. From 1780 to 1857 the members met at SOMERSET HOUSE.

royal yacht   A vessel used by a sovereign for pleasure or for formal state occasions. The early royal yachts of England were associated with Charles II (1630–1685).

rubor   Redness, ruddiness.

rudder   A movable flat fin attached to a vessel vertically below the water line at the STERN by means of PINTLES and GUDGEONS. Directed by the HELM, the rudder turns the vessel using the pressure of the water.

ruff   The male of certain species of the sandpiper family, having a ruff around the neck and ear-tufts during the breeding season. The female is known as a reeve, or ree.

rule of three   Given three numbers, a method of finding a fourth, when the first number is in the same proportion to the second as the third is to the unknown fourth.

rum   Odd, strange, or queer. Bad or spurious. Stupefied or incapacitated through drink. Also, stupid.

rumbowline   Canvas, rope, or the like, well past its prime and used for temporary purposes not demanding strength.

runner   Any line ROVE through a single BLOCK, often with an EYE at one end to which a TACKLE is attached.

running-horse   A racehorse.

rupee   The monetary unit of India. The silver rupee was introduced by Shir Shah in 1542 and varied in weight at different times and places between 170 and 192 grains. Also, the monetary unit of various other countries.

Rüppell, Wilhelm Peter Eduard Simon (*1794–1884*)   German zoologist and explorer who went on major expeditions to the Sudan

(1821–27) and Ethiopia (1830–34) and published maps and scientific accounts of his travels, including the monumental *Travels in Abyssinia* (1838–40). Rüppell's warbler is named after him.

rusa   Either of two deer native to southern Asia.

Russell, Edward, Earl of Orford (*1653–1727*)   A nephew of the first duke of Bedford, Russell was a supporter of William III and commanded the joint Anglo-Dutch fleet in the victory over the French fleet at Barfleur–La Hougue in 1692. He served as First Lord of the Admiralty for three terms (1694–1699, 1709–1710, 1714–1717).

sabretache A leather satchel suspended by long straps from the left side of a cavalry officer's sword-belt. A flat leather saddlebag.

saddle-bow The arched front part of a saddle.

Saffron Walden A market town in northwest Essex, England. The name comes from the purple-flowered crocus, or saffron (*Crocus sativus*), which was at one time an important crop in this town, its stamens being the source of the yellow-orange dye and food flavoring also called saffron.

sagittal suture The front-to-back line of union in the top center of the skull, between the two parietal bones.

sago An edible starch prepared from the pith of the trunks of several genera of palms; a food thickener made by boiling sago in water or milk. Also, the sago palm tree, native to the Indonesian Archipelago, from which sago is obtained.

sagoon *or* seconde In fencing, the second of the eight parries recognized in sword-play.

sahib A respectful title used by the natives of India in addressing a Westerner, roughly equivalent to "sir." In native use, a Westerner.

Also, a title affixed to the name or office of a Westerner and to Indian and Bangladeshi titles and names.

sail or steer large   *See* LARGE.

St. Anthony   Among the several saints of this name, the ascetic St. Anthony of the Desert (250–356) was known for his modesty and courtesy.

St. Augustine (A.D. *354–430*)   One of the greatest early scholars of Christianity, he was from Numidia (today Algeria). Because of his extensive Christian writing, he is considered one of the Fathers of the Church.

St. Brendan (A.D. *484–578*)   Also known as Brendan the Voyager, he was the Abbot of Ardfert in County Kerry, Ireland. Brendan established many monasteries in Scotland and Ireland, including one at Clonfert in the year 561. The medieval legend *Navigatio Brendani* was based on his voyage to the promised land of saints on western islands (Maturin's "Islands of the Blessed"), which lasted eight years beginning in 565.

St. Elmo   A corruption of the name of Saint Erasmus, an Italian bishop who was martyred in 303. His executioners cut open his stomach and wound out his intestines on a windlass, which resembled a ship's CAPSTAN. He became the patron saint of Mediterranean sailors. *See also* ST. ELMO'S FIRE.

St. Elmo's Fire   A light that occurs when low-intensity atmospheric electricity induces an electrical discharge on the MASTHEADs and ends of the YARDARMS of a ship. The light was observed with awe and looked upon by sailors variously as a good or bad omen. Also called corposant. *See also* SAINT ELMO.

Saintes, Battle of the   The last major sea battle of the American Revolutionary War. Fought on April 12, 1782, by Sir George RODNEY with 36 SHIPS OF THE LINE and Vice Admiral Comte de Grasse with 30, in the Saintes passage near the Iles des Saintes, between Guadeloupe and Dominica in the WEST INDIES. Breaking the line of battle, a bold and innovative tactic at that time, the British captured five ships, including de Grasse's FLAGSHIP *Ville de Paris*. This decisive British victory helped to restore the Royal Navy's prestige after a series of defeats and led to the restoration of Britain's possessions in the West Indies in the Treaty of Paris, signed on September 3, 1783.

St. Helena   A small island in the South Atlantic, more than a thousand miles from the coast of Africa, discovered by the Portuguese in 1502. The British EAST INDIA COMPANY established a base there in 1659, and in 1673 the island became a British possession. The British government exiled Napoleon after his defeat and abdication in 1815 to this remote island. He was taken there in H.M.S. *Northumberland* and stayed until his death in 1821.

St. Helen's   Village on the Isle of WIGHT at the entrance to SPITHEAD.

St. Ignatius's bean   The poisonous seed of *Strychnos ignatii*, which contains strychnine. It was occasionally used in strengthening tonics.

St. James's Park   Located near WHITEHALL, this 90-acre expanse of trees and greenery, with a pond—the oldest of London's royal parks—was named for the now-defunct St. James Hospital for female lepers. Before Henry VIII converted it into a bowling alley, the park was a marshy field where the lepers fed their hogs. In 1814 St. James's Park was the scene of a splendid gala celebrating the anniversary of the Battle of the NILE. The view across its pond to the spires, peaks, and domes of Whitehall is said to be one of London's most spectacular.

St. Kitts   One of the Leeward Islands, named St. Christopher by Columbus when he discovered it in 1493 and renamed St. Kitts in 1623 by English settlers who established on the island the first successful English colony in the WEST INDIES. The French also settled there in 1627, but the island became entirely English in 1713.

St. Lawrence   The eastern Canadian waterway of rivers and lakes that connects the Great Lakes at Lake Ontario to the Gulf of St. Lawrence at the Atlantic Ocean. Montreal and Quebec are located along the river.

St. Leger   Held at a racecourse in DONCASTER, the famous St. Leger stakes for three-year-olds, run annually in September, was founded by Colonel St. Leger in 1776.

Saint-Valéry (Saint-Valéry-sur-Somme)   A seaport on the northeastern coast of France, where the Somme River empties into the English Channel. The point of embarkation of William the Conqueror in 1066 for his invasion of England.

St. Vincent   *See* JERVIS. *See also* CAPE ST. VINCENT.

salaam   A salutation or respectful greeting used in the East, meaning "peace be upon you." The ceremonial obeisance that accompanies
the salutation, a low bowing of the head and body with the palm of
the right hand on the forehead.

salamander   A lizardlike animal once thought to live in, or to be able
to endure, fire. Hence, a soldier who exposes himself to fire in battle.
Also, a round shot with a handle, heated and hung up by sailors on
board ship for warmth.

salamander's wool   Asbestos.

salle d'armes   Fencing school (French).

Sallee Rover   From the 16th to early 19th centuries, the most
dreaded of the BARBARY pirates, operating out of the Moroccan port of
Salé (also Sallee or Salli), a suburb of present-day Rabat, on the
Atlantic coast.

sally   To make a vessel roll by having the crew run from one side to
the other. Used to loosen a ship from ice.

Sally Port   The embarkation place at the fortifications on
Portsmouth Point in PORTSMOUTH, reserved for boats and men of the
Royal Navy, particularly for ships anchored at SPITHEAD. Also, sally
port, the opening on a ship's side used for entry, especially on the
LARBOARD side of a warship.

salmagundi *also* **solomongundy** *or* **solomon gundy**   A dish made
of chopped meat, anchovies, eggs, and onions with oil and spices. At
sea, more often boiled salted or cured fish and onions.

salt horse   Salted beef.

Saluting Days   Days on which a salute was fired in celebration. In
this period they included:

Queen's Birthday, January 18...21 guns
King Charles's Restoration, May 29.....................................17 guns
King's Birthday, June 4...21 guns

King's Coronation, September 22 .... 21 guns
King's Accession, October 25 .... 17 guns
Gunpowder Plot, November 5 .... 17 guns

salver   A tray used for refreshments or for presenting letters, visiting cards, and the like.

Salve Regina   In the Roman Catholic Church, an antiphon that begins with "Salve, Regina," recited in the liturgy from Trinity Sunday to Advent or sung as a separate office or devotion. Also, a musical setting for this.

sancta simplicitas   Literally, holy simplicity (Latin). Usually used as an exclamation of astonishment at a person's naïveté.

sandalwood   A fragrant yellowish heartwood obtained from several trees of the genus *Santalum* and used in wood carving and cabinetry; sometimes used medically as a mild stimulating tonic.

sand-grouse   Any of various pigeonlike birds that inhabit arid parts of southern Europe, Asia, and Africa.

Sandwich, John Montagu, fourth Earl of (*1718–1792*)   A British statesman, he served as Lord Commissioner of the ADMIRALTY (1744–1748), twice as Secretary of State for the Northern Department (1763–1765 and 1770–1771), and three times as First Lord of the Admiralty (1748–1751, 1763, and 1771–1782). He was a skilled administrator who attempted to reform the Admiralty and modernize naval practices, advocating coppering ships' bottoms and employing CARRONADEs, but he also achieved fame as a patron of music as well as notoriety as a gambler and rake. Perhaps his greatest contribution to society was culinary: He invented the sandwich as a way to eat supper while gambling.

Sandwich Islands   A chain of Polynesian islands, now called the Hawaiian Islands, discovered and charted by Captain James COOK in 1778 and named by him after the fourth earl of SANDWICH, who promoted his voyage of exploration. Cook was at first treated as a deity here, but later he was attacked and stabbed to death by unfriendly natives.

San Idelfonso Treaty   *See* IDELFONSO TREATY.

San Martín, José Francisco de (*1778–1850*)   An Argentinian soldier and statesman who helped liberate Buenos Aires from Spain. With BERNARDO O'HIGGINS, he then crossed the Andes to liberate Chile. San Martín's army, in which O'Higgins served as a commander, defeated the Spanish at the Battle of Chacabuco on February 12, 1817, and San Martín assured Chile's independence with a victory at the Battle of Maipo on April 5, 1818. With Lord COCHRANE and the Chilean fleet, he then helped liberate Peru, entering Lima in July 1821. San Martín briefly held the title of Protector of Peru, but he resigned in 1822 and retired to France.

sans revanche   No return match (French).

Santa Ana   Built at El Ferrol, Spain, in 1784, she was the most technically advanced 74-gun three-decker built in the 18th century. She had seven sister ships, built during the following decade at El Ferrol and Havana. She saw a number of major actions, including TRAFALGAR, where she fought successfully as Vice-Admiral Alava's flagship and helped recover several British prizes for Spain. She sank at Havana in 1812.

Santander   A province of CASTILE and a major seaport with a spacious harbor on the northern coast of Spain, the city was made a *puerto habilitado* in 1753, which gave it the privilege of trading with America. Santander was ravaged by the French in 1808.

Santissima Trinidad   A colossal Spanish SHIP OF THE LINE with four decks and 140 guns. She was the largest warship in the world when she fought against NELSON at the Battle of CAPE ST. VINCENT in 1797. After fighting bravely at TRAFALGAR, she was captured and sunk.

Sapphic   Of or pertaining to Sappho (*c.* 600 B.C.), the famed poet of Lesbos admired for her beautiful writing. Also, a poetic meter used by Sappho.

saraband   Originally, a dance of Asian origin that first appeared in Spain in the 16th century, accompanied by castanets and tambourines. Cervantes denounced it for its indecent gestures, and it was suppressed. It reappeared in the 17th century in a more dignified form and began to appear as a movement in the instrumental suite.

sardana   A popular CATALAN dance to the music of pipe and drum, closely tied to Catalan national consciousness. It is danced by men and women who join hands in a closed circle.

Sargasso Sea   An area of sea in the southwest quarter of the north Atlantic Ocean, between the WEST INDIES and the AZORES, named for sargassum, a type of seaweed floating over a vast part of the sea. First reported by Columbus, who thought it indicated land, the Sargasso was the source of much fear for later seamen, who told highly exaggerated stories of ships trapped in the seaweed and unable to make their way out. It is also a major breeding ground for eels.

sari   A long, often brightly colored length of cotton or silk worn as a garment by Hindu women. It is wrapped several times around the waist to form a skirt, then passed across the chest over the left shoulder and sometimes over the head.

sassafras   A small North American tree, *Sassafras albidum*, first mentioned by the Spaniards in 1528. The dried root, bark, and wood were used as a flavoring and occasionally as a multipurpose tonic.

satietas vitae   Weariness of life (Latin).

saturnine temperament   Sluggish, cold, gloomy, leaden; Saturn was the astrological symbol for lead. Although most lead-based medicines were meant only to be applied topically, to assist wound healing, the lead could be absorbed into the body through the exposed tissue, sometimes producing toxic effects on the nervous system and elsewhere that could be regarded as typical of the saturnine temperament.

satyr   In Greek mythology, one of a group of woodland gods or demons, part human and part beast, supposed to be Bacchus's companions. In ancient Greek art, the satyr had the ears and tail of a horse. Roman sculptors gave satyrs certain features of a goat, including budding horns. Also, a man who shows excessive sexual desire.

SAUMAREZ, JAMES, LORD DE (1757–1836)
A member of a family of Norman descent on the island of Guernsey that distinguished itself in the British Navy during the 18th century, Saumarez was a LIEUTENANT during the American Revolutionary War, seeing action at the DOGGER BANK against the Dutch in 1781 and with RODNEY at the SAINTES in 1782. In 1793, at the beginning of the war with France, while commanding the *Crescent,* he captured the French FRIGATE *RÉUNION* with no casualties, which earned him a knighthood. Considered brave and bold, Saumarez was made Rear-Admiral in early 1801 and shortly thereafter led his SQUADRON in an unsuccessful

action at Algeciras, where the 74-gun *Hannibal* was lost. The fictitious
Jack Aubrey, in *Master and Commander,* observes the unhappy event as
a prisoner of war from a French warship. But Saumarez quickly refit
his squadron at GIBRALTAR and gained a measure of revenge in an
explosive night action that Aubrey also observes, from a distance, in
Master and Commander. In over 60 years of Navy service, Saumarez
fought in many actions, including those at CAPE ST. VINCENT (in the
ORION with Lieutenant Aubrey on board) and the NILE, where he was
second-in-command to NELSON. With H.M.S. *VICTORY* as his FLAGSHIP,
Saumarez commanded the Baltic Squadron from 1808 to 1812 as a
Vice-Admiral. He was promoted to ADMIRAL in 1814, was COMMANDER-
IN-CHIEF at PLYMOUTH from 1824 to 1827, and in 1831 was raised to the
PEERAGE as Baron de Saumarez of Guernsey.

save-all   Another name for WATER SAIL. Also a drip pan to collect
moisture.

Savoy Chapel   A chapel dedicated to St. John the Baptist, built in
1510 when Savoy Palace, which had been destroyed in the Peasant's
Revolt of 1381, was rebuilt as a hospital for the poor.

Savoy, Liberties of the   A liberty was a district within the limits of a
county but exempt from the jurisdiction of the sheriff. The Liberty of
the Savoy was the property of the English royal house of Lancaster. A
palace on the ground was rebuilt by Henry, first Duke of Lancaster,
between about 1345 and 1370. The Duke also acquired more property,
eventually accumulating what would later be the Savoy precinct. In
1505 Henry VII decided that the palace should be rebuilt as a hospital
for the poor. The area subsequently housed a hospital, barracks, a
prison, and a Jesuit school for boys. Tradesmen moved in, and busi-
nesses were established. In 1772, with most of the buildings now in
ruins, a longstanding dispute over the ownership of the precinct was
resolved. The DUCHY OF LANCASTER retained the outer ring and the
SAVOY CHAPEL, and the Crown took possession of the center part of the
duchy.

   Bounded by the Strand to the north, the Thames to the south, Ivy
Bridge to the west, and the Temple to the east, the Liberties were, as
O'Brian explains in *The Thirteen Gun Salute,* "legally . . . not part of
London or Westminster at all, but of the Duchy of Lancaster, and cul-
turally it was a self-contained village." (From 1816 to 1820, the area

was cleared to build the approach road to Waterloo Bridge.) *See also* LANCASTER, DUCHY OF.

saxifrage   A perennial herb of the genus *Saxifraga* with tufted foliage and small white, yellow, or red flowers, often growing in rock crevices.

Sayers, Tom (*1826–1865*)   Known as the "Brighton Boy" and "Napoleon of the Prize Ring," Sayers was one of the great English heavyweight boxing champions. Weighing less than 160 pounds, he often fought much larger men but beat them with skillful, stiff blows.

scale the shot   To remove the accumulation of rust from the surface of a metal cannonball.

scandalize   To reduce sail in an unusual manner; for instance, instead of lowering throat- and peak-HALYARDs of a GAFF sail together, to drop the peak and perhaps TRICE UP the TACK. Also, when a ship at anchor sets its YARDs askew as a sign of mourning, it is said to be scandalized.

scantling   As applied to timber, the breadth and thickness of a beam, as opposed to its length. In shipbuilding, the scantlings are the dimensions of all structural parts of a vessel regarded collectively.

scapula   Shoulder blade.

scarf *or* scarph   To join the ends of two timbers forming one longer piece, the ends being halved, notched, or cut away to fit together neatly. A ship's KEEL consisted of timbers scarfed together. Also, the joint so formed.

scarper   *Slang,* to leave in haste, escape, bolt.

scaup   Any of several diving ducks having mostly black and white plumage and inhabiting the seas of northern Europe, Asia, and America.

scavenger   A person who is employed to clean streets or to clean a church.

scend   The vertical rise and fall of a vessel caused by the range of the waves; the sudden rising motion when a ship PITCHes in a heavy sea. The scend of the sea is the carrying or upward driving impulse of a sea or wave; also, the surge of the sea into a harbor.

schooner   A FORE-AND-AFT-rigged vessel, originally with only two MASTs, but later with three or more, and sometimes one or more square TOPSAILS. The characteristic schooner RIG consists of two GAFF sails, the after sail not smaller than the FORE, and a HEADSAIL set on a BOWSPRIT. Although British and Dutch prototypes existed in the 17th century, the schooner was developed in the United States, perhaps initially around 1713 ("schooner" possibly is derived from the word "scoon," a local term for skipping a stone). Later developed for speed, particularly at Baltimore, schooners were used in the COASTING trade and in fishing the GRAND BANK off NEWFOUNDLAND. Used also for blockade running and as fast naval vessels.

schuyt *or* **schouw**   A Dutch flat-bottomed boat with a GAFF MAINSAIL, BOWSPRIT JIB, and leeboards, to lessen the leeway (*see* LEE).

Schwarzenberg, Karl Philipp (*1771–1820*)   Austrian field marshal and diplomat who commanded the Austrian army in Russia in 1812, became commander in chief of the allied forces opposing NAPOLEON in 1813, and defeated Napoleon at Leipzig. He drove the French across the Rhine and led the campaign in France that resulted in Napoleon's defeat in 1814.

sciatic nerve   The largest nerve in the human body, which emerges from the spine in the lower back and runs down the back of the thigh to the foot. Sciatica is pain along the sciatic nerve, often caused by pressure exerted on the spinal cord by a ruptured or dislocated disk.

sciatic stay   A strong rope running from the MAINMAST to the FORE-MAST HEADs in merchant ships and supporting a TACKLE that can be shifted over the MAIN or FORE HATCHWAYs when loading and unloading cargo.

Scilly Islands *or* **Scillies**   Thirty miles southwest of Land's End in Cornwall, England, an archipelago of small isles, reefs, and rocks often shrouded in fog and mist and consequently the site of many shipwrecks.

scimitar   A short, curved, single-edged sword, used chiefly by the Turks and Persians.

scoff   To eat voraciously, devour.

Scombridae   The mackerel family. A scombri is a mackerel.

scops owl   Any of a group of small owls, such as *Otus scops* (Old World scops owl) and *O. sunia* (Oriental scops owl), having ear tufts and a whistling call.

scoria   Rough masses formed by the cooling of molten lava when exposed to the air, distended by the expansion of trapped gases.

scow   A large flat-bottomed rowed boat, used as a LIGHTER or PUNT, or to ferry men.

scrag   To wring the neck of; to manhandle; to kill.

scraper   A cocked hat.

scratch   Hastily gathered or assembled.

scratch-wig *or* **scratch-bob**   A small, short wig.

scrim   A thin canvas used for curtains and upholstery lining.

scrofula   Tuberculosis of the cervical lymph glands, resulting in chronic skin ulcers. Often caused by the bovine form of tuberculosis (*Mycobacterium bovis*), it was not as likely to kill the patient as the usual pulmonary form of the disease (caused by *Mycobacterium tuberculosis*). It was also called the King's Evil, because it was supposed to be curable by the touch of the sovereign; the last British monarch to carry out the annual ceremonial touching was Queen Anne (d. 1714).

scroll   In shipbuilding, a curved timber bolted to the KNEE of the HEAD.

scruple   A unit of apothecary weight equal to 20 grains, or approximately 1.3 grams.

scrutineer   One whose job is to examine.

scrutoire *or* **escritoire**   A writing desk made to contain stationery and documents, and in early use, often portable.

scud   To run BEFORE THE WIND in a storm under reduced sail or BARE POLES. In a gale, the Master had the choice of running before the wind if there was enough sea room or lying to if there was not. Also, a loose, vapory cloud fragment drifting rapidly under rain clouds (a fracto-stratus cloud).

scull   An oar worked from side to side over the STERN of the boat, the blade being reversed at each turn. One of two light oars used in a dinghy by a single rower.

This ship is scudding before a heavy wind with only the forecourse set to maintain steering control. (*From Serres's* Liber Nauticus).

scullery A small room next to a kitchen used for washing dishes and other dirty work; a back kitchen.

scunner To shrink back with fear. To feel violent disgust or aversion, to feel sick.

scupper To SCUTTLE. A slang term meaning to confuse or defeat. Also, one of many drain openings in a ship's side at deck level that allow water to run into the sea. To be on one's scuppers means to be sunk or killed.

scurvy *or* **scorbutus** A disease now known to be caused by insufficient ascorbic acid (vitamin C) in the diet and characterized by lethargy, foul breath, extreme tenderness of the gums, loss of teeth, PETECHIAe, and pains in the limbs. Common on long voyages because the diet included few, if any, fruits and vegetables. *See* BLANE.

scut A short erect tail, as of a hare, rabbit, or deer.

scuttle   To sink a vessel deliberately. Also, a porthole in the deck or side of a ship for lighting and ventilation. Scuttle-hatch: a lid or covering of a scuttle.

scuttle-butt   A cask of drinking-water on board ship. Gossip.

sea-coal   Coal, as distinguished from charcoal.

sea-cock   An opening through the hull, with a valve, to let a controllable amount of seawater into the ship.

sea-elephant   An elephant seal, either of two types of large seals with trunklike snouts that inhabit the Pacific coastal waters of the Americas.

Sea-Fencibles   *See* FENCIBLES.

sea-leopard   A leopard seal (*Ogmorhinus leptonyx*), which inhabits the Southern and Antarctic seas.

sealer   A vessel engaged in the sealing trade, killing seals for fur, hides, and oil.

sea (*or* nautical) mile   Equivalent to 6,076 feet, or one minute of latitude. Approximately 1.15 statute miles.

sea-otter   A large marine otter (*Enhydra lutris*) found on the shores of the North Pacific.

sea-pie   A layered dish of meat, vegetables, and fish in between crusts of dough, the number of layers determining whether it was a two- or three-decker. A popular dish on board ship when the ingredients were available.

sear   The part of a gunlock that engages with the notches of the tumbler in order to keep the hammer at full or half cock, and released at full cock by pressure on the trigger.

seat of ease   Latrine seat, located in the Captain's QUARTER-GALLERY or, for all others on a ship, along the BOWSPRIT (therefore the four to eight holes were called the HEAD).

sea-wrack   Seaweed, especially any of the large coarse kinds frequently washed up on the shore.

sebi confectio discolor   A mottled concoction of suet (Latin).

second   A person who represents and assists a principal in a duel and arranges the logistics, such as carrying the challenge, choosing the site, and loading weapons.

second of arc   In angular measure, $\frac{1}{60}$ of a minute, $\frac{1}{3,600}$ of a degree.

secret du roi   Secret service of the king (French).

sectary   A member of a sect or someone who is particularly zealous in the cause of a sect.

seizing   A small cord used in binding two ropes together. Also, the line that results when one rope is "seized" to another.

Selsey Bill   East of PORTSMOUTH, a tongue of land that projects into the English Channel and is surrounded by miles of shallows, which before the seas encroached were roamed by deer and are still called the "park" by fishermen.

selvage *or* **selvedge**   The side edges, or guarding, of a net or sail.

selvagee   A STROP (loop) made of tightly wound rope yarn and used for lifting or securing. A strop made by wrapping small SPUNYARN around two or more nails or spikes and then splicing or tying them together and tarring them. Stronger than a spliced strop, it is used around a SHROUD or STAY to attach a TACKLE.

semaphore   An apparatus consisting of an upright post with one or more arms moving in a vertical plane that was first used for signaling in Britain in 1816, when it replaced an older TELEGRAPH system in use by the British ADMIRALTY. A semaphore code could also be transmitted using handheld flags or lights.

send   *See* SCEND.

senna   A tropical shrub of the genus *Cassia*, bearing yellow flowers and flat greenish pods, used chiefly as a cathartic.

sennet *also* **sennit** *or* **sinnet**   CORDAGE used for making HALYARDS, mats, and LASHings. Also, plaited straw, palm leaves, and the like, used to make grass hats.

sennight   A week.

sensu strictu (*or* **sensu stricto)**   In the restricted sense (Latin). Of a scientific term, in the narrow sense.

sepoy   A native of India employed as a soldier in the command of Europeans, especially the British.

Seppings, Sir Robert (*1767–1840*)   A naval architect, who rose from SHIPWRIGHT's apprentice at PLYMOUTH Dockyard to Surveyor of the Navy. He contributed a number of innovations to shipbuilding, including "Seppings blocks," which improved accessibility to a ship's hull in DRY-DOCK. For this he was made master shipwright at CHATHAM, where he introduced diagonal bracing of frame timbers for added longitudinal hull strength and modified hull design to provide a cleaner run.

sepsis   Putrefaction (though the meaning is more specific today).

septième   Seventh (French).

sequela   An aftereffect of a previous disease or accident.

sequi me   Follow me (Latin).

serang   The BOATSWAIN or captain of a LASCAR (Indian or East Indian) crew.

sercial   A type of MADEIRA wine.

serjeanty   A form of feudalism in which the subject rendered a specified service to the king. In the 13th century, petit serjeanty bound a person to a service "amounting to half a mark or less," such as taking to the king a bag, an arrow, or a bow without string.

Seth   Adam and Eve's third son, who was born after Cain murdered his brother, Abel, and so named by Eve, who said, "For God has appointed [in Hebrew, 'seth'] another seed for me instead of Abel" (Gen. 4:25).

Sethians   According to the 1771 *Encyclopaedia Britannica*: "Christian heretics, so called because they paid divine worship to Seth, whom they looked upon to be Jesus Christ the Son of God, but who was made by a third divinity, and substituted in the room of the two families of Abel and Cain, which had been destroyed by the deluge. These heretics appeared in Egypt in the second century; and as they were addicted to all sorts of debauchery, they did not want for followers, and continued in Egypt about two hundred years."

settee   A decked vessel with a long pointed PROW, carrying two or three LATEEN-rigged MASTS, used primarily in the eastern Mediterranean.

setting-rule *or* **composing-rule**   A brass or steel rule against which a printer sets the type in a composing stick.

settle   A long wooden bench, usually with arms, a high back, and a locker or box underneath.

settle a person's hash   To reduce to order; to silence or subdue.

settling day   A day appointed for settling accounts. The fortnightly payday on the London Stock Exchange.

Seven Dials   Behind the junction of Shaftsbury Avenue and Charing Cross Road, this section of London was built on what was once known as Cock and Pye Fields. It was so named for a column in the center topped by seven sundials, facing the seven streets that radiated out from there. Seven Dials was noted for its poverty and squalor.

Seven Years' War   The third Silesian war (1756–1763), in which Austria, France, Russia, Saxony, and Sweden were allied against Frederick the Great of Prussia. Ended by the Treaty of Paris of 1763.

seventy-four   A third-rate ship carrying 74 guns.

sextant   A hand-held optical instrument invented in 1757 by Captain (later Admiral) John Campbell and used in navigation for measuring horizontal and vertical angular distances between objects, especially for observing the angle of a celestial object above the horizon in determining longitude and latitude at sea. The ultimate refinement of the QUADRANT, a sextant, so called because its calibrated arc, or limb, is one sixth of a circle, is highly accurate.

shaddock   The large pear-shaped citrus fruit of the tree *Citrus maxima,* native to the EAST INDIES and the Pacific. Lemon-yellow in color, it resembles a grapefruit but has a loose rind and pungent, tart, and agreeable but coarse, dry pulp. Also called pompelmous or pommelo. Also, the tree that it grows on. Named after Captain Shaddock, the commander of an EAST INDIA COMPANY ship, who took the tree to Jamaica in the late 17th century.

shag A cormorant, a dark seabird with a hooked bill, long neck, and wedge-shaped tail; especially the crested cormorant, which in the breeding season has a crest of long curly plumes.

shakings Pieces of old rope and canvas used for making OAKUM. The deck sweepings at the end of the day.

shallop A boat powered by oars or by a sail, used in shallow waters or between large ships; a dinghy or SKIFF. Also, a large, heavy boat with one FORE-AND-AFT-rigged MAST, the type that might be built by a ship's carpenters from the salvage of a shipwreck and used to send for help.

sham Short for champagne.

shambling Exhibiting shambles, an awkward, abnormal gait or movement.

Shannon, **H.M.S.** The best-known ship of this name was the fifth-rate 38-gun FRIGATE launched in 1806. In June of 1813, under the command of Captain Philip BROKE and known for her expert gunnery, she fought a brief but bloody battle with the 50-gun U.S. frigate *CHESA-PEAKE* off Boston, an event recreated by O'Brian in *The Fortune of War,* with Jack Aubrey aboard the *Shannon* as a passenger and combatant. Commanded by Captain James LAWRENCE, the *Chesapeake* surrendered with 61 crew lost, including her Captain, and more than 85 wounded. The *Shannon,* whose victory provided a much-needed boost in morale for the Royal Navy, which had recently lost several discouraging actions to the upstart Americans, suffered 33 killed and 50 wounded. Made into a RECEIVING SHIP in 1832, the *Chesapeake* was finally broken up in 1859. Given the fame that Lawrence's encounter with the *Shannon* earned in the United States, it is ironic that the ADMIRALTY unwittingly renamed the ship *St. Lawrence* in 1844.

shanty *See* CHANTERY.

sharper A cheat, swindler, rogue; a fraudulent gamester.

sharp-set Very hungry.

Shaw, George (*1751–1813*) An ordained deacon, Shaw studied medicine at Edinburgh and Oxford and became a botanical lecturer at Oxford. In 1788, he helped found the Linnean Society. He also served as keeper of the natural-history section of the British Museum.

Shawnee   A tribe of Algonquian-speaking American Indians, formerly inhabiting the Tennessee Valley region and now living in Oklahoma. A member of this tribe or its language.

shay   *See* CHAISE.

shears   *See* SHEERS.

shearwater   Any of various long-winged seabirds, related to the PETREL and the ALBATROSS, that skim the surface of the water so closely when they fly that they seem to shear it. Shearwaters are migratory, spending most of their lives over the water, but they nest on land in great colonies.

sheathbill   A white shore bird that inhabits the Antarctic region and has the base of its bill ensheathed in a horny case.

sheave   In a BLOCK, the grooved and revolving wheel over which the rope travels.

shebeen   In Ireland and Scotland, a shop or house where liquor is sold without a licence; a lowly pub.

sheer-hulk   An old ship cut down and fitted with SHEERS, for masting other vessels.

Sheerness   A naval dockyard at the mouth of the Medway in Kent on England's southeastern coast, whose specialty was FRIGATES and smaller vessels. Sheerness was also the site of a small naval hospital.

sheers *or* **sheer-legs**   A device consisting of two or three long poles lashed together at the top, steadied by GUYS, and spread apart at the base, used to support hoisting TACKLE on ships and in dockyards for lifting heavy weights, especially in raising and fixing MASTS.

sheerwater   *See* SHEARWATER.

sheet   A rope attached to either of the lower corners (CLEWS) of a square sail or the BOOM or after lower corner (clew) of a FORE-AND-AFT sail and used to extend the sail or to alter its direction. To sheet home is to HAUL in a sheet until the foot of a sail is as straight and as taut as possible.

sheet-anchor   Traditionally, the largest of a ship's anchors, but in Aubrey's day, similar in size to the BOWER-ANCHORS, which where secured at the CATHEADS. The sheet-anchor (that to which the sheet-cable was secured, ordinarily carried on the STARBOARD side) and a fourth anchor on the other side were secured abreast the FOREMAST, on the CHANNELS, usually set up with tumblers, so they could be dropped in an emergency should the bower anchors fail to hold.

Sheffield plate   A copper plate coated with silver by a process developed in the manufacturing city of Sheffield in Yorkshire, England, about 1742.

Sheikh-al-Jabal   A chief of the ASSASSINS in Syria at a time when they occupied a string of mountain fortresses. French crusaders referred to him as "le vieux de la montagne" ("the Old Man of the Mountain").

shell   The outer casing of a BLOCK. A THIMBLE DEAD-EYE block used to join the ends of two ropes. The dug-out portion of a West Indian canoe.

shellback   A hardened sailor, especially one raised at sea.

Shelmerston   A fictional seaport on the English Channel in southwest England, most likely in Devon on Tor Bay. Facing east in a protected bay that "on either hand . . . curved out in tawny cliffs," the town, home port for the LETTER OF MARQUE *Surprise,* is dominated by houses of both worship and prostitution, and its prime seamen honed their skills largely as smugglers.

Shepton Mallet   A market town in Somerset, 22 miles southwest of Bath.

shift   A change in the direction of the wind. A clockwise shift is said to be veering and a counterclockwise shift, BACKING. Also, an item of men's or women's underclothing, usually made of linen or cotton. Later, a woman's chemise. To change, as in clothes.

shilling   A former English monetary unit and silver coin equal to 12 pence or $\frac{1}{20}$ of a pound sterling.

shilly-shally   Vacillating, irresolute, undecided.

shindy   A spree, merrymaking. Also, a type of dance among seamen.

shingle   Small, smooth stones found by the sea. Also, a beach or other area covered with loose roundish pebbles.

ship Today, any sea-going vessel of considerable size, but in the 18th century, specifically a vessel with three or more MASTS, SQUARE-RIGGED, and suitable for navigating the high seas. To put an object in position to perform its function, as to ship oars. To embark. To take in water from the sea.

ship-chandler A dealer who supplies stores to ships.

ship of the line A RATEd, sailing warship that is large enough and sufficiently armed to be in the line of battle during a fleet action.

ship-rigged Carrying square sails on all three MASTS. *See also* SHIP.

ship's bells The system for telling time on board ship. The ship bell, struck every half hour, indicates by the number of strokes the number of half-hours of the watch that have elapsed. The striking of eight bells indicates midnight. After midnight, one bell is struck at 12:30 A.M., two bells at 1:00 A.M., three bells at 1:30 A.M., and so forth until eight bells are struck again at 4:00 A.M., at which point the above progression is repeated until eight bells are again struck at 8:00 A.M. In this way eight bells ring every four hours around the clock. *See also* WATCH.

shipwright A man employed in the construction of ships. The Company of Shipwrights was incorporated in 1605.

shittim wood The wood of the shittah-tree, acacia wood. See ACACIA.

shiver Of a sail, to flutter or to shake; to cause a sail to flutter in the wind. Sails are said to shiver when a vessel is steered so close in the direction that the wind is blowing from that the air spills out of them. Also, an old word for the SHEAVE of a BLOCK.

shoal An elevation of the sea-bottom to within six FATHOMS of the surface; a shallow; a sandbank or bar. Shoaling: growing progressively more shallow.

shoneen A person inclining toward English rather than Irish standards and attitudes, as in cultural life, sports, etc.

short commons Lacking in rations, scant fare.

short seas When the waves are irregular, broken, and interrupted, frequently bursting over a vessel's side. When the distance between successive waves is abnormally short for their height.

short-weight   Deficient in weight, a means of defrauding the buyer.

shot   Any non-exploding missile fired from a naval gun, including LANGRAGE, CHAIN-SHOT, BAR-SHOT, and the normal cast-iron ball, or ROUND SHOT, which was called by its weight, as in 32-pound, 24-pound, or 18-pound shot. A CARRONADE, also called a smasher, fired a 66-pound shot.

shot-garland   A wooden rack running along the ship's side from one gunport to another and holding the ROUND SHOT for the GREAT GUNs.

shoulder-block   A large single BLOCK, nearly square at its lower end.

shove-groat   The game of shuffleboard, in which a coin or other disk is pushed with a blow of the hand down a highly polished board, floor, or table marked with transverse lines.

Shovell, Sir Cloudesley (*1659–1707*)   English admiral and commander of the Mediterranean fleet during the War of the Spanish Succession (1701–14). Sailing for home in October 1707, his FLAGSHIP, the *Association*, and three other ships met bad visibility in the Channel and were unable to determine their position. Swept by a strong current, four ships, including the flagship, were wrecked near the Bishop and Clerk rocks off the SCILLY ISLANDS, with the loss of more than 1,400 men. Shovell's body washed ashore and, years later, a woman wrecker confessed on her deathbed that she had found him alive and had murdered him for his emerald ring.

show away   Show off.

shrouds   Part of the standing RIGGING of a ship, a range of large ropes extending from the MASTHEADs to the STARBOARD (right) and LARBOARD (left) sides of the ship to provide lateral support to the MASTs, enabling them to carry sail. The shrouds were supported by HOUNDs at the masthead and the lower shrouds were secured by the CHAINs on the ship's side. The shrouds of the TOPMAST and TOPGALLANT MAST ran to the edges of the TOPs. The parallel bands of RATLINES running between the shrouds functioned as ladders by which the TOPMEN climbed up to and down from the mastheads.

shrub   An alcoholic drink usually made with orange or lemon juice, sugar, and rum.

shy To fling, throw, jerk, or toss.

Sic erimus cuncti postquam nos auferet Orcus/ergo vivamus dum licet esse, bene So we will all be after Orcus [Roman god of the underworld] carries us off/therefore let us live well while we may (Latin; an epitaph from the *Satyricon* of Petronius).

Sick and Hurt Office Same as the Sick and Wounded Board; *see* "The Royal Navy During the War of the French Revolution and the Napoleonic War," p. 6.

sick headache A severe headache accompanied by abdominal distress.

side-boy In a warship, a boy whose job is to attend to the GANGWAY or MANROPES, assisting officers and others boarding from or departing to another boat.

side-fish Long timbers dovetailed on either side of a made mast (one constructed of more than one timber).

sidereal Of or pertaining to the stars. Of periods of time, that which is determined or measured by using the stars.

siege-train All the men, guns, and materials gathered to conduct a siege.

Sierra Leone A river in West Africa. Also, a British colony in West Africa in whose capital, Freetown, blacks who had been taken to Britain as slaves were resettled by the Sierra Leone Company in 1787. In 1808, the British government took over direct responsibility for the colony of free blacks. From that year, Sierra Leone was also a naval base for anti–slave trade patrols.

Si la personne qui s'intérrese au pavillon de partance voudrait bien donner rendez-vous en laissant un mot chez Jules, traiteur à Frith Street, elle en aurait des nouvelles If the person who has an interest in the Blue Peter would like to make an appointment by leaving word with Jules, a restaurateur on Frith Street, he will receive information about it (French).

silkstone A type of coal mined at Silkstone near Barnsley in Yorkshire, England.

sill *or* **port-sill** An upper or lower horizontal timber forming the upper or lower edge of a ship's square port.

sillabub   *See* SYLLABUB.

Sillery   A wine of the Champagne region of France produced in and around the village of Sillery, usually the still wine Sillery sec (dry Sillery), formerly made from the grapes of the Sillery vineyards but now chiefly from those of the nearby vineyards of Verzenay and Mailly.

Simia satyrus   The orangutan, a forest-dwelling ape of BORNEO, Sumatra, and Java that is about two-thirds the size of a gorilla and has very long arms.

similia similibus curantur   Like things cured by likes (Latin). The practice of treating a disease by giving the patient small amounts of substances that in a healthy person would cause similar symptoms to those the patient is experiencing.

Simonstown   Near the southern tip of Africa, a port about 30 miles south of Cape Town on the western shore of False Bay, near the Cape of Good Hope. From 1741 Simonstown was a Dutch military and naval base, and from 1814 it was headquarters of the Royal Navy's South Atlantic Squadron.

simoom   A hot, dry, suffocating, and frequently sand-laden wind that blows across the African and Asiatic deserts in spring and summer.

sinecure   An office or position that requires little or no effort but usually provides an income. Of the nature of a sinecure. Involving no duties or work.

single   In cricket, a hit for one run.

sinologist   A Western student of the Chinese language or of Chinese customs, literature, or history.

sippet   Toasted or fried bread, usually served in soup or broth or with meat as a sop.

sirens   In classical mythology, several part-female, part-bird nymphs who lived on an island near Sicily, where they halted sailors' journeys—and eventually their lives—with their enchanting songs. When passing near them, Ulysses plugged the ears of his crew with wax, so they could not listen, and had his sailors lash him to a MAST, so he could listen without succumbing to their call.

siriasis A disease that affects children, causing inflammation of the brain and membranes and burning fever and considered by some to be meningitis. O'Brian uses the term as a synonym for heat stroke.

Sirius, **H.M.S.** A 36-gun fifth-rate FRIGATE that saw action with Sir Robert CALDER in 1805, after which she towed the Spanish 74-gun *Firme* back to PORTSMOUTH. The *Sirius* served at TRAFALGAR in 1805 under Captain William Prowse. In 1810, while serving in the Indian Ocean, she was lost in an attack on the Île de France (MAURITIUS).

sirocco A hot wind from the Sahara Desert that blows from the south or southeast off the north coast of Africa over the Mediterranean and into parts of southern Europe, in the summer sometimes oppressive and bearing sand.

sister block A BLOCK with two SHEAVES, one below the other, sometimes seized between the TOPMAST SHROUDS, and through which were ROVE the TOPGALLANT SHEET and topsailyard lift. Also called a long-tail block.

sixes and sevens, to be at A condition of confusion, disorder, or disagreement. Originally the phrase, from the language of dicing, was "to set on six and seven," which was probably a fanciful exaggeration of "to set on cinque and sice," the two highest numbers.

six-water grog Weak GROG, consisting of six portions of water to each of rum, served occasionally as a punishment to sailors.

Skager Rack A variation of Skagerrak, the broad arm of the North Sea between Norway and Denmark; also known as the SLEEVE, the channel is about 130 miles long and more than 70 miles wide.

skein A length of yarn or thread secured in a long, loose coil. A skein of cotton thread consists of 80 turns on a reel 54 inches in circumference.

skeleton at the feast A reminder of serious or depressing matters at a time of lightheartedness or enjoyment.

skep A beehive.

skid-beam One of the BEAMS over the deck for stowing boats.

skids BEAMS or reserve SPARS kept by a ship usually in the WAIST and used as a support for the ship's boats.

skiff   A small boat equipped with one or two pairs of oars and used for a ship's chores in harbor.

skimmer   A bird of the North American genus *Rhyncops*, especially the black skimmer. These birds use their lower mandibles to skim small fish from the surface of the water.

skink   A small lizard (*Scincus officinalis*) of northern Africa and Arabia. Also, any lizard belonging to the Scincidae family.

skin up   As in "to skin up a sail in the BUNT," to make a FURLed sail smooth and neat using part of the sail to cover the remainder of the furled canvas.

skittles   A game traditionally played with nine pins set to form a square on a wooden frame, with the object being to bowl down the pins in as few throws as possible; nine-pins.

skua   A large dark-plumed predatory seabird (*Catharacta skua*). Growing to about 21 inches long, the skua is a powerful flier and with its hawklike bill often intimidates weaker birds into dropping their prey. They breed primarily along the Arctic and Antarctic shores but wander widely across the open oceans.

skylark   To frolic, play tricks, or roughhouse.

skysail   In SQUARE-RIGGED vessels, a light sail set above the ROYAL, used in a favorable light wind.

skyscraper   A triangular sail set above the SKYSAIL to maximize the advantage of a light favorable wind; a triangular MOONSAIL.

slab   Said of something semisolid, sometimes sticky.

slab-line   A small rope passing up behind a ship's MAINSAIL or FORESAIL used to hold up the sail so that the helmsman had a clear view or to pull in the slack of a COURSE to prevent it from shaking or splitting while it was being HAULed up.

slab-sided   Having long, flat sides.

slack-cask   A cask used for holding dry goods.

slack water   The situation, lasting roughly half an hour, at both high and low water when the tide does not flow visibly in either direction.

slag   Earthen matter separated from metals in the process of smelting, often used in the construction of roads.

slake   To cause a material, as lime, to crumble or disintegrate by the action of water or moisture.

Sleeve, the   An old name for the English Channel and for the SKAGER RACK, possibly originating from their shapes, which resemble sleeves; sleeve is also used to refer to any strait or channel.

slew   To turn (something) around on its own axis; to swing around.

slide   A runner on which a gun is mounted.

sliding keel   A plank of wood or metal that slides through a slot in the bottom of a vessel to increase the depth of the KEEL; a drop keel.

slime-draught   A word not used in everyday medicine of the time, this appears to be a vernacular term for a liquid medicine of unknown composition used sometimes as a stool softener and sometimes as a sleeping medicine.

sling-dog   An iron hook with a fang at one end and an EYE at the other through which to REEVE a rope. Used in pairs for HOISTing and HAULing.

slings   Ropes or chains attached to an object for HOISTing or supporting. YARD slings are ropes or chains used to secure a yard to the MAST.

sloop   Originally, a term used generally for any relatively small ship-of-war that did not fit into other categories; around 1760, heavier three-masted sloops carrying 14 or 16 guns were used in the Royal Navy. By the early 19th century, there were two distinctive classes of SQUARE-RIGGED sloops, the three-masted SHIP sloop and the two-masted BRIG sloop.

slop-book   A register containing a list of the clothing and other articles issued to the sailors to be charged against their pay. *See* SLOPS.

sloppy Joe   A slovenly person.

slops   Ready-made clothing and other furnishings from the ship's stores sold from the PURSER's chest to the seamen, usually at the MAINMAST with an officer present. The cost of slops purchased were deducted from a sailor's pay, with a portion going to the ship's

Purser. There was no official uniform for naval seamen until 1857. The word slops derives from the Old English word *sloppe,* which means breeches, but it also came to cover other commodities sold to the seamen, such as tobacco and soap.

slow-belly   A lazy, idle person; a laggard.

slow-match   A fuse that burned very slowly, used to ignite the charge in a large gun.

slubberdegullion   A worthless, slovenly person.

slush   The fat or grease left over from meat boiled on board ship, from which seamen made a favorite dish. It was also the Cook's perquisite to sell it to the PURSER, who turned it into candles.

small beer   Weak, inferior beer, with 1.2 percent alcohol.

small-bower   An anchor carried at the STARBOARD BOW of a vessel; also the CABLE attached to it. *See also* BEST BOWER.

small-clothes *or* **smalls**   Breeches; knee-breeches; underclothes.

smallpox   An acute contagious disease also known as variola, characterized by pustules on the skin. *See also* POX.

smell-smock   A licentious man, lacking in self-control.

Smith, Sir William Sidney (1764–1840)   Described as daring, vain, resourceful, insubordinate, and imaginative, Admiral Sidney entered the Navy at age 13 and was POST-CAPTAIN by age 18. His life of adventure included action early on at CAPE ST. VINCENT and the SAINTES and two years as a French prisoner after an attack on Le Havre in 1796. After escaping from prison, he was sent to the Mediterranean, where he successfully defended ACRE against Napoleon Bonaparte in 1799 in his most admired action. Promoted to Rear-Admiral in 1805, he returned to the Mediterranean and took part in the DARDANELLES expedition in 1807. After serving on the South American station, he was promoted to Vice-Admiral and was second in command in the Mediterranean from 1812 to 1814.

smiting-line   A line used to break a sail out of STOPS without the necessity of sending men aloft. Its successful execution indicates a good seaman.

smock-frock   A long, loose-fitting garment of coarse linen or the like worn by farmers over or as a coat.

smoke   In common use from roughly 1600 to 1850, meaning to get or understand, to smell or suspect a plot, design, joke, or hidden meaning.

Smollett, Tobias George (*1721–1771*)   A British novelist who drew upon his experiences as a Surgeon's Mate on H.M.S. *Chichester* to write a book entitled *The Adventures of Roderick Random* (1748), which satirized the Navy and the general way of life of British seamen. Smollett, a well-respected figure in 18th-century English literature, also edited the *Critical Review*.

Smyrna asafetida   ASAFETIDA imported from Smyrna (or Izmir), the major port on the west coast of Turkey, whence it came from Persia, Tibet, and other Eastern areas where it grew well.

Smyth, William Henry (*1788–1865*)   A British Rear-Admiral who was a founding member of the Royal Geographic Society in 1830. His surveys and scientific observations in the Mediterranean from 1813 to 1824, made with the help of many Continental scholars and surveyors, were highly praised in Britain and the Mediterranean countries. Compiler of *The Sailor's Word-Book,* published posthumously in 1867.

snack   A share or portion. *See also* GO SNACKS.

snapper-up   One who snaps up or pounces on something quickly.

snatch-block   A BLOCK with a hinged opening on one side so that the BIGHT of a rope could be dropped in, saving a seaman the effort of having to REEVE the whole length of the rope.

sneer   To make all sneer again meant to carry so much canvas that it strained the ropes and SPARS to the utmost.

sniggle   To fish for eels by thrusting a baited hook or other device into their hiding places. A baited hook used in sniggling.

snipe   Any of various wading birds related to the woodcock and characterized by long, straight bills.

Snodgrass, Gabriel   As chief surveyor to the EAST INDIA COMPANY, Snodgrass was an influence for progressive ship design. In 1791, for instance, he proposed the use of iron KNEES, instead of wooden ones, to support a ship's BEAMS and iron riders to reinforce the hull.

snow   The largest type of two-masted sailing vessel of the era, the snow, primarily a merchant ship but also used at war, carried square sails on both masts, with a TRYSAIL on a jackmast known as a snow-mast—which was a SPAR set on the deck about a foot behind the MAIN-MAST and attached at the top to the mainmast.

snub   To stop a running rope or CABLE suddenly by securing it to a post. To halt a vessel sharply, especially by securing a rope around a post or dropping an anchor. Also, when the BOW of a vessel at anchor is held down as the vessel is lifted by a wave, the vessel is said to be snubbed.

snuff-coloured   Of the color of snuff, brown or brownish.

snug *or* **snuggery**   A cosy or comfortable room, especially a small one into which a person retires for quiet or to be alone; a bachelor's den. The bar-parlor of an inn or public-house.

Society Islands   An isolated group of South Pacific islands in French Polynesia that was charted in 1769 by Captain James COOK and named by him after the Royal Society, which sponsored his trip to observe from Tahiti the transit of Venus.

Society of Jesus   The JESUITS.

Socinian   A member of a sect founded by Laelius and Faustus Socinus, two 16th-century Italian theologians who denied the divinity of Christ.

soft soap   A smeary, semiliquid soap made with potash lye; potash soap.

soft-tack *or* **soft tommy**   Sailors' term for bread, as distinct from ship's biscuit, known as HARD-TACK.

Solander, Daniel Carl (*1733–1782*)   A Swedish botanist who studied with Linnaeus and accompanied Sir Joseph Banks on several voyages. He was chosen to catalogue the British Museum's natural history collection in 1763 and was made its curator a decade later.

sole   Any of various flatfishes of the family Soleidae, related to and resembling the flounder, especially several common British and European species highly valued as food. Any of various other flatfishes.

solen The razor-fish, any bivalve mollusk of the genus *Solen*, having a long, narrow shell like the handle of a razor.

Solent, The In the English Channel, the western portion of the strait that separates the Isle of WIGHT and the mainland of England. Between one and three-quarters and four miles wide, It extends eastward for 15 miles from the Needles, the isolated group of rocks to the east of the Isle of Wight, to just beyond Southampton Water, the inlet leading to Southampton. The eastward portion of the strait is called SPITHEAD.

solitaire A large flightless bird (*Pezophaps solitarius*) that once inhabited the island of Rodriguez.

Solomon A person who is profoundly wise or just, like Solomon, the tenth-century B.C. king and son of David, who was celebrated for his wisdom. Also, said of, ironically, a wiseacre.

Somateria mollissima The EIDER. *Somateria spectabilis* is the king eider.

Somerset House One of London's most famous buildings, where the Royal Academy and Navy Board Offices were located. England's first Renaissance palace, it was built between 1547 and 1550 by Lord Protector Somerset. In 1604 peace negotiators from England, Spain, and the Spanish Netherlands met here. After Richard Cromwell's abdication in the mid-1600s, PARLIAMENT tried unsuccessfully to sell Somerset to pay the Army. The ROYAL SOCIETY met in the house's north wing from 1780 to 1857.

sonata A musical composition for instruments, usually the pianoforte or violin, in three or four movements.

soople Supple.

Sophie, **H.M.S.** Aubrey's first command is on board "almost the only QUARTERDECK BRIG in the service." She carries 14 four-pounder guns. The *Sophie* is ficticious but similar in size and armament to the 158-ton converted coasting brig *Speedy*, in which COCHRANE fought heroically (the basis for the action of *Master and Commander*).

sopor A deep unnatural sleep or sleeplike state. *See also* CARUS.

sordes   Filthy or feculent matter on or in a human or animal body. In typhoid or other fevers, the foul matter collecting on the teeth and lips.

sortie   A dash or sally by a besieged garrison to attack the enemy.

sotto i pini   Beneath the pines (Italian; sung by the Contessa and Susanna in act three of Mozart's *The Marriage of Figaro*).

sou   A French coin, formerly ⅟20 of a *livre* and subsequently the five-centime piece.

sounding   The process of finding out the depth of water by means of the LEAD-LINE and LEAD. To be in soundings is to be in a place at sea where it is possible to reach the bottom with the ordinary (up to 20 FATHOMs) or deep-sea (up to 100 fathoms) lead. Derives from the Old English word *sund* for "water, sea, or swimming." *See also* MARK.

soupe anglaise   Trifle, a dessert made by soaking stale sponge cake in wine or liqueur, adding fruit or jam and crushed macaroons, and topping with custard and whipped cream (French).

souse   Various parts of a pig or other animal, especially the feet and ears, that have been pickled. Also, to prepare or preserve by pickling.

South Foreland   A 300-foot headland of chalk on the coast of southeast Kent, England, whose two lighthouses, built about 1620, were particularly important in ensuring a safe transit south of the treacherous shoals and banks known as the GOODWIN SANDS that lie off the coast.

South Sea stock   Stock of the South Sea Company, incorporated in London in 1711 to conduct trade with Spanish America primarily in the South Seas. Its value soared to great heights and then crashed in 1720 following a financial crisis caused by rumors about a plan for the company to take over three fifths of the national debt. The crash ruined many shareholders, some of whom fled the country or committed suicide. The ugly scandal, known as the South Sea Bubble, reached into the top echelons of the government. The company managed to stay in business by changing its focus to other areas, such as the Greenland whale fishery.

south-wester   *See* SOU-WESTER.

Southampton, **H.M.S.** A 32-gun fifth rate built in 1757 whose design became the standard for British FRIGATES through the 1780s, at which point this class began to be outgunned by the French 36-gun frigates. The *Southampton* fought at Bellisle in 1761 and at the GLORIOUS FIRST OF JUNE in 1794. She was wrecked in the Bahamas in 1812.

Southern Cross A constellation with four bright stars in the form of a cross, visible in the Southern Hemisphere.

southing Movement or deviation in a southerly direction.

souviens-toi Remember (French).

sou-wester *or* **south-wester** A wind or GALE blowing from the southwest. Also, a large oilskin or waterproof hat or cap worn by seamen to protect the head and neck during rough or wet weather.

Sovereign Pontiff The Pope.

sow-gelder One whose business is to geld pigs.

span The distance from the tip of the thumb to the tip of the little finger, or sometimes to the tip of the forefinger, when the hand is fully extended; the space equivalent used as a measure of length, averaging nine inches.

Spanish Disturbance *See* NOOTKA SOUND.

Spanish fly An alcohol solution of powdered *Lytta vesicatoria,* a southern European beetle, used externally as a blistering counterirritant to fevers and other internal diseases and, rarely, internally as a diuretic. (Erroneously believed to be an aphrodisiac because its irritant effect on the urethra causes a prolonged erection.)

Spanish Main After Columbus's voyages, the Spanish called the northern coast of South America "Tierra Firma," which in English became known as the "Spanish Main." It was a romantic name for the Spanish possessions in America, consisting of the northeast coast of South America from the Orinoco to the Isthmus of Panama. By the late 17th century, the term also included the Caribbean and its islands.

spanker Originally, a fairweather sail set in place of the MIZZEN COURSE. Later a FORE-AND-AFT sail, set with a GAFF and BOOM on the afterside of the MIZZENMAST of a SQUARE-RIGGED SHIP, BRIG, or BARQUE.

spar   The general term for all the poles in a vessel's RIGGING, such as BOWSPRITS, MASTS, YARDS, BOOMS, and GAFFS.

spar deck   Formerly, a temporary DECK anywhere on a ship, or on the QUARTERDECK or FORECASTLE of a deep-WAISTed ship; also a ship's entire UPPER DECK above the MAIN DECK.

Sparmann   A large hairy shrub of the genus *Sparmannia*, native to southern Africa and bearing heart-shaped toothed leaves and white flowers in clusters.

spate   A flood, especially a sudden one caused by a heavy rain or melting snow, or an inundation, such as a heavy downpour of rain.

speaking-trumpet   A metal tube or megaphone used at sea to carry the voice a great distance or to elevate it above loud noises.

speaking-tube   A tube or pipe used for conveying the voice to various parts of a ship.

specie   Coin; coined money.

specific gravity   A measure of density, expressed as the ratio of the density of a substance to the density of another substance used as a standard (usually water for liquids and solids, and air for gases).

speculum   A mirror or polished metal plate forming part of a reflecting telescope.

spencer   In SQUARE-RIGGED SHIPS, a FORE-AND-AFT TRYSAIL set on the after of the FORE- or MAINMASTS. Also, a tight jacket or bodice worn by women and children or an undergarment, usually wool, worn by women for warmth.

spermaceti   White flakes of a waxy solid that separates from sperm oil when it cools after boiling. Sperm oil is found mainly in the head cavity of the sperm whale, and in some other whales and dolphins, and was used in internal medicines for colds and gonorrhea. From the 18th century, used in the manufacture of candles. Spermaceti whale: the sperm whale (*Thyseter catodon*).

speronara   A large rowing and sailing boat, equipped with a LATEEN sail, used in southern Italy and MALTA.

spica bandage   A bandage formed by wrapping successive overlapping strips of bandaging around a finger, limb, or the chest; so called because the overlaps were thought to give the appearance of an ear of wheat (*spica* is Latin for ear of grain).

spike a gun   To render a gun unusable by hammering a spike into the TOUCHHOLE.

spilling-line   A rope sometimes fixed to a ship's MAINSAIL and FORE-SAIL to assist in REEFing and FURLing.

spindle   The upper part of a wooden made MAST.

spindrift   *See* SPOONDRIFT.

spinet   A musical instrument common in England in the 18th century, similar to the harpsichord but smaller and having a single keyboard and only one string for each note.

spirit-lamp   A lamp burning alcohol or another liquid fuel and used especially for heating, boiling, or cooking.

spirits of camphor   Camphor dissolved in alcohol and used as an analgesic and in treatment of some inflammatory diseases.

spirketing   On the side of a ship of war, the range of planks that lies between the waterways, the planking that connects each deck to the side and forms a gutter for drainage, and the lower edge of the gunports.

Spithead   An anchorage in the east SOLENT, the channel between mainland England and the Isle of WIGHT, offering good shelter for ships near PORTSMOUTH. It was the sight of a famous mutiny in 1797 during the War of the French Revolution, when the sailors of the CHANNEL FLEET refused to go to sea until they were promised better pay and conditions. The sailors succeeded without punishment.

Spitsbergen   The main group of islands in the Svalbard Archipelago in the Arctic Ocean frequented from the early 17th century by whalers, sealers, and fur hunters. Used as a base by the Royal Navy's first polar expedition, under Captain C. J. Phipps in 1773.

splanchnic   Of or relating to the abdominal organs.

splinter-netting   On board a warship, a net or netting of small rope spread above the deck prior to an engagement to protect the men from falling SPARS and splinters.

spoil   SLAG or sludge.

sponge   A mop, or SWAB, for cleansing a cannon-bore after firing. A sponger is one who uses a sponge to clean the bore of a cannon.

sponging house   A detention center for debtors, preceding removal to a debtor's prison.

spoom   To run before the sea or wind; to SCUD.

spoonbill   Any of various long-legged wading birds of the widely distributed genus *Platalea*, which have long spoon-shaped bills.

spoondrift   Spray blown from waves by a violent wind and moving along the surface of the sea. Now also known as spindrift.

spotted dog *or* **spotted dick**   A suet pudding containing currants (the spots) and cooked to a firm consistency in a tightly wrapped pudding cloth.

sprigged   Adorned or ornamented with a representation of plant sprigs.

spring   To split or crack a SPAR; to injure by excess strain. A vessel is said "to spring a butt" when a plank is loosened at the end. Also, in MOORing, the spring lines are the ropes from the BOW of a ship aft to a BOLLARD and from the STERN forward to a bollard, one or the other also being useful in disembarking to help maneuver one end of the ship away from the QUAY. Also, a line made fast at one end to the anchor or CABLE and at the other to the ship's QUARTER, so that by HAULing on it the ship can be brought broadside to the anchor.

springbok   A gazelle (*Antdorcas marsupialis*) common in southern Africa that is known for its habit of springing almost directly upward when excited or disturbed.

springstay   Smaller STAYs placed above the mainstays and intended to serve as temporary substitutes if the mainstays are shot away in battle. Also, spare MAST stays kept on ships-of-war to replace any shot away in action.

spritsail   A four-sided FORE-AND-AFT sail carried on a long SPAR that reaches from the foot of a MAST diagonally across the sail to its upper outer corner.

spruce-beer A fermented beverage made with an extract obtained from spruce needles and branches, and molasses or sugar.

sprung Of a ship timber or SPAR, cracked, split, or warped loose. *See also* SPRING.

spunk-box A tinderbox or matchbox.

spunyarn A line of two or more rope-yarns loosely twisted together, used for a variety of purposes on board ship, including for SEIZING and preserving rope.

squadron A division of a fleet forming one body under the command of a FLAG-OFFICER. The British Navy was divided into three squadrons—the red, the blue, and the white—which in turn were subdivided into sections—the van, the middle, and the rear. Also, a detachment of warships on some special duty. *See also* ADMIRAL.

square To set up in harbor TRIM by laying the YARDS at right angles to the KEEL via the BRACES and to the MAST by trimming with the lifts.

square leg In cricket, a fieldsman's position in which he is square with the wicket to be able to stop balls hit to leg, that part of the on side of the field that lies behind, or approximately in line with, the batsman.

square-rigged Said of a vessel with YARDS and sails set across the MASTS, as opposed to a FORE-AND-AFT rigged craft.

squeaker A child.

squib A small firecracker. A damp squib is something that fails to deliver; an anticlimax, a disappointment.

squill The bulb of the sea onion (*Urginea maritima*), native to southern Europe and used chiefly as a diuretic medicine.

squireen A petty squire; a landowner of little property, or a country gentleman, especially in Ireland.

stag-beetle A beetle of the genus *Lucanus,* the males of which have large and often branched mandibles resembling the horns of a stag.

staging Scaffolding.

stanchions   The posts that support the guardrail on the UPPER DECK. Longer versions are used to support an awning in hot weather and sometimes to support a light deck. Also, a rough log used as a pillar in the ship's hold.

stand   Of a vessel, to hold a course for, as in to stand to sea or to stand into harbor.

standish   A stand containing writing materials. An inkstand; also, an inkpot.

starboard   The right-hand side of a vessel when facing the BOW (as opposed to the LARBOARD, or port, side). The starboard side of a ship was traditionally reserved for the Captain, who took his exercise on the starboard side of the POOP DECK or QUARTERDECK. The word "starboard" derives from "steer board," in early ships a paddle used for steering that was located on this side.

starbowlins *or* **starbolins**   The men of the STARBOARD WATCH.

stargazer   In a SQUARE-RIGGED ship, a small sail set above the SKY-SCRAPER to maximize the power gained from a light wind.

start   To ease away. To start a SHEET means to give it some slack. To start an anchor means to make it lose its ground-hold. Also, to flog with a rope's end or cane, a practice used to prod seamen to work harder, which was outlawed by ADMIRALTY order in 1809.

stateroom   A captain's or superior officer's room on board ship.

station, naval   A naval station consisted of at least one safe harbor for naval and merchant operations, with a dockyard and a place for launching military expeditions. The British Empire's naval stations were: Downs, North Sea and Baltic; English Channel and Coast of France; Jersey and Guernsey; Irish; Spain, Portugal, and Gibraltar; Mediterranean; Coast of Africa; Halifax and Newfoundland; West Indies; South America; Cape of Good Hope and Southward; East Indies.

stave   Each of the thin strips of wood that together form the side of a cask, barrel, or similar vessel. A rung. To stave is to break up into staves or pieces, or to puncture and let out the contents. To stave in is to smash, crush inward, break a hole in, as "to stave in a boat." Also, a musical staff or a verse or a stanza, as of a poem.

stay Part of the standing RIGGING. A large strong rope that supports a MAST, either FORE or AFT. Stays that lead forward are called forestays and those that lead down to rear are called backstays. Stays are named according to the mast they support, as in forestay or mainstay. A ship is "in stays" when her BOW is directly turned to windward when TACKing. A ship is said to miss stays when she fails in the attempt to go about from one tack to another.

staysail (*pronounced* "stays'l") A triangular FORE-AND-AFT sail HOISTed upon a STAY and taking its name from the stay, such as the MAIN TOPMAST staysail.

steel A synonym for iron used in medicines, in the form of either iron filings or, more commonly, ferrous sulfate or other inorganic iron salts. Prescribed chiefly to stimulate the circulation but also for other effects.

Steel's Navy List Officially *Steel's Original and Correct List of the Royal Navy*, first published in 1780. By 1800 the publication served as a complete directory of British maritime activities.

steelyard A balance consisting of a lever with unequal arms in which the article to be weighed is suspended from the shorter arm, and a counterweight moves along the calibrated longer arm until equilibrium is produced.

steep-to Said of a shore that drops off almost vertically with virtually no shoaling, allowing a vessel to come directly up to the land in relatively deep water.

steep-tub A large tub in which salt provisions are soaked, or steeped, before being cooked.

steerage-way A vessel is said to have steerage way when she is moving fast enough for her RUDDER to be useful for steering. When the vessel loses steerage-way, she no longer answers her HELM.

steeve The angle of a BOWSPRIT above the horizontal; to incline upward at an angle instead of lying horizontally. Also, to set a bowsprit at an inclination.

steganopod A bird having webbed toes, such as the pelican, cormorant, FRIGATE-BIRD, and GANNET.

steinbock *or* **steinbok** *or* **steenbok** An African antelope (*Raphicerus campestris*). Also, the ibex (*Capra ibex*) of western Europe.

stem   The curved upright BOW timber of a vessel, into which the planks of the bow are joined. From stem to STERN: from one end to the other. To stem the tide is to make headway in sailing against the tide, current, or wind.

stern   The after, or rear, end of a vessel.

Sterna   A genus of seabirds akin to the gull but with a slenderer body, long pointed wings, and a forked tail.

sternboard   A way to turn a ship when there is not enough room to do so in a forward direction. The HELM is reversed and the sails are BACKED so that the BOW moves in the desired direction. Also, the usually undesired result when the sails are taken ABACK as a vessel is TACKing.

stern-chaser   A gun, often a LONG NINE-pounder, mounted at the STERN of a warship and used to impede a chasing vessel, especially by damaging her sails and RIGGING.

sternpost   A more or less upright BEAM, rising from the after end of the KEEL of a vessel and supporting the RUDDER.

sternsheets   The rear of an open boat or small ship and the seats with which the after portion of a boat is furnished. The area is so named because this is where the SHEET of the sail was worked.

sternway   Movement of a ship in the direction of the STERN, to the rear.

stertor   Heavy snoring.

stertorous   Characterized by noisy inspiration or snoring.

stew   A brothel. In plural, a district of brothels.

steward   A seaman who does the catering for the captain or in the officers' MESS.

stile   A set of steps or rungs or some other contrivance that allows a person to get over or through a fence but keeps animals in.

stilt   Any of several wading birds of the widely distributed genus *Himantopus,* having long spindly legs and a thin sharp bill and inhabiting ponds and marshes. The black-necked stilt, *Himantopus mexi-*

canus, is the common North American species. It has black feathers above and white below, and its reddish legs trail well behind its white tail when it is in flight. It nests from Oregon to the WEST INDIES, as well as in Brazil and Peru.

Stilton cheese   A rich, blue-veined semihard cheese made at various places in Leicestershire since 1750, so called from having been sold mostly to travelers at an inn in the town of Stilton.

stingo   Strong beer or ale.

stinkpot   An earthenware jar filled with combustibles that create smoke and an intolerable stench, used in sea combat to create confusion on the deck of an enemy ship, much as tear gas is used today.

stink-pot petrel   A PETREL that is known for its offensive odor. The term is sometimes used by sailors to refer to any petrel.

stirabout   A porridge of Irish origin made by stirring oatmeal or cornmeal into boiling water or milk.

stirrup   In a SQUARE-RIGGED vessel, one of the short ropes hanging from the YARD with an EYE at its end, through which a FOOT-ROPE, or HORSE, passes. The stirrups support the foot-ropes, on which TOPMEN walk when FURLing and unfurling sails.

stiver   A Dutch coin of small value, originally silver. Something of little value. "Not a stiver": nothing.

stoat   The European ermine, especially in its brown summer coat. A treacherous man. A lecher.

stock   A stiff cloth or band worn around the neck by men, now generally only by those in the army.

stock and fluke   The whole thing, the reference being to either end of an anchor, as in "head to toe."

stock-fish   A fish, such as cod, cured by being split open and dried in the air without salt.

Stockholm tar   A tar made from the resin of pine trees and used as a preservative for RIGGINGs and ropes. Stockholm, the capital of Sweden, was a major exporter of tar made in the Baltic.

stocking   A bandage for a horse's leg.

stockjobbing Stockbroking, usually implying rash or dishonest speculation, especially with reference to abuses in England in the early 18th century, such as those that led to the SOUTH SEA STOCK scandal.

stocks The framework supporting a ship or boat during construction. A ship on the stocks is one still being built.

Stoic A member of the school of Greek philosophers founded by Zeno in about 308 B.C. The Stoics believed that one should be free from passions and submit readily to divine will; hence, one who is unaffected by or indifferent to pleasure or pain, one who practices patient endurance.

stomacher A heavily embroidered and often jeweled covering for the chest formerly worn on the front of a bodice, especially by women.

stone A unit of weight commonly used in Britain, especially for people and large animals, and usually equal to 14 pounds AVOIRDUPOIS but varying with different commodities from eight to 24 pounds. In *The Wine Dark Sea* it is stated that Jack Aubrey weighed 16 or 17 stone (224 to 238 pounds) while Stephen Maturin weighed "barely" nine (126 pounds).

stone, cutting for LITHOTOMY, accomplished by cutting through the skin and bladder above the pubic area. Although many therapeutic successes, including those of Dr. Maturin, are recorded, they were probably outnumbered by postoperative deaths caused by infection or by the shock resulting from the pain of the incisions.

stone-dresser One who dresses, or prepares, stones to be used in building.

stone-horse A stallion.

stone-pine Any of various pine trees with edible seeds common in southern Europe and the LEVANT.

stop Of a CABLE, to check it in order to prevent it from running out too fast. Of a sail, to secure it lightly with SPUNYARN so that it can be used quickly. Square sails already hoisted and in stops can be brought into action in an instant.

stop-cleat A wooden wedge attached on its long side to a SPAR to prevent a line from slipping, for example on YARDARMS to secure the RIGGING and the GAMMONING and on MASTS to hold COLLARS.

stopper   A short rope usually secured at one or both ends and used either to suspend something heavy or to temporarily hold a CABLE, SHROUD, or other part of the RIGGING. The anchor hangs at the CATHEAD by a stopper.

stop-water   A softwood plug used between the KEEL and an adjoining timber, such as the STEM, to block seepage through the joint.

storeship   A government ship used to transport stores for the use of the Army or Navy.

storgé   Natural affection, especially of a parent for a child (Greek).

storm petrel   *See* PETREL. Used figuratively, somebody or something that will cause trouble, as this bird was believed to augur a storm.

storm sail *or* **storm canvas**   A smaller-than-normal sail of especially strong, heavy canvas used in a GALE, for example, a storm-STAYSAIL.

storm trysail   A triangular or quadrilateral FORE-AND-AFT sail, loose-footed (set without a BOOM), used alone in foul weather when there is too much wind for the working sails, even REEFED, to be used.

stove   Past particle of STAVE.

stow   To fill the hold of a vessel with cargo; to load a ship. This task requires expert skill and judgment to ensure that the cargo doesn't shift, which could cause the ship to list, and that it doesn't break loose and damage the ship. Certain kinds of cargo also must be isolated to keep them from tainting others. Also, to fit up a ship.

Strachan, Sir Richard John (*1760–1828*)   In 1805, while commanding a SQUADRON in the BAY OF BISCAY after the Battle of TRAFALGAR, Strachan defeated and captured four French ships (including the third-rate *Scipion*) that had escaped from the British fleet. For this action, he received a hero's welcome in England and a promotion to Rear-Admiral.

strait-waistcoat   A straitjacket.

strake   Each of the continuous lines of planks running from STEM to STERN in the side of a vessel, from the KEEL up to the top of the hull. The breadth of a plank used as a vertical measure: a ship HEELS a strake when a whole plank's breadth rises above the water on one side and falls below on the other.

strand   One of the parts of a rope. Also, the land bordering a body of water, the coast or shore; the part of a shore between the tidemarks. To strand means to run aground or be driven ashore.

strangury   The slow and painful emission of urine, caused most often by bladder stones or an enlarged prostate.

strangulated hernia   A hernia so constricted that blood flow to the segment extruded into the scrotum is cut off.

strap-bound, *or* **strap-bored, block**   A single BLOCK entirely enclosed except for holes left on each side for the rope to pass through. Used with sails to prevent fouling.

Strasburg pie   A pie or pâté made from fatted goose liver.

stray line   The roughly ten or 12 FATHOMs of unmarked LOG-LINE between the LOG-SHIP and the first MARK, allowing the log-ship to get beyond the eddy of the ship's wake before the GLASS was turned and the measuring began.

streak *or* **touch, of the tar-brush**   Said in derision of a person of mixed white and black (or Indian, etc.) origin.

stream (*or*** stern) anchor**   A light anchor stored in the STERN and used with a BOWER anchor when MOOREd in narrow waterways where there is no room for the ship to swing freely with the tide.

stretcher   A piece of wood across the bottom of a boat against which the rowers brace their feet. A short piece of wood used to spread a hammock.

stridulation   A shrill creaking noise, especially that made by certain insects, such as the cricket or grasshopper.

stroke-oar   The oarsman sitting nearest the STERN of the boat, whose stroke sets the time for the other rowers.

Stromboli   An Italian island off the northeastern coast of Sicily and an active volcano located there. Also, the stage of a volcanic eruption in which repeated explosions of moderate force are accompanied by the ejection of gases and bombs of lava. *See* illustration, following page.

strong fives   No such diagnosis was used in regular 18th-century medical practice. O'Brian found the term, along with MARTHAMBLES, in a pamphlet published by a London quack to promote his panacea.

A polacca with a view of the small volcanic island Stromboli (*from Serres's Liber Nauticus*)

strop   A ring or band of wire or rope used for a variety of purposes on board ship, including surrounding the shell of a BLOCK to form an EYE at the bottom, forming a sling for lifting heavy articles, and doubling around a rope or HAWSER to make an eye into which a TACKLE can be hooked for greater advantage. Also, to furnish (a block) with a strop.

studdingsail *or* **stunsail** (*pronounced* "stuns'l")   An extra sail set outside the square sails of a ship during a fair wind.

stuff   A fabric used for clothing, especially a woolen fabric.

stuffing-box   An enclosure packed with fluid-tight elastic material to prevent leakage around a moving machine part.

stuiver   *See* STIVER.

stump   The lower portion of a MAST when the upper part has been broken off or shot away. In cricket, each of the three (formerly two) upright sticks that form the base of a wicket.

stunsail   *See* STUDDINGSAIL.

stupor mundi   The marvel of the world; an object of awe and wonder. The phrase was originally used by the 13th-century English monastic historian Matthew Paris to describe Frederick II, king of Sicily (1197–1250) and later Holy Roman Emperor (1220–1250).

styptic   An astringent applied topically to stop bleeding, usually after shaving.

suave mare magno   The full quotation from Lucretius is: *Suave, mari magno turbantibus aequora ventis, e terra magnum alterius spectare laborem.* It is pleasant to watch from the land the mighty struggle of another in a sea made great by turbulent winds (Latin).

subaltern *or* **subaltern officer**   An Army officer of junior rank, just below that of Captain.

subclavian   Located beneath the clavicle. Subclavian artery: the principal artery of the root of the neck, being the main trunk of the arterial system of the upper extremity. Subclavian vein: the continuation of the axillary vein from the first rib until it joins the internal jugular vein.

sub Deo   By God (Latin).

subfusc   Of drab or somber hue.

Sublime Porte   The Ottoman court at Constantinople; the Turkish government.

subsultus tendinum   Twitching of tendons, often noticeable at the wrist during low-grade fevers.

subtend   In geometry, to be opposite to and to extend under, especially used for a line or side of a figure opposite an angle, or for a chord or angle opposite an arc.

subvention   Assistance or financial support.

sudation   Sweating, perspiration.

sudor insignis   Remarkable sweating (Latin).

suet   The hard fat around the loins and kidneys of cattle and sheep, which is used in cooking, and, when rendered, makes tallow.

suet pudding   A boiled or steamed pudding made from flour, eggs, sugar, bread crumbs, milk, and SUET.

Suez, Gulf of   The northwest arm of the RED SEA between the Sinai Peninsula and Egypt. At the north end of the gulf was the city of Suez, an ancient port and Ottoman naval base that declined after the Suez Canal was built (1859–1869). Napoleon had seen the possibility of building a canal through the narrow isthmus but abandoned the idea when he was defeated at the Battle of the NILE in 1798.

Suffren de Saint Tropez, Pierre André de (*1729–1788*)   One of France's greatest admirals, he served with Admiral Jean-Baptiste d'Estaing in American waters during the American Revolution and fought in five actions against the British fleet under Sir Edward Hughes in the EAST INDIES from 1782 to 1783 without ever losing a ship.

suite   A train of followers or attendants; a retinue.

sulphureous ether   Ether, taken internally as a general remedy or applied externally to stimulate the circulation locally. It was not used as a general anesthetic until 1846.

summat   Somewhat or something.

summum bonum   The highest good (Latin); in an ethical system, the determining principle.

Sunda Strait   A strait, 16 miles wide at its narrowest point, separating the islands of Sumatra and Java in the Dutch East Indies (present-day Indonesia). It links the Indian Ocean and the Java Sea.

sun-dog   A mock sun, parhelion. Also, a small rainbow or fragment of one.

sup   A small quantity of liquid; a mouthful, a sip.

***Superb*, H.M.S.**   A ship name that saw much use in the Royal Navy during the 17th and early 18th centuries. The first ship by this name was a 60-gun French PRIZE taken in 1710 that later participated in the victory over the Spanish fleet off Cape Passaro in 1718, among other actions. The third *Superb*, a third rate of 74 guns, was launched in 1760 and served as the FLAGSHIP at PORTSMOUTH from 1763 to 1770. In 1782 she served well as Sir Edward Hughes's flagship in the EAST INDIES. The fifth ship of the name, also a 74-gun third rate, was built in 1798 and fought at Algeciras in 1801, San Domingo in 1806, and

COPENHAGEN in 1807. She served as Rear-Admiral R. G. Keats's flagship until 1810 and saw action at the bombardment of ALGIERS in 1816. She was broken up in 1821.

supercargo Short for a cargo superintendent, the representative of the owner on board a merchant ship who oversees the cargo and the commercial transactions of the voyage. Also, formerly, an agent in charge of a merchant's business in a foreign country.

supererogation The doing of good works beyond what God commands or requires, held to constitute a surplus of merit that the Church could dispense to others to make up for their lack of it. Doing more than is required by duty, obligation, or expectation.

superfetation A second conception occurring when a fetus is already present in the uterus. Superabundant production or accumulation; an additional product, an accretion, a superfluous addition.

supernumerary A sailor (or LANDSMAN) in excess of a ship's complement.

superstructure The part of the ship above the UPPER DECK.

suppressio veri Misrepresentation of the truth by concealing essential facts. (Latin)

suppurate To form or secrete pus; to bring to a head.

surcingle A belt or girth passing around the body of a horse to bind a saddle to the horse's back.

surd In mathematics, an irrational number, one not expressible by an ordinary finite fraction.

surge To let go or stop pulling, as with a rope being wound around a CAPSTAN.

Surgeon-Major A seldom-used rank for a Surgeon high in the military chain of command.

Surinam toad A large flat toad, the pipa, in which the male fertilizes the eggs on the back of the female, and her skin forms cellules in which the eggs are hatched and in which the young pass their tadpole state. Surinam, formerly called Dutch Guiana, is a country in South America.

surplice   A loose-fitting white vestment with wide, flowing sleeves worn, usually over a cassock, by clergy, choir members, and others participating in church services.

Surprise, **H.M.S.**   This sixth-rate, 24-gun warship, originally the French *Unité*, was captured in the Mediterranean on April 20, 1796, by H.M.S. *Inconstant* and her name changed to H.M.S. *Surprise*. The *Surprise* was involved in a famous incident at Puerto Cabello, Venezuela, in 1799, when her Captain, Edward Hamilton, recaptured the former British ship *Hermione*. The Spanish counted over 200 men killed and wounded, while the British had only 10 wounded. (*See* HERMIONE for an account of the battle.) Hamilton received a knighthood for the exploit, and the *Hermione* was restored to the British Navy. The *Surprise* was sold by the Royal Navy in 1802, making it readily available for service in Patrick O'Brian's naval tales.

swab   A mop made of old rope used for cleaning and drying the deck of a ship. In slang usage, a disagreeable, clumsy person. Also, a slang expression for the epaulet of a naval officer.

swag-bellied   Having a sagging paunch.

swain   A country youth, especially a shepherd. A lover, wooer, sweetheart, especially in pastoral poetry.

sward   Ground covered with grass or other herbage; lawn.

sway up   To HOIST or raise up (especially a YARD or TOPMAST).

sweep   A long, heavy oar used to propel small sailing vessels and to steer barges. To row with sweeps.

sweet biscuit   A cookie.

sweetening-cock   *See* SEA-COCK.

sweetmeat   A dessert or other food that contains a lot of sugar, as candy or candied fruits.

sweet oil   An oil that has a pleasant or mild taste; olive oil.

swift   Any of numerous small, dark birds resembling the swallow but related to the hummingbird and noted for their swiftness of flight. To "swift the shrouds" means to make use of SWIFTERS.

swifter A rope securing the ends of the CAPSTAN bars; a rope snaked back and forth between the lower SHROUDS to temporarily tighten up the RIGGING; also the foremost or aftermost (authorities are divided on which) lower shroud. The word derives from the Dutch verb *zwichten*, or *schwichten*, meaning "to tighten up."

Swiftsure, **H.M.S.** A third-rate ship of 74 guns that was launched at BUCKLER'S HARD, the shipbuilding port in Hampshire, in 1804. She fought at TRAFALGAR in 1805 under Captain William Rutherford and was sold in 1845.

swing clear To ride at anchor without colliding with anything.

swingeing Great or superb; large, immense.

swing out To move something over the ship's side horizontally before lowering, said of an anchor or a boat.

swing the lead To idle, shirk, or malinger (slang).

swipes Poor, weak, or spoiled beer. Also, beer in general.

swivel-gun *or* **swivel** A gun or cannon, usually a small one, mounted on a swivel so that it can be aimed in any direction.

Sybille, **H.M.S.** A 44-gun fifth-RATE PRIZE taken from the French in 1794.

syce A stableman or groom, especially in India and also in parts of Africa and Asia; also, a mounted attendant to a horseman or carriage.

syllabub A drink, or dessert if gelatin is added, made of sweetened milk or cream mixed with wine or liquor.

syncope Fainting. Sometimes fatal if caused by a stroke.

tabby Silk taffeta, originally striped, later of uniform color with a moiré finish.

tabes Wasting of a muscle mass, most commonly applied to the final stage of syphilis when the legs become paralyzed due to progressive loss of their nerves.

table d'hôte In French, "host's table": a communal table for guests at a hotel or restaurant; a public meal served at a stated hour and at a fixed price.

tabling A broad hem at the edge of a sail to reinforce it.

tabor Small drum used to accompany a pipe or trumpet.

Tace is the Latin for a candle *Tace* actually means "be silent" in Latin, while a candle is a symbol of light. The meaning of this paradoxical phrase is "keep it in the dark" or "mum's the word."

tack The lower forward corner of a FORE-AND-AFT sail. On square sails, the lower WEATHER, or windward, corner of the sail and the rope holding down the weather corner of the sail. The course of a ship in relation to the direction of the wind and the position of her sails, as in

"STARBOARD tack," meaning with the wind coming across the starboard side. Also, to alter the course of a ship by turning her with her head to the wind and bringing the wind onto the other side of the ship. To BEAT to windward, or to work or navigate a ship against the wind by a series of tacks.

tackle *Pronounced* "taykle": An arrangement consisting of one or more ropes and pulley-BLOCKs, used to increase the power exerted on a rope in raising or lowering heavy objects, such as guns, cargo, and SPARS, and in TRIMMing sails. *Pronounced* "tackle": The RIGGING of a ship, equipment, gear. Ground tackle comprises anchors, CABLES, and other equipment used to anchor or to moor a vessel.

tackle-fall The entire length of rope in a TACKLE. The end of the rope secured to the BLOCK is called the standing part, the opposite end is the HAULing part.

tack-room A room used for storing horse equipment.

taffrail The upper portion of the after-rail at a ship's STERN, often ornately carved.

tag A brief and usually familiar quotation added for substance or special effect. A cliché, proverb, or other short, conventional idea used to embellish discourse.

tallboy A highboy, or tall chest of drawers usually raised on legs and in two parts, with the upper section smaller than the lower. Also, a chest of drawers on top of a dressing-table.

Talleyrand-Perigord, Charles Maurice de, Prince de Bénévent (1754–1838) French statesman who served as minister of foreign affairs from 1797 to 1807. Quarreled with Napoleon and opposed his Russian and Spanish policy. Helped restore Bourbons after Napoleon's fall.

tally on *or* **tail on** To HAUL taut the SHEETs. Also, to catch hold of, or "clap" on to, a rope.

tamarisk A shrub or small tree of the genus *Tamarix*, native to Europe and Asia, with slender feathery branches, scalelike leaves, and clusters of pink flowers.

tangalung The civet of Sumatra and Java, *Viverra tangalunga*.

Tangiers An ancient seaport on the north coast of Morocco, strategically situated on the Atlantic at the western end of the Straits of GIBRALTAR. In 1661 it was part of the dowry of the Portuguese princess Catherine of Bragança when she married King Charles II of England. It was an English possession until 1684 and became a stronghold of the BARBARY pirates during the 18th century.

Tantalus In Greek mythology, a king who revealed the secrets of the gods and was condemned to Hades, where he was made to stand in water that receded as he stooped to drink and below branches of fruit that evaded his grasp.

Tantum religio potuit saudere malorum Religion can produce such evil (Latin; Lucretius, *On the Nature of the Universe* I).

tap A taproom, or bar.

tapir Any of several chiefly nocturnal ungulate mammals of tropical America or southern Asia of the genus *Tapirus*, related to the rhinoceros and the horse and having a heavy body, short legs, and a short flexible proboscis. Originally referred specifically to the species *Tapirus americanus* of Brazil.

Tapirus americanus *See* TAPIR.

tar A substance made from the resin of pine trees and used to preserve hemp rope, which otherwise would rot when wet, and to preserve a ship's RIGGING; also, a nickname for a sailor from the fact that sailors' canvas coats and hats were tarred against precipitation. An essential for maintaining ships, tar of the best quality came from Sweden, but its high cost drove suppliers to America, where the pine forests of North Carolina became an important source. *See also* STOCK-HOLM TAR.

tarantass A four-wheeled Russian carriage with a flexible wooden chassis and no springs.

Taranto A city, a port, and a bay of the Ionian Sea, inside the arch of the "boot" along the coast of the Kingdom of Naples, what is now southeastern Italy.

tar-bark Bark of various species of pine, juniper, etc., from which tar is obtained by destructive distillation for topical application to various scaly skin conditions.

tar-box   A box formerly used by shepherds to hold tar, which they used as a salve for sheep.

tardigrade   Any of various minute arthropods of the class Tardigrada having four pairs of legs and living in water or damp moss; also called water-bears or bear-animalcules.

tarpaulin   A sheet of canvas made waterproof by a coat of TAR and used to cover and protect things from wetness. Also, other types of waterproof cloth. A sailor's hat made of tarpaulin. Also a nickname for a sailor.

tarsier   Any of several small forest-dwelling nocturnal mammals found in the MALAY Archipelago, related to the LEMUR and having large, round eyes and a long tail.

tartan *or* **tartana**   A small single-masted vessel, varying in size, with a large LATEEN sail and a FORESAIL, used in the western mediterranean for trading and fishing. *See* illustration, facing page.

Tartar   A member of the Mongolian peoples who in the 13th century under Genghis Khan invaded much of central and western Asia and eastern Europe; a descendant of these people, now living in the region of Central Asia extending eastward from the Caspian Sea. Also, an irritable or violent person. To "catch a Tartar" is to grapple with an opponent who proves to be unexpectedly formidable.

Tartini, Giuseppe (*1692–1770*)   An Italian violinist and composer, Tartini composed some 150 violin concertos and more than 200 sonatas and other instrumental works.

tar-water   An infusion of tar in cold water, invented around 1740 by George Berkeley, Bishop of Cloyne, for medical use as a stimulating tonic. Maturin is the author of a highly regarded work called *Tar-Water Reconsidered.*

Tasmanian devil   A burrowing carnivorous marsupial of Tasmania, Australia, about the size of a badger and with a predominantly black coat and a long, nearly hairless tail.

tat   To make a delicate lace, called tatting, by looping and knotting a single cotton thread using a small, flat, spindle-shaped instrument.

Tattersall's   The famous London horse market founded by Richard Tattersall in the late 18th century.

A tartan near Europa Point, Gibraltar (*from Serres's* Liber Nauticus)

tatty   Shabby, worn, frayed.

Tavel   A municipality on the Rhône River in Languedoc, a province of southern France; the highly regarded rosé wine produced there.

tax-cart   An open two-wheeled, one-horse cart, used chiefly for agricultural or trade purposes, on which was levied a reduced duty (later taken off entirely).

Taylor's sermons   Refers to the preaching of the Protestant theologian and Yale professor Nathaniel William Taylor (1786–1858). Born in New Milford, Connecticut, Taylor was known for his temperance preaching and developed a controversial system of theology involving freedom of will.

teal   Any of several small freshwater ducks of the genus *Anas,* widely distributed in Europe, America, and Asia.

tea-wagon   An EAST INDIAMAN used to transport tea.

Te Deum   A Latin hymn that begins *Te deum laudamus* ("We praise you, oh God"), sung on special occasions in thanksgiving, or sung or recited at Roman Catholic matins or, in translation, at Anglican matins. Also, any thanksgiving.

teg   A sheep in its second year, or from the time it is weaned until its first shearing; a yearling sheep.

telegraph   The first chain of telegraphs was employed during the 1790s, linking the Louvre in Paris and Lisle (about 110 miles away), where the French Army was encamped. The plan and alphabet of the machine quickly traveled via Frankfort to England, where it was improved and installed between the ADMIRALTY and the coast in 1795. Each telegraph unit originally consisted of six octagonal boards, rotating on an axis and able to be placed either horizontally or vertically, so as to be visible or not to the next station in the chain. Different combinations indicated different letters of the alphabet or numbers. A succession of improvements altered the telegraph, which was effective in greatly speeding up the flow of information, despite the fact that it could not function in bad weather. In 1806 the Admiralty extended lines to PORTSMOUTH, Chatham, and Deal, and, branching off the Portsmouth line at Beacon Hill, to PLYMOUTH. In 1808 Yarmouth was linked to the system.

tell-tale compass   A compass that is suspended overhead in the captain's cabin facing down so that it is visible from below, enabling the captain to detect any error or irregularity in steering.

Templar   A member of the Knights Templar, a military and religious order consisting of knights, chaplains, and men-at-arms, founded in the early 12th century in Jerusalem chiefly for the protection of the Holy Sepulcher and of Christian pilgrims visiting the Holy Land. So called because they built on or contiguous to the site of the Temple of Solomon at Jerusalem.

tenaculum   A fine sharp-pointed hook used especially to lift and hold arteries or other parts of the body during surgery.

tender   A vessel that attends a MAN-OF-WAR, primarily in harbor, supplying the ship with provisions and munitions and carrying mail and dispatches. A press tender was a small vessel commanded by a LIEUTENANT that was used to round up volunteers and IMPRESSed men and deposit them in RECEIVING SHIPs in home ports, from where they were assigned to naval ships.

tendre   A tender feeling, fondness (French).

tenesmus   A continual but ineffectual urge to void the contents of the bowels or bladder, accompanied by straining.

teniente   Spanish for "lieutenant."

tenuity   Lack of substance or strength; slenderness.

teratoma   A usually benign tumor of the gonads caused by disturbances in the development of germ cells.

teredo   A shipworm, or any of various elongated marine clams that resemble worms and damage the submerged timbers of ships, piers, and sea-dikes by boring into the wood. The shipworm was at first thought to be a worm and was recognized as a mollusk only in 1733. Beginning in 1779, the principal means of combatting it was to copper-sheath the underwater body of a ship.

tergiversation   Turning one's back on or forsaking a cause, party, or faith. Evasion of straightforward action or statement, equivocation.

termagant   An imaginary Muslim deity represented in medieval mystery plays as a boisterous and abusive character. An overbearing or quarrelsome person, especially a woman; a shrew.

tern   Any of various seabirds of the genus *Sterna* or subfamily Sternin, related to the gull but more slender, with long pointed wings and a forked tail; a sea swallow.

terraqueous   Composed of land and water.

tertian   A form of malarial fever that recurs every 48 hours. *Compare* QUARTAN.

tertiary   A monastic third order, especially of lay members not subject to the strict rules of the regulars, originated by St. Francis of Assisi and an established institution among the Franciscans, Dominicans, and others.

tes moeurs crapuleuses ... tu cherches à corrompre mon paresseux ... va donc, eh, salope ... espèce de fripouille Your depraved behavior ... you're trying to corrupt my sloth ... go on, you trollop ... you damn scoundrel! (French).

tesoro Italian for "treasure."

tessera A small piece of marble, glass, tile, or other material used to make a mosaic. Usually used in plural form (tesserae).

Testudo The typical genus of the tortoise family, Testudinidae, or a member of this genus.

tetanic Of, pertaining to, characterized by, or producing tetanus, an acute infectious disease characterized by rigidity and spasms of the voluntary muscles. *See also* OPISTHOTONOS.

Texel One of the small West Frisian Islands in the North Sea off the coast of the Netherlands, site of an important Dutch naval anchorage and blockaded by the British. The sea-fight between the British, under Admiral Duncan, and the Dutch, under Admiral de Winter, known as the Battle of CAMPERDOWN took place near Texel in 1797. Admiral Duncan succeeded in capturing the Dutch commander-in-chief, nine SHIPS OF THE LINE, and two FRIGATES.

thatcher One who thatches, especially one who thatches houses, hay ricks, and the like as a profession.

thaumaturge *or* **thaumaturgist** A performer of miracles, a magician.

thebaic Of or derived from OPIUM. The name refers to Thebes, an ancient Egyptian city, because Egypt was the source of the best opium. Thebaic tincture: LAUDANUM.

Theseus, **H.M.S.** A 74-gun third rate, built in 1786, in which NELSON attacked Santa Cruz, Tenerife, in 1797, and in which his wounded right arm was amputated following the battle. At the Battle of the NILE in 1798, the ship was commanded by Captain Ralph Willett Miller. She was broken up at Chatham in 1814.

thick and dry An order given when WEIGHing anchor for fresh and dry NIPPERS. When the nippers would start to slip, failing to hold to a slimy wet CABLE, sand and ashes were thrown on the cable and "fresh nippers, thick and dry," replaced those in use.

thick-knee Any bird of the genus *Oedicnemus*, especially the stone curlew and the Norfolk, or great, plover. So called from the enlargement of the tibio-tarsal joint.

thick-kneed bustard The stone curlew (*Oedicnemus crepitans*).

thief-taker One who detects and captures a thief, especially one of a company specializing in the detection and arrest of thieves.

thieves' cat A CAT-O'-NINE-TAILS with three knots on each of its tails used for the punishment of theft.

thimble A round or heart-shaped metal ring with a concave outer face around which a rope is spliced, forming an EYE. When spliced into the BOLTROPE of a sail, it makes a CRINGLE. A dog bitch (or dog-and-bitch) thimble is a special pair of thimbles used to prevent a CLEW from developing a half twist, as often happened because of the angle at which a sheet block was placed.

Thirty-Nine Articles The 39 statements or Articles of Religion that define the worship of the Church of England and to which those who take orders in the Church of England subscribe. Originally written in 1571, they were revised in 1662 following the restoration of Charles II to the throne. Similar to the Articles of Religion of the Episcopal Church in the United States, written in 1801.

thole-pin *or* **thole** A wooden peg used as a fastening. One of a pair of pegs set in the GUNWALE of a boat to hold an oar in place and to serve as the fulcrum of its action.

thoracic cage The bones (ribs, sternum, and spine) that make up the thorax.

thorough-paced Thoroughly trained or accomplished; thoroughgoing, complete.

Thousand Islands A group of about 100 small islands that make up part of Indonesia in the southwest Java Sea.

Thrale, Mrs. Henry (*1741–1821*) Born Hester Lynch Salusbury, she was a friend and benefactor of Samuel JOHNSON, the essayist and pioneering lexicographer. Johnson befriended the Thrale family, spent much time at their residence, Streatham Park, and traveled abroad with them. Hester Thrale was the mother of Queeney Thrale (*see* KEITH, LADY), who married Admiral Lord Keith (*see* ELPHINSTONE). After Mr. Thrale's death in 1776, Johnson felt slighted when the widowed Mrs. Thrale became attached to the Italian musician Gabriel Piozzi, whom she married in 1784. Mrs. Thrale wrote several books, including *Anecdotes of the late Samuel Johnson, LL.D., during the last Twenty Years of His Life* (1786), which James Boswell complained was frequently erroneous and unjustly harsh.

three sheets in the wind   Very drunk, deriving from the fact that a ship with her SHEETs in the wind, or loose, is an unsteady, rolling vessel.

threshing   Beating with or as with a flail or whip.

thrum-mat   A piece of canvas or other heavy material into which THRUMS are inserted and which can be wrapped around RIGGING to prevent chafing.

thrums   Short pieces of coarse yarn, used in mops and in THRUM-MATs. To thrum is to insert yarn pieces in a mat.

thrush   An oral infection, chiefly of infants, characterized by white patches in the mouth and caused by a fungus (*Candida albicans*). In the 18th century, any of various throat infections.

Thucydides (*c. 460–395 B.C.*)   A Greek historian who wrote *History of the Peloponnesian War*.

Thule   The most northerly region of the ancient habitable world, conceived by ancient geographers to be a six days' sail north of Britain and variously conjectured to be the present-day Shetland Islands, Iceland, the northern point of Denmark, or some point on the coast of Norway. *See also* ULTIMA THULE.

***Thunderer*, H.M.S.**   A third rate of 74 guns built on the Thames in 1783, she fought in 1794 at the GLORIOUS FIRST OF JUNE and in 1805 at TRAFALGAR with Lieutenant John Stockham as acting Captain. Later, in 1807 she was with Sir John Duckworth in the passage of the DARDANELLES. She was broken up in 1814.

thunder-stroke/thunder-stone   Though Shakespeare does use both terms in his plays, he wrote in *Cymbeline* (a work famously dismissed by

Dr. JOHNSON), "th' all-dreaded thunder-stone," not "thunder-stroke," as Amos Jacob rightly corrects Maturin in *The Hundred Days* (p. 151).

thwart A seat extending across a boat, on which the rower sits.

tib-cat A female cat.

ticket A payment warrant, especially a discharge warrant in which the amount of pay due to a soldier or sailor is written.

ticket-porter A member of a body of porters who were licensed, or ticketed, by the City of London to unpack, load, and transport goods being shipped through the port of London or public markets of the city. Originally called street-porters.

tide-rip A rough patch of sea caused by opposing currents or by a rapid current passing over an uneven bottom.

tie A rope by which a YARD is suspended and the BLOCK on the yard through which the tie passes. A knot of hair; a pigtail. Also, short for TIE-WIG.

tier A coil. A row or layer. Also, a large rack for stowing CABLES, HAWSERS for the KEDGE, anchor gear, RUNNERS, and TACKLES.

tierce A former measure of victuals in casks, equaling 280 pounds of salt beef or 260 pounds of pork until the early 19th century, when casks were made larger and the sizes were raised to 336 pounds and 300 pounds, respectively. As a measure of liquid capacity, equal to a third of a pipe (usually 42 gallons, but varying for different substances). A cask or vessel holding this quantity, usually of wine. Also, in fencing, the third of the eight parries in swordplay or the corresponding thrust.

tierer A sailor who stows the CABLE in the TIER.

tie-wig A wig with the hair gathered in back and tied with a ribbon.

tiger-shark A large gray or brown man-eating shark common in warm seas around the world.

tilbury A light, open two-wheeled carriage, fashionable in the early 19th century.

till A small box, compartment, or drawer in a cabinet or chest of drawers used for storing valuables. A money-box in a store or bank.

tiller   A horizontal wooden bar attached to the head of the RUDDER and working as a lever in moving the rudder during steering.

tiller-rope   A rope leading from the TILLER-head to the wheel and used to steer a ship.

time-bargain   A contract for the purchase or sale of goods or stock at a stated price on a certain day. A stock-market transaction in which the profit or loss is determined by the difference between the prices of the stock on the day the deal is made and on the day it is executed.

timenoguy (*pronounced* "timonoggy")   A rope fastened at one end to the fore-SHROUDS and at the other end to the anchor-stock on the bow to prevent the fore-SHEET from entangling any projection. More generally, a taut rope running between different parts of a vessel to prevent the sheet or TACK of a COURSE from fouling.

timoneer   A helmsman or steersman.

tinamou   Any of various South or Central American game birds of the family Tinamidae that resemble the partridge or quail.

tincture   A solution, usually in alcohol, of a medicinal substance, such as tincture of OPIUM (called LAUDANUM).

tinker   A usually itinerant mender of pots, kettles, and other metal household utensils. The low reputation of tinkers is manifested in such expressions as "to swear like a tinker," "a tinker's curse," and "as drunk/quarrelsome as a tinker."

tint   A taste, a touch, a trace.

tip the go-by to   To leave behind. Also, to give the slip to, elude; to dupe.

tippet   A long narrow slip of cloth attached to a hood, head-dress, or sleeve or worn loose, as a scarf. A cape or short cloak, usually of fur or wool, often with hanging ends; a long black stole worn by Anglican clergymen.

Tippoo (or Tipu) Sahib (1749–1799)   Sultan of Mysore. After his father, Hyder Ali, usurped the throne of Mysore, a region of southern India, in 1761, Tippoo and his father clung to the area, fighting the British and their allies in the Mysore wars. Known as the Tiger of the

Mysore, Tippoo, whose men often dressed in tiger-striped garments, was a fierce and clever warrior but vain and cruel. In 1798, when Napoleon invaded Egypt, he reneged on a humiliating peace treaty he had signed six years earlier and went to war against his neighbors. Tippoo was killed by the British when they stormed the city of Seringapatam, his power center, in 1799.

tipstaff   An officer who carries a staff, as a sheriff's officer, bailiff, or constable.

Tir nan Og   In Irish mythology, a land of eternal youth, an Irish version of Elysium.

titivate   To make small improvements to one's appearance; to smarten or spruce up; to put the finishing touches to.

titmouse   Any of numerous small birds of the family Paridae, common in the northern hemisphere and related to the nuthatch but with longer tails.

tizzy   A sixpenny piece.

toby   The highway as the resort of robbers; also, highway robbery. The high toby was highway robbery by a mounted thief; also, the highway itself. The low toby was robbery by FOOTPADS.

toddy   The sap of various species of palm, especially the wild date, the coconut, and the palmyra, used as a beverage in tropical countries. Also, the liquor produced by its fermentation.

toddy palm   Any palm that yields TODDY.

tog   To clothe, to dress, especially in fine clothing; usually used with "up" or "out."

toggle   A short pin of wood used to connect two ropes so that they can be disconnected quickly. In naval ships, the toggle was particularly useful in the TOPSAIL SHEETS and JEERS to secure the YARDS aloft in case the ropes were shot away.

Tokay   A rich, naturally sweet wine with an aromatic flavor, made near Tokaj, Hungary.

tola   A West African tree (*Gossweilerodendron balsamiferum*).

Toledo A city in Castile, Spain, long famous for its manufacture of finely tempered sword blades.

Tom Cox's traverse The act of an artful dodger, all talk and no work, as in a sailor who goes "up one hatchway and down another" or takes "three turns round the LONG-BOAT and a pull at the SCUTTLE."

tompion (*commonly pronounced "tompkin"*) A disk of wood fit into the bore of a muzzle-loading gun and rammed home as a wad between the charge and the missile. The bottom plate of GRAPE-shot, which serves as a wad to the charge. Also, a block of wood fitting into the muzzle of a gun to keep out rain, seawater, and debris.

Tom Tiddler's ground A children's game in which one of the players is Tom Tiddler, whose territory is marked by a line drawn on the ground, and the other players cross the line, yelling "We're on Tom Tiddler's ground, picking up gold and silver," and try to avoid being caught by Tom Tiddler and having to take his place. Also, a place where money or another form of compensation is acquired readily. A disputed territory, a no-man's-land between two states.

tongs A curling-iron.

top A platform at the head of each of the lower MASTs of a ship, serving to extend the TOPMAST SHROUDs, which help support the topmast. In early fighting ships, the platform, called the topcastle, was fenced with a rail, stocked with missiles, and used by archers during battle. Later, sharpshooters were stationed there.

top-block A large BLOCK suspended below the CAP of the lower MAST, used to HOIST or lower TOPMASTs.

top-chain A chain used to support the YARDs prior to an action to keep them from falling in case the rope SLINGs by which they were hung were shot away.

tope To drink, especially to drink liquor excessively and habitually; to drink large amounts.

topgallant The mast above the TOPMAST, also sometimes the YARD and sail set on it. Topgallant ROYAL was the early name for the royal, the fourth sail above the deck.

topgallant sail The sail above the TOPSAIL and TOPGALLANT, usually the third sail above the deck.

top-hamper Weight and encumbrance aloft, originally referring to a ship's upper MASTS, sails, and RIGGING. Later, also, the burden above the hull.

topi-wallah From the Hindi *topiwala*, "one who wears a hat," the Indian name for a European.

top-lantern A large lantern used on the after-part of a TOP for signaling.

topmast The second MAST above the deck, fixed to the top of a lower mast and surmounted by the TOPGALLANT mast.

top-maul A large hammer used to knock out the TOPMAST FID when striking a topmast and to beat down the EYES of the RIGGING on the mast, when rigging the SHROUDS.

topmen *or* **yardmen** A ship's most agile and best LOWER DECK seamen stationed in one of the tops to work the upper sails. Also, the sharpshooters stationed in the tops during action.

top off To fill up.

top one's boom To start off.

top-rope A rope used to set or lower the TOPMAST.

topsail A sail set above the COURSE, second above the deck, at one time the uppermost sail in a SQUARE-RIGGED vessel. In a FORE-AND-AFT-RIG, a sail set above the MAINSAIL.

topside The upper deck of a ship. In shipbuilding, the upper part of a ship's sides.

torero In Spanish bullfighting, a matador or a member of his team.

tormina Acute wringing and spasmodic pain in the intestines.

torpedo fish The electric ray, a round-bodied, short-tailed fish of the family Torpedinidae, which has a pair of organs that produce a strong electric discharge. Also called cramp-fish, cramp-ray, numb-fish.

torrid zone The region lying between the TROPIC OF CANCER and the TROPIC OF CAPRICORN.

Tory The name of a party in English politics. At the beginning of the 18th century, the name clearly defined a political viewpoint, but by the middle of the century this definition had disappeared, even though the names "Tory" and "Whig" persisted. By 1760, when GEORGE III came to the throne, politics turned on the King's right and practice of choosing his own ministers. In this, there were no parties but only political factions composed of those currently in office, those currently out of office, and independents.

In the declining years of George III's reign, these factions had begun to coalesce into true political parties again, with members who slowly were beginning to share political beliefs. When this occurred, the party names began again to have some meaning. But the differences were not as clearly definable as they had been earlier or would become later, and there was often no clear-cut distinction between parties. When serious political issues arose, groups tended to split into factions. Less than half the members of Parliament could be identified as party members.

A clear distinction between parties began to take shape over the French Revolutionary War. The younger William PITT and his supporters advocated intervention in the war, believing that the revolutionary dictatorship in Paris threatened every other state in Europe.

During the period of the Aubrey-Maturin novels, Tories were generally those who upheld the rights and privileges of the established Church of England and the rights of the King to choose his own ministers, to veto legislation, to dissolve Parliament at his will, and to have an effective voice in government policy.

Although he never labeled himself as such, William Pitt the younger and his followers were Tories. After his death in 1806, the Tories, or "the friends of Mr. Pitt," as they were called, divided for lack of a generally accepted leader into six political subgroups, related in their views but separately led by Addington, Grenville, Canning, Perceval, Wellesley, and Castlereagh. *See also* WHIG.

touchhole A vent in the BREECH of a firearm, through which the charge is ignited.

Toulon France's chief Mediterranean naval base and dockyard, which was involved in many skirmishes between the French and the British. In 1792, it was opened by French Royalists to forces under Admiral Samuel Hood, who commanded the British Mediterranean fleet, but Napoleon, then an artillery colonel, succeeded in driving them out in 1793. Reestablished as a chief French naval base, Toulon was blockaded variously by JERVIS, NELSON, and COLLINGWOOD.

tow A bundle of untwisted fibers.

trabaccolo A one or two-masted medium-sized vessel used primarily for coastal trading and fishing in the Adriatic Sea from the 17th to the 19th centuries. It originated in Chioggia, near Venice.

trace The straps used to attach the collar of a draft-animal to the crossbar of a carriage, coach, or other vehicle.

trade winds *or* **trades** Winds that blow steadily in the same direction from about the 30th parallels on each side of the equator in the Atlantic and Pacific oceans. The trade winds are created as the hot air around the equator rises and cold air is drawn in from the north and south. Because the equator revolves faster than higher latitudes, and in an eastward direction, the air rushing in from the north and south effectively moves in a westward direction, northeast to southwest in the Northern Hemisphere and southeast to northwest in the Southern Hemisphere.

  Although the trades were frequently used by trading vessels in their long voyages, the origin of the term comes from a definition of trade meaning "track." The trade winds are those that keep a fixed track.

Trafalgar A cape on the southern coast of Spain, most famous for the great battle fought just to its northwest on October 21, 1805, between a British fleet (27 SHIPS OF THE LINE) commanded by Admiral Lord NELSON and a French and Spanish fleet (18 French and 15 Spanish ships of the line) under Admiral VILLENEUVE. The British victory followed Napoleon's decision to attack Austria rather than to invade England and prevented the Franco-Spanish fleet from controlling the Mediterranean. The victory was made bittersweet by the death of Nelson, the Royal Navy's greatest commander. Among the warrior's many lucid and inspirational quotations is this from his instructions prior to the battle: "But, in case Signals can neither be seen or perfectly understood, no Captain can do very wrong if he places his Ship alongside that of an Enemy." The British suffered 1,500 men killed or wounded and lost no ships. The Spanish and French suffered 14,000 killed or wounded and lost 18 vessels.

trail one's coat To try to pick a quarrel; to act provocatively (to drag one's coattails so that another will step on them).

train-tackle Used during action, a combination of pulleys hooked to an eye-bolt in the train (after-part) of a gun-carriage and to a ring-bolt in the deck to prevent the gun from running out of the port while it is being loaded.

tramontana In Italy and its coastal area, any cold north wind coming down from the Alps; any cold wind sweeping down from the mountains.

tranquillitas animi et indolentia corporis Peace of mind and indolence of body (Latin).

Transactions More fully, *Proceedings and the Philosophical Transactions,* the publication of the ROYAL SOCIETY of London.

transiens per medium illorum ibat Crossing through their midst he went (Latin).

transom A CROSS-BEAM in the frame of a ship, especially the heavier transverse beams bolted to the STERNPOST and supporting the ends of the decks and the overhanging STERN and QUARTER GALLERIES. The cross-timer that connects the CHEEKs of each of a ship's gun-carriages.

transpierce To pierce through from one side to another, to penetrate.

transport A vessel used to transport soldiers, military stores, or convicts, particularly overseas.

Transport Board *See* "The Navy Board," p. 5.

Traskite A follower of John Trask, who in the early 17th century advocated the Christian observance of certain Jewish ceremonies, such as the Sabbath on the seventh day. The Traskites were forerunners of the Seventh-Day Baptists.

travail de Bénédictin Precise and painstaking work (French).

traveller A ring, THIMBLE, or strap that "travels" or slides along a support.

traverse-board A navigational device consisting of a circular board marked with eight holes radiating outward along each point of the compass. Every half hour of the four-hour WATCH a peg was placed into the hole that corresponded to the ship's course. The record was used to help track the ship's course during each watch.

treacle A sweet syrup, molasses; treacle-crowdy is sweet porridge. Venice treacle is a medicine made with nearly 60 ingredients, the principal one being OPIUM.

treat   To discuss terms; to bargain, negotiate.

tree   A pole, post, stake, BEAM, or SPAR in a ship.

treenail (*pronounced* "trennel")   A cylindrical pin of seasoned oak used in fastening a ship's side and bottom planks to her timbers (ribs) and considered superior to spike-nails and bolts, which could rust, loosen, and rot the surrounding wood. Pounded by mallets into holes created by augers, the treenails—whose size was one inch in diameter for every 100 feet of a ship's length—were sawed off flush and secured with wedges to prevent their splitting.

trend   To run in a certain direction or follow a certain course, as a mountain range or river. To turn in a new direction; to incline; to shift.

trepan   A circular saw used in surgery for cutting out small pieces of bone from the skull. To operate on with a trepan.

trepanning-iron   A TREPHINE.

trephine   An improved trepan, with a transverse handle and a steel pin in the center for support.

trestle-table   A table made of a movable board or boards laid upon trestles, or braced supports.

trestletrees *or* **trestles**   Framing that holds the weight of the TOP-MAST. Two short, strong parallel timbers fixed FORE-AND-AFT on opposite sides of the lower MASTHEAD to support the TOPMAST, the lower CROSSTREES, and the TOP, or similarly fixed at the topmast-head to support the topmast crosstrees and TOPGALLANT MAST.

triangles   Used by the military for punishment, tripods to which offenders were lashed for flogging.

triangulation   The use of a series of triangles to survey and map out a territory or region.

trice *or* **trice up**   To haul something up with a line. In a trice (in a single pull) means in an instant.

trick   A period of time during which a helmsman stands duty at the wheel.

tricorn   The early uniform regulations for the Navy did not mention head gear, but in practice, most officers wore a black tricorn hat. This was a hat with a large, soft brim that was gathered up in three flaps to form three angles. Officers wore the hat with one of the three angles to the front, the edges bound with gold braid and a cockade in the left upturned flap. The regulations first mentioned hats in 1795. From this time only Admirals wore gold-laced hats, and the hats started to be cocked with just two angles. At first the hat was worn with the flaps toward each shoulder. Later, Admirals exercised their prerogative to wear the hat with the points to the shoulders, leaving Captains and other officers to wear them with the points fore and aft.

Trieste   A seaport and Imperial Free City (1719–1891) in the north-eastern corner of the Adriatic Sea on the north side of the Istrian Peninsula and one of the two principal bases of the Austrian Navy. It remained part of the Austrian Empire—except for two periods during the French Revolutionary and Napoleonic wars, when it was held by the French—until the end of World War I.

trilobate   Having or consisting of three lobes.

trim   To prepare a vessel for sailing. To adjust the YARDS and sails of a vessel in relationship to the FORE-AND-AFT line to get the best effect from the wind. The set of a ship on the water—for example, BY THE HEAD or the STERN, or on an even KEEL—by which a vessel is best suited for navigation, and the adjustment of her BALLAST, cargo, and other weight to achieve this.

Trincomalee   Town, district, and seaport in eastern Ceylon (now Sri Lanka). The ancient city of Gokanna, whose first European settlers were the Portuguese in 1612. Possession passed among the Dutch, the British, and the French during the 18th century and was finally secured by the British in 1795. Trincomalee eventually became a valuable naval anchorage that remained in British hands until 1957. H.M.S. *Trincomalee: See* FOUDROYANT.

trireme   An ancient GALLEY (originally Greek, later also Roman) with three banks of oars one above another, used chiefly as a ship-of-war.

trismus   Lockjaw, or spasm of the muscles of the neck and lower jaw, a symptom of TETANUS.

Tristan da Cunha   One of a group of small volcanic islands in the South Atlantic between South Africa and South America, sometimes called Lonely Island because no one lived there for 300 years after it was discovered by the Portuguese Admiral Tristão da Cunha in 1506. It was first settled by the British in 1810. During the War of 1812, the British SLOOP *Penguin* surrendered to the American sloop *Hornet* in 1815 off Tristan de Cunha in what proved to be the war's final naval action. Today, Tristan da Cunha is a dependency of the British colony of ST. HELENA.

trivet   A three-legged metal stand for supporting a pot, kettle, or other cooking vessel over a fire. "As right as a trivet" means thoroughly or perfectly right (i.e., standing firm on its three feet).

trocar *or* **trochar**   A sharp, pointed surgical instrument fitted with a small tube and used to withdraw fluid from a body cavity such as the abdomen.

tromba marina   Italian for marine trumpet, a stringed instrument highly popular in the 15th century and used through the 18th century. It had a long body with only one or two strings, which produced a tone like that of a trumpet.

trompe-couillon   Something that deceives. Literally, trick the fool (French).

tropic line   *See* TROPIC OF CANCER and TROPIC OF CAPRICORN.

Tropic of Cancer   The line of latitude, 23° 27" north of the equator, that marks the northernmost point at which the sun is directly overhead at noon at some point during the year.

Tropic of Capricorn   The line of latitude, 23° 27" south of the equator, that marks the southernmost point at which the sun is directly overhead at noon at some point during the year.

Troubridge, Sir Thomas (1758–1807)   A British Rear-Admiral whose long career included action at CAPE ST. VINCENT, where his ship *Culloden* led the line of battle, and at the NILE. In 1807, sailing in H.M.S. *Blenheim* from Madras to the Cape of Good Hope (*see* CAPE OF STORMS), where he was to take command, Troubridge went down with his ship and all hands in a GALE off Madagascar.

trub   A truffle.

truck   A circular or square wooden cap at the head of a MAST or flagstaff, with small holes or SHEAVES for signal HALYARDs, used to

HOIST signal flags. A small wooden block through which a PARREL, or rope that secures a YARD to the mast, was threaded to prevent its being frayed against the mast. Also, the wooden wheels on which a ship's gun-carriages were mounted.

truckle   To take a subordinate or subservient position; to yield weakly or obsequiously.

trunnions   Short horizontal bars on both sides of a cannon by which it is mounted to the gun-carriage and that provide the axis upon which the cannon pivots when being aimed.

truss   The means of securing a YARD to a MAST, allowing it to slide up and down a mast.

try out   To extract by melting, to render. A try-pot is a pot used in whaling for trying out oil from blubber. The try-works is a brick structure located between the FOREMAST and MAINMAST to hold the fireplaces and the try-pots.

trysail   In a vessel with three MASTS, a small FORE-AND-AFT sail set on a GAFF or a BOOM on the FORE- or MAINMAST. A small, usually triangular sail used in heavy weather. *See also* STORM TRYSAIL.

Tuam   Small Irish town 19 miles northeast of Galway.

tuan   A master or lord. Used by Malays as a title of respect or a form of address, formerly especially to Europeans, similar to "sir" or "mister."

tub   A slow, awkward ship, usually one that is too wide for its length; also, a short, broad boat used for rowing practice.

Tu es là?   Are you there? (French).

tumble-home   The inward inclination of a ship's upper sides, causing the UPPER DECK to be narrower than the MAIN and LOWER DECKS.

tumefaction   The action or process of swelling; a swollen condition, as in a disease.

tumefied   Swollen, distended.

tun   A large cask or barrel, usually for liquids, especially wine or beer. A measure of capacity for liquids (formerly also for other substances), usually equal to 252 gallons.

This ship is beating to windward under TRYSAILS. (*From Serres's* Liber Nauticus)

tundish   A funnel, especially one fitting into the bunghole of a TUN and used in brewing.

tunny   Tuna.

turbary   Land where peat may be dug for fuel; the right to take peat for fuel from common property or from someone else's land.

turbot   A large European flatfish, popular for eating. Any of various related flatfishes.

turkey buzzard *or* **turkey vulture**   An American vulture whose bare red head and dark plumage are similar to a turkey's.

Turkish delight   A confection made from boiled gelatin, cut into cubes and dusted with sugar.

turnip-beetle   A tiny black leaping beetle that feeds on the young leaves of the turnip and other crucifers and whose larvae mine the full-grown leaf.

turpentine enemata   Enemas made with turpentine, among other ingredients.

tussock   A tuft, clump, or matted growth of grass or a similar plant; a tuft or bunch of leaves, feathers, or the like.

Twelfth-night   The eve of Twelfth-day, or Epiphany, a church festival celebrated on January 6 to commemorate the coming of the Three Wise Men.

twice-laid   Of rope, made from the best yarns of condemned old rope. Still, inferior to new rope.

twiddling line   A light line once used to hold the wheel of a ship in a desired position.

twig   To notice, to become aware of, to perceive, to comprehend.

two-pair (*short for* two-pair-of-stairs)   Situated above two flights of stairs, as a room.

Tyburn tree   Slang for the gallows. So called because Tyburn was London's principal place of public hanging from 1388 to 1783. For a time, those condemned to die at Tyburn were given their last mug of ale at the nearby chapel of St.-Giles-in-the-Fields.

Tyneside   The banks of the River Tyne, an important industrial and maritime region on England's northeast coast, including the city of NEWCASTLE-upon-Tyne, known for six hundred years for its export of coal and its shipbuilding.

ukase   A decree or edict from the Russian emperor or government. Also, any proclamation or decree, especially one that is final or arbitrary.

ultima ratio regum   The final argument of kings (Latin). Louis XIV of France had this motto enscribed on all of his cannons.

ultima Thule   The highest point or degree attained or attainable, the acme, limit, but also the lowest limit, the nadir. From Virgil's *Georgics*, in which he names the most northerly land THULE.

unbend   To unfasten, untie, or undo a CABLE, line, or sail.

under hatches   Below deck.

unguent   An ointment or salve.

Union   The Union flag or, officially, the Great Union, Great Britain's national flag. The British Union Flag, designed in 1606, combined the white flag with the red cross of St. George used by England and the blue flag with the white cross of St. Andrew used by Scotland to symbolize the personal union of the two countries under King JAMES I. This union was formalized in 1707 through the Act of Union, which united the two countries under the name Great Britain. With the addition of Ireland in 1801, the country changed its name to the United Kingdom and added the red St. Patrick's cross to the Union Flag. It is called the Union Jack when flown in the BOW of a vessel. In the U.S. Navy, the Union Jack is a small flag that has the stars from the national flag and is flown in the bow.

Unitarian   A member or adherent of a Christian religious sect believing in unipersonality of the Godhead, especially as opposed to an orthodox Trinitarian. Founded in Central Europe in the 16th century and in England and the United States, through a separate movement, in the late 18th and early 19th centuries.

Unité   *See* SURPRISE.

United Irishman   A member of the Society of United Irishmen, a political association formed to promote union between Protestants and Catholics but that became a separatist secret society whose members helped organize the rebellion of 1798.

United States, **U.S.S.**   The first of the U.S. Navy's six original FRIGATES—along with *CONSTITUTION, President,* CHESAPEAKE, *Constellation,* and *Congress.* Armed with 44 guns, she was launched at Philadelphia in 1797 and had an illustrious career. During the Quasi-War with France (1798–1801) she served as the FLAGSHIP of the senior officer, Commodore John Barry, and in 1812, under the command of Stephen Decatur, captured the British *MACEDONIAN.* After peace was made in 1814, she served as flagship in the Mediterranean. Decommissioned in 1849, she remained at Norfolk, Virginia, until 1861, when she was refitted for service in the Confederate States Navy. In 1862, she was scuttled in the Elizabeth River in Virginia as an obstacle against the U.S. Navy. Raised after a short period, she remained afloat until she was broken up in 1865.

unslaked lime   Calcium oxide (lime, quicklime), used therapeutically as a tonic and astringent. Unslaked meant that it had not been exposed to water.

Upper Ossory   A barony in Queens County, Ireland, in what is now County Kilkenny. Ossory was an ancient kingdom that dissolved in 1110.

Upupa epops   *See* HOOPOE.

Urdu   An Indo-Aryan language that originated near Delhi and was earlier called Hindustani. It is written in a modified form of the Persian Arabic alphabet and used by the Muslims in the area of present-day Pakistan and northern India. It is the official literary language of Pakistan.

urinator   One who dives under water; a diver.

Ushant Island *or* **Île d'Ouessant**   A rocky island off the coast of Brittany, France, about 40 miles northwest of BREST. It marks a pivotal point: to the west lies the open Atlantic, to the south the BAY OF BISCAY, and to the north the English Channel. It was a key point in navigation and played a role in the struggles between England and France in the 18th and early 19th centuries. The indecisive action that led to the famous COURT-MARTIAL of Admirals Keppel and Palliser happened off Ushant in 1778. One of the battles of FINISTERRE in October of 1747 is given the name Battle of Ushant. The battle of the GLORIOUS FIRST OF JUNE is sometimes called the Battle of Ushant.

Vade retro, Satanas   Get back, Satan! (Latin).

Vae victis   Woe to the vanquished (Latin).

vail   A profit or emolument in addition to salary, wages, or other regular payment, especially one attached to an office or position; a fee or offering of this nature. A gratuity given to a servant or attendant, especially by a house guest upon leaving. In the 17th and 18th centuries, servants were paid largely by means of these gratuities.

valerian   The root of the plant *Valeriana afficinalis*, used medicinally as both a stimulant and a weak sedative.

Valetta *or* Valletta   A seaport and the capital city of the island of MALTA. Built after 1565, it was named for Jean Parisot de la Valette, grand master of the Order of Hospitalers. It was taken by Napoleon in 1798 from the Knights Hospitalers, and following a Maltese revolt against the French, the British seized the island in 1800. At the end of the Napoleonic War, it became a British colonial possession and served as a strategic base for the British Mediterranean fleet.

vali   A civil governor of a Turkish province, or vilayet.

Valparaiso   A seaport on the Pacific coast of South America in Chile, which was a colonial possession of Spain before the country won independence in 1818.

Vancouver, George (*1757–1798*)   A British naval Captain and explorer who in 1792 made an extensive survey of the west coast of North America from what is now the San Francisco Bay area to British Columbia. Vancouver joined the Navy at the age of 13 and accompanied Captain COOK on his second and third voyages to the Pacific. An island and the city and seaport founded in 1824 on the western coast of Canada were named after George Vancouver.

Van Diemen's Land   The west coast of Tasmania, named after Anthony van Diemen, the Dutch governor-general of the EAST INDIES who sponsored the exploration of Australia by Abel Tasman. Tasman discovered the island and named it in van Diemen's honor in 1642. In 1853, it was renamed Tasmania in honor of the explorer.

vang   GUYS leading from the peak of a GAFF, securing it to the rail and keeping it amidships when the sail was not set.

Vanguard, **H.M.S.**   Nine ships of the Royal Navy bore this name. The fifth, a third rate of 74 guns, was built in 1787 and served as Lord NELSON's FLAGSHIP at the Battle of the NILE in 1798.

Van John   Slang for vingt-et-un, French for the card game "twenty-one."

vapours   Mild nervous disorders, such as hypochondriasis and hysteria, usually seen only in women.

Variables of Cancer and Capricorn or Variables   Regions of the ocean between 23°27″ north and 23°27″ south of the equator (the latitudes of the TROPIC OF CANCER and TROPIC OF CAPRICORN), where variable or shifting winds are normally found. In between the TRADE WINDS and the Westerlies. Also called the Horse Latitudes.

vast (*short for* **avast**)   Hold! Stop! Stay! Cease!

Vathek   *See* BECKFORD.

vaticination   An oracular or inspired prediction, a prognostication, a prophetic forecast. Also, divine or inspired apprehension or knowledge. Intuition, insight.

Vauban, Sébastien Le Prestre de (*1633–1707*)   A Marshal of France and the French military engineer who revolutionized the design of fortifications during the reign of Louis XIV.

Vega   A star of the first magnitude, the brightest in the constellation Lyra and the fourth brightest in the night sky.

velleity   A mere wish, desire, or inclination without an action or effort to realize the objective.

Vendée   A department of western France on the BAY OF BISCAY that gave its name to the insurrection of 1793 to 1796. The peasants of the Vendée opposed the Revolution after it turned against the Roman Catholic Church. An army of more than 50,000 men attempted to clear the region of revolutionary authorities. However, they were routed by the republican army. In 1796, British-backed royalist émigrés tried to land here, at Quiberon. Under heavy opposition, the comte d'Artois (later Charles X) abandoned the Vendéan leaders to capture and execution. Isolated royalist uprisings occurred in the Vendée in 1799 and 1815.

venerem omitte   No sex (Latin).

vent-bit   A tool used for clearing the vent of a gun when it is choked.

***Venus*, H.M.S.**   This 36-gun fifth rate, built in 1758, fought at the battle at Quiberon Bay in 1759. Reduced to 32 guns, she fought at the GLORIOUS FIRST OF JUNE in 1794. She was renamed *Heroine* in 1809 and sold in 1828.

verdigris   Copper acetate, a green rust naturally forming on copper, brass, or bronze, used as a pigment and used in surgical dressings because of its antiseptic property.

verge   An area subject to the jurisdiction of the Lord High Steward, a distance of 12 miles around the King's court.

verjuice   The sour juice of green or unripe grapes, crab apples, or other fruit, especially when made into an acidic liquor. This liquor was once much used in cooking, as a condiment, and for medicinal purposes.

vermiform appendix   The appendix. A vestige of some early stage of human evolution, it now has no known function.

vermilion   Cinnabar or red crystalline mercuric sulphide, valued for its brilliant scarlet color and used as a pigment or in the manufacture of red sealing wax. Also, any similarly colored red earth used as a pigment.

verminous   Worm-infested.

vesical   Pertaining to the bladder; *see* CALCULUS.

vestry   A room or part of a church, usually situated in close proximity to the chancel or choir, in which the vestments, vessels for the service, and records are kept and in which the clergy and choir dress for service. A similar room at any church, chapel, or place of worship. In parish churches, also a meeting place for the transaction of certain parochial business. In Anglican parishes, another name for the parish council, an assembly or meeting of the parishioners to deliberate or legislate the affairs of the parish or certain temporal matters connected with the church.

veuve   Widow (French).

vicar-general   In the Roman Catholic Church, an ecclesiastical officer, usually a cleric, appointed by and representing a bishop in matters of jurisdiction or administration.

viceroy   One who acts as the governor of a country, province, or territory in the name of and by the authority of the supreme ruler. Literally, a vice-king.

Victory, **H.M.S.**   A 100-gun first rate and one of the most famous ships in British naval history. Built in 1765, she had a long career, participating in the American Revolution and in the French Revolution, when she was commanded by Lord HOWE. Rebuilt in 1801, she is best known for being the FLAGSHIP of Vice-Admiral Lord NELSON. At the battle of TRAFALGAR in 1805, Nelson was mortally wounded on the QUARTERDECK of the *Victory*. The ship was permanently drydocked in 1922 and can be visited by the public at PORTSMOUTH, England.

victualler   One who furnishes a vessel or navy with provisions. A merchant ship employed to carry provisions for a fleet or SQUADRON, a victualing ship.

Victualling Office   The office of the Victualling Board, the agency of the Royal Navy concerned with the provisioning of ships and responsible for the contracting, purchasing, and distribution of all SLOP clothing and food, as well as appointing to all ships a PURSER, who issued these provisions and kept accounts. In this period, the Victualling Office was located with the Navy Board at Somerset House.

Victualling Yard   In the Royal Navy, a place where provisions, such as SLOP clothing and food, were deposited and held for distribution to the fleet.

vicuña   An undomesticated relative of the llama and alpaca, the vicuña lives in the Andes Mountains in what is now Ecuador, Peru, and Bolivia. Its coat yields a fine, lustrous wool.

Viennese treatment   Antisyphilitic treatment, introduced in 1750, with the strong mercurial drug CORROSIVE SUBLIMATE. *See* MERCURY.

Vigo   A port and naval station on the northwestern coast of Spain with an excellent sheltered anchorage and a substantial shipbuilding capacity. In British naval history, Vigo is remembered as the site of a battle in 1702, during the War of the Spanish Succession, where a combined Anglo-Dutch fleet under the command of Sir George Rooke attacked a fleet of Spanish treasure GALLEONS.

Ville de Paris, **H.M.S.**   The original *Ville de Paris* was a first-rate prize, De Grasse's FLAGSHIP, taken at the SAINTES in 1782; she foundered in a hurricane en route to England. In 1795, a second rate.

Villeneuve, Pierre-Charles-Jean-Baptiste-Silvestre, Comte de (1763– 1806)   A French Admiral who participated in many fleet actions under Napoleon. Villeneuve commanded the rear division of the French fleet at the Battle of the NILE in 1798, and his FLAGSHIP, *Guillaume Tell*, and three other French ships were the only ones to escape from the British at that action. In 1804, Villeneuve became commander of the TOULON squadron. Having heard the unwelcome news that he was to be replaced as commander, Villeneuve sailed from CADIZ and met NELSON's fleet at the Battle of TRAFALGAR on October 21, 1805. Villeneuve was taken prisoner by the English in the battle. Later paroled, he was found stabbed to death at a hotel in Rennes, France, in 1806. It is believed he committed suicide.

vinolent   Tending to drunkenness, especially on wine; a drunkard.

vinous   Like wine, tasting or smelling like wine. Made with wine. Resulting from indulgence in wine.

violoncello   The complete name of the cello, a large four-stringed instrument of the violin class; a bass violin.

virgoes intactoes   Aubrey's pidgin Latin for "untouched virgins."

viscacha   Either of two large burrowing rodents of South America, related to the chinchilla, one inhabiting the upper Andes from Chile to Ecuador and the other the southern Argentine pampas.

Visigothic   Of or belonging to the Visigoths, members of the Western branch of the Goths that entered Roman territory toward the end of the fourth century and subsequently established a kingdom in France and Spain that was overthrown by the MOORs in 711.

visto   Vista.

Vite, vite . . . à gauche. Tu l'attraperas. . . . Allez, allez. . . . Fouette. . . . Arré. . . . Fouette toujours. . . . A gauche. A gauche, je te dis. . . . A droite.   Quick, quick . . . to the left. You'll catch him. . . . Go, go. . . . Crack the whip. . . . Giddyap. . . . Keep cracking. . . . To the left. To the left, I said. . . . To the right (French).

Vive l'Empereur   Long live the Emperor (French).

Vixi puellis nuper idoneus   Until recently I was able to conquer girls (Latin, from Horace, *Odes* III, 26).

vitriol   Sulfuric acid, or any of various sulphates of metals used as paint pigment or, medicinally, chiefly as stimulating tonics.

vizier   In the Turkish empire, Persia, or other Muslim country, a high state official or minister, often with vice-regal authority. A province's governor or VICEROY. The sovereign's chief minister.

Vlach   A Slavic name for a member of the Romani or Roumanians, a Latin-speaking people occupying portions of southeastern Europe, who migrated to various parts of the Balkan Peninsula, including Macedonia, Dalmatia, and Istria.

vol-au-vent   A puff-pastry pie (French).

voyal-block *or* **viol-block**   *See* MESSENGER. A massive SNATCH-BLOCK secured to the MAINMAST and used with the VOYAL in weighing anchor.

wad   A plug of rope-yarn, cloth, or green wood rammed down the barrel of a gun to keep the powder and shot in position. Also, a similar device used in a cartridge.

wader   Long-legged birds that frequently wade in shallow water, such as the HERON, PLOVER, and SNIPE.

waft   A flag, or ENSIGN, used to indicate the direction of the wind or to convey various signals, depending upon where it is hoisted. Also, to convoy, a "wafter" being an escort vessel.

Wager, **H.M.S.**   This 24-gun sixth rate was purchased in 1739 and wrecked in the South Atlantic on the southern coast of Chile in 1741 during ANSON's voyage around the world. O'Brian's novel *The Unknown Shore* is set on this grim voyage.

waist   The middle part of the upper deck of a ship, between the QUARTERDECK and the FORECASTLE.

waistcoat   A garment worn by men under a doublet, coat, or jacket partly exposed to view. The earliest waistcoats were often very elaborate and expensive. They sometimes had sleeves and reached over the hips.

waister   One who worked in the WAIST of a ship, where the duties were principally unskilled, like hauling on ropes. A LANDSMAN or other person good for only menial labor.

waiting-woman   A female servant or attendant.

Walcheren   A Dutch island at the mouth of the Scheldt River that played a role in a misconceived British enterprise in 1809. The British government dispatched a force of 235 armed vessels with 44,000 troops to divert the French troops fighting the Austrians in the Danube valley. The island of Walcheren was captured, but the Austrian armies failed to defeat the French. All British ships and forces were withdrawn with heavy casualties, among them some 4,000 dead of disease and 11,000 listed as sick.

wall-eye   An eye with an iris that is whitish and barely distinguishable or that is streaked or different in hue from the other eye, presumably because of cataract formation. An eye with a divergent squint.

wall-knot   A knot that acts as a stopper at the end of a rope, made by unlaying and intertwining the strands.

Walmer Castle   One of the three castles (Walmer, Deal, and Sandown) built by King Henry the VIII in 1539 to defend the English coast near the town of Walmer, which is between Dover and Deal. Situated near the shore, it has an uninterrupted view of the DOWNS and the English Channel as far as the French coast.

wand   A fishing rod.

wardroom   The messroom on board ship for the commissioned and WARRANT OFFICERS, who were said to be of "wardroom rank." As a group, the officers who used the wardroom.

Ward's Drops   A medicine devised by Joshua Ward, a famous 18th-century London quack, it was an ANTIMONY salt dissolved in wine and promoted as a panacea.

Ward's Pill   A medicine devised by the maker of WARD'S DROPS, it was made with an ANTIMONY salt and the exotic East Indian extract DRAGON'S BLOOD, and promoted as a panacea. It is unlikely that either of Ward's medicines was truly helpful in any condition, although any panacea could be credited with the recovery that followed an illness, thanks to what Maturin and his colleagues knew as the *vis medicatrix naturae*, the "healing power of nature."

ware   Short for beware, used as a warning cry or call to animals during a hunt.

wariangle   A shrike, especially the red-backed shrike, *Lanius collurio.* The wariangle nests in thick clumps of brambles or hedgerows and breeds in the late spring.

warp   A rope or light HAWSER attached to a KEDGE ANCHOR or fixed object and used for pulling on in order to move a ship from one place to another in a harbor, road, or river. A rope used to secure a vessel to a QUAY or to another vessel. Of sails, a lengthwise measurement of canvas. Also, the threads along the length of sailcloth. In fishing, a unit equal to four fish, used by herring fishermen on the east coast of England. To warp means to measure and lay out a ship's RIGGING prior to cutting it. Also, to move a ship along by pulling on a warp, sometimes used with "out." Of wind, to toss or drive a ship violently around.

warrant   An official certificate of appointment issued to an officer of lower rank than a commissioned officer.

warrant officer   One of a varied group of officers below commissioned rank, holding a WARRANT from an authority such as the NAVY BOARD, the ADMIRALTY, or the Ordnance Board. Among the warrant offices were the MASTER, Surgeon, PURSER, BOATSWAIN, Gunner, and Carpenter. These were the warrant sea officers, the heads of specialized technical branches of the ships' company. Below them was a second category of warrant officers who were considered "inferior officers." These included the Cook, Chaplain, Armorer, Schoolmaster, Master at arms, and Sailmaker. This system remained in effect until the mid-19th century. *See also* "Sea Officers: Commissioned and Warrant," page 13.

washboard *or* washstrake   A thin board attached to the GUNWALE of an open boat to keep out the spray. Also, a board on the SILL of a LOWER DECK port, for the same purpose.

watch   The period of time that each division of a ship's company alternately remains on deck, usually four hours, except for the DOG-WATCHes, which are two hours each and serve to prevent the same watch being kept by the same men every day. The names of the watches are:

Middle (graveyard watch): midnight to 0400 hours
Morning: 0400 to 0800 hours
Forenoon: 0800 to 1200 hours
Afternoon: 1200 to 1600 hours
First dog: 1600 to 1800 hours
Second, or last, dog: 1800 to 2000 hours
First: 2000 hours to midnight

See also SHIP'S BELLS.

Also, those of the officers and crew, usually half and sometimes a third, who work a vessel during a given watch. When the crew is divided into two parts, they were known as the LARBOARD (or port) and STARBOARD watches, and when the crew was divided into thirds, they were usually known as the red, white, and blue watches.

watch and watch   The arrangement in which the two halves, or watches, of a ship's crew are on duty alternately every four hours.

watch-bill   A list of the officers, seamen, and Marines of a ship-of-war and their corresponding WATCHes and stations for battle and other purposes.

watchet   A light blue color. A cloth or garment of this color.

watch-glass   An hour-glass used on board ship to measure the remaining time of a WATCH.

water-butt   A large cask with an open top set to receive rainwater.

WATERLOO, THE BATTLE OF   On June 18, 1815, the decisive showdown of the Napoleonic War, in which the allied forces under the duke of WELLINGTON and BLÜCHER defeated NAPOLEON. Facing Napoleon's 72,000 troops, Wellington's advance position lay a mile south of his headquarters in the village of Waterloo, Belgium, along the ridge Mont Saint-Jean, where he had three outposts: to the west, at Château Hougoumont; in the center, at La Haye Sainte, a farm and gravel quarry; and to the east, at the houses and farms of Papelotte and La Haye, beside the Bois de Paris. Behind this ridge and interlaced with these positions were his two main corps under General Sir Rowland Hill and the Prince of Orange (later William II, king of Holland). His main force of cavalry, under Field Marshal Lord Uxbridge, lay in reserve in the center. Wellington's army numbered 68,000, only a third British and many of the others raw recruits and former French allies.

Napoleon's goal was simple: to decimate Wellington's army and to march on to Brussels, the Belgian capital, by nightfall. Wellington's was also simple: to hang on until Blücher and his army of 89,000 Prussians arrived. In this, he was aided by heavy rainfall, which delayed Napoleon's attack. Under the battle command of Marshal Ney, the French bombarded the allied lines, then sent Jerome Bonaparte's division against Château Hougoumont in the hopes of drawing Wellington's reserves. The allied forces held without the reserves, resulting in Ney's first major setback of the day. At 1:30, Ney launched the Comte d'Erlon into his attack in the center, but he was repelled and then routed by Lord Uxbridge's cavalry charge. Uxbridge advanced too far, however, and was pounded by the French grand battery, losing a third of his men before regaining the allied lines. At around 3:30 Ney sent a cavalry assault against Wellington's right, which he believed was breaking, but Wellington's infantry squares stood fast, and Ney's cavalry were defeated.

In the meantime, the Prussians, led by Bülow's corps, had arrived, diverting French troops to the village of Plancenoit, where Napoleon was forced to commit the IMPERIAL GUARD. At 6:00, Ney had at last taken La Haye Sainte, and Wellington was in trouble. At this point, the Imperial Guard could have easily delivered the knockout blow, but they were still engaged at Plancenoit. Wellington, on the other hand, learned of the arrival of ZEITEN's corps on the left, and was able to draw reinforcements from that side to his center. By the time the Imperial Guard arrived to attack Wellington's center, it was too late, and the Guard's thrust was not well aimed. Maitland's Guardsmen met the Imperial Guard with volley after deadly volley, and the Frenchmen reeled back down the hill.

The allies lost 22,000 men in the fighting and Napoleon 41,000. Politically, he would not recover, and he soon abdicated and was exiled to Elba.

waterman   A man working on a boat or among boats, as a boatman, ferryman, or someone who assists in berthing a vessel.

water sail   A small fairweather sail set under a lower STUDDINGSAIL or below the DRIVER BOOM to take advantage of a following wind. A triangular sail set under the BOWSPRIT of a Cornish fishing LUGGER.

wax-moth   A moth whose larvae prey on the honeycomb.

way   The progress of a vessel through water; the rate of progress, velocity. A vessel gathers way as it increases speed and loses way as it slows. It has way on when it is moving. A vessel is under way when it has lifted its anchor from the bottom or left its MOORINGs, even though it is not moving. *See also* WEIGH.

wear *or* **wear round**   Of a vessel, to come around on the other TACK by turning the head away from the wind, the opposite maneuver being to put a ship about by bringing her head toward the wind, which is to TACK. *See* illustration below.

weather   Situated on the side that is toward the wind; to windward. To weather a ship is to get to windward of her, and to weather a shore is to pass it to windward.

weather-awning   *See* AWNING.

This ship is wearing, turning downwind with her main course brailed up to the yard and her foresails braced around to catch the wind to help bring the bow around on a new course. (*From Serres's* Liber Nauticus.)

WEATHER GAUGE *OR* GAGE

A situation in which a ship or line or ships is WINDWARD of another ship or line of ships. To have or keep the weather gauge of something is to be to windward of it. In a line of battle or single-ship action, the fleet or ship that has the weather gauge is generally considered to have the advantage, although that is arguable. The advantages of having the weather gauge or the lee gauge, as described by *Falconer's* (1815):

Advantages of the Weather-Gage:

1. The weather-gage is the sooner clear of smoke; and, of course, that line can better observe the signals which are spread, than the ships to leeward can, which must have the continuance of both its own and of the enemy longer.

2. If the weather-ships are more in number than the enemy's, they can detach some from their squadron; which, bearing down upon the rear of the enemy, must infallibly throw them into disorder.

3. The fire-ships of the weather-line can, when they are ordered, more easily bear down upon the enemy than those of the lee can ply to windward, which can never be done against a line in action; but the weather fire-ships can bear down against all the resistance that can be made by the enemy.

Disadvantage:

The weather-line cannot decline the action, without the dangerous expedient of forcing through the enemy's line; and if it keeps the wind, the lee-line may inclose and totally destroy it, especially if it is inferior in number to the latter, or if the ships thereof are in bad condition; for it then can find no other source but in the dexterity of its maneuvers, unless it is favored by the wind, or any oversight of the enemy.

Advantages of the Lee-Gage:

1. If one, two, or more of the ships to windward should be disabled, they must inevitably drive to leeward, and become a prey to the enemy.

2. The ships of the lee-line can more readily bear away before the wind, and have their places supplied by ships from the corps-de-reserve, in case of being disabled or meeting with any disaster.

3. The line to leeward can keep their ports longer open in a strong wind with a high sea, when those to windward in all probability, may be obliged to shut the ports of their lower tier of guns, to prevent the water from rushing in between decks, which may be attended with the most fatal consequences.

4. The lee-line can more easily observe the men on the decks of the ships to windward, as they heel, and when the smoke does not interrupt their sight; at which time the marines and topmen may easily take aim at and destroy them with muskets and carbins.

Disadvantage:
It cannot decide the time and distance of the battle, which may commence before it is sufficiently formed; and it will, perhaps, be attacked by an enemy, who bears away upon it in regular order.

weatherly   Capable of sailing close to the direction from which the wind is blowing.

Wedgwood   The bone china and other pottery made by Josiah Wedgwood (1730–1795) and his successors at Etruria, the factory-village he built in Staffordshire. Their best-known vases, plaques, medallions, and the like are of fine clay lightly glazed, with classical designs in white relief on a blue or black background.

weevil   Any beetle whose larvae, and sometimes the beetles themselves, bore into grain, fruit, nuts, and the bark of trees, causing severe damage. Especially a beetle of a species of the family Curculionoidea, the true weevils.

weigh   To lift; to weigh anchor is to lift or HAUL up a ship's anchor from the sea floor before sailing. The words "weigh" and "WAY" both derive from the Old English word *wegan*, "to carry or move," which later came to mean to lift as well.

well-found   Fully furnished or equipped.

Wellington, Arthur Wellesley, First Duke of (*1769–1852*)   The commander of British troops during the Peninsular War (see p. 27), he defeated NAPOLEON at WATERLOO in 1815, ending the Napoleonic wars. Wellington entered the army in 1787 and, aided by his brother Richard (later Earl of MORNINGTON), rose rapidly in rank. After service in India, he returned to England in 1805 and was knighted. The following year, he was elected to Parliament, and he was appointed Irish secretary in 1807.

In 1808 he led an expedition to assist Portugal in its revolt against the French. In 1809 he returned to the Iberian Peninsula and ultimately assumed command of the British, Portuguese, and Spanish forces in the Peninsular War. Though his campaign received poor support from the British government, he took advantage of the irregular terrain, Portuguese and Spanish nationalism, and Napoleon's preoccupation with other theaters to drive the French north of the Pyrenees by 1813. He had invaded southern France as far as Toulouse when news of Napoleon's abdication arrived in April 1814.

Returning to England, he received many honors and was created duke of Wellington. When Napoleon returned from Elba, Wellington took command of the allied armies and, together with the Prussian general, Gebhard Leberecht von BLÜCHER, defeated the French at WATERLOO. Wellington then took charge of the army of occupation in France, exerting his influence to restrain harsh treatment of the defeated French.

He served as prime minister (1828–30), foreign secretary (1834–35), and again as minister without portfolio (1841–46). In 1842 he was made commander in chief for life. He is buried in St. Paul's Cathedral.

wenching   Associating with common women.

were-   The first element of, for example, the word "werewolf," used with names of animals to indicate a human being imagined to be transformed into a beast, as in "were-bear."

wery   Obsolete form of "very."

West Indies   The long chain of islands arcing from the coast of Florida to the coast of South America and separating the Caribbean Sea from the Atlantic, discovered by Columbus and so named because he believed that he had reached India from the west. The West Indies consist of the Greater Antilles, including Cuba, Jamaica, Hispaniola, and Puerto Rico; and the Lesser Antilles, comprising the Windward and Leeward Islands, Barbados, Trinidad, and Tobago. Fought over by Spain, England, France, and the Netherlands because of their rich trade, the West Indies were the site in 1782 of a victorious British battle against the French known as the Battle of the SAINTES. NELSON pursued VILLENEUVE here in 1805. Britain's success in this region helped to establish a decisive maritime and commercial supremacy over France.

wet   A drink of an alcoholic beverage.

wether   A male sheep, or ram, especially a castrated one.

whale-back   A large mound in the shape of the back of a whale; any land mass with an appearance similar to that of the back of a whale.

whale-bird Any of various birds that inhabit the places where whales live, particularly ones that feed on whale oil or offal, including certain PETRELS, the turnstone, the red or gray PHALAROPE, and the ivory gull.

wheatear A small songbird widely found in the Old World, having a blue-gray back, white belly and rump, and blackish wings. It is considered a delicacy.

wherry A wide sailing BARGE with a single MAST and a large MAINSAIL, used to transport freight on the Norfolk Broads in England. Also, a light rowboat used chiefly on rivers to carry passengers. *See* illustration, below.

Whig Although there was no clear distinction between Whigs and Tories during the era of O'Brian's Aubrey-Maturin novels, in general terms, a Whig was one who upheld the supremacy of PARLIAMENT and, while acknowledging the King's theoretical right to appoint his own ministers, in practice wanted to deprive him of it. The Whigs stood for civil and religious liberty all over the world, including Catholic Emancipation at home. In 1792, Charles J. Fox and the Whigs opposed entering the war as an unjustifiable interference by a reactionary power in the rights of an independent country. The Whigs were in opposition for more than 20 years after 1807. Their leaders included Fox, Lord Grey, and Ponsonby. *See* TORY for general background.

whinchat A small brown and buff European songbird, closely allied to the stonechat and found in grassy meadows.

whip A TACKLE, or pulley, consisting of a single BLOCK and a rope, used on board ship primarily for light hoisting.

A Thames wherry (*from* Naval Costume *by Sir William Symonds, R.N.*)

whist   A card game, played by four people in pairs, in which points are scored according to the number of tricks won. It was a forerunner of bridge.

Whitehall   In the district of Westminster in London, Whitehall houses the chief government buildings, including the ADMIRALTY, the Treasury, the Prime Minister's residence at 10 Downing Street, and the HORSE GUARDS. The site was originally the location of the huge, rambling Whitehall Palace, which in 1532 became Henry VIII's premier royal residence in London. The palace expanded over the years until 1698, when a fire destroyed everything but the Renaissance-style banqueting hall, designed by the architect Inigo Jones in 1619–1622. The ADMIRALTY Office (*see also* page 4), a brick building with a large Ionic portico built between 1722 and 1726, is on the west side of Whitehall.

white letter   In printing, the type of print now called roman.

white pudding   A type of sausage made of oatmeal and suet. Also, pudding made of milk, eggs, flour, and butter.

White's   The oldest and grandest of the St. James's gentlemen's clubs in London, White's was infamous as a gambling spot where anything was worthy of a wager. (Legend has it that Lord Arlington bet £3,000 on which of two raindrops would be the first to reach the bottom of a window pane.) By 1814 the club had 500 members and a lengthy waiting list.

white squall   A squall or sudden gust of strong wind that is not accompanied by clouds, as opposed to a black squall, which is, and a thick squall, one usually with hail or sleet.

white-tailed eagle   The European sea eagle.

wicket   A gate for pedestrians, frequently one to be used when an adjacent larger gate is closed.

widdershins   In a direction opposite to the usual; in a wrong or contrary direction.

widow's cruse   A supply that, though apparently meager, is or seems to be inexhaustible. It is an allusion to I Kings 17:12–16, in which a widow feeds the prophet Elijah for many days from only a small pot of oil and a handful of meal.

wigeon   Either of two wild ducks with brown plumage found in North America, Europe, and northern Asia.

wight   A live creature, especially a human being. Brave, valiant.

Wight, Isle of   A diamond-shaped island off the southern coast of Hampshire, across the strait known as the SOLENT from PORTSMOUTH and Southampton. It protects the harbor of Portsmouth.

Wilkes and Liberty   The rallying cry for the London-born politician and journalist John Wilkes (1727–1797), who became known as a champion of liberty and an upholder of press freedom. An MP, he attacked the ministry in his weekly journal *North Briton.* In 1762, Wilkes was found guilty of seditious libel, imprisoned, released, then expelled from the House of Commons. He was reelected and expelled on several occasions, his rioting mob of supporters shouting the slogan "Wilkes and Liberty." Wilkes pushed for parliamentary reform, including the suppression of rotten boroughs and the protection of individual liberty. Supported by London merchants, he became Lord Mayor of London in 1774 and regained admission to Parliament, where he championed colonial rights in the American Revolution.

William, Prince   *See* CLARENCE, Duke of.

William III (*1650–1702*)   *See* DUTCH WILLIAM.

Willis, Thomas (*1621–1675*)   Physician of Oxford and London who made several important neuroanatomical discoveries.

Winchester   A city in the county of Hampshire in southern England. It was the capital of the ancient kingdom of Wessex and later the seat of the Danish King Canute's government (1016–1035). Winchester is famed for its cathedral, the longest in England, and Winchester College, a boys' school founded by William of Wykeham in 1382 to prepare students for New College, Oxford.

Winchester quart   A quart (two pints) in Winchester measure; four Imperial pints (80 fluid ounces). Also, a bottle holding four pints.

windage   A space between the inner wall of a firearm and the SHOT or shell that it is charged with to allow for the expansion of gas in firing, the size of which is determined by the difference between the diameters of the bore and the shot.

wind-gall A fragment of a rainbow or colorful halo, supposed to presage windy weather.

windlass A mechanism operating on the same principle as the CAP-STAN but on a horizontal axis, used on board merchant ships and some smaller vessels of the Royal Navy for weighing the anchor, hoisting, and hauling.

windsail A long wide tube or funnel of sailcloth with wings at one end that is suspended from a STAY to direct fresh air below deck.

Windsor English city in the county of Berkshire on the Thames River, 20 miles west of London. Location of the principle residence of England's sovereigns since the time of William the Conquerer, Windsor is the home of St. George's Chapel, the burial place of many English kings.

wind-suck Of a horse, to noisily draw in and swallow air, often associated with CRIB-BITING.

windward Situated in the direction from which the wind blows; the WEATHER side of a vessel. At sea, the windward side of the QUARTER-DECK was reserved for use by the Captain.

wine-cooler A vessel equipped to carry bottles of wine immersed in ice or iced liquid.

wing-transom The uppermost and longest TRANSOM in the stern-frame of a ship.

wireworm A worm that is the slender hard-skinned larva of any of the click beetles, which destroy the roots of plants. Also, similar larvae, especially the leatherjacket grub of the crane fly.

wisent The European bison, *Bison bonasus,* once found throughout Europe, including Great Britain, and still living in some protected forests on the Continent.

Witch of Endor A medium who can call up the dead; a witch. An allusion to 1 Samuel 28:7, in which King Saul consults with a divining woman.

with a run Rapidly.

Withering, William (1741–1799) Clinician and medical botanist of Birmingham, England. His *Account of the Foxglove* (1785) introduced DIGITALIS for the treatment of DROPSY.

withy A flexible willow branch used for tying or binding, as in a halter, leash, or hoop.

wizened To be shrunken and dried up, shriveled, as from aging. Also, to have a parched throat.

wombat Any of the stocky burrowing marsupials native to South Australia and Tasmania and resembling small bears.

woodcock A European and British migratory game bird, allied to the SNIPE, with a long bill, large eyes, and brownish variegated plumage. Also, a related American game bird.

wood-louse A small terrestrial isopod crustacean found in old wood and under stones, which often rolls itself up into a ball. Also called cheeselip, hog-louse, pill bug, slater, or sow bug.

Wool A town in the county of Dorset, England, southeast of Dorchester.

woolding Binding a MAST, YARD, or other SPAR with several turns of a rope to strengthen it where it is broken or where, being made of two or more pieces, it is FISHed or SCARFed. Also, the rope used to do this.

worm Any of many species of intestinal worms, but usually the easily visible tapeworm (other species are difficult to see without a microscope, which did not enter common medical usage until the late 19th century). However, MAGGOTS might also be meant, especially in reference to a cadaver. Also, a double or single screw at the end of a rod, used to withdraw the charge or WAD from a muzzle-loading gun. Of a rope, to fill the lay between strands with tarred SPUNYARN or filling to give it a smooth surface or to prevent moisture from getting inside.

wrack Marine vegetation, especially seaweed, cast ashore by waves or growing on the tidal seashore.

wring a mast To bend it beyond its natural position by setting up the SHROUDs too tight.

wryneck Either of two species of woodpeckers, distinguishable by their habit of contorting the neck and head.

xebec *also* **xebeque, jabeque, sciabecco, chebeck**   A small, fast three-masted (originally two-masted) vessel with a shallow draft and a distinctive overhanging BOW and STERN. In the 18th and early 19th centuries, a large xebec carried a square RIG on the FOREMAST, LATEEN sails on the others, a BOWSPRIT, and two HEADSAILS. It was frequently used in the Mediterranean by CORSAIRS, carrying a crew of up to 400 men and mounting up to 24 guns. *See* illustrations, next page and page 57.

A xebec with a view of the lighthouse on the mole at Naples (*from Serres's* Liber Nauticus)

yacht A light, fast, sailing ship, originally used as a vessel of state to transport royalty, ambassadors, and other important people. Later applied to vessels used exclusively for pleasure.

yard A long and narrow wooden SPAR, slung at its center from before the MAST in a SQUARE-RIGGED ship and serving to support and extend a square sail that is BENT to it; a yard that crosses the MAST diagonally is known as a LATEEN yard.

yardarm Either of the ends of a YARD, the outer QUARTERS, where on SQUARE-RIGGED ships signal flags were flown and where men sentenced to death by a COURT-MARTIAL were hung. Often incorrectly used for the yard as a whole.

yardarm to yardarm Of ships, so near to one another that the YARDARMS are touching, as in a battle fought at close quarters.

yard-tackles TACKLEs attached to the FORE and MAIN YARDs and used to HOIST and lower a ship's boats.

yataghan A long knife or short sword of Turkey and other Muslim countries, with no cross guard and often with a double-curved blade.

yaw Of a vessel, to deviate temporarily from the desired course as a result of a powerful following wind or sea reducing the control of the RUDDER, or sometimes as a result of poor steering. Also, to turn to one side or from side to side in her course.

yawl A small craft with two MASTS, FORE-AND-AFT rigged, that resembles a KETCH; a ship's boat resembling a PINNACE but smaller, usually with four or six oars.

yearth Earth.

yellow To make a YELLOW ADMIRAL.

yellow admiral A POST-CAPTAIN who is simultaneously retired and promoted to Rear-Admiral "without distinction of squadron," having not served as a Rear-Admiral and having not been attached to one of the Red, White, or Blue SQUADRONS, and so deemed a "yellow" ADMIRAL. The practice, begun in 1747, was used to recognize distinguished service while weeding out less able leaders and also decreasing the logjam of officers eligible for promotion.

yellow fever A viral disease found in most tropical climates and transmitted by mosquitoes. It caused epidemics in cold climates when infected mosquitoes were transported in ships' water casks, but such epidemics died out, along with the responsible mosquitoes, in the first frosts of autumn. Mortality varied from about 10 percent to as high as 80 percent, but the higher extreme was rarely approached. Typical symptoms included a bright red facial rash, black vomiting, severe diarrhea, liver destruction, and jaundice.

yellow flag A yellow-colored flag flown on a ship formerly as a signal that capital punishment was being carried out on board; later as a signal of the presence of infectious disease or of quarantine.

yellow Jack Slang for YELLOW FEVER and also for the yellow-colored quarantine flag. A nickname of certain pensioners at Greenwich Hospital who were made to wear a coat with yellow in it to warn others of their proclivity to drink.

yeoman In the British and U.S. navies, a PETTY OFFICER who is in charge of the stores of a particular department, such as a BOATSWAIN's or GUNNER's yeoman or the yeoman of the SHEETS.

ye thrawn, ill-feckit gaberlunzie   You perverse, misbegotten beggar (Scots).

York, **H.M.S.**   A third rate built in 1796. She foundered in 1804.

Young, Arthur (*1741–1820*)   A prolific English writer on agriculture, politics, and economics, Young advocated farming innovations such as the seed drill and enclosure of open fields. In 1771, he published the first of many editions of *The Farmer's Calendar,* and in 1774, the widely translated *Political Arithmetic.* He published the periodical *Annals of Agriculture,* which included articles from GEORGE III under the pseudonym "Ralph Robinson." His famous *Travels in France* (1792) gave accounts of the French just prior to the Revolution.

younker   A youngster; a boy or junior seaman on a ship.

Zealous, **H.M.S.** The 74-gun third rate, built in 1785, that led the British fleet at the Battle of the NILE in 1798. She was commanded by Captain Sir Samuel Hood and afterward used by Hood when he commanded the force blockading the French army in Egypt. She was scrapped in 1816.

Zeiten (*also* Zieten *or* Ziethen), Count Hans Ernst Karl von (*1770–1848*) A Prussian field marshal whose corps engaged in intense fighting at LIGNY on June 16, 1815. Two days later, at WATERLOO, his crucial 6:30 P.M. arrival compelled NAPOLEON to send his reserve troops into the battle in a desperate and failed attempt to break WELLINGTON's line.

Zelenka, Jan Dismas (*1679–1745*) A little-known Bohemian composer of sacred vocal music as well as some chamber and other instrumental works. He studied in Prague and played the double-bass in the royal orchestra at Dresden, where he became kapellmeister. Zelenka died lonely and bitter because of his lack of recognition as a composer.

Zenata One of three tribes of northern Africa (along with the Sanhaja and the Masmoda) constituting the Berbers, a generic name imposed on them by the Arabs and meaning "those who are not Arabs." The Berbers were well established in North Africa before the Phoenicians arrived in 1200 B.C.

zephyr   The west wind, especially as personified, or the god of the west wind. A gentle breeze.

APPENDIX:

A Time Line of the Napoleonic Wars, the War of 1812, and the Fight for Independence in Chile

1793

January 3   French batteries at Brest fire on H.M.S. *Childers.* These are the first shots in the Anglo-French naval wars of 1793–1815.

January 21   Louis XVI executed.

February 1   France declares war on England and Holland.

March 13   H.M.S. *Scourge* takes the *Sans Culotte* off the Scilly Isles in the first engagement with the French at sea.

September 22   New French calendar begins on this date, renamed as 1 Vendèmiaire, Year II of the Republic.

December 19   Earl Spencer succeeds the Earl of Chatham as First Lord of the Admiralty.

December 19–23   British evacuate Toulon.

1794

March 22   Capture of Fort Bourbon and all of Martinique by General Sir Charles Grey and Vice-Admiral Sir John Jervis in H.M.S. *Boyne.*

May 21 Capture of Bastia, Corsica, after a siege of 37 days, by troops under Lieutenant-Colonel William Villettes (69th Regiment) and seamen under Captain Horatio Nelson in H.M.S. *Agamemnon*.

June 1 The Glorious First of June. Admiral Earl Howe in his flagship H.M.S. *Queen Charlotte* defeats Rear-Admiral Villaret-Joyeuse (*Montagne*) west of Ushant.

June 10 (22 Prairial, Year II) The Terror begins in France.

June 12 Captain Nelson blinded in right eye while besieging Calvi, Corsica. Nelson writes, "At present I can distinguish light from dark, but no object: it confined me one day, when thank God I was able to do my duty."

July 27 Death of Robespierre. End of the Terror.

1795

March 3 Evan Nepean succeeds Philip Stephens (in office since 1763) as Admiralty Secretary.

August 22 Directory established in France.

September 16 Vice-Admiral Sir George Elphinstone, later Lord Keith, and General Alfred Clarke capture the Cape of Good Hope in the name of the Prince of Orange.

1796

January 28 The Admiralty telegraph system, based on Murray's shutter system, begins working between London and Portsmouth and London and Chatham. (It extends to Plymouth in 1806 and to Yarmouth in 1808.)

May 24 St. Lucia falls to Lieutenant-General Sir Ralph Abercromby and Rear-Admiral Sir Hugh Cloberry Christian, in H.M.S. *Thunderer*.

August 19 First Idelfonso Treaty signed, allying France and Spain. As a result, British leaders decide to withdraw from Toulon and evacuate the Royal Navy from the western Mediterranean, moving to Gibraltar.

October 8   Spain declares war on Britain.

December 15   Expedition leaves France for Ireland.

December 21–27   Landing at Bantry Bay fails.

1797

February 14   Battle of Cape St. Vincent, 24 miles west by south of Cape St. Vincent. British fleet under Admiral Sir John Jervis in H.M.S. *Victory* defeats 27 Spanish sail of the line under Vice-Admiral Don José de Cordoba, flying his flag in *Santissima Trinidad*.

February 18   Lieutenant-General Sir Ralph Abercromby and Rear-Admiral Henry Harvey in H.M.S. *Prince of Wales* capture Trinidad.

May 1   First Spithead mutiny ends with issue of Admiralty orders against abuses.

May 7   Second Spithead mutiny begins.

May 8   Parliament passes Sailors' Bill to improve conditions of naval service.

May 12   Mutiny at the Nore begins in H.M.S. *Sandwich*.

May 15   Second Spithead mutiny ends.

June 14   Mutiny at the Nore ends. Many of the mutineers, including their leader, Richard Parker, are subsequently tried and executed.

July 3   Rear-Admiral Sir Horatio Nelson's boat action with Spanish gunboats at Cadiz.

October 11   Battle of Camperdown. Admiral Adam Duncan in H.M.S. *Venerable* defeats the Dutch fleet under Vice-Admiral Jan de Winter, flying his flag in *Vrijheid*.

1798

July 1   Napoleon lands in Egypt.

August   Battle of the Nile. Rear-Admiral Sir Horatio Nelson in H.M.S. *Vanguard* defeats Vice-Admiral François Brueys (*Orient*) at Aboukir Bay.

December 29   Second Coalition formed against France.

1799

March 1   War breaks out between Second Coalition and France.

August 23   Napoleon leaves his troops in Egypt and returns to France on October 9, arriving in Paris on October 14.

November 11 (20 Brumaire, Year VIII)   Provisional Consulate formed.

December 14   Napoleon made First Consul.

1800

February 18   H.M.S. *Leander* captures the French Généreaux.

March 14   Pope Pius VII elected.

June 14   Battle of Marengo.

September 5   Major-General Henry Pigot captures Malta, after a naval blockade begun in May. Captain, later Admiral, Ball becomes Governor.

October 7   Second Treaty of Idelfonso. Spain cedes Louisiana to France.

December 18   Second Armed Neutrality. In response to British claims of the right to search neutral shipping, Denmark, Sweden, Russia, and Prussia revive the Armed Neutrality of 1780, threatening the effectiveness of Britain's naval blockade of France, cutting off British supplies of timber and naval materials, and halting grain imports from the Baltic at a time of poor harvests at home.

1801

January 1   Current form of Union flag and naval ensigns established upon the union of Great Britain and Ireland.

February 19   Earl of St. Vincent succeeds Earl Spencer as First Lord of the Admiralty.

March 17   Henry Addington succeeds William Pitt the Younger, who has been Prime Minister since 1783.

March 23   Czar Paul I assassinated; succeeded by Alexander I.

April 2   First Battle of Copenhagen. When Vice-Admiral Nelson's Commander-in-Chief, Admiral Sir Hyde Parker, orders the ships to break off the action, Nelson puts his spyglass to his blind eye and says, "I really do not see the signal."

May 6   Captain Thomas Cochrane in the *Speedy* captures the much more powerful Spanish *Gamo* southwest of Barcelona.

May 25   Admiralty Hydrographic Office publishes its first dated Admiralty charts, which are of Alexandria and the Egyptian coast. (The previous year it had published its very first chart, Quiberon Bay.)

July 3   French squadron under Linois takes H.M.S. *Speedy.*

July 6–12   Battle of Algeçiras. Rear-Admiral Sir James Saumarez, in H.M.S. *Caesar,* defeats Franco-Spanish squadron of nine ships under Vice-Admiral Don Juan de Moreno and Rear-Admiral Durand-Linois, both in *Sabina,* in the Gut of Gibraltar.

October 1   Preliminaries of Peace of Amiens signed.

1802

March 25   Peace of Amiens.

May 8–14   Plebiscite on Life Consulship; proclaimed on August 2.

1803

March 18   Resumption of hostilities between Britain and France.

May 3   France sells Louisiana to United States.

May 17   Britain declares war on France.

August 23   Invasion camps form at St. Omer and Bruges. French invasion flotilla assembles.

October 9   Franco-Spanish alliance signed.

1804

January 7   Commodore Samuel Hood (*Centaur*) seizes the Diamond Rock, an island southwest of Martinique. Fortified and commissioned by Lieutenant Maurice.

March 11   French Navy ordered to prepare to invade England.

March 21   William Marsden succeeds Evan Nepean as Admiralty Secretary.

May 5   Commodore Samuel Hood, in H.M.S. *Centaur*, with troops under Brigadier-General Sir Charles Green, captures Surinam.

May 10   Succeeding Addington, William Pitt forms his second administration as Prime Minister.

May 15   Viscount Melville succeeds the Earl of St. Vincent as First Lord of the Admiralty.

May 18   Napoleon proclaimed Emperor.

October 5   H.M. ships *Lively, Indefatigable, Medusa,* and *Amphion* intercept, off Cadiz, Bustamante with four Spanish frigates carrying treasure from Montevideo.

December 2   Napoleon's coronation.

December 14   Spain declares war on the United Kingdom.

1805

March 29   Admiral Villeneuve and his fleet evade the blockade of Toulon and pass Gibralter en route to the West Indies on April 9.

April 11   Anglo-Russian Alliance signed.

May 2   Lord Barham succeeds Lord Melville as First Lord of the Admiralty.

June 2   After enduring three days' bombardment, Commander James Maurice surrenders the island called H.M.S. *Diamond Rock* to a strong French squadron under Captain Cosmao-Kerjulien, in *Pluton*.

July 22   In a precursor to Trafalgar, Vice-Admiral Sir Robert Calder, in H.M.S. *Prince of Wales*, reinforced by Rear-Admiral Stirling with five ships, fights Vice-Admiral Pierre Villeneuve with 19 French and Spanish ships, 150 miles west-northwest of Ferrol.

August 9   Austria completes formation of the Third Coalition against France.

October 20   Capitulation of Ulm.

October 21   Battle of Trafalgar, eight leagues off Cadiz. Vice-Admiral Viscount Nelson in H.M.S. *Victory* defeats the Franco-Spanish fleet of 33 sail of the line under Vice-Admiral Pierre Villeneuve and Admiral Don Federico Gravina. British ships destroy 16 ships and capture four, but Nelson is killed.

December 2   Battle of Austerlitz.

December 26   Surrender of Austria under the terms of the Treaty of Pressburg.

1806

January 9   Funeral of Vice-Admiral Lord Nelson in St. Paul's Cathedral.

January 10   Cape Town capitulates to British forces under Major-General Sir David Baird and Commodore Sir Home Riggs Popham in H.M.S. *Diadem*. The entire Cape Colony surrenders on January 18. (It had been previously taken on September 16, 1795, but was returned to the Dutch in 1802.)

January 23   Death of William Pitt. The "Ministry of All the Talents" formed, headed by Lord Grenville as Prime Minister.

February 6   Battle of San Domingo. Vice-Admiral Sir John Duckworth in H.M.S. *Superb* defeats a French squadron of five under Rear-Admiral Leissegues in San Domingo Bay.

February 10   Hon. Charles Grey (from April 1806, Viscount Howick) succeeds Lord Barham as First Lord of the Admiralty.

April 6   Cochrane in H.M.S. *Pallas* drives the French vessels *Garonne, Gloire,* and *Malicieuse* ashore at the mouth of the Gironde, while most of his men were in boats engaged upstream in cutting out *Tapageuse*.

May 16   Royal Navy begins blockade of French ports.

June 27   Commodore Sir Home Riggs Popham, in H.M.S. *Diadem*, and Major-General William Carr Beresford capture Buenos Aires.

July 20   Peace treaty between France and Russia signed; Czar Alexander refuses to ratify it on August 24.

September 29   Thomas Grenville succeeds Viscount Howick as First Lord of the Admiralty.

October 6   Formation of Fourth Coalition against France.

October 14   Battle of Jena-Auerestadt.

October 27   Napoleon enters Berlin.

November 21   Napoleon issues Berlin Decree, closing European ports to British goods and inaugurating the Continental system.

1807

January 1   Captain Charles Brisbane in H.M.S. *Anson*, with *Arethusa, Fisgard*, and *Latona*, captures Curaçao.

January 7   British Orders in Council against contraband aim to further isolate France but increase tension with neutrals.

February 3   Brigadier-General Sir Samuel Auchmuty and Rear-Admiral Charles Stirling, in H.M.S. *Diadem*, capture Montevideo.

February 19   Vice-Admiral Sir John Duckworth in H.M.S. *Royal George* forces the passage of the Dardanelles and anchors off Constantinople, destroying 11 Turkish ships and capturing two.

March 24   Whigs leave office for the last time in the reign of George III. Duke of Portland succeeds as Prime Minister.

April 6   Lord Mulgrave succeeds Thomas Grenville as First Lord of the Admiralty.

June 22   After sailing from Hampton Roads, Virginia, U.S.S. *Chesapeake* refuses to be searched for British deserters, and H.M.S. *Leopard* fires into her, killing three, including the captain, and wounding 18 American seamen.

September 2   The fleet under Admiral James Gambier in H.M.S. *Prince of Wales* and shore batteries erected by Lieutenant-General Lord Cathcart bombard Copenhagen.

September 7   Seventy Danish ships surrender to Admiral Gambier.

June 24   Hon. William Wellesley Pole succeeds William Marsden as Admiralty Secretary.

July 7–9   Peace and treaties of Tilsit.

September 7   British forces seize Danish fleet.

November 11   British Orders in Council require British vessels trading with Europe to stop first at a British port to unload, pay duties, and reload.

December 17   Napoleon issues Milan Decree, authorizing French ships to seize any vessel stopping in a British port or that has been searched at sea by British warships.

December 22   In response to French and British attacks on neutral American shipping, U.S. Congress enacts Embargo, prohibiting U.S. vessels from sailing to foreign ports until March 1809.

1808

April 17   Napoleon issues Bayonne Decree, authorizing French authorities to sequester American vessels in Europe.

August 30   Convention of Cintra signed.

November 5   Napoleon takes personal command in Spain.

December 24   General Sir John Moore begins his retreat.

1809

January 16   Battle of Corunna. General Moore killed while covering the embarkation of the Army.

February 24   Lieutenant-General George Beckwith and Rear-Admiral the Hon. Sir Alexander Cochrane in H.M.S. *Neptune* capture Martinique.

March 1   U.S. Embargo repealed and replaced by Non-Intercourse Act, prohibiting American trade with both belligerents until May 1810 or until repeal of their restrictions on U.S. commerce.

April 9   Fifth Coalition against France formed.

April 11   Captain Lord Cochrane's fireship attack on the French fleet at Basque Roads.

May 18   Occupation of the island of Anholt in the Kattegat.

July 5–6   Battle of Wagram.

July 26   Admiral Gambier court-martialed for his conduct at Aix Roads.

July 30-December 23   The Walcheren Campaign. The Royal Navy supports a large invasion force that attempts to seize control of the mouth of the River Scheldt, where the French have established a naval base. The French force the expedition to withdraw.

October 12   John William Croker succeeds William Wellesley Pole as Admiralty Secretary. (He remains in office until 1830.)

December 2   Spencer Perceval succeeds the Duke of Portland as Prime Minister.

1810

February 5   Lieutenant-General Sir George Beckwith and Vice-Admiral the Hon. Sir Alexander Cochrane, in H.M.S. *Pompee*, capture Guadeloupe.

February 17   Captain Tucker in H.M.S. *Cornwallis*, with the *Dover* and the *Samarang* and a detachment from the Madras European Regiment, capture Amboina, in the Molucca Islands.

March 7   Vice-Admiral Lord Collingwood dies at sea in the Mediterranean, off Minorca, on his way home after being granted sick leave.

March 23   Napoleon issues Rambouillet Decree, authorizing confiscation of ships and cargos sequestered under the Bayonne Decree.

May 4   Charles Philip Yorke succeeds Lord Mulgrave as First Lord of the Admiralty.

July 8   The island of Bourbon (Réunion) captured by H.M. ships *Boadicea, Iphigenia, Magicienne, Nereide,* and *Sirius,* along with British troops, including the Bombay Artillery Pioneers and the Madras Native Infantry.

August 23–28   Battle of Grand Port, Mauritius, in which the French capture H.M.S. *Neride* and H.M.S. *Iphigenia,* and the British burn H.M.S. *Magicienne* and H.M.S. *Sirius* to avoid capture.

September 12   The British ships *Bodicea, Africaine, Otter,* and *Staunch* engage the French *Iphigenie* (ex-British *Iphigenia*).

September 17   Action between H.M.S. *Ceylon* and H.M.S. *Bodicea* with the French *Vénus.*

December 3   Vice-Admiral Albermarle Bertie in H.M.S. *Africaine* and Major-General the Hon. John Abercromby capture Île de France (Mauritius).

1811

February 5   Parliament passes the Regency Act and the Prince of Wales is accepted as Regent by hereditary right. Royal assent to the act was signified by a commission.

May 16   The U.S.S. *President* takes H.M.S. *Little Belt.*

September 18   Lord Minto, with Rear-Admiral the Hon. Robert Stopford in H.M.S. *Scipion* and Lieutenant-General Sir Samuel Auchmuty, captures Java.

December 23   Napoleon begins preparations against Russia.

1812

March 25   Viscount Melville succeeds Charles Philip Yorke as First Lord of the Admiralty, remaining in office until 1830, except for 16 months in 1827–1828.

May 11   Bellingham assassinates Prime Minister Spencer Perceval in the House of Commons.

June 8   Earl of Liverpool becomes Prime Minister and remains in office for nearly 15 years.

June 18   The United States declares war against Britain.

June 20   Sixth Coalition formed against France.

August 13   Wellington enters Madrid.

August 19   U.S.S. *Constitution* takes H.M.S. *Guerriere* about 55 miles southeast of Halifax, Nova Scotia.

September 7   Battle of Borodino.

September 14   Napoleon enters Moscow.

October 19   French begin to leave Moscow.

October 25   U.S.S. *United States* takes H.M.S. *Macedonian* about 600 miles west-southwest of Madeira.

December 18   Napoleon returns to Paris.

December 29   U.S.S. *Constitution* takes H.M.S. *Java* 30 miles east of Bahia, Brazil.

1813

February 24   U.S.S. *Hornet* takes H.M.S. *Peacock* off the mouth of the Demerara River, British Guiana.

March 16   Prussia declares war on France.

April 29–May 9   Boats from the squadron under Rear-Admiral George Cockburn destroy American shipping and stores in Virginia.

June 1   H.M.S. *Shannon* takes U.S.S. *Chesapeake* off Boston, killing her captain, James Lawrence, whose dying words—"Don't give up the ship!"—become an American battle cry in the War of 1812.

August 10   Commodore Sir James Yeo in H.M.S. *Wolfe* engages an American squadron under Commodore Isaac Chauncey on Lake Ontario, capturing the American schooners *Growler* and *Julia*.

August 17   Austria declares war on France.

September 10   The American Lake Squadron on Lake Erie under the command of Oliver Hazard Perry defeats the British Lake Squadron.

October 16–19   Napoleon defeated at the Battle of Leipzig, pushing all his forces west of the Rhine.

1814

February 3   H.M.S. *Majestic* gives up pursuing U.S.S. *Wasp* to capture the French *Terpsichore*, 300 miles north-northwest of Madeira.

March 13   The allies at Vienna declare Napoleon an outlaw.

March 25   Seventh Coalition formed against France.

March 31   Allies enter Paris.

April 4   Wellington arrives in Brussels.

April 6   Napoleon abdicates at Fontainbleau.

April 28   Napoleon surrenders to Captain Ussher in H.M.S. *Undaunted* for his passage to Elba.

May 1   First Navy List published officially by the Admiralty.

May 3   Louis XVIII enters Paris.

June 28   U.S.S. *Wasp* takes H.M.S. *Reindeer* 240 miles west of Ushant.

August 24–25   Detachments under Rear-Admiral Sir Alexander Cochrane and General Robert Ross capture and burn Washington, D.C.

September 11   The American Lake Squadron under Captain Thomas MacDonough defeats the British Lake Squadron in Plattsburg Bay, halting the British advance in New York.

September 13–14   Rear-Admiral Cochrane in H.M.S. *Surprise* unsuccessfully bombards Fort McHenry at Baltimore, Maryland, leading Francis Scott Key, an American observer on the deck of H.M.S. *Minden*, to compose the poem "Defence of Fort M'Henry," later set to music as the "The Star-Spangled Banner."

November 1   Congress of Vienna opens.

December 24   Peace of Ghent signed, ending the War of 1812 between the United States and Britain, but the news does not arrive in the United States until February 11, 1815.

1815

January 8   Major-General Sir Edward Pakenham and Vice-Admiral Sir Alexander Cochrane attack New Orleans.

January 15   H.M.S. *Endymion*, with *Pamone* and *Tenedos*, defeats U.S.S. *President*, 70 miles southeast by south of Montauk Point, Long Island.

February 17   Peace between United States and Britain proclaimed in United States.

March 20   Napoleon returns triumphantly to Paris.

June 18   Wellington defeats Napoleon at Waterloo.

July 15   Napoleon surrenders at Basque Roads to Captain Maitland of H.M.S. *Bellerophon*.

July 26   The *Bellerophon* arrives at Plymouth with Napoleon on board.

August 7   Napoleon sails from Plymouth in H.M.S. *Northumberland* to be exiled on the Island of St. Helena in the South Pacific.

October 16   Napoleon arrives at St. Helena.

1816

July 4   Commodore Sir William Bowles arrives in Rio de Janeiro as commander-in-chief, South American Squadron. He is succeeded by Commodore Sir Thomas Masterman Hardy in October 1819.

August 17   A combined Anglo-Dutch fleet under Edward Pellew, Viscount Exmouth, bombards Algiers.

1817

February 12   Forces under José de San Martín invade Chile and take Chacabuco. Two days later they enter Santiago, where Bernardo O'Higgins is named Supreme Director of Chile and leader of the revolutionary forces.

<u>1818</u>

February 12   Chilean Independence is declared.

November 28   Lord Cochrane arrives at Valparaiso to take command of the embryonic Chilean navy.

Selected Bibliography

In addition to the volumes of *The Naval Chronicle* and the novels of Patrick O'Brian, the following sources were used in writing this book:

Bagar, Robert, and Louis Biancolli. *The Concert Companion: A Comprehensive Guide to Symphonic Music.* New York: Whittlesey House/McGraw-Hill, 1947.

Borer, Mary Cathcart. *The City of London: A History.* New York: David McKay, 1977.

Boswell, James. *Life of Johnson.* [A New Edition Corrected by J. D. Fleeman.], edited by R. W. Chapman. Oxford: Oxford University Press, 1970.

Brewer's Dictionary of Phrase and Fable. 15th ed. Revised by Adrian Room. New York: HarperCollins, 1995.

Brown, Anthony Gary, ed. *A Guide for the Perplexed: Translations of All "Non-English" Phrases in Patrick O'Brian's Sea-Tales.* World Wide Web site, 1997. E-mail dr_gary_brown@geocities.com for current location.

Chandler, David G. *Dictionary of the Napoleonic Wars.* New York: Simon and Schuster, 1993.

Clowes, William Laird. *The Royal Navy: A History from the Earliest Times to the Present.* Vols. 4–6. London: Sampson, Low, Marston and Company, 1899–1901.

Clunn, Harold P. *The Face of London*. Revised by E. R. Wethersett. London: Spring Books, n.d.

Coad, Jonathan. *The Royal Dockyards*. Aldershot: Scolar Press, 1989.

Cochrane, Thomas. *Autobiography of a Seaman*. 2 vols. London: R. Bentley, 1859, 1860.

Colledge, J. J. *Ships of the Royal Navy: A Complete Record of all Fighting Ships of the Royal Navy from the Fifteenth Century to the Present*. Annapolis: Naval Institute, 1987.

Connelly, Owen, ed. *Dictionary of Napoleonic France, 1799–1815*. Westport: Greenwood Press, 1985.

Cunningham, A. E., ed. *Patrick O'Brian: Critical Essays and a Bibliography*. New York: Norton, 1994.

Da Ponte, Lorenzo. *Le Nozze Di Figaro: Libretto*. Translated by Judyth Schaubhut Smith. New York: Metropolitan Opera Guild, 1990.

Davies, David. *Fighting Ships: Ships of the Line, 1793–1815*. London: Constable, 1996.

Eagle, Dorothy, and Hilary Cranell, eds. *The Oxford Literary Guide to the British Isles*. Oxford: Oxford University Press, 1977.

Encyclopaedia Britannica; Or, a Dictionary of Arts and Sciences Compiled upon a New Plan. Edinburgh: C. Macfarquhar, 1771. Three-vol. facsimile.

Estes, J. Worth. *Dictionary of Protopharmacology: Therapeutic Practices, 1700–1850*. Canton, Mass.: Science History Publications, 1990.

Falconer, W. A. *A New Universal Dictionary of the Marine* (also known as *Falconer's Marine Dictionary*). Modernized and enlarged by William Burney. 1815. Reprint. London: Macdonald and Jane's, 1974.

Harland, John. *Seamanship in the Age of Sail: An Account of the Shiphandling of the Sailing Man-Of-War, 1600–1860, Based on Contemporary Sources*. Annapolis: Naval Institute Press, 1984.

Harvey, A. D. *English Literature and the Great War with France: An Anthology and Commentary* (London: Nold Jonson Books, 1981).

Hattendorf, John B., et al. *British Naval Documents, 1204–1960*. Publications of the Navy Records Society. Vol. 131. Aldershot: Scolar Press, 1993.

Haythornthwaite, Philip J. *The Napoleonic Source Book*. New York: Facts On File, 1990.

Heinl, Robert Debs, Jr. *Dictionary of Military and Naval Quotations*. Annapolis, Md.: United States Naval Institute, 1966.

Henderson, James. *The Frigates: An Account of the Lesser Warships of the Wars from 1793 to 1815*. New York: Dodd, Mead, 1970.

Hill, J. R. ed. *The Oxford Illustrated History of the Royal Navy*. Oxford: Oxford University Press, 1995.

Jarrett, Dudley. *British Naval Dress*. London: J. M. Dent, 1960.

Joy, Norman H. *How to Know British Birds*. London: H. F. and G. Witherby, 1936.

Kemp, Peter, ed. *The Oxford Companion to Ships and the Sea*. Oxford: Oxford University Press, 1993.

Kennedy, Michael, ed. *The Concise Oxford Dictionary of Music*. 4th ed. Oxford: Oxford University Press, 1996.

Kerchove, René de. *International Maritime Dictionary*. Princeton, N.J.: Van Nostrand, 1961.

King, Dean, with John B. Hattendorf. *Harbors and High Seas: An Atlas and Geographical Guide to the Aubrey-Maturin Novels of Patrick O'Brian*. New York: Henry Holt, 1996.

Lavery, Brian. *The Ship of the Line*. Annapolis: Naval Institute Press, 1983.

———. *Nelson's Navy: The Ships, Men and Organization, 1793–1815*. Annapolis: Naval Institute Press, 1989.

Little, George. *Life on the Ocean; Or, Twenty Years at Sea: Being the Personal Adventures of the Author*. Boston: Waite, Peirce, and Company, 1845.

Lloyd, Christopher. *Captain Marryat and the Old Navy*. London: Longmans, Green, 1939.

———. *Lord Cochrane: Seaman—Radical—Liberator: A Life of Thomas, Lord Cochrane, 10th Earl of Dundonald*. London: Longmans, Green, 1947.

———. *The British Seaman*. London: Longmans, Green, 1968.

Lyon, David. *The Sailing Ship List*. London: Conway Maritime Press, 1994.

Maclay, Edgar Stanton. *A History of American Privateers*. 1899. Reprint. New York: Burt Franklin, 1968.

Manning, Captain T. D., and Commander C. F. Walker. *British Warship Names*. London: Putnam, 1959.

Morriss, Roger. *The Royal Dockyards During the Revolutionary and Napoleonic Wars*. Leicester: Leicester University Press, 1983.

Parkinson, C. Northcote. *Portsmouth Point: The Navy in Fiction, 1793–1815*. London: Hodder & Stoughton and The University Press of Liverpool, 1948.

Pivka, Otto von. *Navies of the Napoleonic Era*. Newton Abbot: David and Charles, 1980.

Price, Anthony. *The Eyes of the Fleet: A Popular History of Frigates and Frigate Captains, 1793–1815*. London: Hutchinson, 1990.

Rees, Abraham. *Rees's Naval Architecture (1819–1820)*. Annapolis: Naval Institute Press, 1970.

Rodger, N.A.M. *The Admiralty*. Lavenham: Terrence Dalton, 1979.

———. *Articles of War: The Statutes which Governed Our Fighting Navies, 1661, 1749 and 1886*. Havant: Kenneth Mason, 1982.

————. *Naval Records for Genealogists.* London: Public Record Office, 1984.

————. *The Wooden World: An Anatomy of the Georgian Navy.* New York: Norton, 1986.

Rogers, John G. *Origins of Sea Terms.* Mystic, Conn.: Mystic Seaport Museum, 1984.

Rose, J. Holland. *William Pitt and The Great War.* 1911. Reprint. Westport, Conn.: Greenwood Press, 1971.

Sainsbury, A. B. *The Royal Navy Day by Day.* New Ed., revised and expanded. London: Ian Allen, n.d.

Sainty, J. C. *Admiralty Officials, 1609–1815.* London: Athlone Press, 1975.

Scott, Samuel F., and Barry Rothaus. *Historical Dictionary of the French Revolution.* Westport: Greenwood Press, 1985.

Serres, Dominick and John Thomas. *Liber Nauticus: and Instructor in the Art of Marine Drawing.* London: Scolar Press, 1979.

Smyth, William Henry. *The Sailor's Word Book: An Alphabetical Digest of Nautical Terms.* London: Blackie and Son, 1867.

Steel, David. *Steel's Naval Chronologist of the War.* Printed for David Steel at the Navigation Warehouse, 1803. Reprint. London: Cornmarket Press, 1969.

Symonds, Sir William. *Naval Costumes.* Privately printed, 1840.

Tunstall, Brian, edited by Nicholas Tracy. *Naval Warfare in the Age of Sail: The Evolution of Fighting Tactics, 1650–1815.* Annapolis: Naval Institute Press, 1990.

Uden, Grant, and Richard Cooper. *A Dictionary of British Ships and Seamen.* New York: St. Martin's Press, 1980.

Weinreb, Ben, and Christopher Hibbert. *The London Encyclopaedia.* Rev. ed. London: Macmillan, 1993.

Werstein, Irving. *The Cruise of the Essex: An Incident from the War of 1812.* Philadelphia: Macrae Smith, 1969.

Wilson, P. W. *William Pitt, the Younger.* New York: Doubleday, Doran, 1933.

The Oxford English Dictionary magnetic tape, 2d ed. Oxford: Oxford University Press, 1992.

Academic American encyclopedia computer file. New York: Grolier Electronic Publishing, 1994.

About the Authors

DEAN KING is the author of eight other books, including the acclaimed biography *Patrick O'Brian: A Life Revealed*, and the editor of the Henry Holt series Heart of Oak Sea Classics. His articles have appeared in *Art & Antiques, Esquire, Men's Journal*, the *New York Times*, and *Travel & Leisure*. He is a graduate of the University of North Carolina at Chapel Hill and earned a Master of Arts degree in English at New York University. He lives with his wife, Jessica, and their four daughters in Richmond, Virginia.

JOHN B. HATTENDORF is the Ernest J. King Professor of Maritime History and Director of the Advanced Research Department in the Center for Naval Warfare Studies at the U.S. Naval War College, Newport, Rhode Island.

J. WORTH ESTES is a professor of pharmacology at the Boston University School of Medicine, where his research specialty is 18th- and 19th-century medicine on land and at sea. Editor of the *Journal of the History of Medicine and Allied Sciences*, he is the author of the *Dictionary of Protopharmacology: Therapeutic Practices, 1700–1850* (1990) and *Naval Surgeon: Life and Death at Sea in the Age of Sail* (1997).

Patrick O'Brian: A Life Revealed
by Dean King

"King's book is the Rosetta stone to Patrick O'Brian."
—*Europe* magazine

"King casts a sober eye but not a cold heart on this secretive writer whose followers lionize him for his 20-volume sequential novel of British seafaring life during the age of Napoleon. . . . His devotees should rejoice at this account of his life, written with appreciative balance, rich with literary insight. King seems to pull no punches, nor does he deny that the quality of the art can, at times, surpass the character of the artist. . . . His analysis is crisp and engaging. Even devout readers will deepen their understanding of O'Brian's wondrous 2 million-word magnum opus and the author's studious techniques. . . . O'Brian endures and captivates readers for reasons this biography sets forth lucidly. . . . Dean King does his memory justice."
—*Los Angeles Times*

"A generous portrait by a true believer that sets much of the record straight."
—*The New York Times Book Review*

"King's diligent research yields pleasing details. . . . O'Brian addicts will be grateful for King's efforts."
—*The New Yorker*

"Excellent."
—*The Star-Ledger* (Newark)

"King dares to ask the impertinent questions others did not, and as a result makes an important contribution to understanding a writer's complicated life."
—*Seattle Weekly*

"A fascinating look at the late novelist Patrick O'Brian and the mythic persona O'Brian himself created . . . Engaging and full of surprising details."
—*Kirkus Reviews*

"Intriguing and extraordinarily detailed . . . King argues that O'Brian's prolific and knowledgeable writing owes more than a little to his divided life, his failures, and his need to reinvent himself. A worthy biography." —*Library Journal*, starred

"[King's] admiration of O'Brian did not trump his obligation as a biographer to present a balanced view, and thus his book likely will stand as *the* definitive biography of one of the century's more interesting writers." —*Richmond Times-Dispatch*

Heart of Oak Sea Classics

Peter Simple by Frederick Marryat
Doctor Dogbody's Leg by James Norman Hall
The Black Ship by Dudley Pope
Mr Midshipman Easy by Frederick Marryat
The Wing-and-Wing by James Fenimore Cooper
Lord Cochrane: Seaman, Radical, Liberator by Christopher Lloyd
Percival Keene by Frederick Marryat
Decision at Trafalgar by Dudley Pope
The Rover by Joseph Conrad
Tom Cringle's Log by Michael Scott